AMERICAN SOCIOLOGY SERIES

Kimball Young, *General Editor*

AMERICAN SOCIOLOGY SERIES

Wilbur B. Brookover
A Sociology of Education

Ernest W. Burgess and Harvey J. Locke
The Family, Second Edition

Paul K. Hatt, editor
World Population and Future Resources

J. L. Hirning and Alma L. Hirning
Marriage Adjustment

Paul H. Landis
Population Problems, A Cultural Interpretation, Second Edition
(prepared by Paul K. Hatt)

Charles F. Marden
Minorities in American Society

Lowry Nelson
Rural Sociology, Second Edition

James A. Quinn
Urban Sociology

James M. Reinhardt, Paul Meadows, and John M. Gillette
Social Problems and Social Policy

Herbert H. Stroup
Social Work, An Introduction to the Field

Carl C. Taylor
The Farmers' Movement, 1620-1920

R. Clyde White
Administration of Public Welfare, Second Edition

Arthur E. Wood and John B. Waite
Crime and Its Treatment

Kimball Young
Sociology, A Study of Society and Culture, Second Edition

MARRIAGE

ADJUSTMENT

J. L. Hirning
Roosevelt University

Alma L. Hirning
Kendall College

AMERICAN BOOK COMPANY - NEW YORK

Hirning-Hirning: *Marriage Adjustment*

MADE IN U.S.A.   E. P. 1

PREFACE

There are about forty million married couples in the United States. Most of them have made a satisfactory adjustment to marriage and are happy and contented. There are others, however, who find marital adjustment so difficult that their marriage is not something to be enjoyed but something to be endured. Often they remain married only because of conditions beyond their control. There is also an ever-increasing number of couples who find it impossible to make their marriage work at all and who therefore escape from it either by desertion or by divorce.

It is our conviction that people fail in their marital adjustment not so much because of improper motivation as because of inadequate information about the intricacies of modern marriage. Some of this information we hope to make available in this book. We are not writing an encyclopedia on marriage, however, nor are we endeavoring to enumerate a set of rules to be followed. Rather, we hope to give the reader insight into the meaning of marriage and to acquaint him with guiding principles, so that he may be more qualified to solve his marital problems. On some aspects of premarital and marital adjustment there are sincere differences of opinion in our society. Where this is true, we have tried to present opposing views as objectively as possible.

While this book is intended primarily as a text for college classes or for various other groups endeavoring to make a systematic study of marriage, we believe that it can be read with profit by any intelligent, enlightened person, married or single.

The content of the book is the product of both theoretical considerations and practical experience. The practical experience has been of four types. First, from many years of dealing clinically with the serious problems of individuals has come a deeper understanding of the complexities of personality adjustment. Second, from many years of premarital counseling with young people has come a recognition that there is a real need for more knowledge about marriage. Third, from many years of counseling with married couples in conflict has come first-hand knowledge of the complex problems involved in proper mate selection and marital adjustment in our time. And fourth, from many years of teaching the college course in marital adjustment has come a knowledge of what questions young people most need answered, of what may stimulate careful and critical thinking on their part.

The literature on marriage has been increasing in recent years at such a rapid rate that to keep up with it has become a considerable task. We have consulted most of the publications, and our thinking has been influenced and enriched by many of them. In fact, it would have been difficult to write this book without the ideas gained from others. To acknowledge all general sources of help is impossible, of course, but it is possible to give credit for direct quotation. We therefore wish to express our appreciation to the authors and publishers for permission to quote from their publications.

In addition, we wish to extend our special thanks to George W. Hartmann, Irwin A. Berg, Maurice H. Kraut, and Emery W. Balduf, who have been good enough to read the entire manuscript. Their suggestions and constructive criticisms have been especially beneficial.

To the editor of this series, Kimball Young, we are deeply indebted for his patient co-operation and suggestions for improvement in form and enrichment in content of the book.

All cases reported have been selected from our personal files and have been sufficiently disguised so as not to reveal the identity of individuals involved. We have their permission to incorporate their experiences for the benefit of others.

J.L.H.
A.L.H.

CONTENTS

1

MARRIAGE TODAY

Marriage in the United States today is in a state of transition. Within the last century, both its structure and its basic meaning have been modified. In fact, marriage as interpreted by our culture is still so much in a process of change that, though we know what it has been in the past, that knowledge alone will not tell us what it will be in the future. Nevertheless, we may surmise in what direction marriage is moving by noting some basic trends. First, marriage is changing from a partnership to a companionship. Second, it is moving in the direction of greater equality between mates. Third, modern marriage shows greater instability. Fourth, mates tend to stress marital happiness more than in former years. Fifth, there is a noticeable relaxing of forces which make for permanency in marriage.

These changes alone indicate that marriage is becoming less an institution which exists for its own sake and more a union in which men and women seek self-realization, self-expression, and effective personal adjustment. This kind of union becomes ever more complex, intricate, and intimate. To be successful in modern marriage, both mates must possess, more than ever before, a high degree of personal maturity, the ability to understand each other, and the capacity to develop compatability. These observations will become clearer as we examine in detail the essential characteristics of marriage as it exists today.

From Partnership to Companionship

About a century or more ago, the emphasis in married life was on co-operative work—actual physical labor shared by husband and wife in the creation and maintenance of a home. The couple were primarily partners in this undertaking, with which, indeed, they were so occupied that there was little time or energy left for companionship not directly associated with work. Insofar as companionship existed in former years, in most cases it was secondary. But as more and more functions were taken away from the home, it was only natural that those functions which were left became more central. Thus there has been a shift from partnership to companionship, a shift which is still in progress.

The changes in the functions of marriage depend even today much upon whether a couple lives in a rural or an urban area; and in urban families, much depends upon whether a couple lives in its own home or in an apartment. The greatest changes are taking place in the urban areas.

Typical functions which have been or are being taken away from the home are the following:

Production of Economic Goods. Several centuries ago, cloth was woven exclusively in the home. Later, materials were available through purchase, and only sewing was done in the home. Now, more and more families buy almost all cloth products "ready-made." Similarly, once all food was raised and prepared by the family. For example, the average family once ground its own grain for flour with which to make bread. Subsequently, this primitive process was eliminated when prepared flour became available; and today, most households go one step further by depending upon prepared breads and other ready-to-eat foods, available at any grocery or delicatessen.

Religious Education. In former years, father and mother together transmitted to their children religious traditions. Now this task is performed by the "Sunday school," summer church school, and other similar training centers under the direction of the churches. The religious influence of parents often is limited to precept and example.

"Dinner isn't started, dear. I'm becoming a mental companion to you."

George Clark and the Chicago Tribune–New York News Syndicate, Inc.

Education. Parents no longer play a considerable part in the formal education of their children. Formal education has been taken over almost completely by the public and private schools.

Recreation. Only a few generations ago, the family itself created its recreation, which centered in such activities as playing musical instruments, singing, playing games, reading, and conversing around the fireside. All this has changed, and today most recreation is found outside the home. Radio and television are modifying this trend, it is true, but still the home is not the major locale of recreation.

Protection. The sick, the weak, and the old were formerly taken care of in the home. Today an increasing number of specialized institutions have assumed this function.

All these changes have affected the wife more than the husband, for many of her functions have lessened or even disappeared. In her greatly altered role, she must find new values for herself. She is still responsible for giving her children an early start in life (though even here the nursery school steps in), but she no longer performs many of the functions that formerly made her of value to her husband. To replace these lost values, she has tended to become a companion to him, functioning now more on the psychological level. In this period of transition, neither husband nor wife is fully prepared for the wife's new role.

Unfortunately, there are at present several hindrances to the effectiveness of companionship. Husband and wife spend less time together than in the past. As a rule, the husband spends all day away from home, so that the couple see each other only evenings and over week ends—and even these times may be shared with relatives and friends. Furthermore, a considerable number of married women (one in seven) are gainfully employed outside the home; and, unless they are in business together, husband and wife seldom work at the same place. Moving in different areas of activity, they develop interests so diversified that they may not be able to share them. They may, indeed, make new friends and acquaintances with whom they can share interests and values more satisfactorily than with each other. Thus their companionship suffers if the only hours left them to spend together are those when fatigue is at its peak. They may then be so tired and irritable that they cannot fully enjoy and benefit from each other's company.

GREATER EQUALITY BETWEEN HUSBAND AND WIFE

Marriage does not exist in a vacuum. On the contrary, it is constantly influenced by its cultural surroundings. Therefore, as culture changes, marriage changes; and as women are granted greater equality with men outside the home, they demand and receive more freedom within the home. It is generally true that modern society is granting women more and more rights and privileges. In the economic sphere, the woman is permitted to own property, to enter into business and industry, and to earn her own living as she pleases. Increasingly, she is receiving the same pay as a man for the same work. In the political sphere, she may vote and hold office. She is being admitted to institutions of higher learning and, gradually, to all the professions. More and more social restrictions are being removed to give her opportunity for greater self-realization. The introduction of contraceptive devices has relieved her from the burden of excessive childbearing. All these changes have enhanced woman's status.

In this period of transition, woman is not quite ready for her new role; nor is the husband ready to understand it in full. Both cling to the old while at the same time striving for the new. To be successful, both need a new orientation, one based largely upon a better understanding of their own personalities.

GREATER INSTABILITY OF MODERN MARRIAGE

Marriage today is characterized by increasing instability, which manifests itself in separation by mutual consent, desertion, and divorce. Folsom estimates that the number of families affected by desertion is about half the number affected by divorce.[1] Since a greater number of desertions than divorces involve children, the undesirable effects of desertion are greater than mere statistics indicate. Exactly how many separations there are, no one knows,

[1] Joseph K. Folsom, *The Family and a Democratic Society*, New York, John Wiley & Sons, 1943, p. 509.

since some of these "separations" are permanent. According to the best estimates, a large proportion of the more than two million persons living apart are permanently separated. It is common knowledge that the divorce rate in the United States has been rising steadily for years. In 1900 there was only one divorce for every twelve marriages, whereas at present the rate is about one divorce for every four marriages. In some localities, the rate is even higher.

How much suffering and unhappiness are caused by desertion, separation, and divorce can be fully understood only by those involved in such situations. Ordinarily, people get married because they are certain they are in love and are loved. This feeling builds up their self-respect. They anticipate a great deal of happiness in their marriage. As a consequence of marital instability, they not only become frustrated in the love which they feel as a basic need but also are forced to lower their opinion of themselves. There results the most unpleasant feeling a person can have—the hurt ego. Thus, in proportion as the couple expected happiness, they become disillusioned about themselves and about life in general. The degree of such effects depends, of course, upon the personalities involved.

Publicity and the airing of private matters in a divorce court generally bring loss of status and feelings of shame and humiliation. Friends and relatives are often affected adversely. The consequences are even more serious when children are involved, for they are deprived of security and affection. The psychological wounds thus created in many persons may never fully heal; even when they do, the scars often remain during a lifetime. There are other painful effects of forceful and unnatural termination of a marriage, but probably enough has been said to show that everything possible should be done to remove the causes of disrupted marriage.

The causes for divorce, separation, and desertion are many. Here we are concerned primarily with the adjustment factors involved, and these are by no means insignificant. Indeed, some authorities regard them as major causes. Christensen states: "Legal grounds for divorce are often not the same as actual causes, and state laws on the subject vary greatly. Legally, the three most commonly used reasons for divorce are cruelty, desertion, and adultery. Actually, this tells almost nothing. It is probable that most divorces are by mutual agreement, as evidenced by the fact that very few divorce suits are ever contested by the defendant. Since state laws require that there be some reason, with the implication of guilt, married mates wanting a divorce will frequently resort to collusion, hatching up a case that will get them by the law. Of all the real causes, incompatibility is the most basic, and behind that usually lie personality inadequacies. Authorities agree that successful marriage is one of the best evidences of a good adjustment to life and unsuccessful marriage of a poor adjustment." [2] Insofar as this analysis of the causative factors of divorce is correct (and the authors believe that it is), the divorce rate will decrease to the extent that mates are equipped to evaluate personality characteristics before marriage and to adjust after marriage. Enlightenment about these two major factors is one of the primary objectives of this book.

MORE STRESS UPON MARITAL HAPPINESS

One can safely say that most people who enter marriage have as their aim greater personal happiness. This aim can be primary or secondary, but in our country there is a strong tendency to make it primary. While our forefathers were also glad to be happy in marriage, in most cases other reasons for marrying or for staying married were equally or even more important for them. Such considerations as economic welfare, the security of a home, the prestige of having and rearing children, the desire to marry a person of one's social and economic status, either attracted them to marriage or aided them in keeping their marriage intact. At present, an increasing number of persons tend to make these reasons secondary and, consequently, either do not get married if they cannot foresee happiness in a marital state or get out of marriage if they cannot find the happiness they anticipated.

Let us examine a number of available studies dealing with

[2] Harold T. Christensen, *Marriage Analysis*, New York, The Ronald Press Company, 1950, pp. 13–14. Reprinted by permission.

marital happiness. The following tables do not show how many of those who felt they were unhappy got a divorce later, so that the percentages for unhappy couples may also, in part, cover divorced couples. But a sufficient number of unhappy couples remain married to make unhappiness of married couples a distinct problem. The tables will indicate how married people rated themselves regarding their happiness or how they were rated by others.

Tables 1 and 2 are based upon self-ratings, and Tables 3 and 4, on ratings by friends and acquaintances. Interestingly enough, the ratings are very much alike. While the sampling for some of

TABLE 1[3]

Happiness Ratings	*902 Husbands* Per Cent	*644 Wives* Per Cent
Extraordinarily happy	25.5	27.2
Decidedly more happy than average	29.4	28.0
Somewhat more happy than average	13.1	10.1
About average	18.2	16.3
Somewhat less happy than average	6.6	7.3
Decidedly less happy than average	3.2	4.0
Extremely unhappy	4.0	7.1
Total	100.0	100.0

TABLE 2[4]

Happiness Rating	*526 Couples* Per Cent
Very happy	42.6
Happy	20.5
Average	14.4
Unhappy	13.5
Very unhappy	8.0
No reply	1.0
Total	100.0

[3] By permission from *Psychological Factors in Marital Happiness*, by Lewis M. Terman *et al.* Copyright, 1938. McGraw-Hill Book Company, Inc. P. 78.

[4] Ernest W. Burgess and Leonard S. Cottrell, Jr., *Predicting Success or Failure in Marriage*, New York, Prentice-Hall, Inc., 1939, p. 32. Reprinted by permission.

TABLE 3 [5]

Happiness Rating	2,080 Men Per Cent	2,176 Women Per Cent
Very Happy	58.0	58.0
Doubtful	15.0	15.0
Unhappy	27.0	27.0
Total	100.0	100.0

TABLE 4 [6]

Happiness Rating	Number of Cases 17,533 Per Cent
Very happy or happy	61.6
Average	18.9
Unhappy, very unhappy, or divorced	19.5
Total	100.0

the tables is small, the percentages given are almost uniform. If these percentages are representative for the population in general, one may conclude that about 65 per cent of married couples are happy or very happy, about 20 per cent just get along, and about 15 per cent are more or less unhappy. Translated into actual numbers, the picture thus presented would be impressive. In 1952 there were 76,500,000 married persons living in the United States. Of these, 49,725,000 would be happy or very happy in their married life; 15,300,000 would just get along; 11,475,000 would be unhappy or very unhappy. It must be unpleasant for 15,300,000 to get less out of marriage than they expected, but the sufferers are the 11,475,000 who would frankly admit that they are definitely unhappy.

In some cases, marital unhappiness may lead to personality

[5] Paul Popenoe and Donna Wick, "Marital Happiness in Two Generations," *Mental Hygiene*, 1937, 21:218–223.
[6] Data by Richard O. Lang, reported in Burgess and Cottrell, *op. cit.*, p. 139. Reprinted by permission.

disorders, which are more or less serious, depending upon stability of personality before marriage and upon the intensity of the conflicts in marriage. Physicians, psychiatrists, clinical psychologists, and marriage counselors encounter many such cases. Here are a few examples:

Mrs. F. finds married life painful and inescapable and, as a consequence, builds up a world of phantasy in which she is happily married, worshipped by her husband, showered with gifts from him, and given endless attention. At first, such imaginings are infrequent and she recognizes them as products of phantasy; but after a while they are accepted as real, and Mrs. F. lives constantly in a dream world.

Mrs. W. feels antagonistic toward her husband. For some time she can endure intimacies, but after a while they upset her so much that her physiological processes lead to all kinds of aches and pain. She becomes ill, and this condition helps her to escape unpleasant attention. In due time she becomes a chronic invalid.

Mr. S. lives in almost constant overt conflict with his wife. He tries to forget his worries by getting drunk and ultimately becomes an alcoholic.

Even if these consequences were based upon personality deficiencies before marriage, the fact remains that marital maladjustment could have precipitated them. The opposite of this picture is equally true. Some persons have personality inadequacies before marriage which happiness after marriage helps them overcome.

CAUSES OF MARITAL UNHAPPINESS

There are many reasons why people are unhappy in their marriage. Let us consider four basic ones. The *first* is ignorance. A number of people do not know what constitutes happiness, so that they can neither give happiness to others nor receive it themselves. This is especially true because of the unconscious factors involved in human relationship. The *second* is the utopian idea of marriage. Such a concept is fostered in modern society by magazines, novels, movies, the radio, and television. There is nowhere a perfect state in this world; yet too many young people are encouraged to believe that marriage is such a state. "They lived happily ever after" is a pat conclusion too often accepted. Many people develop their own illusory idea of "living happily," and if reality later does not conform to this notion, they become disillusioned. One would think that examples of marital unhappiness which young people see around them would disabuse them, but most people persist in believing that somehow *their* marriage will be "different." Such a belief is prevalent perhaps because it is satisfying to the ego.

The *third* reason for unhappiness involves marked differences 3 between the personalities of husband and wife. While two young people are in love, these differences are frequently minimized, but later they assert themselves with full force. Examples are differences in religion, race, education, taste, status, and general systems of value. These differences often produce frustrations, guilt feelings, worries, and deep feelings of self-depreciation and loneliness. The *fourth* reason is personal immaturity, which mani- 4 fests itself especially in dependency and autonomy. When an adult still depends, like a child, upon the service of other people, he is immature. He merely receives without being able or willing to give anything in return. A person is autonomous when his needs must be satisfied regardless of inconvenience or discomfort to anyone else. Such an immature mate is indeed a "ball and chain."

RELAXING OF FORCES MAKING FOR PERMANENCY OF MARRIAGE

Once a couple is married, they are not entirely free to dissolve their union should they so desire. They must first confront those forces—such as public opinion, law, and religion—which have a tendency, through pressure and control, to make marriages endure. In former years, such pressures were so great that voluntary dissolution of marriage was practically impossible. At present, though controls are less rigid, public opinion is far from unanimous in approving divorce. We find extreme attitudes. At one extreme are those who do not condone divorce under any circumstances; at the other are those who glamorize divorce. For the latter, divorce has almost become a fashion. Between these extremes are various degrees of acceptance of divorce as unavoidable. Many persons are beginning to regard divorce as a normal phenomenon of our modern age. No longer are divorced persons looked upon as necessarily immoral or devoid of good character. Evidence of this attitude is found in the fact that divorced persons are respected and accepted in all walks of life. They continue in their professions, remain members of their clubs, and, with few exceptions, retain membership in their churches. Generally, they do not find social stigma against them sufficiently strong to prevent them from selecting a new mate.

A century ago it was almost impossible to obtain a divorce in any state in our country under any circumstances. At present, all states permit divorces, the last state to enact a divorce law being South Carolina, in 1950. While the grounds for divorce were few at first, they are increasing in number in many states. Though five states still grant divorce only on grounds of adultery, seven states recognize fourteen different grounds. These are adultery, desertion, cruelty, alcoholism, impotence, failure to provide, conviction of a felony, insanity, imprisonment, separation, pregnancy by another at marriage, bigamy, indignities, and drug addiction. A couple wishing to be divorced for a reason not recognized by their state may establish residence in another state and thus obtain a decree. In some sections of the country, there has been a tendency to simplify and speed up divorce procedures.

There has also been a noticeable change in the religious attitude toward divorce. While the Catholic Church and extremely conservative branches of the Protestant and Jewish faiths still do not approve of divorce under any circumstances, on the principle of "what God hath joined together, let no man put asunder," other, more liberal branches are gradually accepting divorce as inevitable under certain circumstances. At first, an attempt was made by some Protestant churches to punish only the "guilty" party in a divorce by not permitting him or her to remarry. Now it is recognized that the causes of an unhappy marriage leading to divorce are not so easily isolated and that "guilt" cannot be ascertained in every instance. At present, divorced persons are permitted to remarry, even with the sanction of the church, provided the officiating minister understands and passes on the case. Several ministers and religious workers known to the writers have continued in their profession after obtaining divorces themselves. Sometimes persons who, after obtaining a divorce, find themselves not accepted by their church, form another religious connection to help them toward adjustment.

The over-all effect of the relaxation of outside pressures is to make marriage more and more a voluntary union of two persons. Permanency of marriage thus depends increasingly upon the judgment of the two persons involved, and success or failure in marriage is becoming a personal responsibility. This fact becomes highly significant when it is realized how adequate personal adjustment is increasingly required to meet the demands of modern marriage.

PREPARATION FOR MARRIAGE

In these times we are quite aware of the fact that preparation is necessary for success in various vocations and professions. Similarly, the individual is trained in social skills so as to be able to meet the demands of society. Commendable efforts are made to discover and develop in him interests and hobbies and to provide him with diversified information aimed toward preparing him for the specific roles he must perform in the future. With all our enthusiasm to protect and educate the "whole personality" so that the individual will be ready to meet various problems in life and to play all roles effectively, one would assume that everything possible is also being done to prepare him for marriage. Indeed, since so much more is required of two individuals to be successful in marriage today, one would expect preparation for this role in life to be given top rank in importance.

Unfortunately, relatively little is being done at present to inform, train, and prepare youth for one of the most significant roles of their lives. Some work along this line has been done, it is true, and credit should be given to those institutions—some schools, young people's groups in churches, and clubs—which are making a brave and helpful start in this direction. More and more enlightened persons with a deep understanding of personality structure and an appreciation for the adjustment needed in marriage have spoken up forcefully for the growing need of such training. Stagner says:

> "The remarkable stupidity of a nation which sends children to school for ten or fifteen years to learn a profession, and lets them learn absolutely nothing about marriage, which is far more important than any profession, is a mystery to the logical mind. When we consider that the very core of American social structure is the institution of marriage, it is more than amazing that children not only receive no positive training, but are actually filled with false notions about it." [7]

In the past, preparation for marriage was left, on the whole, to incidental learning and more or less informal tutoring. In the matter of selecting a mate, incidental knowledge came from the frequent association with other members of the community from which mates were chosen. Young people grew up together and thus learned to know each other. But today, there is more freedom in the choice of a mate, and, consequently, young people must be better equipped to make their choices. Geographical, economic, social, educational, and religious barriers are breaking down; as a result, young people often marry without sufficient time for learning to know each other. Actually, even association for some time is rarely sufficient. One needs insight and skill in order to appreciate important personality patterns. Ideally, one should be able to predict how a person will behave in the future under circumstances about which one knows very little at the moment.

Another change is also worthy of consideration. In the past, parents had much more to say about the selection of mates for their children than they do today. The early Puritans arranged marriages between their children, primarily on an economic basis. At present it is considered the prerogative of any young man or woman to choose a mate without parental intervention. To give primary concern to parental choice in this matter is open admission that one is tied to "mother's apron strings" and that father is

[7] By permission from *Psychology of Personality*, 2nd ed., by Ross Stagner. Copyright, 1948. McGraw-Hill Book Company, Inc. P. 379.

nearby. The important thing is not economics, but love and happiness. Unfortunately, the nature of love and happiness is little understood.

As long as family life was relatively simple and husband and wife were partners, the roles that each had to play in the future could be learned merely by growing up in a family. The young woman often received some special training from her mother in her future duties as a wife and mother. Today, such tutoring has become inadequate. Some of the more important areas in which special preparation is needed will be discussed in the following chapters. Before proceeding to a discussion of these topics, however, a few words need to be said concerning the notion held by some individuals that marriage is not a topic for study, that it is too personal to be treated in an objective analysis.

Two Arguments Against an Objective Study of Marriage

First, we encounter the argument that young people fall in love and marry, that love is an emotion, that it is blind, and that no amount of objective consideration will alter this condition. Second, there is the argument that if one examines objectively and critically the whole matter of getting married, one destroys the romantic element of marriage and thus removes from marriage its pleasant features. These points are made so frequently by older as well as younger people that they should be dealt with here, even though we thereby anticipate some matters to be discussed later. For if the reader carries these objections in the back of his mind, he may look upon what follows as idle speculation and a waste of time.

The first argument assumes that falling in love does not conform to the general principle of behavior: that for every effect there is a cause. Just as nothing happens in the physical world without a cause, so nothing happens in behavior without an adequate cause. Many of the causes, especially in human behavior, are often hidden and unknown. And human behavior is more often the result of several causes than of a single cause. Some of these may be completely unconscious in the individual, so that only a trained specialist can discover them.

Why one falls in love with a specific person and not with another can be known only when both are studied as individuals, but the fundamental causes of falling in love are fairly well known. A person falls in love because of his personality make-up at a particular time. He considers himself love-worthy because he was loved as a child. He is used to being accepted rather than rejected. He also has a need to experience the love relationship. Consciously or unconsciously, or in both ways, he has built up a concept of the kind of person with whom he can fall in love. This concept becomes his "ideal." The sources of the concept are (1) previous associations with persons of the opposite sex who have given him pleasure—a mother, sister, aunt, other girls; (2) the reading of fiction; (3) daydreams about girls; (4) movies and television; and (5) observation of the behavior of others. As a rule, when he meets a person who in one way or another possesses the characteristics implied in such a concept, he will fall in love. At the time of falling in love, he may be "in the mood"; that is, psychologically he may be especially longing for companionship with the opposite sex, or his repressed sex urges may have made him so tense that he seeks relief from this tension. The whole experience may arouse such a strongly pleasant emotion that he cannot think clearly. Since it is so pleasant, he tries to prolong it and therefore resorts to phantasy thinking in which all the aspects of a love relationship are embellished. In order to enjoy this state to the utmost, he endows the object of his love with all the attributes his ideal possesses. He will not see her as a real person but as his idealized person. From this point of view, one may say that "love is blind."

The more a person knows *beforehand* about the process of falling in love and what transpires in that process, the less he will be overcome by emotion and the more he will be guided by reason. Reason and emotion are forever antagonistic; the more insight a person possesses, the less he will be dominated by any emotion, pleasant or unpleasant. Not that reason ever completely destroys or removes emotion in anyone. It is rather a matter of limiting the frequency, intensity, and duration of emotion and, on the whole, refining an emotion so as to make it appropriate to a given situation.

The same principle applies to the second objection, that objective study will destroy the pleasant emotion present in romantic love. Such a study will not at all destroy the pleasant sensations, feelings, and ideas connected with romance, but, on the contrary, will refine, enrich, and prolong them. To most persons in our society, romance is a necessary element in the pattern of life. Without it, they would be unhappy, and life for them would be dreary, drab, and empty. Merrill states:

> "Romantic love is the principal prerequisite to marriage in the United States. Courtship and marriage without romance are considered unthinkable, ridiculous, and a little immoral. Actions committed in the name of romance are morally condoned, if not always enthusiastically accepted. Actions committed without the protecting sanction of romance are often considered reprehensible. Romantic love is necessary to the public welfare." [8]

In spite of the fact that romantic love is of such significance to millions in our society, some persons wish to do away with it completely. They regard the whole experience as an illusion, as the cause of many unhappy marriages and, at best, as only a temporary phenomenon, which should be replaced as soon as possible with an adjustment to "reality." We believe that these criticisms apply not to romantic love as such but to its extreme manifestations. When romantic love is characterized as glamorous, dreamlike, ecstatic, "out of this world," we are dealing indeed with unrealities. But when we speak of romantic love as being thrilling, exciting, exhilarating, and adventuresome, it has a definite place in the experience of any normal person, both before and after marriage. To remove romance in the latter sense of the word from marriage would be to convert it into a cold business arrangement.

How can the romantic element of love be refined, enriched, and prolonged in marriage? The answer lies in the selection and cultivation of those elements of romantic love which are consonant with a normal, happy marriage. What, then, are the romantic

[8] Francis E. Merrill, *Courtship and Marriage*, p. 23. Copyright 1949 by Francis E. Merrill. Reprinted by special permission of The Dryden Press, Inc., New York.

elements in a love experience? First, there is the element of adventure—something is happening which one hoped for only in phantasy thinking or daydreams. Popularly expressed, "one sees a dream walking." Second, there is the impression of being singled out from millions of people as "the one and only." One might say to himself: "I can't believe it is happening to *me*." Third, one is convinced that there are greater things to come—that this is only the beginning. One is filled with great anticipation for the future. Fourth, the thinking is of the pleasant kind. Consciously or unconsciously, one remembers all the pleasant things that ever happened in his life and realizes that the experience of "falling in love" is the greatest of all. Cinderellalike images are common. Fifth, a great deal of projection is present. The person romantically affected will ascribe to the loved one all kinds of beautiful and wonderful characteristics which his or her love-ideal possesses. In other words, one does not see the real person, but a person endowed with a halo. Sixth, there is a conviction that, since all this happened without any effort but by merely exposing oneself to an opportunity, so all one has to do in the future is to wait for more and more similar experiences. Seventh, undoubtedly there is present some sexual excitement; it may not come directly from the genital areas, but from the sex hormones, which are poured into the blood stream. All in all, the experience is one which puts the individual in a state of well-being or euphoria.

Not all marriages begin with romantic love, nor will all romantic love experiences eventuate in marriage; but however marriage begins, it will be happier if it contains some romantic elements. Let us look at the above points. First, marriage is an adventure, a joint adventure, in living together, in sharing the new experiences of founding a home and rearing children. In order to be stimulating, there must always be some element of novelty in any marriage. Second, a husband and wife should always feel that each has been singled out as *the* one. To feel that anyone else might perhaps have been just as good does not contribute to one's need for feeling important. Third, each mate should always encourage the other to realize his or her potentialities for growth and development, thus stimulating the promise of greater things for the future. Fourth, many couples find not only that reliving pleasant past experiences is invigorating but also that it puts them into a hopeful mood for the future. Fifth, projection has no place in a marital relationship, for it leads to misunderstanding; but to look for actual good qualities in the other and to give recognition to them promotes successful marriage. In other words, the projection of romantic love must be replaced in marriage by a realistic understanding of the mate. Sixth, a mate should be exposed to pleasant stimulation from the other; that is, good things should be expected, for such expectation will encourage the other to do his or her best. More important, one must try to make a mate happy by satisfying as many needs as possible. Seventh, a well-adjusted couple will know how to get romantic satisfaction from their intimate association with each other.

All these remarks indicate that romantic love can be and should be present throughout married life. A more detailed discussion of marital adjustment will show specifically how romantic love in marriage can be maintained.

INTERPRETATIVE SUMMARY

1. The very nature of modern marriage is changing. It is still in a state of transition; therefore, young people entering marriage do not get a clear-cut picture of the kind of union expected of them.

2. Young people formerly could learn everything they needed to know about marriage in their own homes; now, because of the changing nature of marriage, they need more systematic preparation than the home can provide. At present, society is not sufficiently aware of such needs and, consequently, does not satisfy them.

3. Marriage is changing from an institution to a relationship in which companionship is the principal motif.

4. The old idea of the husband as an absolute ruler is giving way to that of a democratic relationship.

5. "Until death do us part" in marriage is being replaced more and more by "until our legitimate personal interest do us part."

6. The emphasis is more on mutual happiness than on the per-

manence of a marital union in which either spouse may be forced to make unwarranted sacrifice.

7. Yet the roles which a husband and wife must play in modern marriage are not well defined.

8. More and more, public opinion, law, and religion are approving divorce as an acceptable method of dissolving some marriages.

9. Education about marriage can be of great value, in spite of the emotional element involved in mate selection.

10. A scientific and objective analysis of love need not destroy its romantic elements. In fact, these elements can be refined and prolonged.

THOUGHT QUESTIONS AND PROJECTS

1. There is a marked decline in the production of economic goods in the modern home. With this fact in mind, compare the bases for mate selection of seventy-five years ago with those of the present.

2. Religion in family life is said to be decreasing. Do the members of your group believe that modern families are less religious? Do they express their religion differently today? Have they more individual freedom in religious expression?

3. Do you believe that the church plays an important role by bringing young people together in youth organizations?

4. Discuss pro and con: Members of a family need to spend more of their recreational time together.

5. Schools have virtually taken over the formal education of children. What practices are now being used to keep parents informed about and interested in their children's educational progress?

6. The modern home does not carry as much responsibility for protection of its members as in former years. Can you name local, state, or federal agencies and organizations represented in your community which assist the family in the care of the aged, the handicapped, and the sick?

7. Ask each member of the class to list his or her reasons for

wanting to marry, ranking them 1, 2, 3, etc., according to importance. Leave each list anonymous except for M (male) or F (female). Tabulate reasons submitted, noting duplication and rank of importance given to reasons. Check differences and similarities in responses given by men and women.

8. What factors may have encouraged the element of romantic love between courting couples fifty years ago? What factors aid today in building up a romantic concept of love?

9. Find out what is currently being done in your community to help young people prepare more adequately for marriage. If you discover that nothing is being done, what do you suggest as primary steps to be taken toward meeting that need?

10. Do you believe that genuine love alone is adequate for a successful and happy marriage? Defend your point of view.

SUGGESTED READINGS FOR FURTHER STUDY

Adams, Clifford R., *Preparing for Marriage*, New York, E. P. Dutton & Company, 1951.
    Chapter 1. Why Should You Marry?
Bowman, Henry A., *Marriage for Moderns*, 3rd ed., New York, McGraw-Hill Book Company, 1954.
    Chapter 2. The Reasons for Marriage.
Burgess, Ernest W., and Harvey J. Locke, *The Family*, 2nd ed., New York, American Book Company, 1953.
    Chapter 16. The Family in Transition.
Burgess, Ernest W., and Paul Wallin, *Engagement and Marriage*, New York, J. B. Lippincott Company, 1953.
    Chapter 1. Marriage in Transition.
    Chapter 2. The Study of Modern Marriage.
Christensen, Harold T., *Marriage Analysis*, New York, The Ronald Press Company, 1950.
    Chapter 1. Introduction and Orientation.
Goldstein, Sidney E., *Meaning of Marriage and Foundations of the Family*, New York, Bloch Publishing Company, 1942.
    (An interpretation of Jewish marriage.)
Harper, Robert A., *Marriage*, New York, Appleton-Century-Crofts, 1949.
    Chapter 1. Marriage in Modern Society: Romance and Realism.
Landis, Paul H., *Your Marriage and Family Living*, New York, McGraw-Hill Book Company, 1946.
    Chapter 2. The Seven Important Social Functions of the Family Have Changed.

Magoun, F. Alexander, *Love and Marriage*, New York, Harper & Brothers, 1948.
Chapter 2. The Nature of Marriage.
Merrill, Francis E., *Courtship and Marriage*, New York, The Dryden Press, 1949.
Chapter 1. Courtship as a Social Relationship.
Chapter 2. Courtship and Romantic Love.
Schmiedeler, Edgar, *Marriage and the Family*, New York, McGraw-Hill Book Company, 1946.
(A book dealing with marriage from the Catholic point of view.)
Skidmore, Rex A., and Anthon S. Cannon, *Building Your Marriage*, New York, Harper & Brothers, 1951.
Chapter 1. Why Prepare for Marriage?
Winch, Robert F., *The Modern Family*, New York, Henry Holt & Company, 1952.
Chapter 1. Definition of the Family and of the Area of Study.
Chapter 14. Romantic Love in American Life.

2

PERSPECTIVES OF MARRIAGE

Marital adjustment is much more complex than it may at first appear. Two persons entering marriage must adjust to each other on various levels. On the organismic level, they must adjust to each other's sensory, motor, emotional and intellectual capacities and needs. On the personality level, they must adjust to each other's habits, skills, attitudes, interests, values, traits, ego concepts, and spiritual beliefs. In addition, the couple must adjust together to their total environment, including such matters as a new household, children, provision and preparation of food, relatives, friends, recreation, and work. This adjustment is by no means static; it is a dynamic process. Mutual needs of the couple must be satisfied in sickness and in health; in good and in depressed moods; in prosperity and in times of shortage; in a friendly and in a hostile environment; in success and in failure.

Marital adjustment is thus so varied and many-sided that it must be considered in several perspectives to be appreciated and understood. We shall present here eight perspectives. We do so with full awareness that not even all these put together can do justice to the unique experiences a couple may have in married life. We recognize that the pattern of adjustment of any married couple remains always a highly individualized one.

LITERARY PERSPECTIVE OF MARRIAGE

Novelists and short-story writers from ancient to modern times have shown interest in the adjustment between a man and a woman. There is not a facet of this interrelationship that has escaped the attention of authors. They write about ecstasy, love, hate, jealousy, devotion, domination, enslavement, loyalty, unfaithfulness, selfishness, monogamy, polygamy, divorce, and a

"Darling, this is the happiest day of my life! Wait'll you see the car dad gave us!"

George Clark and the Chicago Tribune–New York News Syndicate, Inc.

host of other features of marriage. Sex is treated from many angles —attraction, compulsion, continence, convention, curiosity, experimentation, fear, disgust, ignorance, incest, inhibition, intimacy, perversion, and promiscuity. Love affairs, triangles, and illegitimate children are common in the pages of literary creations.

Literary authors are not interested primarily in informing and instructing the reader, as are scientists. Consequently, they need not be hampered by facts. They can create characters and conditions. Their limits are only the limits of their own imagination and their desire to portray essential truth as they see it. They can dramatize any aspect of marriage until it stands out in great relief and vividness. The reader may become so interested that he forgets himself completely. He is prepared to enjoy; therefore, he is not critical. Scientific treatment, compared with a more entertaining approach, may seem drab and boring. The creative writer cannot be concerned with an accurate analysis of cause and effect. He can create both of these as he desires, whereas the scientist must strive constantly for accurate analysis of actual situations. What has been said does not imply, however, that the products of literary authors have no scientific value. On the contrary, in many cases the insights revealed by some of them bear up quite well under present psychological and psychiatric analysis.

ANTHROPOLOGICAL PERSPECTIVE OF MARRIAGE

Anthropologists have contributed much to a better understanding of the meaning of marriage. They have collected a rich storehouse of information about the types of marriage in a great variety of both modern and ancient cultures. These facts make an interesting background for the study of our own society's interpretation of marriage in that they bring to attention cultural contrasts. We are often not aware of our own mores and beliefs until we meet people who differ from us. These contrasts are brought vividly to the attention of anyone who travels among peoples of different cultures. Each person seems to be convinced of the innate "rightness" of his own culture. Seeing other cultures often compels an individual to examine his own and helps him attain greater objectivity in his thinking.

A few examples will illustrate cultural contrasts. In our society, the only form of marriage recognized and approved is monogamy. In other parts of the world, the established form of marriage is polygamy, in which a man may have two or several wives. Polyandry, one wife having several husbands, is also found, though not as commonly as polygamy. A still rarer form is group marriage —several men mated to several women.

In our society, an individual is free to select any mate, except for a few legal restrictions concerning such matters as blood relationship, age, and health. In many other societies, in contrast, there are very strict rules, or taboos, which regulate mate selection. Under endogamy, marriages outside the tribe or village are strictly forbidden. Under exogamy, one *must* marry outside the tribe. In some areas of the world, instead of merely asking a girl to marry him a man must buy his wife, the price often being determined by the social position of the bride. In some regions, the young people concerned have nothing to say about the choice of a mate; their marriage is arranged exclusively by parents. In other parts of the world, child marriages are common.

Our mores stress virginity, especially for women, at the time of marriage; but the enforcement of these mores is left to the discretion of the persons concerned. Among some people, virginity is made a prime requisite for marriage. There are, on the other hand, some tribes which pay scant attention to the premarital sex experiences of young people. And in some areas, no one will marry a girl until she proves that she can become pregnant.

We regulate the termination of marriages by law: divorce can be granted only by a court. In certain other parts of the world, a man can divorce his wife by the simple process of publicly announcing that he is so doing.

Thus there are in the world deviations from every single aspect of marriage as it is practiced in our society. The bigoted or narrow-minded will dismiss all these deviations as inferior practices; the objective person will try to understand the basic, underlying factors of marriage in general. To an objective person, such deviations from our own forms of marriage and such differences in mores are not only interesting but also instructive and important. He is encouraged to treat every aspect of marriage with greater objectivity and to try to determine which aspects of marriage are incidental to culture and which are more universal and therefore more basic.

BIOLOGICAL PERSPECTIVE OF MARRIAGE

From the biological point of view, marriage is an outgrowth of the mating drive between the male and the female. It is, in effect, an invention by man to regulate the animal sex drive and to provide for the rearing and education of offspring. While the cultural superstructure has undergone many changes throughout the centuries, the biological function naturally has remained the same.

Biologists have done much to dispel ignorance, superstition, and fear concerning the normal processes of the body. Because of their work, we are better informed than were our forefathers about reproduction, heredity, genetics, and health. Because of their study of the structure and function of the reproductive apparatus of men and women, we understand better the nature of the sex drive, the process of conception, fertility and infertility, and the possibilities of intelligent birth control. Through their study of hereditary forces, the biologists have dissipated superstitions concerning sex determination of offspring and the inheritance of acquired characteristics. The discovery of the laws of heredity has contributed to the possibility of ultimate improvement of the race through eugenics. The biologists' contribution to the general improvement and maintenance of health is inestimable. In many ways, then, the work of the biologists has greatly increased the possibility of happiness in a modern marriage.

ECONOMIC PERSPECTIVE OF MARRIAGE

While it is true that man does not live by bread alone, it is true also that he must have bread in order to live. There is an intimate relationship between economics and successful marriage, because income is necessary to satisfy many physiological needs. Economic contentment in marriage appears to depend not on the amount of economic goods a couple has at its disposal but on the adequacy of these goods to meet what it regards as important needs.

The economist recognizes an important movement still in progress, one in which the family is changing from a unit concerned with both production and consumption of economic goods to one primarily concerned with consumption. As a result of this shift, the home economist has become an important person in education for marriage. In order to assist couples in the establishment and maintenance of a family, special departments of home economics or home management have been created in our colleges and universities. Typical courses of study listed in these departments are Food Economics, Meal Planning, Food Preparation, Nutrition, Interior Design, Textiles, Household Buying and Budgeting, and Clothing Construction.

The need for information and guidance in economics is recognized by numerous other organizations, institutions, and business firms, many of which offer courses in the management of a household. It is interesting to note that even our popular magazines for women are today devoting more and more space to the economic problems which every woman must face in directing her home and family.

Legal Perspective of Marriage

In the eyes of the law, marriage is primarily a legal contract. The aim of marriage laws is to preserve and protect the institution of marriage. In actual practice, of course, emphasis is on the permanence of any particular marriage. Once a union has been consumated, it can be broken only by establishing that one or the other member is guilty of not fulfilling the conditions laid down by the laws. The happiness or unhappiness of either or both mates is of very little concern to the law. (Only within recent years have a few states granted divorce for mental cruelty.) It knows only of duties, obligations, and responsibilities, which it enforces by threat or punishment. Because of this fact, the law can and does deal only with the external manifestations of marriage; the true essence of marriage is beyond its reach. One might say that the law deals with the shell and not with the kernel of marriage. It covers such aspects of marriage as age of marital partners (but only insofar as one or both may be minors), physical and mental health, blood relationship, racial differences, property rights, legitimacy of children, fraud and duress, licenses to marry or to perform the marriage ceremony, and annulment or divorce.

It is significant that, though the law does little to regulate the entrance into marriage, it is very much concerned with its termination through any means other than death. By fulfilling only a few requirements, any couple can get a license to marry, but should they decide to end their marriage by divorce, they encounter many legal difficulties.

It should be noted that divorce laws, on the whole, do not precede, but follow, public opinion. As a rule, such laws originate in the following manner. Couples will run into a problem which makes their union unbearable. In due time, public opinion, concerning itself with their problem, becomes crystallized. The next step is to enact such crystallized opinion into a law. Since considerable time elapses in the process just described, many couples are forced to endure much unhappiness before they can get legal relief. Because of these conditions, many couples resort to all kinds of deception to obtain a divorce. It is well known that the legal grounds given for divorce are, in many instances, not the actual causes.

RELIGIOUS PERSPECTIVE OF MARRIAGE

In speaking of religion, we have in mind only religion as it is taught by the major faiths in our country—the Jewish, Protestant, and Catholic faiths. All three agree, in the main, on the origin, nature, purpose, and moral character of marriage.

Origin of Marriage. According to these religions, marriage is a divine institution, founded by God. God created man and woman, and then decreed that they live as husband and wife. Thus, marriage (the *institution* of marriage) is made in Heaven. This is not the same, however, as saying that a particular marriage is arranged in Heaven. Contrary to what some people suppose, the three major faiths do not hold to this notion.

Nature of Marriage. Marriage, having been created by God, has therefore a spiritual quality, in addition to being a physical, biological, legal, social, and psychological union. Just what is meant by *spiritual quality* is hard to determine, since precisely what is meant by spirit is not understood. Speculation about spirit has sought to explain it as a level of being over and beyond mind. Reality is assumed to include four levels. The lowest is that of matter, the inorganic world; the second is the level of life, or organic world; the third is the level of mind, the thought world; and, finally, there is the level of spirit. What constitutes the spiritual world is beyond the full comprehension of the human mind, for just as mere organic life cannot "understand" mind, so mind cannot, in the fullest sense, understand spirit. The qualities of spirit are the same as those ascribed to God. Since each human being possesses these qualities in some degree, the union between man and woman is a spiritual union.

Purpose of Marriage. The purpose of marriage is the consecration of individual lives, since marriage is regarded as sacred or holy, or as a sacrament. In the Jewish faith, marriage is *kodosh*, meaning that it is sacred, or a consecration. Protestant churches use the term *holy:* marriage is a holy estate. The words *holy* and *sacred* characterize that which is set aside for divine use. Any object can be made holy or sacred. Thus ordinary bread, when used in a religious ceremony, becomes sacred or holy. The Catholic Church thinks of marriage as a sacrament, a visible means by which Divine grace is sought and conferred.

In any one of the three religions mentioned, marriage performed by its official representatives is endowed with an element of sacredness. It becomes an institution in which its members are instruments in the service of God. Thus husband and wife do not seek primarily their own happiness but carry out God's function in creating a religious home. If husband and wife are happy in their marriage, so much the better; but they marry for "better or worse." On the whole, the emphasis of all three faiths is on the marriage union, and not on the individuals who enter into it.

Moral Character of Marriage. Theoretical religion and theoretical morality are not identical, but applied or practical religion implies morality. The three faiths agree in teaching that man is of great value; that, by virtue of having been created by God, men constitute a universal brotherhood; and that the highest principle of interpersonal relationship is love. These three beliefs are the bases of religious ethics and supply the best motivation for moral living. Marriage, as an intimate union between two persons, cannot function successfully without the application of moral principles. In fact, marriage has a threefold moral function. First, the daily life of husband and wife should be a practical application of ethical principles. Second, marriage adjustment should be training in the acquisition and perfection of moral character. Third, it should be the duty and responsibility of husband and wife so to rear their children that they become moral persons.

Religion as a Factor in Successful Marriage. In view of the attitude of the faiths toward marriage, one might reasonably ask whether marriages in which religion is an important factor are more successful than marriages not so characterized. Certain research studies indicate that the answer is affirmative. A study of 13,000 young people in Maryland lists the following percentages for separation, desertion, and divorce according to religious affiliation: Jewish 4.6; Catholic 6.4; Protestant 6.8; mixed 15.2; no religion 16.7.[1] Burgess and Cottrell find a positive correlation between good marital adjustment and (1) attendance at Sunday school beyond the age of eighteen, (2) church attendance two or three times a month, and (3) marriage in a house of worship by a minister, priest, or rabbi.[2] Terman and associates state: "Certainly attitudes congenial to Christian teaching should be favorable rather than unfavorable to successful marriage provided that the mate chosen were sympathetic in viewpoint."[3] They also say, however: "There is nothing in our own investigation or in the investigations of others to warrant the belief that religious training during childhood has much effect one way or the other on marital happiness."[4]

[1] Judson T. Landis, "Marriages of Mixed and Non-mixed Religious Faith," *American Sociological Review,* 1949, 14:403.

[2] Ernest W. Burgess and Leonard S. Cottrell, Jr., *Predicting Success or Failure in Marriage,* New York, Prentice-Hall, Inc., 1939, pp. 122–126.

[3] By permission from *Psychological Factors in Marital Happiness,* by Lewis M. Terman *et al.* Copyright, 1938. McGraw-Hill Book Company, Inc. P. 163.

[4] *Ibid.,* p. 236.

We may conclude that, insofar as religion is a factor in marital success or happiness, it is so for two reasons. First, a person who, because of religious teachings, regards marriage as a permanent union will make a greater effort to adjust to a mate than he otherwise might. Second, a person who incorporates within himself certain religious traits—love, sympathy, kindness, understanding, respect for others, loyalty, unselfishness, and trust—will possess characteristics favorable to a happy and successful marriage.

SOCIOLOGICAL PERSPECTIVE OF MARRIAGE

Sociologists, regarding the family as the basic social institution, are interested primarily in its organization and function. For sociologists, what differentiates marriage from mere biological mating is the fact of social approval. Formerly, marriage was considered an institution preserved by external forces; now, it is regarded more and more as a companionship held together by social and psychological forces operating between husband and wife. Burgess and Locke state that "the family in historical times has been, and at present is, in transition from an institution to a companionship. In the past, the important factors unifying the family have been external, formal, and authoritarian, such as the law, the mores, public opinion, tradition, the authority of the family head, rigid discipline, and elaborate ritual. In the new emerging form of the companionship family, its unity inheres less and less in community pressures and more and more in such interpersonal relations as the mutual affection, the sympathetic understanding and the comradeship of its members." [5]

In spite of this shift from institution to companionship, cultural forces are still of primary importance, since, as sociologists point out, personality itself is a cultural product. According to Faris, "Culture is the collective side of personality; personality the subjective aspect of culture." [6] While not all sociologists would subscribe to this statement, they agree that the basic traits of per-

[5] Ernest W. Burgess and Harvey J. Locke, *The Family,* 2nd. ed., New York, American Book Company, 1953, p. vii. Reprinted by permission.

[6] By permission from *The Nature of Human Nature,* by Ellsworth Faris. Copyright, 1937. McGraw-Hill Book Company, Inc. P. 278.

sonality are formed in the family, and that the basic function of the family is creating and maintaining a common culture. Husbands and wives enact roles that have been prescribed by society.

Interested as they are in the organization and maintenance of the family, sociologists are particularly alert to any forces which either prevent the formation of family life or disrupt it after it is formed. Of special interest, therefore, are such matters as family income, legal prescriptions about marriage, public opinion, customs, mores, childlessness, divorce, personality inadequacies, and character defects.

Since sociologists regard marriage as a basic social institution, it is natural that they have devoted a great deal of time, energy, and skill to research on anything pertaining to marriage. This is evidenced by the great number of books, monographs, and journals written by sociologists about the family.

Sociologists are interested also in teaching youth about marriage. The first course in marriage ever to be taught in this country was that given by Ernest R. Groves at the University of North Carolina in 1933. Other schools rapidly followed his example, and by 1950 five hundred and fifty colleges and universities were offering six hundred and ninety-seven courses taught by one thousand nine hundred and sixty-eight professors. Most of these courses are offered in departments of sociology.

The interest of sociologists in this field manifests itself not only in teaching but also in marriage counseling. Sociologists have been active in supplying information about proper mate selection and methods of resolving marital conflicts. They have greatly enriched the service of family agencies by stimulating interest in and actively participating in marital counseling.

PSYCHOLOGICAL PERSPECTIVE OF MARRIAGE

Psychology is currently defined as the science of behavior. For the psychologist, marriage is just one form of behavior. About any behavior, the following questions may be asked: What is happening? Where it is happening? Why does it happen? How and when does it happen? The psychologist is interested primarily in the questions of the "why" and the "how" of behavior. The "what," the "when," and the "where" give him only its data and their setting.

The "Why" Question in Psychology. The psychologist explains behavior by motives, which are, for him, the mainsprings of human action. Motives are not simple units, however, but may be further analyzed into needs, drives, and goals. The basic elements are needs. No human being is complete in himself; at all times he draws from his environment and he protects himself from its destructive aspects. Thus he has a need for food and must protect himself from extremes of temperature. It is not our intention to give an exhaustive list of human needs, but merely examples. Man has visceral needs—for food, liquids, air, elimination, sex; sensory-motor needs—to see, hear, touch, taste, act, and rest; emotional needs—sympathy, affection, love, freedom from fear and anxiety; ego needs—security, recognition, power, and self-realization. Needs may be innate or acquired, universal to the species or individual and unique.

The human organism is so constituted that, whenever a need is present, tension of some sort is produced, manifesting itself in an activity. This activity is called a *drive*. It may be explicit or implicit, localized or generalized. An organism has as many drives as it has needs; for this reason, the words *need* and *drive* are often used interchangeably. The relation between need and drive can be illustrated by examining what happens when an organism experiences hunger. When blood sugar falls below a certain level, the stomach, by a mechanism yet not fully understood, begins its churning movement. If no food is introduced from the outside, the sensations arising from stomach activity will activate more and more of the organism, until a person can do nothing but think of and look for food.

Perhaps none of the drives are directed by heredity toward any one object or condition in the environment which will satisfy a need and thus stop a drive. The objects or conditions which possess the capacity for stopping a drive are called *goals*. Learning which goals will satisfy which needs is often a long and slow process. In many cases, there are several goals which may satisfy a particular need. The psychologist calls a goal-directed drive based upon some need a *motive.*

In passing, some other causes of behavior must be briefly defined. An *urge* is practically synonymous with a drive but is slightly more conscious than a drive. An *impulse* is a quick, unexpected expression of a drive. A *desire* is a more or less strong feeling for an object or condition which will satisfy a need. A *wish* is very similar to a desire, except that the object or condition is more conscious. A *want* is a need with an unpleasant feeling tone. A *purpose* is very closely related to motive. Perhaps the best definition is that given by Shaffer: "A purpose is the symbolic representation of a motive. Purposes involve not only the existence of a motive and its recognition, but also the knowledge of the end-result of activity by which the motive may be satisfied." [7]

The "How" Question in Psychology. The "how" pertains primarily to the methods, ways, and means of attaining goals which will satisfy needs or stop drives. This is by no means a simple process. Drives quite often conflict; the satisfaction of one may mean the suppression of another. Since many objects or conditions may satisfy a particular drive, there must be selection of the "best." A certain drive may be so complex that the individual must master intricate techniques and skills to satisfy it. Above all, needs must be satisfied in such a manner as not to interfere with the rights and privileges of others. In fact, in a civilized society, each person must know how to help others achieve satisfaction of their needs. In an intimate marital relationship, all of the above matters are of great significance.

PSYCHOSOCIAL PERSPECTIVE OF MARRIAGE

In order to present a complete picture of marriage, one must view it from all of the above perspectives. This can be done either by having specialists of each orientation write treatises on marriage from their viewpoint or by taking one or more of these orientations

[7] Laurence F. Shaffer, *The Psychology of Adjustment,* Boston, Houghton Mifflin Company, 1936, p. 110. Reprinted by permission.

as basic and organizing the others around them. Much can be said in favor of either of these approaches, but the latter approach, for reasons given below, appeals most to us. When we examine books on marriage written by sociologists, we find that they cannot proceed far without bringing in psychological considerations. It is equally true that a psychologist cannot say much about marriage without referring to the sociologist for data. The logical consequence is to integrate these two approaches. This we are endeavoring to do. Our orientation can therefore be regarded as psychosocial. Biological, legal, religious, anthropological, and economic points of view will not be disregarded. On the contrary, they will be incorporated at appropriate places in order to present a total and unified picture of marriage. Our emphasis, then, is upon marriage as a product of the interaction between social and psychological forces. The cardinal concepts are (1) personality and interaction, and (2) society and its culture.

Definition of Marriage. From the psychosocial point of view, marriage is a more or less permanent, culturally determined union between a man and woman for the purpose of attaining mutual happiness. The detailed meaning of this definition will become clear as the reader proceeds through this book. Here we wish to make a few general observations on basic terms. The union is a companionship rather than a partnership. The union is characterized by feelings of oneness and of belonging which manifest themselves in sharing and participation. It involves adjustment of one person to another. Adjustment has two aspects: (1) adapting oneself to another, and (2) changing the other to suit oneself. This process is accompanied by many problems, because it is hard to determine where adaptation to the mate should cease and change of the mate should begin. Even when this point can be determined, there is still the problem of the method of change.

The union is in part culturally determined. Society not only provides the cultural atmosphere within which a couple must function but also sets up definite expectancies in the form of laws, religion, mores, and public opinion, to which a couple must conform. To the extent that a couple abides by these cultural requirements, the union will be sanctioned and approved by society.

The marriage involves two personalities. It may begin with merely physical attraction, perhaps sexual attraction; but if it is to persist, it will involve the adjustment of two entire personalities. Since each personality is not only extremely complex but also unique, to match two personalities and then to make them function harmoniously requires much insight. To complicate this problem further, there are some innate personality differences between men and women. Since we regard the adjustment of two personalities as central in marriage, we must devote considerable space to the nature of personality, to the proper selection of a mate, and to an analysis of adjustment.

The purpose of marriage, from our point of view, is the increased happiness of both mates. It is rather significant that the first thorough research in marriage by a psychologist concerned itself with the isolation of factors which contribute to happiness in marriage.[8] We consider happiness so central to marriage that we regard any marriage from which happiness has disappeared not as a marriage but as some kind of business arrangement. Any legal marriage for any purpose other than happiness is not marriage in the sense in which we use the term.

The Meaning of Happiness. Terman says: "Marital happiness . . . is not a single variable but rather an omnibus name that embraces an infinitude of interrelated satisfactions no one of which can be described in purely quantitative terms. . . . Happiness of any kind is admittedly a very complex phenomenon, and marital happiness is no exception to the rule. Its elements are in the strict sense qualitative rather than quantitative and can never be measured as linear distances are measured." [9] Two phrases stand out in this quotation—"an infinitude of interrelated satisfactions" and "qualitative." These phrases, as we interpret them, suggest the basis for the meaning of happiness. Happiness is a pleasurable condition resulting from the merging of a great number of pleasant experiences. These many pleasant feelings are cumulative in their effect, and their summation is retained by the

[8] We refer to Lewis M. Terman *et al., op. cit.*

[9] By permission from *Psychological Factors in Marital Happiness,* by Lewis M. Terman *et al.* Copyright, 1938. McGraw-Hill Book Company, Inc. P. 5.

organism just as complex intellectual experiences are retained. The experiences which channel or feed pleasant feeling tones into the ego or self in married life are of three kinds: sensory, emotional, and intellectual. Many pleasant stimulations come from the eyes, ears, tactual sense, and sex organs. Others result from such shared emotional experiences as joy, delight, and pleasant surprises; still others come from sharing thoughts, memories, and adventures. In the course of years, there will be an "infinitude" of such elements of happiness.

These experiences do not come to the individual in a chaotic or senseless pattern. Rather, they center on basic needs which the husband and wife seek to satisfy in their marriage. Each one will measure marital happiness according to the satisfaction of what each regards as his or her basic needs. Since people do not agree about what they regard as basic needs and since these needs are arranged according to their concepts of values, it is not possible to draw up a universally accepted list, nor to arrange needs in an order acceptable to all. Nevertheless, an enumeration of what most people consider basic needs in marriage will further illustrate what is meant by marital happiness. These are (1) security, financial as well as emotional; (2) respect for one's personality; (3) sharing of experiences; (4) love or affection; (5) sexual satisfaction; (6) degree of physical comfort; and (7) ability to satisfy the mate's needs. (Each of these is further explained in Chapter 5, Why People Marry.) It is obvious that each of these needs can be satisfied to varying degrees. Thus a person can rate the degree of his satisfaction on each item, from 1 to 100 per cent. Having

MARITAL HAPPINESS SCALE

	1	25	50	75	100
1. Security					
2. Respect					
3. Sharing					
4. Love					
5. Sexual satisfaction					
6. Physical comfort					
7. Ability to satisfy mate					

rated himself, he can plot his happiness curve, and he also can determine the average degree of his happiness.

Individuals will vary greatly in their ideas about the relative importance of each of the above needs. In fact, some individuals will consider one or the other of no importance at all. Nevertheless, a conscientious self-rating will give a reasonably objective picture of one's inner state of being. It may also indicate to one's mate or to oneself any unsatisfied need that may be preventing greater happiness.

It cannot and should not be expected that all experiences the husband and wife will have with each other will be accompanied by pleasant feeling tones. There will be many which are definitely unpleasant and painful. Naturally, for a couple to be happy, their pleasant experiences should outnumber the unpleasant. Such unpleasant and painful experiences should not be regarded as completely without value, provided they do not outnumber the pleasant ones and are not too intense. They alert a couple to possible underlying differences which, if not periodically resolved, can become dangers or threats to their marital happiness. The occasional unpleasant experience between mates can provide a sharp contrast to their peaceful harmony. Such experiences may call their attention to the possibility that they may be losing their happiness, and this realization may encourage them to increase their effort to maintain a harmonious union.

INTERPRETATIVE SUMMARY

1. Marriage is such a complex and many-sided relationship that no single approach to it offers adequate explanation. Eight possible approaches are sketched briefly in this chapter.

2. Novelists and short-story writers have portrayed many aspects of marriage. While they have been interested primarily in entertaining the reader, many of them nevertheless have contributed richly to a better understanding of marriage.

3. Anthropologists have described vividly and accurately the cultural forms and manifestations of marriage from ancient times

to the present. Their studies have stressed the great diversity in marital form and practices.

4. Biologists see marriage primarily as an institution for the procreation of offspring and the preservation of the human race.

5. In former years, the family was primarily a center of the production of economic goods; in modern times, it has become primarily a consumer of goods. As a result, the present-day housewife must be much better informed about the economics of buying and financial management than was her grandmother.

6. Marriage laws are all enacted with the intent of preserving the institution of marriage and therefore deal with entrance into marriage, the rights of husband, wife, and children, and the conditions under which a marriage can be dissolved.

7. Religion is concerned primarily with the ethical, moral, and spiritual aspects of marriage.

8. Sociologists view the family as the basic social unit. They are especially interested in the dynamic interaction of this unit with other social and cultural forces.

9. Psychologists stress marriage as an interaction between two persons of opposite sex and regard the happy marriage as dependent upon the satisfaction of basic personality drives.

10. The authors' primary orientation toward marriage is psychosocial.

Thought Questions and Projects

1. Think of five married couples in whose home religion appears to play an important role. What aspects of their daily life seem to be affected by religion?

2. Would there be advantages or disadvantages in having uniformity of marriage laws for all states? Support your opinion.

3. According to present laws, it is usually easier to enter into marriage than it is to get out of it. Is this desirable?

4. What kinds of services are there in your community to which you may go for budgetary advice and economic counseling?

5. Discuss at least two well-known novels which deal with economic problems of the family.

6. Discuss the following:
 (a) The treatment of the sex-love marriage theme in five widely read "pulp" magazines.
 (b) How the "family situation" plot is handled by two or three television or radio presentations.
 (c) Current commercial films in which marriage problems are presented. Evaluate any proposed solutions.

7. If you were an anthropologist and wanted to study behavioral patterns of married couples in other societies, where would you prefer to make such a study? Why?

8. What kinds of services has the sociologist made available to couples in solving their marital and family problems?

SUGGESTED READINGS FOR FURTHER STUDY

Bowman, Henry A., *Marriage for Moderns,* 3rd ed., New York, McGraw-Hill Book Company, 1954.
 Chapter 13. The Use of Money and Leisure Time.
Jung, Moses, ed., *Modern Marriage,* New York, Appleton-Century-Crofts, 1947.
 Chapter 13. A Religious Approach to Marriage, by Leland Foster Wood.
 Chapter 8. The Legal Aspects of Marriage, by Mason Ladd.
Koos, Earl L., *Marriage,* New York, Henry Holt & Company, 1953.
 Chapter 2. The Purposes of Marriage.
Locke, Harvey J., *Predicting Adjustment in Marriage,* New York, Henry Holt & Company, 1951.
 Chapter 13. Economic Factors.
Mace, David R., *Hebrew Marriage, A Sociological Study,* New York, Philosophical Library, 1953.
Mead, Margaret, "The Contemporary American Family as an Anthropologist Sees It," *Journal of Social Case Work,* November, 1947, 28:323–330.
Merrill, Francis E., *Courtship and Marriage,* New York, The Dryden Press, 1949.
 Chapter 8. Economic Roles: The Homemaker.
 Chapter 9. Economic Roles: The Working Wife.
Pilpel, Harriet F., and Theodora Zavin, *Your Marriage and the Law,* New York, Rinehart & Company, 1952.
Stone, Hannah M., and Abraham Stone, *A Marriage Manual,* rev. ed., New York, Simon and Schuster, 1952.
 Chapters 2 & 3. The Biology of Marriage.
Young, Kimball, *Personality and Problems of Adjustment,* 2nd ed., New York, Appleton-Century-Crofts, 1952.
 Chapter 17. Some Problems of Marriage and Divorce.

3

THE NATURE OF PERSONALITY

In 1932, Murphy and Jensen made the following statement about our knowledge of personality: "Considering the fiendish complexity of the human organism, it seems to us very improbable that this century or even the next will succeed in systematizing our knowledge and in giving us a conception of personality as clear and as sound as the conceptions of contemporary physical science." [1]

Fifteen years later, Murphy concluded a new study of personality with these significant words:

> "The psychology of personality as it exists today will be crushed and pulverized and a new creation made from the débris, not because of the wisdom inherent in criticism of it but simply because in grappling with the problems of man it will be weighed in the balance and found wanting. Even the increasingly fascinating materials which the present methods are found to produce will leave man dissatisfied. The task of the psychology of personality today is to apply ruthlessly, and to limit, every promising suggestion of today, but always with the spice of healthy skepticism which will know how infinite are nature the macrocosm, and man the microcosm, how infinitesimal our knowledge of it and of him." [2]

It is with such respect for the complexity of our subject and the awareness of the limitations of our present knowledge of it that this chapter is written. What can be said about personality in one chapter is necessarily only fragmentary, but we hope that even a limited presentation will help toward a better understanding of the subject.

[1] Gardner Murphy and Friedrich Jensen, *Approaches to Personality*, New York, Coward McCann, Inc., 1932, pp. 57–58. Reprinted by permission.

[2] Gardner Murphy, *Personality*, New York, Harper & Brothers, 1947, pp. 926–927. Reprinted by permission.

DEFINITION OF PERSONALITY

Allport has enumerated and examined fifty definitions of personality. Finally, he gave his own definition, which has become almost a classic: "Personality is the dynamic organization within the individual of those psychophysical systems that determine his unique adjustment to his environment." [3] The essence of personality, according to Allport, is *organization*. An organization consists of many units arranged in a systematic fashion or pattern.

In personality, what are these units? They are called psychophysical units. In common terminology, they are needs, drives, motives, habits, attitudes, traits, interests, values, and so on. All of them, separately and together, are to be thought of as dynamic and active. Each unit contains energy, and, integrated into one whole, all units form a great storehouse of energy. A simple analogy may help. We know that atoms, the units of our physical world, contain energy—as do any new atomic combinations. In a similar way, our personality, being made up of a great number of individual dynamic units, is not inert but is an active, driving, searching entity.

The definition stresses adjustment to environment—the fact that personality cannot be understood in isolation but is merely a nodal point, a focus of energy, which is a product of forces of the universe. What personality is in its essence, we do not know. We know it only in its interaction with environment and especially with other personalities in that environment.

Personality definitely cannot be thought of as confined within an organism; it radiates in every direction, and it interacts with everything with which the organism comes in contact.

Another important word in the definition is *unique*. Unique adjustment is based upon the uniqueness of personality structure. In all the millions of years of the existence of the human race, there have not been two personalities exactly alike, nor are there two today, nor will there ever be two perfectly identical personali-

---

[3] Gordon W. Allport, *Personality: A Psychological Interpretation*, New York, Henry Holt & Company, 1937, p. 48. Reprinted by permission.

ties. This fact can be understood easily if one remembers that every individual begins life with a chance combination of millions of genes, which have come not only from parents but from grandparents, great-grandparents, and so on. The environment which shapes the individual can also happen but once. The child is born

"I like you a lot, Jerry, but they say everyone has the perfect mate somewhere, and it just doesn't seem possible that he'd be right next door, does it?"

Reproduced by permission. Copyright 1951 by The New Yorker Magazine, Inc.

into a certain family, whose environment changes from hour to hour.

The unique structure of personality may be made more meaningful by the use of analogy. Everyone has a torso, arms, legs, head, hair, eyes, nose, and mouth; yet each human being looks somewhat different from all others. So also, though every personality contains many similar "psychophysical structures," these are integrated in each person in a unique fashion. Of course, one might extend the analogy by pointing out that as every unit of the body, such as the heart or the lungs, differs from individual to individual, every "psychophysical system" differs from a parallel system in another person. From all this, we should draw the conclusion that while one can learn a great deal by studying personality in general, such observation can never be a substitute for studying one individual by himself. This fact is of great importance in the selection of and adjustment to one's mate.

DEVELOPMENT OF PERSONALITY

Nature-Nurture. Personality is the product of the process of learning. All learning depends upon one's innate capacity and upon one's differentiated experiences—in other words, upon heredity and environment, or, as it has been expressed, upon nature and nurture. No one has been able to demonstrate how much each factor contributes to any one aspect of personality, much less to personality as a whole. We do know that both are important. It is obvious, for example, that no one could ever learn to play the piano, no matter how great his musical capacity might be, unless his environment afforded him an instrument and the opportunity to use it.

For our practical purpose, we need not concern ourselves with the proportion of heredity and environment in any trait, especially since a certain trait in one individual may be due largely to heredity, and the same trait in another individual may result primarily from training. For example, one person may tend to be aggressive because of innate vigor, drives, and tempo, whereas another person may become aggressive as a result of situations he encounters. It should be kept clearly in mind that throughout this book it is accepted as a fact that personality as a whole, or any one aspect of it, is a product of both heredity and environment, and that no effort will be made to determine the relative importance of the two.

There is a certain parallel between the growth of the body and the growth of personality. The body begins as a fertilized ovum, which at first develops rapidly. Growth continues from birth until the person reaches maximum size in his early twenties.

Personality also has a beginning. Whether or not a child has a personality before birth is still a disputed question; however, most psychologists seem to agree with Allport, who believes that a new-born infant is devoid of personality.

Whenever it first appears, the personality grows quite rapidly at first and reaches a certain state of maturity at about thirty years of age. Other, less perceptible changes follow, until senility is reached, when the personality begins to disintegrate. Ordinarily, there is a gradual modification of personality, although an intensely disturbing experience may bring about its complete reorganization. We may better comprehend personality in its full development if we first trace the process of its growth and change.

Despite their limitations, we shall use diagrams in tracing this development. If not taken too literally, they may help toward clearer visualization of the evolving structure of personality. We shall start with a simple, basic part of the diagram and add to it as the discussion progresses, until the complete picture is presented.

The Beginning of Personality

Biological Organism. Personality begins with the individual, the living organism as we find it at birth. This organism is extremely complex, but, for practical purposes, we may say that a new-born infant is made up of three closely fused parts, physique, chemique, and intellectual endowment, with their needs, drives, and capacity for growth. The innate elements of personality present at birth are represented in Figure 1 (p. 47).

Physique. The physique depends upon an individual's heredity and upon climate, food, exercise, and possibly other less-known factors. By physique, we mean sex, height, weight, general body contour, facial features, color, complexion, absence or presence of deformities, and so on.

The physical make-up of man was studied for many centuries on the assumption that it was the basis of personality. For instance, the ancient Greeks believed that if a man in any way resembled an animal, he had the characteristics of that animal. A man whose face was slim and pointed, a little like that of a fox, was assumed to be sly as a fox. Even today, many persons imagine that the character of an individual can be ascertained merely by studying his facial features. Thus, a man with a protruding chin is supposed to possess strong will power and determination, while

FIGURE 1. Hereditary endowment. Physique—the physical make-up of the child. Chemique—biochemistry and physiological functions, including emotional predispositions. Intellectual endowment—innate intelligence. In addition, there are the capacities for growth and learning.

the unfortunate person with a receding chin is dubbed a weakling. A person develops attitudes toward his body as he does toward other things, and these attitudes become important factors in his evaluation of himself. For the growing child or budding adolescent, physique is a significant source of inferiority feelings. During these crucial years of development, the smallest blemish or physical defect takes on exaggerated significance. Girls worry about being too fat or too tall and become concerned about the quality and color of their hair and of their complexion. Nor do young males escape periods of anxiety over their physique. At an early age, boys become "muscle-conscious." They want to be strong, muscular, and capable of competing in rugged sports. A person's physique determines also the attitudes of others toward him. His status in his peer group during childhood and early adolescence is almost completely dependent upon his physical appearance and skills. Physical appearance becomes a significant factor in the selection of a mate, especially in the later teens and early twenties.

Chemique. Body chemistry is undoubtedly of great importance in the development of personality, but, unfortunately, it remains a field of limited knowledge. Briefly, the chemique of the body involves, among other things, metabolism and the hormones from the glands of internal secretion, such as the pituitary, thyroid, parathyroid, adrenals, and gonads. According to our best knowledge, body chemistry is largely the product of innate factors. Upon these rest motility and temperament, neither of which is clearly defined at present. In general, though, by motility we mean energy, speed, and intensity and control of muscular activity. Many studies, especially by Gesell and his co-workers, show that motility remains constant through the years of growth and therefore very probably is innate.[4] Energy output, talkativeness, human social responsiveness, and emotional expressiveness, though influenced by training, certainly have their roots in innate motility.

Temperament has been defined in many ways. Were it not such an important aspect of personality, we would prefer to avoid the word altogether. We are confronted, however, with the fact that there is no personality without temperament. Warren's *Dictionary of Psychology* defines temperament as follows: "The general *affective* nature of an individual as determined by his inheritance and life history." Allport gives a better, although involved, definition:

> "Temperament refers to the characteristic phenomena of an individual's emotional nature including his susceptibility to emotional stimulation, his customary strength and speed of response, the quality of his prevailing mood and all peculiarities of fluctuation and intensity in mood; these phenomena being regarded as dependent upon constitutional make-up and therefore largely hereditary in origin."[5]

The three important terms in these definitions are *affective, emotional,* and *mood*. They all refer to a *quality* which an organism contributes to any experience. Since this concept of quality is of great importance in marital adjustment, further explanation may be helpful.

For example, sweetness is a quality. It exists for the individual

---

[4] Arnold Gesell *et al.*, *Biographies of Child Development*, New York, Paul B. Hoeber, 1939.

[5] Gordon W. Allport, *op. cit.*, p. 54. Reprinted by permission.

because his tongue has taste buds supplied with nerve ends which, when stimulated, report sweetness to the brain. When novocaine or a similar anesthetic is injected into the tongue, sugar no longer has sweetness for the otherwise sensitive buds.

Colors are qualities. Outside of an organism are light waves of varying lengths. When a certain wave length strikes the retina of our eyes, we see red. A color-blind person exposed to the same wave length cannot see the red color. Redness, then, is a quality added by our sense organs to objective events.

In a similar way, *affects, emotions,* and *moods* are qualities added to experiences by the human organism, not by a sense organ but by the nervous system, especially the autonomic (the system that regulates the internal organs). Thus, if a gun is fired near an infant, he will respond with excitement or perhaps with fear. Objectively, there were only sound waves, which came to the brain by way of the ear. The response of the organism is due to its make-up. Every human being is equipped by nature to respond qualitatively to his environment. What situation will produce affect in him depends not only upon innate equipment but also and largely upon his training and his momentary mood. Thus, a kiss from one person may be a thrill, from another a great annoyance; or a kiss from the same person at different times may be pleasant or unpleasant, depending upon mood. As this illustration implies, the qualities we add to any experience may be pleasant or unpleasant. This idea will receive further elaboration in Chapter 6.

Mood requires brief explanation. Every emotion has a cycle. We get angry when we meet with an intensely frustrating experience but, after a while, we "cool off," so to speak. If the emotion aroused persists longer than it ordinarily would, then this persistent form of emotional state may be called a "mood." Some persons seem predisposed to have lingering emotions or moods.

Intellectual Endowment or Intelligence. By *intelligence* is meant ability to adjust to novel situations. This implies that one perceives a situation clearly, is able to analyze it, sees familiar elements and new elements, and can draw upon the fund of previous information and devise new methods of attack. Intelligence, then, is concerned with problem-solving, thinking, judgment, and learning. That this capacity is of tremendous importance in the development of personality is self-evident. In fact, without it there is no personality. The higher the intelligence, other things being equal, the better an organism can deal with environment or make adjustments to it. Intelligence is intimately related to the nervous system, especially to the cortex—a thin outer layer of the brain which, in man, is made up of approximately nine billion neurons.

So far, we have stressed the equipment of the biological organism—its physique, chemique, and intelligence. In addition, the organism has capacity for physical and mental growth. Physical growth consists primarily of the multiplication of cells, their individual growth and integration. Mental growth is very similar. Here the unit is a pattern of neurons. These patterns are multiplied, strengthened, and integrated. In a sense, the sum total of these integrated patterns is the structure of personality.

Needs, Drives, and Motives

Nothing is more obvious than the fact that an infant depends upon its environment for survival. He needs many substances and special conditions in order to live and to grow; he needs to avoid injurious and destructive aspects of environment. As he matures, new needs arise. Whenever a need is present, tensions are produced in the organism. These tensions eventuate into some form of implied and/or explicit activity. This activity is known as a drive. (Since the two are so intimately connected, the terms are often used interchangeably.) A drive persists until some substance or condition is found which satisfies the need. What these substances and conditions are must be learned by the human organism, for at first drives are not directed toward these goals. When one's goals have been learned, drives are directed toward them. Drives now become motives. A motive, then, is a goal-directed drive.

Learning consists essentially in connecting needs and drives with goals. Thus, all learning is motivated. Since new needs may be built on old needs by this process of learning, it becomes clear that the process of motivation is extremely complex. Personality depends ultimately upon learning, and one may say that the study of personality is the study of motivation.

The importance of motivation in personality is recognized in the following statement by Gardner Murphy: "As the story unfolds it will become evident that this whole volume is about motivation; every aspect of personality is conceived in terms of the molding, the complication, the interpretation, the concealment, the indirect expression of motives." [6]

Classification of Drives and Motives. One would think that, since there is so much emphasis on drives and motives, there would be universal agreement among psychologists as to their number and their classification. Actually, however, there is considerable difference of opinion. Some psychologists accept a few basic motives; others, a great number. Some classify them into two groups; others divide them into several.

Since our purpose is not to study personality exhaustively but merely to acquaint the reader with its basic structure, we will select the most important drives for our purpose and classify them into physiological and psychological drives, realizing that this division is somewhat arbitrary because of overlapping. The list given below stresses the more important drives in the development of personality.

Comparison of Physiological and Psychological Needs or Drives. Physiological drives are segmental, whereas psychological drives involve adjustment of the entire organism to the environment; that is, physiological drives can be localized in certain areas of the organism, while psychological drives are felt "all over." Physiological drives have definite cycles. Psychological drives are more constant and differ in intensity from one time to another. For example, the hunger drive persists until food is taken, only to be felt again after a period of time. Drive for recognition is less crucial but, nevertheless, persistent, expressing itself more keenly at certain times than at others. Both types are much modified by

[6] Gardner Murphy, *op. cit.*, p. 86. Reprinted by permission.

environment; in fact, we do not know of any drive which does not manifest a reaction to external objects and situations.

Physiological drives depend more on internal stimulation than do psychological drives. The physiological needs must be satisfied if the organism is to live. Lack of satisfaction in any of the basic needs, except sex, means death. And if sex needs were not satisfied, the human race would die out.

Physiological Drives. The potency of physiological drives is well known to anyone who is at all familiar with the behavior of men and animals. It is not our purpose to discuss each of these drives

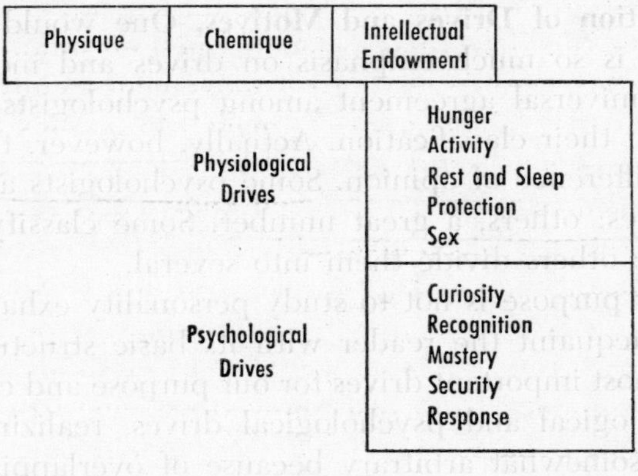

Physique	Chemique	Intellectual Endowment
	Physiological Drives	Hunger Activity Rest and Sleep Protection Sex
	Psychological Drives	Curiosity Recognition Mastery Security Response

FIGURE 2. Basic physiological and psychological drives having roots in heredity and environment. They are considered the central dynamics in personality development.

in detail. In fact, no drive can be studied completely by itself, because drives are all interrelated. From experimentation, we have fairly exact knowledge as to how these drives operate in animals. Since the human organism functions very much like that of an animal, we can draw many conclusions about physiological drives in man from these studies.

Let us first consider *the food or hunger drive.* Hunger produces restlessness and activity. When a hungry rat is put into an activity cage (a revolving cage especially constructed for laboratory tests), the greater degree of activity can be recorded and compared with normal activity. A hungry animal will cross an electric grid and take much punishment in order to get to food. It will learn to solve many problems in order to obtain this food. In fact, the hunger drive is used by trainers as an aid in teaching animals almost any trick. To evaluate the strength of the hunger drive in man, one has only to be reminded that there are thousands of things man will do to satisfy it; he spends much of his time in pursuing its satisfaction, and he seeks pleasure in the actual process of eating.

Activity is the very essence of life; in fact, it is one basic characteristic of protoplasm. A large proportion of our life, waking or sleeping, is taken up with activity caused by tensions in the nervous system and in the striped as well as unstriped muscles. The intense force of this drive may be seen when an infant's arms and legs are forcibly held to restrict his movements. Only a few moments of such treatment suffice to make the infant's face redden as he squirms, screams, and makes violent attempts to free himself.

Rest and sleep are drives too well known to need much comment. Deprivation of sleep invariably causes discomfort, suffering, and even illness. Puppies kept awake over an extended period of time are unable to survive more than ten days. Experiments have been made with college students as volunteer subjects who, after abstinence from sleep and rest, showed extreme irritability, irrational forms of behavior, actual illness, and of course final submission to sleep.

An organism will make every effort to gain *protection.* There are many reflexes, such as the pupilary winking, sneezing, coughing, and vomiting reflexes, whose primary function is to protect the organism from injurious substances or conditions. Almost any intense stimulus will produce some avoidance behavior. A loud noise will produce a startle response in the new-born infant. Living organisms, both animal and human, are capable of throwing off many toxins and germs. Only a short span of experience is necessary for man to learn to shrink away from dangerous situations, especially those producing pain.

The strength of the *sex drive* has been studied in animals and invariably has been found to be powerful. Most adults are personally aware of the acute force of this drive. Psychoanalysts have stressed the strength of the sex drive in infancy and childhood, and more will be said about this drive in other sections of the book.

Psychological Needs or Drives. *Curiosity,* in general, is a drive. However, curiosity in any specific thing is an attitude and is due greatly to experience. For instance, curiosity in astronomy or biology is an acquired attitude.

Is there such a thing as innate curiosity? Our answer is yes. There appears to be a basic drive found invariably in animals and human beings to explore any new environment in which they are placed. Attention is constantly shifted from one new element to another, until a feeling of satisfying familiarity is attained. An individual in a new situation starts immediately to investigate. Rats placed in a maze start at once to investigate their surroundings. Infants begin at an early age to explore their bodies. The astronomer explores the universe; the atomic scientist explores matter. In each case the same basic drive is present—a powerful curiosity about the unknown. We seek knowledge not merely for practical application, but also for the sake of knowing, for the sake of satisfying our curiosity. This curiosity is most commonly recognized in the form of need for new experience: all of us become bored with any daily routine if it is not occasionally spiced with some elements of newness. Obviously, there is a great variation in the strength of this drive from individual to individual, but it is present in everyone to some degree.

By *recognition* we mean that each individual wants to be counted as a separate entity, as a person in his own right. It is the psychological counterpart of the drive for survival which Darwin discovered in every living organism. This drive manifests itself in animals as well as in children when they use all kinds of attention-getting devices. Training largely determines from *whom* and for *what* in particular a person wants attention. Each individual wants to be recognized for what he is or for what he has or for what he can do. The satisfaction of this drive is invariably accompanied by pleasant feelings or emotions; and being deprived of that satisfaction can cause discomfort and unhappiness.

Mastery is closely related to recognition. It means essentially that an individual wants to count more than do his fellows; he wants to control. (Whether or not mastery is truly a drive has been questioned by anthropologists,)because some primitive tribes do not show competition such as is found in the Western societies. These anthropologists mistake a drive for an attitude. Primitive tribes may not compete for the same things for which Western man competes, but every human society shows some form of dominance behavior.

Every living organism seeks *security*—a state of harmony with its environment. There are objects and conditions in the environment which promote and those which threaten the existence and welfare of an organism. Every organism is so constituted that it will approach and align itself with a favorable environment and will seek to escape its unfavorable aspects. Insofar as these goals are achieved, the organism is in a state of security. The need for security is present from infancy to old age, and the fear of its loss is ever-present. Whether security needs are emotional or economic makes no difference. People are willing to do almost anything in order to be secure. No doubt the desire to possess either objects or persons is based upon this need for security.

The psychological drive remaining for consideration is difficult to name; for want of a more precise term, we shall call it *response*. The response drive is the tendency of one organism to be close to another, to attract others, to be emotionally united with them. In general, we mean what Angyal calls "a trend toward homonomy," [7] or what has been called "primitive satisfaction in the presence of others." On this drive are built many modes of interaction between individuals, such as identification, sympathy, affection, and love.

ENVIRONMENTAL FACTORS

It is conceivable that there is some influence on the organism by its prenatal environment, but thus far there is little reliable knowledge as to the extent and intensity of that influence. By concentrating on postnatal environment, we do not mean to preclude

[7] Andras Angyal, *Foundations for a Science of Personality*, New York, The Commonwealth Fund, 1941, pp. 167–207.

the possible important prenatal environmental effects. Our major concern is how postnatal environment affects the development of personality.

We regard environment only as a source of stimulation, a kind of stimulation which brings about changes in the organism, and especially within the nervous system. In the figure below, environment has been divided into three parts.

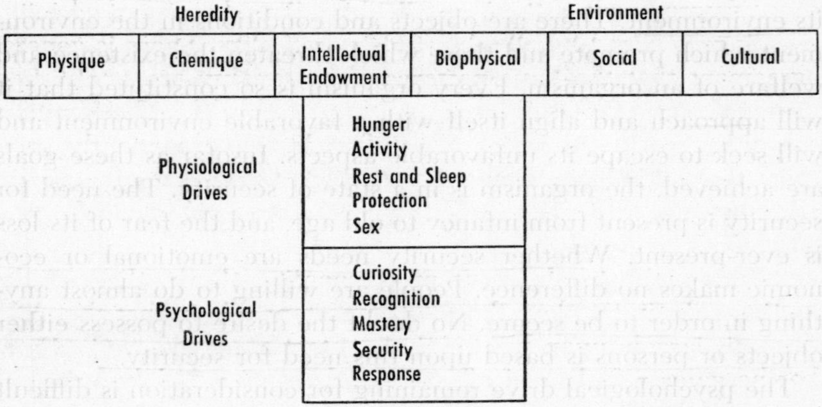

Heredity			Environment		
Physique	Chemique	Intellectual Endowment	Biophysical	Social	Cultural

Physiological Drives	Hunger Activity Rest and Sleep Protection Sex
Psychological Drives	Curiosity Recognition Mastery Security Response

FIGURE 3. Aspects of environment which influence development of personality.

In dividing environment into biophysical, social, and cultural, we do not claim that it is the only way of looking at environment; nor do we think of these three aspects as distinct units. We simply consider this division convenient and helpful in studying personality.

Biophysical Environment. Biophysical environment includes such matters as geographic location, climate, weather, fertility of soil, animals, especially domesticated animals, and all the material culture created by man. The significance of these for the development of personality has been amply revealed by anthropologists. On the whole, man has gradually been relieved from concern about his physical existence and has been able to devote more time to psychological satisfactions. Think of the contrast: to be born into an environment where all effort, energy, and time had to be expended in order to eke out a mere existence; or to be born into an environment which provides adequate means for better health, nutritious foods, physical comforts, more security, and general opportunity for ego-expansion.

Social Environment. Social interaction is of inestimable importance in the growth and development of personality. The first social environment is the immediate family, whose marked influ- *Basic* ence is recognized by all who study personality. There is general *patterns* agreement that the basic patterns of personality are established *of personality* during the first three to five years of a person's life. The family is the only "world" in which he at first lives; consequently, it is there that all his needs must be satisfied. To what degree and in what manner they are satisfied will determine the general trend of his personality.

In this early development of personality, the mother, or the mother substitute, plays the most important role in that the child depends largely upon her for the satisfaction of his needs. From her he gains a feeling of affection and security and from her he learns to accept discipline. The child discovers that his varied attention-getting devices fail to elicit consistently the response he desires, and he may at times become frustrated. In short, he finds himself in a world of rewards and punishments, one in which his needs are not always of primary importance. The father, too, confuses the child with "dos" and "don'ts" of his own. These varied experiences of the child make him both love and fear his parents.

The siblings likewise play an influential role in the development of a child's personality. From them he learns many skills, such as speech and types of play; from them he learns (often through painful experience) how to deal with his equals, how to co-operate, how to reconcile hostility and affection, when to speak and when to be quiet, when to dominate and when to submit, and even when to reveal and when to conceal his feelings.

Personality is molded not only by a person's immediate family but also by smaller or larger groups with which he may come into contact. From birth on he is in indirect contact with a larger group, for his parents are a product of group life. As he grows up, he will come into more direct contacts with groups outside his own family. These groups further direct the development of his personality. He acquires more and more "group memberships." In a sense he is a member of a group as an organ is a part of the body. Within a group he has meaning and purpose; without such membership he could never become a personality. However, it must not be thought that an individual is completely molded by society, for he also reaches out on his own, accepts some things and rejects others. He makes compromises and integrates all of his experiences in his own unique fashion.

Cultural Environment. Culture is a complex whole which includes knowledge, belief, values, art, law, morals, mores, traditions, customs, and many other capabilities discovered and created by man. Each society has its own culture, which it transmits from generation to generation. Therefore, every child born into a society is influenced and molded by a specific cultural system. This influence is so potent that he gradually becomes largely a "subjective aspect" of his culture. To what extent he becomes a "subjective aspect" or "replica" of his culture will depend upon the pressure exerted by his society on him and upon his individual make-up. If every individual were to submit completely to social pressure, there would be no chance for individualists and for progress.

ORGANIZATION OF PERSONALITY

The organization of the personality is a product of the interaction between the biological organism, on the one hand, and environment, on the other. The organism constantly seeks satisfaction for its needs from the environment into which it is born. In the process of getting satisfaction, it has many experiences. Such experiences are not to be regarded merely as temporary events; each experience leaves a more or less permanent imprint in the organism. These imprints, or records, are not retained in haphazard fashion—they are constantly organized and reorganized into a great variety of systems or units. These systems range all the way from very simple to highly complex ones. All of them are progressively integrated into one total unit or system—personality. In ascending order of complexity, the systems are designated as response patterns, habits, attitudes, traits, roles, and self or ego.

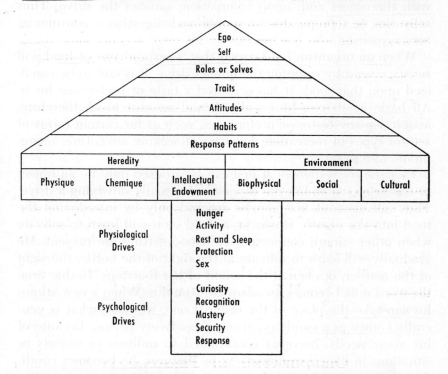

FIGURE 4. Diagrammatic representation of total personality integration. The various levels of response patterns, habits, attitudes, traits, roles or selves, and ego are conceived as modified drives as they are shaped by hereditary endowment and environmental factors.

(These levels should not be regarded as distinct, but as shading into each other.)

We are now prepared to examine the organization of the psychological elements of personality.

Response Patterns. According to Sherrington, there are two types of response connected with any need or drive.[8] They are the preparatory response, which consists of activities preparing the organism for contact with a drive-activating stimulus, and the consummatory response, which brings the organism into contact with the object and, upon completion, satisfies the drive. Thus salivation is a preparatory response and digestion a consummatory response.

When an organism has learned that a certain type of food will satisfy a need by stopping the hunger drive, it is said to be canalized upon that food. It has acquired a taste or preference for it. All basic needs can be canalized, and an individual, therefore, acquires many tastes or preferences, such as for certain forms of art, for types of recreation, for ways of seeking adventure, recognition, and so on.

Preparatory responses at first can be aroused only by an object or condition which has the capacity of actually satisfying a drive. Thus salivation at first can be aroused only by introducing the food into the mouth. However, a child soon will learn to salivate when other stimuli connected with food-getting are present. He gradually will learn to salivate at the sight of the bottle, the sight of the mother, or even at the sound of her footsteps. In due time the word *milk* becomes an adequate stimulus. When a new stimulus can take the place of the original one, we have what is generally known as a conditioned response. Every person, because of his many needs, becomes conditioned to millions of objects or situations in his environment. As he matures, he becomes conditioned to more and more abstract symbols.

Canalizations are seldom, if ever, eradicated. Conditionings may sometimes disappear, but as a rule they last throughout a person's lifetime. For these reasons, canalizations and conditionings form a stable and permanent foundation of personality.

Habits. A great many of the response patterns become firmly established and function almost automatically. Such response

---

[8] Charles S. Sherrington, *The Integrative Action of the Nervous System,* New York, Charles Scribner's Sons, 1906, Lecture IX.

patterns are called *habits*. Every person has innumerable habits or ways of dealing with physiological and psychological drives. Thus we have habits of eating, drinking, sleeping; habits of achieving protection and sexual satisfaction; habits of seeking security, new experiences, recognition, and response. Habits are often interlinked with each other into a chain or system. In this manner, people acquire *skills*, by which is meant performing an act with ease and precision. Many of these skills are of the motor type: riding a bicycle, driving a car, typing, or playing an instrument. Other skills are primarily intellectual: solving mathematical problems, reasoning logically, or thinking about politics.

Attitudes. An attitude is a learned mental and emotional predisposition to act positively or negatively toward a person, object, condition, or symbol. The mental and emotional elements are blended in varying proportions. On the one hand there are attitudes which are strong feelings of likes, dislikes; approval, disapproval; pleasantness, unpleasantness concerning a person, an object, or symbol. For this reason we sometimes try to discover a person's attitude by asking, "How do you feel about this matter?" On the other hand, there are attitudes which result more from cognitive processes—thinking and reasoning. Such attitudes are more closely related to opinion.

Attitudes are always directed toward a goal or an objective. One has attitudes toward generalized categories, such as government, religion, education, marriage, nationalities, children; and one has attitudes toward specifics, such as one's country, wife, child, the neighborhood church, or the Frenchman down the street.

When an attitude is well established, it predetermines an individual's behavior. Because of his attitudes, a person's actions are not so much guided by the immediate situation as influenced by his established or set way of responding to such stimuli. Therefore, it is often helpful to know an individual's attitudes toward certain matters, because we can then predict, with at least a fair degree of accuracy, what his behavior is likely to be in given situations.

Attitudes are intimately related to interests and values. When a person has a favorable attitude toward a person, thing, or situation, he will be interested in it. Interests are positive; therefore, whatever one is interested in must have value for him.

Most of our attitudes are acquired unconsciously. A great many are adopted "ready-made" from one's social environment—that is, from our parents, friends, teachers, and so on. These may undergo reorganization but, nevertheless, they remain essentially constant. Other attitudes are acquired by a person in the course of the variety of his experiences.

Traits. The word *trait* may indicate any means by which one person can be distinguished from another, or it may indicate "a generalized tendency to evaluate situations in a predictable manner and to act accordingly." [9] It is in the latter sense that the term is used here. If I am loyal in any situation in which loyalty is demanded, I possess the trait of loyalty. I am loyal not only to my friends but also to my family, my church, my school, my country. There are a great many traits. The reader will recognize the following common ones: co-operativeness, submission, dominance, persistence, extroversion, introversion, conscientiousness, gregariousness, and altruism. Allport and Odbert counted the designating trait names in the 1926 edition of Webster's New International Dictionary and discovered that of the 400,000 words listed, 17,953, or 4½ per cent of the total English vocabulary, were trait names.[10] Many of these terms overlap, but even so there remain a great number of traits.

No one person possesses all the traits, naturally, especially since many are contradictory. But the number and type of traits and their generality and integration are very important indicators of personality make-up. We shall come back to traits repeatedly in our discussion. Traits are usually considered to be the "significant" units of personality.

Roles. Every person plays a number of roles in his life. He plays the role of a child, a sibling, a pupil, a friend, a sweetheart, a

---

[9] By permission from *Psychology of Personality*, by Ross Stagner. Copyright, 1940. McGraw-Hill Book Company, Inc. P. 143.

[10] G. W. Allport and H. S. Odbert, "Trait Names: A Psycho-Social Study," *Psychological Monograph*, 1936, No. 211.

mate in marriage, a parent. As an adult, he may play several roles at the same time: a husband, a parent, a businessman, a friend. All these roles are defined by society, very often in a rigid fashion. As a person plays different roles, he will show different traits, attitudes, and habits. When the roles are played for some time, they become a fixed part of the personality.(They constitute, in effect, segmental selves.) In many cases, these selves are well integrated with one another; in others, they may contradict one another. A gangster may be very ruthless with society, yet very loyal to fellow gangsters and a model husband and father. In some rare cases, the selves may be incompatible with one another to the extent that there results the phenomenon of dual or multiple personalities.

Self. The apex of personality organization is the self; it is the highest integration of everything a person is by hereditary endowment and by experience. It is by no means a passive organization. It is the summation and focusing of all the drives of the organism as they have been modified by environment. Subjectively, it is the concept the individual has of himself as an entity in relation to his environment, especially his social environment. For what people think of him and the way they treat him are basic in his concept of himself.

The nature of the self will become clearer when we understand its origin. The child at first is not aware of himself as a *self*: there is no distinction between a *self* and a *not-self*. He plays with his hands and feet as he plays with toys. Gradually, through many experiences, he learns to discriminate between himself and his environment. A number of factors contribute to this discrimination. He gets sensations when pinching parts of his body. The name given him is not used for anyone else. There are many objects—his clothes, toys, and milk cup—which belong only to him. He bumps into objects which give him pain. He meets with many frustrations. All of these experiences and observations set him apart from his environment, and he is able to perceive himself as being "different." This self grows as he grows, as he has more and more experiences.

It should help the reader to understand the nature of the self still more by examining the accompanying diagram, in which the "roots" of the self are emphasized.

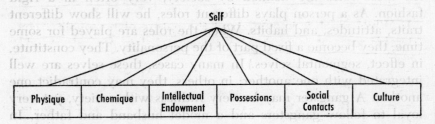

Physique	Chemique	Intellectual Endowment	Possessions	Social Contacts	Culture

FIGURE 5. The "roots" of the ego or self. What a person ultimately thinks of himself will depend upon his evaluation of his physical structure, his health and emotion, his intelligence, possessions, social contacts, and the acquisition of his culture.

In conclusion, it should be stressed that personality is dynamic, not passive, and is characterized by a constant growth and striving toward self-integration and self-realization, on the one hand, and a modification of environment, on the other.

CHARACTER

The reader may be somewhat disappointed because nothing has been said thus far about character, in spite of the fact that one hears of character more often than of personality as the most desirable attribute in a mate. Character has not been discussed because an individual does not possess personality *and* character as two separate entities; nor is character even a substructure of personality. It is merely personality evaluated by a moral code. In other words, it is the sum total of all those persistent or enduring personality aspects to which society applies the terms "good" or "bad," "right" or "wrong." When the aspects conforming to a moral code predominate, a person is said to possess a good moral character; when they do not conform, he is said to possess a bad character.

Interpretative Summary

1. While much is known about the nature of personality, considerable research is needed before we can claim to understand it thoroughly.

2. Personality is not the mere summation but an integration of a great number of units.

3. The material which enters into the structure of personality is derived from heredity and environment. Just how much is contributed by each is not known.

4. The growth of personality depends upon physical maturation and learning.

5. The raw material supplied by heredity can be classified into physical elements, body chemistry, and intellectual endowment.

6. The physical elements comprise body tissues, organs, their interaction, and the total body structure.

7. Body chemistry is determined by metabolism, glandular secretions, and the like. Physical growth, motility, and temperament are largely the product of this chemistry.

8. Temperament may be regarded as the "emotional climate" in which a person lives.

9. Intelligence is an innate capacity upon which all learning ultimately depends.

10. Physiological and psychological needs and drives underlie the growth and development of personality.

11. The more important physiological drives influencing personality are hunger, activity, rest and sleep, protection, and sex.

12. The significant psychological drives considered are curiosity, recognition, mastery, security, and response.

13. Not only is a child born into an environment, but he also reacts to it and internalizes such elements as ideas, beliefs, attitudes, values, and so on. In this sense, the organism makes the environment a part of itself.

14. Instead of speaking of environment as a whole, it is more meaningful to subdivide it into biophysical, social, and cultural aspects.

15. By interacting with environment, an organism creates within itself more or less permanent behavior patterns, which range from the simple to the complex: experiences, habits, attitudes, traits, selves, and the self.

16. All these behavior patterns are organized and integrated into a unified and unique structure.

17. The "focal point" of this integration is the self.

18. Character is made up of those aspects of personality which can be evaluated according to a moral code.

Thought Questions and Projects

1. Write your own definition of personality.
   (a) Next consult Gordon W. Allport's book on *Personality*, in which (Chapter 2) he presents and examines fifty definitions of personality.
   (b) Evaluate your definition in the light of the discussions of these definitions.
2. To what does the term *nature-nurture* refer?
3. Differentiate between character, personality, and temperament.
4. Elaborate on the interrelationship of need, drive, and motive. What are the *physiological needs* of a human organism?
5. What are the psychological needs? Can you mention societies in which the psychological needs differ from those of your own?
6. What is a trait? Give examples.
   (a) It is possible for a personality to be so completely organized around a single, cardinal trait that the individual becomes known for that quality. For instance, one speaks of "honest Abe." What central trait do you associate with the names of the following personalities?
      Shakespeare's Othello? Macbeth?
      Swift's Gulliver?
      Dickens's Scrooge?
      Hugo's Quasimodo?
      Mitchell's Scarlett O'Hara?

Bunyan's Christian?
Balzac's Grandet?
Daudet's Tartarin?
Robinson's Miniver Cheevy?
Lewis's Babbitt?

(b) Are you acquainted with a person whose entire personality seems to exemplify one cardinal trait?

7. What is an attitude? To what extent do children have attitudes similar to those of their parents? Compare your attitudes with those of your parents.

8. How does a child develop the concept of a "self"?

9. What is meant by a "neurotic" personality? Do you consider the age in which we live "an age of anxiety"?

10. Can personality be judged accurately by facial features, as is implied in the expression "he has an honest face"?

11. Are you influenced by quality of voice as a clue to traits in personality? Do you attribute certain traits to persons whom you know only by way of telephone or radio voices?

12. Sometimes when an individual has suffered a serious loss— a member of the family, all of his property, faith in mankind or in God—the difference is said to have "changed his entire personality." In the light of what you now know about the more detailed structure of personality, what changes may have taken place?

Suggested Readings for Further Study

Allport, Gordon W., *Personality*, New York, Henry Holt & Company, 1937.
Part III. Structure of Personality.
Chapter 9. The Search for Elements.
Chapter 10. The Theory of Identical Elements.
Chapter 11. The Theory of Traits.
Chapter 12. The Nature of Traits.
Chapter 13. The Unity of Personality.
Burgess, Ernest W., and Harvey J. Locke, *The Family*, 2nd ed., New York, American Book Company, 1953.
Chapter 7. Culture and Personality.
Cole, Lawrence E., *Human Behavior*, Yonkers-on-Hudson, World Book Company, 1953.
Chapter 7. The Style of Life: A Bio-social View of Needs and Purposes.

Chapter 24. The Normal Personality.

Horney, Karen, *The Neurotic Personality of Our Times,* 1937; *The Struggle Toward Self Realization,* 1950, New York, W. W. Norton & Company. (All chapters deal with personality from psychoanalytical point of view.)

Lindgren, Henry Clay, *Psychology of Personal and Social Adjustment,* New York, American Book Company, 1953.

Chapter 2. The Development of Personality: The Self.

Chapter 8. The Forces that Mold Us: Determinants of Personality.

Murphy, Gardner, *Personality,* New York, Harper & Brothers, 1947.

Sargent, S. S., *Social Psychology,* New York, The Ronald Press Company, 1950.

Chapter 3. Culture and Personality.

Chapter 4. Social Influences on Personality.

Chapter 11. Social Roles.

Thorpe, Louis P., *The Psychology of Mental Health,* New York, The Ronald Press Company, 1950.

Chapter 6. Mental Health—The Organization of Personality.

Chapter 7. Physiological Factors in Personality and Mental Health.

Chapter 8. Development of Personality.

Young, Kimball, *Personality and Problems of Adjustment,* 2nd ed, New York, Appleton-Century-Crofts, 1952.

Part I. The Foundations of Personality.

Chapter 1. Personality, Society and Culture.

Chapter 2. Constitutional Foundations of Personality.

Chapter 3. Motivation and Affective Processes.

Chapter 4. Some Aspects of Social-Cultural Learning.

Chapter 5. Internal Organization and Interactional Processes.

Chapter 6. The Development of Language in the Individual.

Chapter 7. The Rise and Function of the Self.

Chapter 8. Symbolic Behavior and the Self.

4

COMPARING MEN AND WOMEN

Marital adjustment is influenced not only by the personalities of the partners but also by the culture of which they are a part. One aspect of this culture which will have great influence on their mutual relationship is the concept of the relative status of men and women.

While women are moving toward a higher status in our society, they still have not achieved complete equality with men. There still exists great disagreement about this matter. We continue to hear about the "war between the sexes." Many men are not yet willing to concede equality to women; others accept equality in theory but not in practice. In this period of transition, each couple must decide on ways of bringing about a workable and harmonious life between them. To reach an intelligent decision, they need accurate information about each other. Careful study will reveal many similarities between men and women, but also real differences. The important questions are: What are these differences, and what is the proper attitude toward them?

Differences between the sexes result from both heredity and environment. In our present state of knowledge, it would be futile to try to ascertain the proportion of each factor in a given trait. The geneticists are likely to overstress the importance of heredity; the cultural anthropologists, the importance of environment. That both factors are important has been amply shown by many studies. Physical traits, such as the general shape of the body and the reproductive apparatus, are primarily due to the germ plasm; but just how much heredity contributes to what we generally call masculine and feminine traits is still unknown. How important environment can be in determining traits has been shown by anthropologists, especially by Margaret Mead.[1]

The layman in our society assumes, for example, that dominance is a masculine trait; yet among the Tchambuli it is the women who are dominant and aggressive. There the roles and statuses of the sexes are almost completely reversed. Men depend on women for economic support and affection. Men take care of

Reverse of our culture

"You have the wrong number, but my wife will be glad to talk to you anyway."

J. Monahan and The Saturday Evening Post.

the children and show what we think of as "feminine" interest in artistic and ceremonial matters. In relations with women they feel inferior, shy, and timid. There is rivalry between men over women, but it takes the form of backbiting, suspicion, spying, and petty gossip.

In comparing men and women, we shall follow the general outline of personality in the previous chapter. We shall begin by

[1] See *Sex and Temperament in Three Primitive Societies,* New York, William Morrow and Company, 1935.

comparing men and women first in physique, then in chemique, and then in the other aspects of personality.

SEX DIFFERENCES IN PHYSIQUE

Differences in physique begin with the germ plasm. The human organism begins its life with the fertilization of an ovum from the mother by a sperm from the father. The nucleus of the ovum contains twenty-four rodlike units, called chromosomes. One of these, which is larger than the others, is called the X chromosome. The sperm also contains twenty-four chromosomes, but half of the sperms contain an X chromosome and the other half a smaller, Y chromosome. If a male sperm containing an X chromosome fertilizes an ovum, the offspring will be a girl; if it contains a Y chromosome, the offspring will be a boy. Thus, the sex of a child is determined by the father.

The fertilized ovum grows by fission, each new cell containing forty-eight chromosomes, the same number as the fertilized ovum. Finally, every cell in the body contains forty-eight chromosomes, with this difference: In every cell of the female body there is a pair of X chromosomes and forty-six other chromosomes (called autosomes). In every cell of the male body there are forty-six autosomes and a pair of XY chromosomes. Thus the trillions of cells which make up the male and female organisms differ in their very basic structure.

The chromosomes are made up of thousands of smaller units— the *genes*. To what extent these differ in the two sexes is not known, but it is fairly well established that the genes in the forty-six autosomes slant the organism in the direction of maleness and the genes in the X chromosomes counteract this tendency. When there are two X chromosomes in the germ cell, they overpower the contrary genes in the other chromosomes and pull the individual toward female development.

In the process of growth, cells not only multiply in number but also change in their inner structure. They produce the various tissues, such as bone, muscle, nerve, and skin. These tissues arrange themselves in the characteristic outline of the male or female body. The average male body differs from the female in height, weight, and general contour. In over-all contour, the male body has a greater tendency to squareness and angularity, the female to more curves. The male reaches physical maturity at about twenty-four years of age, the female at about twenty.(At that time, the man is on the average 6 per cent taller and from 20 to 25 per cent heavier than the woman)

The most significant physical difference between man and woman is in the structure of the reproductive apparatus. ✔

Male Sex Organs. Visible on the outside of the male body are the *penis* and the fleshy pouch (called the *scrotum*), which contains the two testicles. The front part of the penis looks somewhat like an acorn and is called the *glans penis*. Well supplied with nerves, it is the most sensitive part. If circumcision has not been performed, it is covered with a foreskin—the *prepuce*. Near the underside is a tube—the *urethra*—through which passes the urine, as well as the seminal fluid. Throughout the muscular structure of the penis, there is a complex network of blood vessels, which fill up during the period of sexual excitement.

The *testicles* are of unequal size: the left is larger and hangs slightly lower than the right. The mature testicle has the shape of a bird's egg and is about an inch and a half long and about an inch thick. The testicles develop in the body cavity and descend into the scrotum before birth. In some individuals, they do not descend, with a resulting condition known as cryptorchism. The testicles must be outside the body, body temperature being too high for sperm production.

The cross section of a testicle looks somewhat like the cross section of a kidney. The inside consists of a very complex network of tubes, in which the sperms, or spermatozoa, are produced in prodigious numbers. The rate of production varies from man to man and also with age. The average, according to careful estimates, is three billion a month, or about a hundred million a day. The spermatozoa, which can be seen only with a high-powered microscope, are shaped like tadpoles and are about two ten-thousandths of an inch long. It takes two to span a thin hair.

When released, they can swim their own length in a second—an Olympic record.

Beside and attached to each testicle is the *epididymis*, which serves as a sort of finishing shop and storehouse for the sperms. It also adds a fluid to the sperms and sends them into the *vas deferens*, a tube with a pin-sized channel, through which the fluid is propelled along its course. This channel extends from the testicle into the groin of the body around the base of the bladder to the urethra. Close to its end it widens into the *ampulla*, which, as recent study has revealed, is the chief storehouse for the spermatozoa. The ampulla also produces a mucus. Just beyond the ampulla is the *seminal vesicle*, which, until recently, was considered the main storehouse for the spermatozoa. Its main function seems to be the production of mucus; it may, however, also store sperms. Close to the seminal vesicle is located the *prostate gland*, the size and shape of a horse chestnut. It secretes a thin, milky, alkaline fluid and functions to preserve the sperm from destruction by the uric acid, which previously had passed through the urethra. Close to where the vas deferens empties into the urethra, there are two more glands—the *Cowper's glands*. They also give off a lubricant which prepares the way for the sperms in the urethra.

During the height of sexual excitement, the orgasm, propellant muscles from the base to the top of the penis ejaculate the sperms with their fluids. The total amount ejaculated at one time is about a teaspoonful, containing from two hundred million to five hundred million sperms. In rare cases, there are as many as two billion.

Female Sex Organs. The outer, visible part of the female sex apparatus is called the *vulva*. Its outer rim is composed of two tapering cushions, covered with hair, called the larger lips, or *labia majora*. Just inside is the *vestibule*, which varies in depth and length, depending upon the thickness and length of the outer lips. It serves as the funnel access to the vaginal opening. On the inner side of the vestibule, there are two smaller lips, the *labia minora*. While the labia majora are firm, the labia minora are flabby. This makes it possible for them to cover wholly or in part the opening to the vagina. During erotic excitement, they become turgid and stand somewhat apart. Just above where the labia minora meet is the *clitoris,* which corresponds to the male penis—or perhaps more to the glans penis. The clitoris also varies in size, but ordinarily it is the size of a small pea. Its tip is supplied with many sensitive nerves. The whole organ is covered with skin, the *prepuce,* which sometimes is too thick or tough to allow proper stimulation of the clitoris. During sexual excitement, the clitoris becomes more rigid.

A short distance below the clitoris and between the inner fold is the opening of the urethra coming from the bladder. In the female, the urethra serves only for the passage of urine. The next larger opening leads to the *vaginal canal.* This opening is partly closed by the *hymen,* which varies considerably in size, shape, and thickness. In some women, it is little developed; in others, it covers the vaginal opening almost completely. There is also a great variation in thickness and toughness.

The female sex apparatus also possesses lubricating glands. There are two pairs of these: the *Skene glands,* near the opening from the bladder, and the *Bartholin glands,* near the vaginal opening. Without secretion from these glands, intromission of the penis is difficult and painful. The vaginal entry is surrounded by a group of muscles, which are subject to voluntary and involuntary contractions. This area is also supplied with sensitive erotic nerves. During orgasm, these muscles manifest a series of involuntary contractions, which are considered by many to be the "real" orgasm. Orgasm may be experienced, however, without such contractions.

While the size of the vaginal entry differs a great deal among women, the average is about three quarters of an inch in diameter. After some months of sexual activity, it is usually stretched to about an inch and a quarter. At childbirth it stretches to five or six inches.

Just inside this muscle "bridge," the vaginal canal forms an elastic tube extending three to four inches into the lower body cavity. During intercourse it may lengthen to more than six inches. While the area of the vagina just inside the opening is also supplied with sensitive nerves, these are absent in the upper region. In this upper region of the vagina is the pear-shaped womb, or *uterus*. It is composed of muscles, is hollow inside, and is lined with a mucous membrane. At the tip of the uterus is a small opening, the *cervix.* The uterus is suspended by rubber-like ligaments, which permit its movement during sexual activity. At the upper end of the uterus, at either side, are two small openings which lead into the *Fallopian tubes.* These are from four to six inches long and curve first out then in, toward the ovaries. Near the uterus, the tube measures about one hundredth of an inch across. It widens as it approaches the upper end, where it opens like a funnel.

Close to this funnel, but not connected with it, are two *ovaries,* located on either side of the abdominal cavity. These are almond-shaped, about an inch and a quarter long. Whereas the testicles *produce* the spermatozoa, the ovaries are merely a *storehouse* for eggs, or *ova.* At birth, each ovary contains from twenty-five thousand to thirty thousand immature eggs. One or more ripen each month up to the menopause. As a rule, the ovaries alternate in this function from month to month. Each egg is encased in a follicle, which bursts when the egg is ripe. At this time the egg is only about one hundredth of an inch in diameter, the thickness of a sharp pin point. (The egg finds its way by an unknown process into the funnel.) From here, at the wider end of the Fallopian tube, it is moved by hairlike projections toward the uterus. At the narrower part of the tube, it is moved along by peristaltic action, similar to that in the intestines, until it comes close to the opening of the uterus. This journey takes about a week. Exactly how long an unfertilized egg is able to sustain life is not known. Two days is a fair guess. Fertilization takes place in the Fallopian tubes. This means that the spermatozoa must find their way into the cervix and traverse the entire length of the uterus into the Fallopian tube. But no matter how many spermatozoa find their way to the ovum, only one can enter its nucleus.

Sex Differences in Chemique

Hormones. The ovaries and the testes, in addition to giving off eggs and sperms, also function as glands of internal secretion. They produce *sex hormones,* which are important in the development of primary and secondary sex characteristics. These hormones affect the quality, intensity, and frequency of the sexual urge. Other sex hormones are given off by the pituitary gland, located at the base of the brain, and the adrenal glands, located on top of the kidneys. Both sexes produce male and female hormones, but in different proportions and at different rates. On the average, a man produces two and a half times more male hormones than a woman, a woman eight to ten times more female hormones than a man. (The male produces from 20 to 70 units of male hormones and 80 to 150 units of female hormones; the female produces from 10 to 20 units of male hormones and from 30 to 1,500 units of female hormones.) In the woman, the rate of production changes considerably with the menstrual periods and childbearing cycles.

Rate of Maturation. There is considerable difference in the rate of physical maturation of the two sexes. It may hurt the male ego somewhat to read that women mature more rapidly than men, but it is nevertheless true. As was stated above, men mature physically at twenty-four years of age, women at twenty. This difference begins at birth, when a girl is biologically one month older than a boy, even in the case of fraternal twins. The girl stays ahead of the boy throughout their biological growth. At two, she is six months ahead of him; at five, one year; and at thirteen, two years. This means that she reaches puberty about two years sooner than the male, a fact which is important for our understanding of adolescence. It explains why girls at this age find boys of their own age uninteresting.

The Menstrual Cycle. Women have two distinct functions—menstruation and childbearing. A sure sign of puberty in women is the menstrual cycle, which appears, on the average, every 28 days until menopause, except during pregnancy. However, there are variations. At the beginning, menstruation may skip some months. Some women menstruate every three weeks, others every five weeks. No woman seems to have a rigid cycle. The periods between menstruations may be longer one month and shorter the next. There are many causes for this, both physical and emotional. Any serious emotional tension may delay menstrual flow. In extreme instances, menstruation may be stopped completely for six months or longer. The average length of the menstrual flow seems to be three days, with variations from one to seven days. In ill health, the flow may be prolonged beyond seven days.

What is the purpose of this monthly cycle? As the ovum ripens in the ovary, the lining in the uterus is prepared to receive it. But when no impregnation takes place, the lining becomes useless and is discharged from the uterus into the vagina and thence to the outside. In spite of the redness of the discharge, little blood is lost —about two ounces during the whole cycle. Contained in the flow are broken-down tissue cells, mucus, some lime, and a few other substances needed by the embryo.

Climacteric. Both men and women experience a climacteric in later life. In women, there is a cessation of menstrual flow known as menopause. After menopause, she cannot conceive, because no ova are produced. Sexual desire at this period does not cease, though usually it decreases. However, some women who were afraid of pregnancy before may then enjoy the sex act more. There are some who experience increased sex desire before the onset of menopause. The climacteric, on the average, is attained earlier by women than by men. In women, it comes between the ages of 38 and 50, although deviations from these years occur. In men, the climacteric usually begins in the fifties. The effects on physical health and emotional balance are, as a rule, more serious for women than for men.

Other Differences in Body Chemistry. A woman's body can adjust better to temperature variations than a man's. To begin with, women are about two degrees cooler than men. If temperature increases, a man will perspire sooner and more profusely than a woman. Because of better body insulation, better adjustable metabolic rate, and the presence of a sex hormone (Theelin), a woman can adjust better to lower temperature.

The two sexes also differ in blood composition. Men have proportionally more red blood corpuscles and correspondingly fewer white corpuscles than women. Men have 5,200,000 red corpuscles per cubic millimeter; women have about 4,900,000. The hemoglobin content in the blood is also about 10 per cent higher in men than in women.

Men, on the whole, need more food than women. A very active man needs about 50 per cent more nutriment than a very active woman—about 4,500 as compared with 3,000 calories. When only moderately active, a man needs about 3,000 calories, a woman about 2,500. No wonder many a husband wants meat and potatoes when his wife is satisfied with a salad!

SEX DIFFERENCES IN EMOTIONAL MAKE-UP

It is commonly assumed that women are more "emotional" than men. Since "emotional" can mean many things, the assumption needs careful examination. Emotional experience can be analyzed, like any experience, into stimulus, organism, and response (usually indicated as S-O-R). Emotions are evaluated or measured by three criteria: frequency, intensity, and duration. Frequency may result either from more emotion-inducing situations or from greater sensitivity to stimulation. Intensity is a matter of degree, but it may also refer to the extent of overt, or outward, expression of an emotion. Emotional experiences have a certain cycle—that is, one gets angry and after a while "cools off." The length of the cycle determines the duration of a particular emotion. If a woman is more emotional, it may also mean that her emotional cycle lasts longer than does that of a man.

Thus far, we have no means of obtaining evidence which differentiates accurately between the emotional states of men and those of women. Perhaps the best answer to this question could be obtained by measuring emotions under carefully controlled situations. So far, we have not been able to produce lifelike emotions in a laboratory setup. Nor have we been able to devise scientific instruments to measure accurately and completely such emotional states as can be produced experimentally or as can be found in actual life situations. There are a number of other means of measuring emotions, however, and while these means are not as reliable and valid as we would like them to be, they still give some indications of emotion.

Johnson and Terman summarized fifty of the best statistical studies of emotions made over a period of twenty years. The following quotation lists the methods used and the conclusions reached in these studies: "True samplings of the nervous behavior of nursery school children, observational records by parents, laboratory studies of fear responses, self-ratings by associates, clinical data on incidence of the psychoneuroses and quite a number of paper and pencil tests . . ." "The results of such studies are almost unanimous in indicating less emotional balance in the female." [2] As to the causes for the emotional imbalance in women, the authors list "greater frustration produced in the female by the kind of training she receives," and "possible influences of original constitutional equipment."

Just how important the constitutional equipment may be in a woman's emotional life, we do not know; but we do know that her training from childhood on is conducive to frequency, intensity, and longer duration of emotions. All infants manifest their needs by emotional expressions, but boys, as soon as they are old enough, are exhorted to act like little men—that is, to restrain emotional expression. Girls, on the other hand, are *expected* to show emotional sensitivity; consequently, it is not surprising that they persist in using emotional appeals, especially since they find that emotions are a very effective means of attracting attention to themselves and of getting what they want. Having learned this through many experiences, it is only logical that some women occasionally should resort to tears to get what they want.

A growing girl soon will meet with more frustrations than will

[2] Winifred B. Johnson and Lewis M. Terman, "Some Highlights in the Literature of Psychological Sex Differences Published since 1920," *Journal of Psychology*, 1940, 9:317. Reprinted by permission.

a boy. Her life is much more restricted than is a boy's. Is it any wonder that girls develop more nervous habits, such as nail biting, gum popping, hair twisting, and kicking shoes on and off? At adolescence, even more restrictions are enforced, especially with reference to sex. The girl soon finds that many forms of recreation and many professions are closed to her. She finds her urge for self-realization restricted in many ways.

This state of affairs has important consequences. Insofar as her experiences are more colored by emotions, a woman's entire personality structure will take on a more emotional coloring than does a man's. Her perceptions, reasonings, judgments, and actions will also be more motivated by emotions than are those of men. Since emotional satisfactions are derived more from other human beings than from any other source, the greater emotionality of a woman may explain in part her greater interest in people.

SEX DIFFERENCES IN INTELLIGENCE

Men have always claimed intellectual superiority over women. This claim is not supported by intelligence tests: The average I.Q. for both men and women is the same—100. There is, however, a difference in performance on subtests. College women do better in the linguistic part of the tests and men in the mathematical part. Women excel in reading, word knowledge, opposites, sentence completion, and color naming; men, in spatial perception and arithmetic. These differences can be observed in early childhood. Girls begin to talk at least one month earlier than boys; they pick up new words sooner and use longer sentences. They have fewer speech difficulties: More boys than girls stutter. In general aptitude, girls tend to excel in skills in which language is the central factor; boys, in anything in which mechanical skill is important. One could easily construct tests which would be to the advantage of either sex by stressing one or the other of these factors. In tests constructed to measure adjustment to social situations, women definitely rate higher than men. Such tests would measure the ability to appreciate factors involved in social situations and in doing what society considers "proper."

An interesting study of differences in I.Q. between the sexes was that of 1,300 gifted children in California grade and high schools by Terman and associates. It shows that as these gifted children attained maturity, girls began to lag behind boys. "Boys not only become increasingly more likely than girls to have a high I.Q. as they advance in age, but they are more likely than girls to retain a high I.Q. earlier evidenced." [3] Even at this age, however, girls retained their superiority in grades. Just why gifted girls fall behind boys in I.Q. at maturity has not been explained. One possibility is that the change may result from biological factors. Glandular secretions may interfere with intellectual functioning, or girls may become mentally set sooner, just as they become physically mature earlier. It is more than likely, however, that gifted girls, seeing only very restricted opportunities for them in the professions, may become discouraged about developing their minds further in such areas as are measured by intelligence tests. As a result, they may then concentrate on "social intelligence."

In support of their argument for superiority, men often mention the fact that there have been more male than female geniuses. Woodworth and Marquis define genius thus: "Geniuses are exceptionally intelligent persons who, with favorable opportunities, reach outstanding intellectual achievement." [4] If this definition is correct, the reason women fall behind men in later adolescence may also explain why there are fewer women geniuses. Women so far certainly have not had the same "favorable opportunities" as men.

Thus, we must conclude that there is no basis for man's claim to intellectual superiority over women. It must also be remembered that there are great individual differences in intelligence within each sex and that while certain men are more intelligent than certain women, the reverse is also true.

[3] Reprinted from *The Promise of Youth* (Volume III of *Genetic Studies of Genius* edited by Lewis M. Terman) by Barbara Stoddard Burks, Dortha Williams Jensen, Lewis M. Terman with the permission of the editor and of the publishers, Stanford University Press. Copyright 1930 by the Board of Trustees of Leland Stanford Junior University.

[4] R. S. Woodworth and G. G. Marquis, *Psychology*, New York, Henry Holt & Company, 1947, p. 58.

SEX DIFFERENCES IN PHYSIOLOGICAL NEEDS AND DRIVES

General Activity. There are many differences between the sexes in general activity throughout life. At infancy, boys show more gross muscular movements than girls. Though they are slower than girls in general maturation, they are one month ahead of them in creeping and other movements which require muscular strength and physical activity. Girls manifest more head and hand movements. They sit longer at an early age and engage in sedentary activities which require fine rather than gross muscular co-ordination. Adolescent boys and mature men engage much more than girls and women in play and work requiring the use of gross muscles. Even in sleep, men are more restless than women; they toss and turn more and with greater force. Man's greater general activity is explained by his somewhat higher metabolism, greater energy, and muscular strength.

Foods and Liquids. It was stated above that men need 50 per cent more food per body weight than women. Thus food is more important in a man's life than in a woman's. There is some truth in the statement that the way to man's heart is through his stomach! A man also tends to consume more liquids in almost any form than does a woman.

Health. It seems that the male organism is not as well equipped to deal with substances and conditions which affect its health and existence as is the female. In general health, the male is definitely the weaker sex. This is true for any period of his life. More boys die at birth than girls, and in the year after birth, 27 per cent more boys die than girls. Women live, on the average, four to six years longer than men. The average life expectancy for white males in the United States at present is 66.65 and for nonwhite males, 59.2, whereas for white females it is 72.9 and for nonwhite females, 63.2.

Sex Drive. There are considerable differences between men and women in their sexual needs and satisfactions. These differences will be discussed in Chapter 16.

Sex Differences in Major Interests

In our society, there are sex differences in degree of interest in the various aspects of the environment. On the whole, men are more interested in things, women in people; in other words, men are more preoccupied with the biophysical environment, women with the social. Men like to explore, travel, fish, hunt, seek adventure, be active; women prefer to settle down in one place, establish a home, and rear children. Even from childhood, women are more responsive to people. As to culture, men are more interested in its abstract, speculative aspects; women in its practical and moral aspects, and in etiquette. These conclusions are derived from general observations and from vocational choices made by the two sexes. On the Kuder Performance Record, the first choice for men is science, and for women, social service. According to Edward K. Strong, Jr., author of the well-known "Vocational Interest Blank," the following interests are distinctly masculine: (1) mechanical and scientific activities; (2) physically strenuous, adventuresome activities; (3) legal, political, and army occupations; (4) selling activities; (5) certain forms of entertainment, such as smokers, rough-house initiations, and chess; (6) certain other preferences, such as for outside work and for working for oneself. The distinctly feminine interests include (1) musical and other artistic activities; (2) literary activities; (3) certain kinds of people, especially the unfortunate and the disagreeable; (4) certain forms of entertainment—going to fortune tellers, full-dress affairs, and social-problem movies; (5) clerical work; (6) teaching; (7) social work; (8) shopping and window-shopping; (9) certain school subjects; and (10) miscellaneous matters.[5]

[5] Leona E. Tyler, *The Psychology of Human Differences,* New York, Appleton-Century-Crofts, Inc., 1947, p. 83. By permission.

SEX DIFFERENCES IN QUALITY AND RANGE OF EXPERIENCE

Personality, as we have seen (Chapter 3), is a product of the interaction of heredity and environment mediated by experiences. The major elements of any experience are perception, thought, and affect. Insofar as women are more emotional than men, their experiences are more colored by affect. Every aspect of their personality—habits, attitudes, interests, values, traits, selves and ego —shows more emotional coloring. We speak here only of the average male and female. In actual life, there are, of course, many individual women who are much less emotional than certain men.

The differences in physique between men and women lead to distinct experiences. The differences in physique result in different sensations, conations, and feelings. Greater muscular development gives a man experiences a woman can never have. His sensations from his reproductive apparatus are very likely different from those of a woman. The woman, on the other hand, has sensations and experiences the male can never understand. She receives sexual pleasures from many parts of her body. She has experiences from her menstrual cycle and from pregnancy and giving birth which are completely foreign to him. About these matters, there is surely a greater understanding between woman and woman or man and man than there is between the sexes.

In spite of the fact that we have greater equality between men and women in our society than ever before, it still is true that a woman is much more limited in her freedom of movement than a man, and that the range of her experiences thus is considerably narrower. She is still more guarded and protected than the male. On the whole, she lives in a less stimulating environment.

In addition, the lives of men and women are steered into different areas. From childhood, a woman's activities are made to center in the home, whereas those of a man are directed toward things outside the home. All these things result in such different experiences and interests that men and women live in quite different worlds and speak different "languages."

Sex Differences in Habits and Skills

There are notable differences between men and women in habits and skills. These are due in part to heredity and in part to training.

Women excel in many visual skills, such as color vision and perceptual discrimination. They have fewer eye defects, such as extreme near-sightedness, eye muscular paralysis, eye tremors, enlarged cornea, and optic atrophy. Total and partial color blindness is much more common among men than among women. Women are more skilled in types of work which require fine, quick, and deft muscular co-ordination. They excel in tests involving manual dexterity, finger dexterity, and tweezer dexterity.

Women are much more proficient than men in clerical work. They are quicker, more accurate, and more satisfied with their work. Men almost invariably excel in mechanical aptitudes. For this reason, psychologists use two different sets of industrial norms for the two sexes.

Each sex excels in skills which are required by its particular vocation or profession. Thus, women possess many skills pertaining to housekeeping and homemaking, such as cooking, sewing, planning and decorating the home, and all aspects of work pertaining to the care of children. Men acquire the skills in the vocations and professions in which they are primarily engaged, such as business, industry, journalism, government, medicine, and law.

Sex Differences in Attitudes and Values

As was pointed out above, attitudes contain rational and emotional elements. One or the other element may predominate in certain attitudes. On the whole, the emotional element predominates in women's attitudes. When challenged, women do not feel quite as much as men the need to justify their particular beliefs, likes, and dislikes. Both sexes rationalize, of course, but women, when pressed, do not persist in rationalization as much as do men. (Rationalization can be defined as giving "good" reasons for "true" reasons.) Women quite often are satisfied to justify a certain attitude or belief by answering "I believe so and so—oh, because!" This type of answer often annoys a man—not because the word "because" makes a sentence incomplete, but because he feels one must be "rational" and must have reasons for his attitude.

Attitudes are *for* or *against* something. Women, on the whole, are more conservative than men. Several studies have shown that women are more conservative in matters relating to religion, morals, domestic problems, labor, and government. The reason for these attitudes is, perhaps, that women feel a greater need for security. A woman knows what she has now. In bringing about a change, she is not as free as a man to make her opinions felt in this "man's world." Consequently, she feels uncertain as to the direction which "reform" will take. What happened in Spain in 1931 is often mentioned as an example of woman's conservatism. The Spanish Socialists were elected to power by promising women the right to vote, only to be thrown out of power at the next election by women, who had found their policies too radical. Women are more pacifistic. This, in our present world, is considered radical. But they favor pacifism because war will disrupt their ordered and more or less secure world.

We do not possess the information needed to compare women with men in a great number of attitudes. We do have, however, a statistical study of differences between the sexes in attitudes toward themselves. Both men and women have inferiority feelings or "complexes," but a greater percentage of women have such feelings. From a study of a group of college students, Allport[6] reports inferiority feelings in the following areas:

TABLE 5

	Percentage	
	Men	Women
Physical	48	55
Social	58	65
Intellectual	29	64
Moral	17	18
None at all	10	9

[6] Gordon W. Allport, *Personality: A Psychological Interpretation*, New York, Henry Holt and Company, 1937, p. 174. Reprinted by permission.

These statistics become more significant when we compare the ratio of inferiority feelings during the subjects' high-school years. At this age, 58 per cent of boys reported feelings of intellectual inferiority, a percentage which, in college, decreased to 29 per cent. Girls in high school reported 25 per cent of such feelings, which increased in college to 64 per cent. It would seem that feelings of inferiority tend to increase in women with age.

Men and women also differ from each other in their value systems. This observation is based upon results obtained by the administration of the Allport-Vernon "Study of Values Test." According to this test, men are primarily interested in theoretical, economic, and political values while women manifest more interest in social, religious, and aesthetic values.[7] This test is an outgrowth of Eduard Spranger's theory of values,[8] according to which there are the following six classifications:

(1) The theoretical. The person dominated by this value is interested in the discovery of truth. He seeks to order and systematize knowledge.

(2) The political. The aim of the political person is power, influence, and renown. He uses people as a means to achieve this end.

(3) The social. Persons having this value look upon people as an end rather than a means to an end. They love people and devote their lives to the service of mankind.

(4) The economic. The aim of a person dominated by this value is the accumulation of property. He stresses what is useful in the struggle for self-preservation.

(5) The religious. The religious person seeks to know the ultimate nature of the cosmos and his relation to it.

(6) The aesthetic. The aim here is to discover the beautiful. Form and harmony are of central importance.

Sex Differences in Roles and the Self

Role-taking with reference to the development of the self ordinarily means that a person's general behavior, his words, and

---

[7] The original test was constructed by Gordon W. Allport and P. E. Vernon. *Study of Values*, rev. ed., by Allport, Vernon, and Gardner Lindzey was published in 1951 (Boston, Houghton Mifflin Company).

[8] Edward Spranger, *Types of Men*, Authorized Translation of the Fifth German Edition by Paul J. W. Pigors, Halle (Saale), Max Niemeyer Verlag, 1928, Part II, pp. 109–246.

various relationships to others follow a pattern as prescribed by the group to which he belongs. The roles he plays depend upon what he thinks or imagines is expected of him. The interpretation and enactment of his roles may bring him approval or disapproval. Certain roles appear to be conventional and stable, while others are in process of modification as affected by social change.

In the past, the roles of men and women were clearly defined; but at present there is less rigidity and clarity in the delineation. Especially is this true for women, who, in consequence, are somewhat uncertain within themselves and insecure about their place in life. Since the roles one plays in life are important in the development of the concept of one's self, it follows that woman is less at peace and in harmony with herself than is man.

We have seen in the preceding chapter that the self has its roots in physical make-up, body chemistry, intellectual endowment, physical environment, material possessions, relatives, friends, and culture. There is no difference between the male and female concepts of the self in this regard, except in the emphasis on various aspects of these roots. Thus, man's self is markedly influenced by his size and physical strength and by the fact that he is male rather than female. When woman thinks about her physical make-up, she thinks of her figure, her attractiveness or unattractiveness, and the fact that she is a woman rather than a man. Man is made more aware of his emotional experiences than is woman, since he is expected to manifest more emotional control. He is also inclined to pay more attention to his intellectual endowment, which he almost invariably overestimates. Regarding material possessions, women build their self-respect on more personal possessions, such as clothes, jewelry, and collector's items, while men build their self-respect on more impersonal possessions, such as automobiles, real estate, and money. There is very little difference, if any, with regard to significance of relatives and friends. Both sexes take great pride in making our culture their own by the process of education. In general, however, women seek satisfaction in the fine arts and in social service, whereas men look for it more in the various sciences. At present, more men than women seek to build their self-respect through higher education.

All in all, the constituent elements of the self concept of men and women are sufficiently different to require special effort for mutual appreciation and understanding.

INTERPRETATIVE SUMMARY

1. Differences between men and women are due to both hereditary and environmental factors. How much each contributes to a specific trait is unknown.

2. On the whole, physical traits are influenced more by heredity, and behavioral traits more by environment.

3. In general physique, men are on the average 6 per cent taller than women and 20 to 25 per cent heavier.

4. The sexes differ radically in the structure and function of their reproductive organs.

5. Biologically, the function of the male sex organ is to deposit the germ plasm inside the female body.

6. Men and women produce both male and female hormones.

7. Women have two distinct functions—menstruation and childbearing.

8. Insofar as women are more emotional than men, it is because of training rather than heredity.

9. There is no basic difference between men and women in I.Q. However, men excel in one type of intelligence and women in another.

10. Men are physically more active than women throughout life, a fact which explains why men need 50 per cent more food than do women.

11. There is considerable difference in the kinds of interests manifested by men and women, a difference due largely to cultural training.

12. Comparable differences are also found between men and women in habits and skills, attitudes, values, traits, roles, and self concepts.

Thought Questions and Projects

1. Compare the typical attitudes of men and those of women toward marriage.

2. Would you like to see equality between men and women extended to further areas of our way of life? Justify your answer.

3. To what extent does our society encourage sex differences? Sex equality?

4. Discuss: Are women more emotional than men?

5. Have you observed the difference in interests between men and women? The next opportunity you have to watch an informal, "chatty" party of married couples, observe whether the following situation takes place. At first, the conversation may be quite general and diversified, appealing to the interests of both sexes; gradually, the men drift to one corner of the room or even to another room, and the women congregate in the opposite direction. The men take up their "pet" topics of interest and the women theirs. What subjects would you anticipate hearing discussed by each group?

6. Give specific illustrations to show how misunderstandings may arise between couples as a result of their not knowing basic differences between men and women.

7. Girls mature at an earlier age than boys. What social problems may result from this fact?

Suggested Readings for Further Study

Christensen, Harold T., *Marriage Analysis*, New York, The Ronald Press Company, 1950.
    Chapter 4. Men and Women.
Dickinson, Robert L., "Anatomy and Physiology of Sex Organs," in *Successful Marriage*, edited by Morris Fishbein and Ernest W. Burgess, Garden City, New York, Doubleday & Company, 1947.
    Part II, Section 1, pp. 69–91.
Koos, Earl L., *Marriage*, New York, Henry Holt & Company, 1953.
    Chapter 12. Roles in Marriage.

Mead, Margaret, *Male and Female,* New York, William Morrow & Company, 1949.
(Entire book is a comparative study.)
Scheinfeld, Amram, *The New You and Heredity,* New York, J. B. Lippincott Company, 1950.
(Especially Chapters 1 through 8.)
Scheinfeld, Amram, *Women and Men,* New York, Harcourt, Brace & Company, 1944.
Young, Kimball, *Personality and Problems of Adjustment,* 2nd ed., New York, Appleton-Century-Crofts, 1952.
Chapter 18. Psychology of Modern Woman.

5

WHY PEOPLE MARRY

When people are asked why they marry, the greatest number will answer that they seek happiness—or at least greater happiness than they now possess. This answer is satisfactory as far as it goes, for happiness naturally is a desirable goal in marriage, but it is too general and too vague to be of much use. When we ask for more specific aims of marriage, we get several typical answers, such as the following: It is the "proper" thing to do, it gives one prestige, or it fills one or more of a variety of needs or desires—for security, and so on.

Individuals differ markedly in their motives for marriage. First of all, there is a difference in motives between men and women, perhaps not so much in the types of motives as in the degree of emphasis on them. According to Magoun, "The husband wants a combined companion, cook, hostess, dressmaker, purchasing agent, mistress, bridge partner, nurse, governess, and comforter among other things. The wife wants a combined lover, protector, household handyman, provider, squire, and father of her children." [1] There is also a difference in the number of motives which people seek to satisfy in marriage, and in the importance of these motives. For instance, security may be most important for one person, whereas for another the most important motive may be "the proper thing to do." There is a difference also in the degree of awareness of the motives. It is obvious, then, that the various motives for marriage cannot be ranked from least to most important.

[1] F. Alexander Magoun, *Love and Marriage*, New York, Harper & Brothers, 1948, p. 49. Reprinted by permission.

Since not every individual may be aware that he possesses unconscious motives for his behavior, before discussing any motives for marriage, something should be said about unconscious motivation.

UNCONSCIOUS MOTIVATION

Modern psychology accepts the fact that some behavior is due completely to unconscious factors; other behavior may be partly conscious and partly unconscious. Such is to be expected when behavior is influenced not only by present events but also by the person's previous experiences.

As a background for behavior, the total organism may be involved, to a greater or lesser degree, in any kind of experience. It may function on either the conscious or the unconscious level. One analogy which has been used to stress the ratio between these two levels is that of the iceberg. Just as seven-eighths of the iceberg is below the water, leaving only one-eighth above, so it is said that seven-eighths of our mind is unconscious and only one-eighth is conscious. Or one can think of a lake illuminated at night by a searchlight; the part exposed to the light is analogous to the conscious and the rest to the unconscious. The latter analogy is especially apt: now one, now another part of our mind may be conscious, while some parts are never brought into consciousness, just as the deeper areas of a lake are never reached by the light.

One must guard against thinking of *two* minds, the conscious and the unconscious. Both are part of one, just as we do not have two icebergs, one above and one below the water, or two lakes. There is no hard and fast line between the two levels of the mind; one shades into the other. Every person knows from his own experience that there are degrees of awareness. We often say "I was keenly aware of such and such," or "Now as I recall it, I was not aware of it at that time." Such reactions indicate that our states of awareness are not always of equal degree.

What is the content of the unconscious part of our mental processes? First, there are the innate drives, like hunger, sex, and

so on, which operate long before we are conscious of their significance and which continue to function throughout life, often
considerably below the level of awareness. The rest comes from
our varied experiences. There are the experiences in the first years
of our life, which we can never consciously recall. There are other
experiences of which we were only partly aware. These, as we
have seen, lie at the foundation of our personality. In this "content
of mind" are also many kinds of experiences which we have sup-
posedly "forgotten." Much of the so-called forgotten material is
still in our mental activity, however, influencing our behavior
even though remaining beyond conscious recall. In addition, there
are experiences which are so painful to our mind that we repress
them. Thus we say of an experience that we "have to get it out of
our mind." We succeed, of course, only in getting it out of our
conscious thought processes. This process of "putting something
out of mind" is often tried with painful love experiences.

Finally, there is much which gets into our being through peripheral impression. Everyone has had the experience of finding
in a newly developed snapshot objects and peculiar relationships
which he did not perceive when he focused the camera. In the
same way, when we look at a total situation, we are aware of
only a few aspects of what we see; but the rest gets into our brain,
where a record is made of it. The principle of perception applies
to each of our sense organs. Whenever we receive impressions
through several of our sense organs simultaneously, we may pay
attention to one only, but the others also make a record in our
nervous system.

The *operation* of unconscious motivation can be demonstrated
easily by hypnosis. A person hypnotized and made completely
unaware of what goes on around him can be told that upon awak-
ening he will open an umbrella and hold it over himself. When
he wakes, he will promptly carry out the suggestion, even though
he is inside a room, in front of an audience, and obviously without practical reason for raising the umbrella.

As we shall see, the unconscious is a significant element in the
process of falling in love. It is a vital factor also in marital adjustment and plays a very significant role in either achieving or not
achieving happiness. As a rule, no one is fully aware of all the

factors which contribute to happiness, nor is one aware of all the causes for unhappiness. The fact that the unconscious factors are beyond the individual's control does not mean that they are not of great consequence. The very fact that they are unconscious makes them more potent than ever. To become aware of unconscious factors is the first step in gaining control over them; therefore, knowing what factors or motives are present in marital adjustment should give one considerable control over the elimination of undesirable and mastery of desirable motives.

"Yes! Now get off your knees—that suit is going to have to last you for awhile."

Salo and the Chicago Tribune–New York News Syndicate, Inc.

MOTIVES FOR MARRIAGE

In the discussion of the following motives, we shall make no attempt to classify them in any particular order or hierarchy. Such classifications usually prove unsatisfactory because of great individual differences in value systems.

As we have seen, a motive is a goal-directed drive. In naming motives, one can therefore identify them either according to the drive involved or according to the goal one seeks to achieve. In listing the following motives we have designated them either according to the drive aspect or goal aspect, depending on which alternative seemed to be most appropriate in terms of brevity and clarity.

Doing the Proper Thing. It is generally accepted by authorities that preparation for marriage begins in childhood. Almost every child grows up in a home where there is a father and a mother, and he learns to accept this fact as naturally as he acquires his native language. Just as it is "natural" for the child to acquire the language spoken in his home because it is the only language he hears, so it is "natural" for him to think of the world in which he lives as being made up of couples. As he grows older, he becomes increasingly aware of the fact that practically all adult men and women live as couples. What then is more normal for him than to regard marriage as the established pattern of living? Evidence that he is impressed by the marriage relationship in early childhood is the fact that he and his playmates "play house," where the roles of father and mother are enacted. This "natural" tendency to accept marriage as desirable will be reinforced by much of what he learns in the home, at school, at church, and from his friends.

Sexual Satisfaction. One important reason for marriage, but only one of many, is the desire for sexual satisfaction. The sex drive is one of the potent drives of man. This fact has been recognized and stressed, especially in the last century, by such men as Krafft-Ebing, in his *Psychopathia Sexualis;* Havelock Ellis, in his important studies on the *Psychology of Sex;* and Sigmund Freud, in many of his writings on psychoanalysis. At present, it is a fact accepted by leaders of thought in almost all fields.

Evidence for the potency of the sex drive comes from many studies of animals and man. Various experiments have been devised to test the strength of the sex drive in animals. One is the obstruction method, in which two cages are separated by an electric grid in such a manner that the male or female can be given a shock when crossing the grid to reach the other. The strength of the shock may be left constant, to observe how often an animal will subject itself to the shock to reach another of the opposite sex; or the voltages of the shock may be increased, to [*Animals*] determine how much pain one animal will endure to reach the other. In this manner, it has been discovered that only the maternal, thirst, and hunger drives are stronger than the sex drive. The female has also been placed in a revolving drum and its activity compared when in heat and when not in heat. Being in heat increases activity markedly.

We cannot experiment with human beings in similar fashion. However, there are a number of factors from which the strength of the human sex drive can be inferred. At least three important endocrine glands give off hormones which have to do with the sex drive—the pituitary, the adrenals, and the gonads (testes and ovaries). The effect of these hormonal secretions can be gauged by comparing such secondary sex characteristics as the vigor and strength of a normal man with their lack in a eunuch.

The sex drive in man is so strong that its regulation requires many social controls. In our society, taboos, mores, convention, ethics, and religion are used as means of controlling the sex drive. [*Cultural system*] The punishment for deviation is very great under our cultural system. An important, perhaps a major, part of this system revolves around sex.

Sex is also linked to the most powerful emotions of man. When the sex drive is frustrated in some persons, anger, jealousy, and hate are overpowering. Some are driven to rape and murder. When the drive is repressed and not permitted normal expression, it may take abnormal forms of behavior, such as kleptomania, pyromania, or homicidal mania. Freud and many psychiatrists have shown that many types of abnormal behavior result from repression. It should be noted here that by repression is meant, not abstinence from sexual intercourse, but rather inability to accept one's sex urges as normal, human drives.

Man may be said to have two basic objectives in life—self-preservation and race preservation. The first has a tendency to make him selfish; the second, altruistic. If he is blocked in his struggle for existence, he experiences anger and hate and, as a consequence, becomes destructive of others. In order to perpetuate the race, he needs the help and co-operation of others. He is therefore inclined to help promote their welfare; in so doing, he learns to experience tender emotion toward them. Sex thus can become a source of kindness, affection, sympathy, and love. These emotions are the bases of much that is fine and noble in our society: they lead to devotion, service, and sacrifice. Freud has used the term *sublimation* for the redirection of a drive from socially unacceptable modes of expression to socially approved forms of behavior. Many forms of creative self-expression in the fine arts, in science, in industry, and in religion are due to such sublimation.

It is the strong sex urge that often is a deciding factor in getting married. According to our mores, a young couple may engage in almost any activity before marriage except sexual intercourse. Whatever the reasons for this belief or attitude, it has the tendency to make sex central in getting married. It also accounts for the fact that many look upon marriage as mere license for intercourse, an attitude which frequently becomes a hindrance to a happy marital relationship.

Such an attitude blocks out other purposes of marriage or makes them at least secondary. The strong sex urge often induces a young couple to rationalize away disadvantages in marrying each other. When sex is central, it becomes a sort of entrance permit to marriage.

In this connection, students' reaction to the importance of sex in marriage is of interest. At Cornell University, Rockwood and Ford submitted the following question to 364 students: "Is sex the most important factor in marriage?" Seventeen per cent—25.3 per cent of the men and 8 per cent of the women—replied yes. The majority of the Cornell group (81.3 per cent) replied that, in their opinion, sex is not the most important factor in marriage, and 1.7 per cent did not answer the question. The comments, especially those made by the men, indicate that the subjects may have responded to the question as they thought they ought to feel, rather than as they actually felt. Typical comments were: "Perhaps not *the* most important but *very* important!" The same authors quote a study made by Bernard at the University of Colorado. Here, of 500 students, 33 per cent answered yes.[2]

[2] L. D. Rockwood and M. G. N. Ford, *Youth, Marriage and Parenthood*, New York, John Wiley and Sons, Inc., 1945, p. 117. By permission.

It is the common experience of marriage counselors, psychiatrists, clinical psychologists, minsters, and others that often where sex is the only or the most important factor in marriage, unhappiness soon follows. This result is to be expected, for marriage is the adjustment of two total personalities to each other. There may be sexual satisfaction and harmony; yet when personalities clash on other levels, it may follow that sexual relations become impossible. As a result, all reasons for marriage may disappear. It is common sense that sex should be only one aspect of marriage—a very important one, but nevertheless only one.

Security. At present, everyone is "security-conscious." During World War II, numerous restrictions were imposed for "security reasons." Since the end of the war, we have spent billions of dollars on "national security." Congress and the nation are stirred up over "social security." What is the nature of this all-powerful drive?

In order to exist and achieve stability and success, every individual, as well as every group or nation, must be in harmony with the environment, an environment which may be favorable for, or destructive of, any unit living within it. Man as a unit, a *microcosm*, is constantly acted upon and must react continuously; his existence, or at least his inner piece of mind, is in constant danger. It is small wonder that he seeks the security which comes from being in harmony with his environment.

Marriage is sought by many as a source of security because it adds strength to the individual and provides a fairly stable environment. Perhaps every individual suffers from some degree of inadequacy or inferiority. Alfred Adler has made an important contribution to the understanding of man by bringing into clear relief the fact that every individual begins life with inferiority feelings because of dependency in childhood and possible organic or psychological handicaps. Life is a struggle to overcome this inferiority feeling. Few master the feeling completely; many suffer defeats which leave a permanent imprint on the personality structure. It is no wonder that the individual seeks strength by close association with someone else. Marriage provides this reinforcement. It promises the individual a mate who will join forces in battling the exigencies of life, who is willing to share victory and defeat, and who, above everything else, believes in him.

In addition, marriage has been made into a fairly stable and permanent institution in a constantly changing world. All the forces available to human society have been enlisted to bring about this result. Once marriage has been entered into, public opinion immediately operates to preserve the union. Fulfillment of the obligations incurred in marriage is rewarded by public approval in the form of acceptance of the married couple as respectable members of society, of status, and of prestige. The married couple is given opportunities to enjoy the benefits of social life. Nonfulfillment of marriage obligations often leads to loss of respect, rejection, and even social ostracism. No couple can safely disregard public opinion. It is true that public opinion is not as strict as it once was, but couples who deviate from the established conventions must prove to society that they are justified in getting out of their marriage status.

Law is also on the side of permanence of marriage; numerous laws have been enacted to preserve a marriage. They regulate individual rights in marriage, control of property and offspring, and so on. Divorce is made difficult, if not impossible. In order to obtain a divorce, one party still must prove in court that the other is guilty of cruelty, desertion, adultery, or some such charge.

As was shown above, religion reinforces public opinion and laws by stressing moral and spiritual factors. The Divine Being is enlisted in the interest of a lasting marriage.

People also often seek financial security through marriage. They feel financially secure when they have enough money to provide for the satisfaction of such basic needs as food, clothing, shelter, health, education, and recreation. Men and women believe that marriage provides greater opportunity for the satisfaction of these needs. It is usually claimed that women, more than men, marry for economic reasons. Insofar as this is true, it is probably because of one or both of the following reasons: First, women are more handicapped than men in earning an adequate income. Second, as a rule, women want children, and marriage usually makes it financially possible to have them.

One may seek greater financial security in marriage by selecting a mate who either has already accumulated some financial means or is capable of earning an adequate income. There is also the advantage of pooling resources and saving by joint housekeeping. While it is not true that two can live as cheaply as one, it is true that two can live together for less than if they lived apart. In addition, there is the assurance that if one becomes ill, the other is ready to help in any way possible.

Recognition, Status, Prestige. A person's concept of himself ultimately depends upon what he thinks of himself and what he believes others think of him. In order to feel secure in his self-esteem, he needs to have his opinion reinforced by others. It is for this reason that he is sensitive to the reactions of others to him. Since he wants to count as at least *one* in society, he wants to know how he is being evaluated. This evaluation by society is his status, and it is one of his prized possessions. Without it, he has no friends, no fellowships; he is a nobody. He would rather have a negative status than none at all, for then he is at least noticed. Prestige indicates a man's position relative to others in his group. This relative position is all-important to him, for it indicates his privileges and responsibilities.

One argument often advanced by either party for getting married runs like this: "Everybody of our age is getting married. It is implied that, if we do not get married, others will believe we are not as good as they are."

Since marriage is a milestone of achievement, it is a determiner of status and prestige. Not to attain it in some sense implies low prestige, especially for a woman. It may, in the minds of some people, connote that she was unable to attract or hold a male. Conversely, it is a source of proud satisfaction when she attains it. This is evident in the pride shown in an engagement ring and in the attention received from friends and relatives. The future groom and bride are showered with good wishes, congratulations, and presents. They are granted many privileges and are the object of admiration from single as well as married people. Before, they were just members of society in general; now they are in the limelight. They are admitted and accepted as full-fledged members of adult society.

Among other things, to get married implies having grown up, having someone who believes in you, being physically mature, being a desirable personality, being capable of giving and receiving happiness, being reasonably healthy, being attractive, having sex appeal, and being ready to become parents.

Need to Belong. The need to belong is closely related to status, but differs from it in that it gives the individual the satisfaction of being accepted by society as a mature member. Marriage is the accepted and approved mode of life in our society; therefore, an individual not conforming to it is considered "different." Unmarried persons of marriageable age are often put on the defensive. Questions are raised about reasons for not marrying.

This desire to belong, to be a part of another, is extremely strong. In former years, psychology assumed the existence of an instinct of gregariousness to account for it. At present, this assumption is no longer held. However, the desire to belong is considered a basic drive, the potency of which is explained on the basis of conditioning throughout life. Each human being begins life, before birth, as an intimate part of the mother. In the first years of his life, the existence and the satisfactions of each human being depend on the nearness and ministrations of other individuals. Neglect or rejection would mean death; hence, there develops in every individual a sense of dependence upon others. Fear of losing this support is terrifying; on the other hand, its presence becomes very satisfying. Thus, the individual develops the urge or desire to be with others, to be a part of others, to be a part of a larger group. This desire manifests itself throughout life in a greater or lesser degree. Children want to play with other children; they want friends. The adolescent belongs to societies or "gangs." The adult joins organizations. It is said that we are a nation of "joiners." Men and women list with pride the organizations to which they belong.

Loyalty is considered a virtue. It means that the individual is willing to sacrifice his own interests to those of society. He will conform to folkways, customs, and mores, even though conformity may bring personal inconveniences.

Conformity and loyalty are enforced by society through rewards and punishments. The rewards take many forms: respect, prestige, privileges, good reputation, admiration. Loyalty often continues to be recognized even after the individual's death, in various ways, from elaborate monuments and memorials to modest tombstones inscribed with words of praise.

Nonconformity or disloyalty is punished in numerous ways. Children in the home are isolated by being locked into a room, or are kept from playing with their companions. In school, they are made to stand by themselves, and, in extreme cases, are expelled. A church may excommunicate. Society at large may ridicule or ostracize. Governments may send a person to prison and there punish him with solitary confinement, or may banish him from his country, or may send him to a penal colony. These forms of isolation are painful to the individual. They are ego-hurts, which are more unpleasant even than physical pain. Prolonged, complete isolation, as in solitary confinement, often leads to mental and emotional disorganization.

The need for belonging having thus been acquired by an individual and conformity to the codes of society having been impressed upon him, it is only natural that he will seek satisfactions in life in ways acceptable to society. In our society, marriage is one of those ways. It goes without saying that many individuals may be unaware, or only partly aware, of this motive.

Great and important as are the satisfactions which an individual derives from being a member of society at large, membership in society does not fully satisfy his deep-seated need of belonging, especially since primary groups are more and more supplanted by secondary groups. These latter groups, on the whole, stress rationality almost to the exclusion of emotional satisfaction; they are impersonal. They bring loss of intimacy and security; the individual still feels lonely. Marriage, being highly intimate and personal, satisfies more fully the need for belonging. It becomes a place of refuge in a turbulent world. In marriage a person seeks "to unite with," to belong.

Possession. The male wants the satisfaction of being able to say of the woman he chose, "She is *mine;* she is *my* wife." The female also seeks the satisfaction of being able to say of her chosen man, "He is *my* husband." At present, we do not know much about the origin of this drive of possession. It may be innate, at least in part. Evidence for this conclusion may be the fact that most birds and animals mate either temporarily or permanently. The drive of possession among them is extremely strong, as is evidenced by the fact that in case of competition there is often a struggle unto death. Another evidence for its innateness is the universality of mating among human beings at all times, in every society. The differences are only as to the number of mates a male or female may possess. The basis for the desire to possess a mate is perhaps a tendency toward self-expansion. Whatever the origin of the desire to possess, culture has a great deal to do with the forms it takes. Even among animal societies, there is some recognition of the "rights" of mates. In every human society, there are a great number of mores, taboos, and laws which protect an individual in his possession of a mate. All in all, desire to have one's own mate is extremely strong and is therefore either a conscious or an unconscious factor in marriage.

Having Children. Closely related to possession of a mate is the desire for offspring, a desire found almost universally among mankind. Many individuals feel this desire before marriage, while in others it comes to consciousness only after marriage. The strength of the desire is evidenced by the fact that many couples undergo sacrifices to have children. Gynecologists and obstetricians are familiar with the great effort made by many women to have offspring. Often, of course, when unable to have their own children, a couple will make tireless efforts to adopt one or more children. Some will even go so far as to secure a child by illegal methods. Just what lies behind this desire to have children, we do not know. It may be a drive for self-perpetuation. It may even go beyond the couple or individual and be a characteristic of life as such, for only by means of offspring can a particular stream of life perpetuate itself.

Establishing a Home. All living organisms have their habitat. Human beings are no exception; they also seek a home. Our country is an aggregate of millions of homes—in cities, towns, hamlets, and on farms. Young people, in maturing, develop strong longings to establish a home of their own. Since homes center on marriage, young people wish to get married and begin the establishment of a home which will be "theirs." They seek the pride that comes with ownership.

Desire for Sharing. Closely related to the desire for belonging is the desire for sharing. Every individual is more or less aware of an inner isolation. No one can be so aware of his feelings, thoughts, ambitions, strengths, and weaknesses as he is himself. To contain these within himself, not to share them with anyone else, leads progressively to a feeling of isolation and possibly rejection. Not everyone is permitted to look into this private world. It must be a person whose interests can be identified with his own; otherwise, self-revelation may be accompanied by criticism, rejection, and various ego-hurts. A good mate is ideal for this purpose. To him one can relate secrets not meant for the ears of others.

There is a desire to share both unpleasant and pleasant things. Joy, happiness, elation also must be shared, and in this sharing the pleasures are increased. Telling others about one's inner feelings gives one an additional reward. A mate who understands will not interpret such sharing as boasting but as the natural expression of normal excess psychic energy.

Common goals

Participation. Participation is closely related to sharing, but the two are not the same. Sharing means essentially that A possesses something and wants to impart it to B; participation means that A and B have common goals. Participation means doing things together. There are hundreds of activities that one can engage in alone, but one gets immeasurably more pleasure by sharing them with a sympathetic, understanding mate. For instance, a person can attend a concert alone, but somehow the pleasure is greater if one listens with a partner at his side. Well-adjusted couples quite often find that neither mate can enjoy anything as completely by himself as when in the company of the mate. Incidentally, this motive is an important factor in the acquisition of common interests, or in making the interests of one mate common to both.

Curiosity. Curiosity is such a strong and universal tendency among animals and men that, in former years, it was classified as an instinct. While psychologists have discarded the concept of instinct in man, they regard curiosity as a strong tendency or desire, whatever its origin may be. It manifests itself in numerous ways, from exploration of the minutest object to probing into the mysteries of the universe as a whole. Marriage offers so many unknown aspects that it is not surprising to find curiosity about it as one motive for it. Even before one has found a mate, he begins to show curiosity by such questions as: "I wonder whom I am going to marry? I wonder what kind of a person he or she will be?" As one approaches marriage, all kinds of new questions come up: "I wonder how we will get along with each other? How happy will we be? What kind of a home will we have? What friends will we have? What kind of children?"

Escape. There are some who regard marriage as a refuge, a means of escaping a more or less unpleasant situation. The most important thing for them is not to marry a certain person, but to get away from something. It may be an unpleasant home situation, such as extreme poverty, parental domination, tension between parents, conflicts with siblings, and the like; or, especially for women, it may be an unpleasant work situation. It may be extreme isolation—that is, being without close relatives and friends. For some, indeed, this may be the primary motive. All too often, though, the marriage counselor will be told: "I am very unhappy in marriage; I did not marry him for love but because I simply had to get away from home. The way I felt at that time was such that I could have married anybody." On the whole, women use the escape motive for marriage more often than do men.

Money. Marrying someone who, in addition to desirable personality characteristics, also possesses money is considered by many in our society the height of achievement. Many still believe that possession of enough money to provide a home is a prime requisite for marriage. But to marry someone solely for money is regarded by others as immoral. Many a melodrama has been written around the plot in which the heroine is in love with a poor man but must marry the villain who owns the mortgage on her parents' home. Since it offers so many privileges, however, there are individuals who voluntarily marry solely for money. Because of our mores, this motive is seldom, if ever, admitted in public. In fact, many an individual will rationalize it away in his own thinking.

Improvement of Status. A person may select and marry a mate in order to enhance his status. Thus, a young man may marry a particular girl because she enjoys a higher economic status than he: she may move in the upper social circles; she may be the daughter of a professional man; her father may have achieved a great reputation as an artist, scientist, or inventor; or she may belong to one of the "old" or "noble" families. A girl may marry a young man for the same reasons. If the social level of the two families is approximately the same and if the motive to marry for status is a secondary one, then the marriage may work out satisfactorily. On the other hand, if there is a marked difference in social rank between the families and if to gain status is the primary motive, the success of the marriage is doubtful.

Aid to a Career. This motive is closely related to marrying for money and improvement of status; yet it is somewhat different, in the sense that the individual wants these things as aids to the advancement of his career. Since men in our society are more career-conscious than women, it is a motive more commonly found among men. Most people know of some young man who married the boss's daughter to make sure of promotion. Whether this motive will lead to successful marriage depends upon the objectives set by the two persons. If they mutually agree that their marriage is primarily a business arrangement or for the enhancement of a career, then it may result in a satisfactory union. However, if close companionship is the ideal, a marriage created as an aid to a career or business advancement is likely to fail.

Fear of Loss of Reputation. Here and there one finds a couple who have been sweethearts since childhood. "Everybody" knows they have been going together for years. Not to marry each other would start "everyone" wondering and questioning. To avoid these consequences, the couple gets married. This type of situation sometimes arises among young immigrant couples, for whom prospective marriages are often arranged by members of their families. When two persons marry each other chiefly to satisfy parents and friends, they run great risk to their happiness. They may live together in the same house, but unless each is the other's choice in marriage their lives do not merge. They will not experience the satisfactions and happiness which come from close, intimate intercommunication. In fact, such superficial living side by side may become extremely difficult to endure. The forced relationship is likely to result in increased frustration and tension.

Feeling Sorry for the Other. A man and woman may spend so much time together that they become used to, and dependent on, each other; they must get married in order to avoid pain and disappointment. In some cases, the attachment becomes one-sided. For example, a man, after having been taken for granted over a long period of time, may actually prefer not to enter into marriage. Yet he realizes that the girl is still deeply attached to him. She may claim that a termination of the relationship will mean loss of reputation, isolation, and severe ego-hurt for her. She may even threaten suicide. He is overpowered by pity and, as a consequence, marries her primarily out of sympathy and a desire "to save face." (Obviously, the reverse of this case is equally true; men, too, know how to coerce and threaten suicide when jilted!) It is possible to feel sorry for a person for a reasonable period of time, but not indefinitely. After a while, the feeling is bound to disappear or to turn into resentment, annoyance, disgust, and even hate. It is psychologically just as impossible to give constantly without receiving anything in return as it is to expend physical energy without replenishing it.

Obligation or Duty. A man may feel himself duty-bound to marry a particular girl for several reasons. A couple may have been "going together" for so many years that the girl has reached an age when it is very difficult for her to find another mate. The man may feel that it would be unjust to leave her now, and so he marries her, even when he no longer cares for her. A similar situation arises when it is felt that the man has "compromised" the woman. He may conclude that the only "decent" thing to do is to get married to remove a stigma from the girl and give a prospective child a name and a home. Again, the threat of suicide on the part of one party may make the other feel "duty-bound" to prevent such tragedy. There are other similar conditions which tend to force a couple into marriage. Such unions seldom work out happily and satisfactorily.

Love. Love is such an important and complex motive for marriage that an entire chapter will be devoted to it (see Chapter 6).

While the above list of motives for marriage is not exhaustive, it covers the major ones operative in our society. Probably it is rare that one person marries another for any single reason. As a rule, marriage is entered into for a number of reasons, some of which may be unconscious. Since happiness in any marriage depends upon the degree of satisfactions achieved in marital adjustment, it is desirable that man and woman discover and understand their motives for marrying each other. Just what motives will bring greatest happiness certainly depends upon the personalities of the mates. (For a discussion of undesirable motives, see Chapters 18 and 19.)

INTERPRETATIVE SUMMARY

1. The over-all motivation for marriage is usually happiness.
2. Specific motives for marriage may be conscious as well as unconscious.

3. Happiness or unhappiness may be due just as much to unconscious as to conscious motives.

4. Motives may be due to innate needs, or they may be culturally determined.

5. Individuals differ considerably in the number of needs they wish to satisfy in marriage and in their emphasis on particular needs, as well as in the intensity of those needs.

THOUGHT QUESTIONS AND PROJECTS

1. Try this project:

Step A. Divide the class into "buzz-session" groups to discuss the topic "Why Marry?" Following discussion by the smaller groups, bring together all reasons submitted. Let the class compile, revise, and condense them if necessary. Write the final selection of reasons for marrying on the blackboard. The class may then as a group agree upon the rank order of the reasons by numbering them 1, 2, 3, etc. Or each student may make his own evaluation as to rank. Such data should be recorded for later reference in step C. When the reasons are selected and ranked, each student should make a set of cards by writing one reason on a separate index card. (Note: Rank numbers should be omitted from the cards.)

Step B. Each student is then ready to present his shuffled set of cards to a married couple of his acquaintance whose age range is between 60 and 75. (The couple's name may be kept anonymous.) The couple is instructed to read the reasons and to decide together the order of importance in their own marriage. One or two blank cards may be included in the set to be used in cases where a couple wishes to add reasons not mentioned by the class. As soon as the couple has stacked the cards according to their preferred rank order, number them.

Step C. Report the returns to the class. Compare the rank order given by the couples with that agreed upon by the class or with individual ranks as the case may be. Are there marked differences? Are there similarities? Did any couples appear to have difficulty in reaching agreement as to the rank order of the reasons? Were any couples reluctant to include certain reasons given by the students? Let the class discuss and share any helpful observations made during the interviews.

2. Do you think girls tend to marry more for love than do men? Discuss.

3. Why do business firms sometimes give preference to married men when filling positions? Are there positions for women which are more likely to be given to married applicants?

4. What are some conditions which cause a person not to choose to marry?

5. Do you think many individuals marry primarily because society expects them to do so?

SUGGESTED READINGS FOR FURTHER STUDY

Adams, Clifford R., *Preparing for Marriage*, New York, E. P. Dutton & Company, 1951.
Chapter 1. Why Should You Marry?
Bowman, Henry A., *Marriage for Moderns*, 3rd ed., New York, McGraw-Hill Book Company, 1954.
Chapter 2. The Reasons for Marriage.
Chapter 3. The Permanently Unmarried.
Burgess, Ernest W., and Harvey J. Locke, *The Family*, 2nd ed., New York, American Book Company, 1953.
Chapter 10. Wishes as Motivation.
Foster, Robert Geib, *Marriage and Family Relationships*, rev. ed., New York, The Macmillan Company, 1950.
Chapter 11. Basic Needs and Human Behavior.
Harper, Robert A., *Marriage*, New York, Appleton-Century-Crofts, 1949.
Chapter 2. Why People Do and Don't Marry.
Landis, Judson T., and Mary G. Landis, *Building a Successful Marriage*, New York, Prentice-Hall, 1953.
Chapter 4. Why People Marry or Do Not Marry.
Waller, Willard, *The Family* (rev. by Reuben Hill), New York, The Dryden Press, 1951.
Chapter 6. The Sentiment of Love.

6

MARRYING FOR LOVE

In our society, love is considered a very important, perhaps the most important, motive for marriage. By many it is regarded as so essential that marriage without love is looked upon as undesirable, if not indeed immoral. For this reason, those in love may disregard factors that may cause serious difficulties in marriage and make adjustment impossible. Not only is love considered prerequisite for getting married, but it is also assumed to be essential for remaining married. The absence of love is often given as the reason for seeking a divorce.

DEFINITION OF LOVE

Since love is considered imperative for a successful marriage, one would assume that the meaning of love was clear and definite. Yet this is far from true. The word *love* is used very loosely, and has a great variety of meanings. Thus one can "love" almost any object, such as food, clothing, or an automobile. People speak of "loving" many activities, such as work, play, and various sports. They speak also of love between various individuals, such as love of parents for children and children for parents, love between siblings, and love between neighbors. The concept of love is also central in most religions. Religious people love God, and feel they are loved by Him; and God Himself is defined as love.

It is obvious that in many cases where we use the word love it would be more appropriate to use such words as *liking* or *affection*. The quality of love between parents and children obviously cannot be the same as that between sweethearts or between husband and wife. In our discussion of love, we shall confine our-selves to this latter type.

Even this type of love is difficult to define, since it is a complex relationship. In Warren's *Dictionary of Psychology,* it is defined as follows: ". . . a feeling or sentiment of attachment toward some person, often growing out of sexual attraction, relations, or situations, and exhibiting a great diversity of psychological and physiological manifestations." [1] This definition posits feeling or sentiment as the essential characteristic of love. Magoun defines love in the following words:

> "Love is the passionate and abiding desire on the part of two or more people to produce together the conditions under which each can be, and spontaneously express, his real self; to produce together an intellectual soil and an emotional climate in which each can flourish, far superior to what either could achieve alone. It is an intimate re-latedness based on the mutual approval and affirmation of the charac-ter and integrity of the personalities involved." [2]

The word *passionate* is explained in a footnote in these words:

> "Passion is being in the grip of an emotional experience so big that it possesses you and you can do nothing about it, like the feelings which possess a person in the presence of birth, or death or love." [3]

This definition, too, stresses very much the quality of feeling and regards it as all-powerful in the creation of conditions which serve to perpetuate it.

The element of feeling is undoubtedly essential in any concept of love; however, it seems more realistic to regard feeling as only one component of the love experience. Love is a complex experi-ence which results from the blending of feeling or emotion, men-tal processes, and sexual attraction. Together these components produce a single pleasant quality which we call love.

While these definitions are helpful in delimiting the concept of love, they are far from satisfactory in explaining its true nature. The whole concept should become clearer when we consider the genesis of love in an individual, the experience of love, and the nature of the love relationship.

[1] Howard C. Warren, *Dictionary of Psychology,* Boston, Houghton Mifflin Com-pany, 1934. Reprinted by permission.
[2] F. Alexander Magoun, *Love and Marriage,* New York, Harper & Brothers, 1948, p. 4. Reprinted by permission.
[3] *Ibid.,* p. 4.

GENESIS OF LOVE IN AN INDIVIDUAL

As we have defined it so far, love is possible only for persons who have reached a certain degree of maturity. No child possesses the ability for such love, and some individuals, regardless of age, are incapable of experiencing love. As far as is known, every normal child is born with a *capacity* for love, whereas the *ability* to love requires time and training.

In the acquisition of this ability, one can roughly distinguish three stages: (1) self-love, (2) object-love, and (3) love for a person. In infancy and early childhood, love is directed only to the self; it depends upon the pleasures which are derived from body and ego satisfactions. The bodily satisfactions are produced by the stimulation of many pleasure zones, such as the tongue, lips, nipples, ear lobes, palm of the hand, forehead, and genital organs. The psychoanalysts consider the reactions to such stimulation to be of sexual nature, but many psychologists regard them as being merely pleasurable.

At first, the child is not aware of himself as an organism distinct from the environment. Only at the age of eighteen months to two years does the concept of self begin gradually to emerge. At this stage come new experiences which contribute pleasurable satisfactions: heightened self-feeling, increased sense of values, and self-esteem. Not knowing the sources of his satisfactions, all the child can do is enjoy them. We may say that, in effect, he is in love with himself. He is said to be in the "narcissistic" stage.

The second stage of love begins when a child becomes aware that his satisfactions depend upon objects and conditions in his environment. He now becomes attached to the sources of his satisfactions.

"Just as the puppy or kitten makes contact with everything that does not injure it, so the child is primarily "positive"; he reaches out to, snuggles up against, immerses himself in nearly everything with which he is free to make contact. As soon as anything clearly recognizable as *love* (in the sense of a strong personal attachment) appears, it begins to serve as a powerful dynamic in living. Unless he is starved or frustrated, the child lives his life in terms of the people, the things, and the activities he loves. Such a torrent of loving cannot remain un-directed; the persons and things and activities which satisfy the love impulse are *canalized,* and those that do not are crowded out, ig-nored." [4]

In this manner a child becomes attached to objects and condi-tions in his environment, not for their own intrinsic value, but because they give him satisfaction. At this stage, the child be-comes attached to his mother, or to any other person who takes care of him, merely as a source of his satisfactions.

The third stage begins when a child learns not only to receive satisfactions from others but also to give them. This period begins with the child's awareness that he cannot always receive what he wants when he wants it. He learns that those who serve him also have needs which must be met. Many experiences teach him that his reaction to the favors received cause pleasure in those who give them: he perceives that he also is a source of satisfaction. The beginning of this awareness is the beginning of mature love. He will now do things to please those who take care of him, in part because he notices that his giving of pleasure increases the amount of pleasure he himself will receive.

This process of learning to satisfy the needs of other people and thus to give them satisfaction is facilitated by several conditions. First, there are many *rewards,* such as praise, recognition, accept-ance, and love, for attempts to give satisfaction to others, and various *punishments* for not making such attempts. Second, as the child matures, he becomes capable of guilt feelings which he experiences whenever he does not accede to the wishes of others. Third, the child observes the love relationships in his immediate environment—between his brothers and sisters, his parents, and many other persons with whom he comes in contact. This observa-tion of love relationships is important: Many studies show that most couples who are happy in marriage come from homes in which true happiness prevailed. Other sources of learning to love are literature, the school, and the church.

[4] Gardner Murphy, *Personality,* New York, Harper & Brothers, 1947, p. 555. Re-printed by permission.

ANALYSIS OF LOVE EXPERIENCE

We have shown that love is a complex experience, and that the ability to love another is acquired gradually. It is now of value to analyze the subjective experience of love—to determine, as best we can, what a person experiences within himself when he is in love.

We have stated that love is composed of three components— the mental, the affective, and the sexual. Graphically, it might be presented in the following manner:

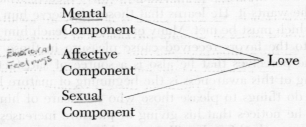

Mental Component

Affective Component → Love

Emotional Feelings

Sexual Component

Let us examine more closely each of these components.

The Mental Component. The mental processes in love are of the pleasant and easygoing type, such as recall, phantasy, and optimistic planning for the future. Since the present experience is pleasant for the one in love, he will recall pleasurable experiences from his past. This is shown by the fact that conversation centers on happy events in the past life of lovers. Especially enjoyable are memories of childhood, so that the person feels almost like a child. Probably that is why many people in love engage in "baby talk."

As common pleasure-giving experiences accumulate, they are relived again and again, so that recall becomes enriched with time. Imagination is usually given free reign. One visualizes himself in the company of the loved one in a great number of situations, such as working together, playing together, making friends together, building a home, and rearing children. Many plans are made for the realization of these imaginings, always with the feeling that they will result in great happiness.

The Affective Component. Affective components are the feel-ings and emotions aroused by the excitation of the autonomic nervous system. The feelings and emotions ("affects") are experi-enced as either pleasant or unpleasant. The pleasant affects pre-dominate in the love experience. An understanding of the func-tioning of the autonomic nervous system should aid us consider-ably in a greater appreciation of the affective quality of love. An examination of the figure on page 118 will reveal that the auto-nomic nervous system is divided into two parts: the parasympa-thetic and the sympathetic. Pleasant affect, such as love, depends upon the dominance of the parasympathetic; unpleasant, such as hate and jealousy, upon the dominance of the sympathetic.

When we experience emotions, there is not only an awareness of affect but also a series of definite physiological changes in the organism. When the sympathetic nervous system is in ascendance (accompanied by unpleasant feelings and emotions), the follow-ing changes take place: The pupils of the eyes dilate, the retina becomes more sensitive, and the organism becomes more respon-sive to visual stimuli. Digestion is either stopped or slowed down: No saliva is secreted, and no digestive fluids are given off from the walls of the stomach. However, there may be an increase of hy-drochloric acid. Peristaltic movement also stops. The liver gives off concentrated sugar, which, as concentrated nourishment, is poured into the blood stream. At the same time, adrenalin is given off by the adrenal glands. All this activity exerts an influence on the circulatory system. The heart beats faster and with greater force, the blood pressure rises, and the pulses beat faster. The tissues of the body absorb more food, and the muscles become tense, ready for action. Since more food is absorbed, more waste products are produced, thereby creating a condition which affects the respiratory system. The individual breathes more deeply and at a faster tempo. Elimination is also affected. There is more frequent urination. In an extremely unpleasant emotion, the bowels may be emptied involuntarily. If, however, an unpleasant emotion persists, constipation will result. Sex functions are altered. There may be an increase of the sex urge because of the secretion of hormones, but sex expression is impossible, because sufficient blood is not supplied to the genitals.

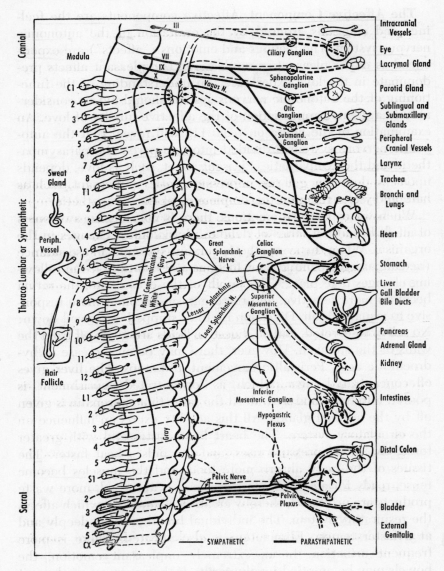

FIGURE 6. Autonomic Nervous System.[5]

[5] After Frank H. Netter, M.D., The CIBA Collection of Medical Illustrations. By permission.

When the parasympathetic nervous system is in ascendance, all the physiological processes are facilitated. Digestion proceeds easily; circulation is so enhanced that the individual becomes aware of a pleasant sensation in the chest. (This sensation has popularized the illusion that love is centered in the heart.) Elimination becomes quite normal, and the whole reproductive system is activated to a greater or lesser degree. Sex hormones are poured into the blood stream, and the sex organs are prepared for their function. This fact is indicative of the close connection between the pleasant emotion of love and sex.

One should not get the impression that the parasympathetic nervous system functions in complete independence of the sympathetic. In many cases, there are all kinds of combinations between them. This fact explains why the quality of affect experienced in love is not always the same. The intensity of affect is greater in the early stages of love than in some later stages. We have said above that in pleasant emotion digestion is facilitated, and yet quite often when people are in love, they lose their appetite. Ordinarily, when one has been in love for only a short time, he cannot quite believe that it is true; in other words, he is afraid of losing his beloved. In the early stages of love, there is usually a greater element of thrill, which results from the alternation between doubt and certainty, that is, between the dominance of the sympathetic nervous system and that of the parasympathetic.

The Sexual Component. The sexual components of love involve the sensations experienced as a result of stimulation of the erogenous zones of the body. These zones are stimulated whenever a person is physically attracted to an individual of the opposite sex. The sensations may be caused merely by thinking of the other individual or by actual physical contacts of varying degrees of intimacy. The total sexual element, therefore, may be of greater or lesser frequency, intensity, and duration. Occasionally, people use sex as a term almost synonymous with love, as when sexual stimulation is designated as "making love." From what we have said so far, it should be clear that love does not comprise either sex *or* feeling *or* thought, but a fusion or coalescence of all three.

While adult love between the sexes contains these three components, there are great differences from person to person. These differences are primarily of two kinds: first, in the emphasis or predominance of one of the three factors; and second, in the quality of each of these factors. Thus in one individual the mental element may be all-important, while in another the affective may pre-

"Maybe Prof. Bixby is right about love being simply a chemical reaction between a fellow and a girl and I'm just dating the wrong chemicals!"

Salo and the Chicago Tribune—New York News Syndicate, Inc.

dominate, and in still another, the sexual. Or again, any two components may be highly significant and the third may be unimportant. It is also true that the emphasis on one or the other of these components varies from one period of life to another. There is a definite tendency in almost all individuals for the sexual and affective components to decrease and for the mental element to increase with age.

The quality of each component may also vary from individual to individual and from one period of life to another: from phantasy to realistic thinking in the mental element; from great emotional excitement to emotional calm; and in the sexual component, from great intensity and frequency to occasional moderate enjoyment.

CHARACTERISTICS OF THE LOVE RELATIONSHIP

The over-all characteristic of the love relationship is the unification, merging, and coalescing of two personalities. It is not implied that the two personalities disappear in this union, but that they are simply so much alike in motivation, attitudes, values, interests, and viewpoints that the differences between them are reduced to a minimum. There results a strong feeling of oneness; each person feels fully accepted, protected, and secure.

This state expresses itself in an intense desire for physical closeness. Sir Francis Galton has observed that two persons in love, even when sitting on chairs side by side, appear to lean toward each other. He suggested, somewhat facetiously, that by attaching pressure-recording instruments to the legs of their chairs, one would discover that greater weight was exerted on the legs nearest each other!

Persons in love like to look at each other, especially into each other's eyes. There is also a great desire to touch the loved one, to hold hands, to kiss, and to caress.

A number of processes operate to facilitate this feeling of oneness.

Sharing. A person in love opens up his entire personality to the loved one. There is an intense desire to have the loved one "look" into him or her. Each one wants the other to see him as he is. Corresponding to this, there is also a tremendous *curiosity* about each other. One wants to know all the experiences the other has had, from childhood to the present. Any picture of the other, even a baby picture, is regarded with great delight. All this takes place without fear or hesitancy, because each one feels fully accepted by the other.

Identification. Putting oneself in another's place and playing his role in order to experience life as he does is characteristic of identification. The aim is to be as nearly as possible identical with the other; similarities are stressed and differences are minimized or overlooked.

Empathy and Sympathy. The emotions in a person's life are of extreme importance; consequently, people in love have an urge to participate in each other's emotions. By the process of empathy, one seeks to reproduce within himself the same emotions—mostly the pleasant ones—experienced by the other, thus experiencing them vicariously. Through the process of sympathy, one seeks to share the other person's mostly unpleasant emotions and thus to feel *with* him in any given situation. The total effect is that the pleasant emotions are increased by sharing them, and the unpleasant are decreased by dividing them. The general result is to bring the two persons closer together emotionally.

Giving. We have said that mature love is attained only when a person can not only receive satisfactions but also give them. In a sense, therefore, the essence of love consists in the sincere desire of one person to make another person happy by giving of himself and of his possessions. Evidence for this is found in the innumerable sacrifices the lover makes for the loved one and in the many presents and gifts exchanged between them. Since the desire to give of oneself and of one's possessions is so sincere and intense, not to have them accepted causes great pain and discouragement. This kind of love approaches altruism.[6] However, love should not be looked upon as completely devoid of self-interest. One still seeks the pleasure derived from giving, and while a reward for specific sacrifices and gifts is not expected, there is still the anticipation of being loved more as a result of having contributed to the happiness of the loved one.

Forgiving. When a person attains the third stage in the development of love, in which he can give and receive satisfactions freely,

[6] Altruism is defined as "the type of conduct based on the consideration of the welfare of other beings rather than one's own advantage." See Warren, *op. cit.*

it does not mean that the first two levels have been completely outgrown and discarded. On occasion, he may regress to either one of the first two levels. Sometimes he may seek satisfactions without thinking of the needs of the loved one. Or he may be so preoccupied with self-satisfaction that the loved one may feel slighted or even discarded. At other times, he may use the loved one only as a means of getting greater satisfactions. His giving may be motivated by the desire to flatter his ego. He may demand sacrifices in the name of love. It is an axiom that just as soon as one demands in the name of love, genuine love disappears. For this reason, the statement "If you love me, you will do this or that for me," indicates that love is beginning to wane.

Reversion to either of the first two levels may manifest itself in unwillingness to accept expression of love for fear of dependence or enslavement. Any reversion or regression to the first levels becomes a source of pain and irritation for the loved one. It is expected in a real love relationship that regressions be recognized as such by the person regressing and that the hurt or offended person be willing to forgive just as soon as such insight is expressed. This is all the more important because either member of the love relationship may experience such regressions.

Participation. Two persons in love like to be with each other, to do everything possible together. They like to be with each other because of the pleasant interstimulation and interaction. The increasing number of new experiences will bind them together, not only while the current experiences are in progress, but also after they have become rich memories.

The general effect of the love relationship is that each one feels himself completely free, although interacting intimately with another person. There is an intense and satisfying feeling of greater self-realization and expression, as well as a feeling of having one's own personality reinforced and strengthened and enriched.

In conclusion, love, as it has been delineated above, can well be the motive for marriage, because persons so motivated will do everything in their power to bring about a successful, and therefore happy, adjustment in marriage.

SOME SPECIFIC QUESTIONS ABOUT LOVE

Infatuation and Love. On the basis of what has been said about love, it should not be difficult to differentiate between infatuation and love. Infatuation involves only the first and second stages of the love development. The infatuated person does not see the other individual as a person possessing needs of his own, but merely as a stimulus which arouses within him the pleasant qualities accompanying a love experience. The affective and the sexual elements predominate over the mental element, and the mental element consists primarily of phantasy thinking. The infatuated person is really in love with "love," and the other person is merely incidental in arousing his reactions. Consequently, it is not surprising that infatuation is temporary, and that the individual can be infatuated with a number of persons in rapid succession.

The following case illustrates infatuation. An attractive and intelligent white co-ed, aged 17, met an Oriental student at a dance. He was in this country on a temporary permit of nine months. Her report ran as follows:

> "I never met a finer young man. He is kind, refined, considerate, and exceptionally polite. I was immediately overwhelmed by him and loved him right away. I can't see why a white American girl should not marry an Oriental. I believe the only way to solve our international problem is through intermarriage. My girl friends can't see it that way and they don't want to double-date with me. In fact, some of them have dropped me completely. On the other hand, his friends accept me fully; they treat me like a queen. I know how my parents would react if they knew about it; they would not only forbid my seeing him but I am sure my father would disown me. I have a younger sister who, I think, would understand. I know, if we get married, we shall move from C. Perhaps we should move to the Orient. However, I don't care; I'll be glad to live with him anywhere. My features and coloring are somewhat Oriental, so I know I would not have any trouble."

About two months later, while on a vacation trip, this girl met a young man of her own race, whose background was very similar to her own. Now she was just as strongly convinced that this time it was real love. She now saw what a mistake her previous affair had been and wondered how she could have been so blind. Now, she claimed, her eyes were open and she knew that she truly was in love. But this affair, too, ran its course, and within a short time there was a new hero in the picture for her. Clearly this girl received her thrills from "falling in love," rather than from staying in love.

Love at First Sight. Love at first sight is actually impossible, because love between two individuals is always a product of intimate and complex interaction, which depends upon varied types of experiences. Prior to the time a person falls in love, he unconsciously builds up his "love ideal," or he has loved some other individual—a father, mother, siblings, or others. Falling in love at first sight really involves a transfer of attachment from an ideal or a loved one to a new person because of some consciously or unconsciously observed similarity. Such "love at first sight" will persist only if a continued relationship shows that each person possesses the desirable personality characteristics attributed to him at the first meeting.

Persons who believe in love at first sight sometimes claim that they are capable of judging another personality instantaneously by "intuition"—in other words, that they can know the other person completely at a glance. It is extremely doubtful that this capacity is actually possessed by any individual. And even if such a capacity should exist in one person, it is inconceivable that two individuals should possess it simultaneously and because of it be able to fall in love with each other.

Inability to Love. It is sometimes stated that a particular man or woman is incapable of love. It is true that some individuals whose personality development is arrested have not reached the third stage in the growth of their love development—the ability not only to want their needs satisfied by someone else but also to be willing and effective in the satisfaction of the needs of others. They cannot get beyond the stage of looking upon other people as only means for their own gratification. Such persons possess one or more of the following characteristics: self-centeredness, overdependency, excessive self-sufficiency, and overdominance.

Occasionally one also meets a person who cannot believe that he or she may be loved by anyone. Such a conviction, in most cases, is due to the fact that he has not experienced real love from another. Either the person was rejected in childhood and now cannot believe that he is love-worthy, or he has been loved only because he served to gratify the selfish interests of his parents. These experiences have created the feeling that he has no value in himself but is only a tool for the satisfaction of others. As a result, when such a person is told that he is loved, he looks for hidden selfish motives.

MATURE LOVE

We should not assume that the growth of love stops when a person attains the third stage. Actually, in this stage, there are many levels. When love between two persons has once taken root, it will continue to grow because of the maturing of their individual personalities and because of the increasing intimacy of their relationship. For this reason, a couple may feel at some time that their love has reached its maximum growth, only to discover months or years later that it is capable of still further growth. This continuing growth is an important factor in the enrichment of their personalities.

The mental component is modified from excessive idealization of the mate to a realistic perception, which involves awareness and acceptance not only of strengths but also of weaknesses in character and personality. To living in the past and present is added careful planning for the future. And phantasy thinking is replaced by logical reasoning.

The affective component likewise manifests progressive changes in that it moves from excitement and turbulence to calm and peaceful contentment.

The sexual component is changed from the early forms of anticipatory sex pleasure to one of mature gratification which comes from actuality and the aggregate effect of many pleasant intimacies.

Modified subjective love leads to a closer and more intimate union of mates. They grow in mutual respect for the uniqueness of their personalities and, therefore, to a more tolerant and understanding attitude toward each other. Their love becomes increasingly characterized by the qualities of love mentioned by the Apostle Paul in his first letter to the Corinthians, Chapter 13, Verses 4–7 (The Modern Reader's Bible, by Richard G. Moulton):

"Love suffereth long, and is kind; love envieth not; love vaunteth not itself, is not puffed up, doth not behave itself unseemly, seeketh not its own, is not provoked, taketh not account of evil; rejoiceth not in unrighteousness, but rejoiceth with the truth; beareth all things, believeth all things, hopeth all things, endureth all things."

INTERPRETATIVE SUMMARY

1. In our society, love is considered *the* real motive for getting married.

2. In spite of the fact that love is considered to be so essential, one looks in vain for agreement as to its meaning.

3. In this chapter, an attempt is made to explain love as a product of growth, as an experience, and as a relationship between a man and a woman.

4. A person usually goes through three stages in attaining mature love. First, he loves himself; next, he loves others, but only as a means to his own satisfaction; and finally, he loves others for their own sake. At first, he only receives; later, he learns to give.

5. In heterosexual love, one experiences a fusion of thoughts, feelings, and sexual sensations.

6. The mental element in love is made up of recall of pleasant experiences, phantasy thinking, and optimistic planning for the future.

7. The affective component of love centers in the effects of the parasympathetic nervous system.

8. The sexual element consists of the pleasant sensations arising from the stimulation of the various erogenous zones.

9. Two persons in love seek unification of their personalities and, to effect this, are likely to disregard differences between themselves.

10. To promote unification, they will use several mechanisms, such as identification, sympathy and empathy, giving, forgiving, and sharing.

11. Infatuation is self-centered. An infatuated person enjoys his own "inner" experiences and uses the other person chiefly as a stimulus.

12. Love at first sight is merely transfer and attachment of love experienced for another person, or transfer of a "love ideal."

13. A person who has not reached the third stage in the growth of love is incapable of really loving another person.

14. In mature love, altruism is at least as strong as self-interest.

Thought Questions and Projects

1. Try to write your own definition of "love."

2. What is implied in the statement that "we learn how to give and how to receive love"?

3. What are the basic components of the love experience?

4. What are some chief characteristics which distinguish "infatuation" from love?

5. Do you think modern movies, television, radio, popular love-story magazines, encourage "infatuation" among teenagers? If you do, can you give specific examples from these sources to support your conclusion?

6. Is there such a thing as "love at first sight"?

7. What type of individuals appear never to develop the capacity to love another person?

8. What are indicators of mature love?

9. Members of the class who have read *Swann's Way,* by Marcel Proust, may find it interesting to discuss the author's presentation of immature, romantic love.

Suggested Readings for Further Study

Adams, Clifford R., *Preparing for Marriage*, New York, E. P. Dutton & Company, 1951.
  Chapter 4. Is It Love or Infatuation?
Burgess, Ernest W., and Paul Wallin, *Engagement and Marriage*, New York, J. B. Lippincott Company, 1953.
  Chapter 7. Love and Idealization.
  Chapter 13. Looking Forward to Marriage.
Duvall, Evelyn M., and Reuben Hill, *When You Marry*, rev. ed., New York, D. C. Heath & Company, 1953.
  Chapter 2. It's Love.
Landis, Paul H., *Your Marriage and Family Living*, New York, McGraw-Hill Book Company, 1946.
  Chapter 6. Finding Your Proper Mate Should Not Be Left to Chance.
Merrill, Francis E., *Courtship and Marriage*, New York, The Dryden Press, 1949.
  Chapter 4. Dating and Courtship.
  Chapter 5. The Courtship Process.
Skidmore, Rex A., and Anthon S. Cannon, *Building Your Marriage*, New York, Harper & Brothers, 1951.
  Chapter 3. What Is Love?

7

SELECTION OF A MATE

Concept of the Ideal Mate. The *first* step in mate selection should be to examine one's concept of a mate. As has been pointed out in our discussion of "falling in love," almost every individual has some ideal of a possible mate. This ideal is often largely unconscious, because it has been acquired unconsciously. It should now be brought into consciousness in order to see just how realistic it is. Too often it is found to be fantastic, a product of vivid imagination fed by "love literature" and by the Hollywood version of "they lived happily ever after."

Self-analysis. The *second* step, equally important, should be to ask oneself: "Am I capable of making a mate happy?" Since love is a mutual relationship, one must think also of his ability to satisfy the needs of a mate; otherwise the desire to marry may be merely an urge to return to the conditions of childhood, when everything was centered on making oneself happy, with little or no obligation to give anything in return.

In this connection, the authors are reminded of a man, thirty-two years of age, who came to see them about personality problems. He had no friends or companions; he had been constantly alone, even in childhood. The authors suggested, among other things, that he try to get acquainted with some young lady. Special effort was made to help the man meet several groups of people, including interesting girls. He dated several girls, but never the same girl twice. Inquiry into his "social progress" and into the type of person he was looking for revealed that he had a "fixed ideal" in mind. He wanted a very young girl with a beautiful figure, a good education, highly developed social skills, refinement, dignity, and a worshipful love for him. When asked whether or not he could make such a girl happy with what he had to offer her, he was surprised and momentarily speechless. Finally he confessed that he had really never thought about that. He was one of those persons who actually do not want a true mate, but someone in whose admiration they can bask and who can make *them* feel happy and important.

On the other hand, some people marry with the intention of reforming their mate. This is true of many women, particularly of women who have a strong "motherly" tendency which gives them the conviction that they can reform wayward men. If any reforming is to be done, it must be done before marriage, when the motives for change are stronger than afterwards. Prior to marriage, a young man may be willing to change in order to please his prospective wife; after marriage, when he is sure of her, he usually may not be so inclined to change. He is likely to use subterfuge and alibi to avoid modifying his personality. As an excuse for not complying, he may resort to finding flaws in the personality of his mate. The same problems hold true for a male would-be-reformer. There is also the danger that either mate may want to create the other in his or her own image. It must be remembered that it is not easy to change personality. Even clinical psychologists, psychiatrists, and psychoanalysts find extreme difficulty in modifying some aspects of personality.

Motives in Selecting a Mate. In selecting a mate, one should also keep in mind one's motives for marriage. The motives of mates should be similar. In general, the personalities of mates should be somewhat alike, in spite of the popular saying that opposites attract each other. They may attract, but they may also repel. The attraction to an extreme opposite may be based largely on curiosity or a desire for completion—that is, one wishes to acquire a characteristic which he does not possess but for which he has a hidden longing. For this reason, a "moral" person may be attracted to an "immoral" person, or a quiet, nonsociable person to a socially active one. But when the range of differences between mates is too great, it can only lead to conflict. As we have already pointed out, the highest manifestations of love are oneness, belonging, sharing, and participation—four qualities in a relationship which cannot exist when the differences between mates are very great.

When we say that mates should be alike, we do not imply that they should be identical. Too much duplication in personality structure would result in boredom and monotony. When two persons differ, the all-important question is: Can they adjust to each other? Adjustment, it will be remembered, implies, on the one hand, fitting and adapting oneself to the environment and, on the other, changing the environment. Additional questions would be: Is the difference important? Can I accept this difference without feeling frustrated or annoyed? In reality, any point of difference is not important in itself; it is primarily the reaction to it that is important.

In considering differences in personality, it is also essential to realize that the modern conception of marriage considers the partners equal—in the sharing of rights and privileges as well as in the assumption of responsibilities. To be equals, they should start out without serious handicaps. An overworked argument holds that if one of the mates is submissive and the other dominant there will be perpetual peace. Such indeed may be the peace between master and slave when the slave accepts his position. But this type of relationship is most undesirable for partners in marriage. The submissive person will never be able to realize his own personality, and the dominant person will not benefit from the guidance and direction of the other. Similar criticism can be made of other extremes in traits.

Homogamy. Most modern researchers in marriage agree that the greatest happiness in marriage is found in homogamy—marriage of like with like. Adams suggests that mates be reasonably alike in the following twelve traits: "sociability, conformity, tranquility, insight, stability, tolerance, calmness, flexibility, seriousness, balance, conservatism and motivation (deriving from family upbringing and previous experience)."[1] Terman con-

---

[1] Clifford R. Adams, *Preparing for Marriage*, New York, E. P. Dutton & Company, 1951, p. 100. Reprinted by permission of the author.

cluded from his intensive study of 792 married couples that the more mates tended to be alike in the characteristics given below, the happier they were in their marriage:

> "(1) Superior happiness of parents; (2) Childhood happiness; (3) Lack of conflict with mother; (4) Home discipline that was firm, not harsh; (5) Strong attachment to mother; (6) Strong attachment to father; (7) Lack of conflict with father; (8) Parental frankness about matters of sex; (9) Infrequency and mildness of childhood punishment; (10) Premarital attitude toward sex that was free from disgust and aversion." [2]

Burgess and Wallin, in a study of 1,000 engaged couples living in the Chicago Metropolitan region, found that there is a greater tendency of mates to select spouses who are like themselves. They conclude:

> "Homogamy is an intriguing aspect of mate selection. It is probably an interesting outcome rather than a significant factor in choosing a mate. The study of 1,000 engaged couples confirms the findings of previous studies that in many physical, psychological, and social characteristics the tendency of like to mate with like is greater than that of opposites to be attracted. So far not a single instance of the reverse has been established. Interesting as this fact is, it does not imply that people have an homogamous impulse. The factors already considered —propinquity, image of the ideal mate, parental image, and personality need combined with family and social pressure—are all that seem to be needed to explain the preponderance over chance of homogamous unions. This assumed finding should, however, be demonstrated by research." [3]

In recent years, Winch has questioned the theory that homogamy is the determining factor in mate selection. He believes that homogamous factors so far studied as basic in mate selection merely determine the field in which selection operates, whereas actual selection depends more upon basic personality needs. His hypothesis can be presented best in his own words:

> "In one sense many of the factors which have been studied either under the heading of 'homogamy' or 'assortative mating' represent conditions which operate to delimit and to define the field of eligible mates. In part these conditions function positively to facilitate association with 'one's own kind,' and in part they function negatively to

[2] By permission from *Psychological Factors in Marital Happiness*, by Lewis M. Terman *et al.* Copyright, 1938. McGraw-Hill Book Company, Inc. P. 372.

[3] Ernest W. Burgess and Paul Wallin, *Engagement and Marriage*, Philadelphia, J. B. Lippincott Company, 1953, pp. 212–213. Reprinted by permission.

designate persons of different background as unavailable and undesirable." [4]

Thus a Catholic is more likely to meet a Catholic, a college
student another college student, and a person interested in music
is more likely to associate with another person interested in music.
This merely means that persons having similar interests are likely
to be thrown together.

However, "there is no evidence that persons with similar need
patterns tend to marry" [5] Need-satisfaction in marriage is important. The question is merely, what kind of needs? The answer
is, Winch believes, complementary needs.

> "The theory of complementary needs presents the hypothesis that
> mate selection takes place in part on the basis that persons whose need
> patterns provide mutual gratification tend to choose each other. An
> extreme example of this is the dependent, infantile person who marries
> a quite self-sufficient, nurturant person." [6]

Winch states further that the operation of the theory of complementary needs "can be seen most clearly in rather unusual
(and some pathological) cases." [7]

On the basis of the authors' observation, it would seem that
Winch's theory applies only to a limited number of marriages. It
is to be expected that, in view of the uniqueness of personality,
one will find in marriage complementary, as well as similar, needs.
But this fact does not prove that two persons marry each other
primarily because of such complementary needs. However, final
judgment upon this matter must await the outcome of Winch's
rather intensive and long-term research.

Evaluation of Aspects of Personality

Since failure or success in marriage depends upon the personality adjustment of mates, it is very important that each partner
assess the other's personality accurately before marriage. Some

[4] Robert F. Winch, *The Modern Family*, New York, Henry Holt & Company,
1952, p. 402. Reprinted by permission.
[5] *Ibid.*, p. 403.
[6] *Ibid.*, p. 433.
[7] *Ibid.*, p. 412.

available methods will be mentioned in Chapter 8. Here we are concerned with what to look for in a mate. First, we shall consider the various aspects of personality, and then personality as a whole. In the examination of personality, we shall follow in general the structural outline given in Chapter 3.

Physical Appearance. The significance of size, weight, and beauty is likely to be overemphasized during the adolescent period, since these are the factors which largely determine a person's status at this time of life. Later in life, the emphasis will be more on the quality of personality. One's estimation of another person will first rest upon the more visible and tangible factors, but later will shift to the more intangible. Size is not very important; however, it is desirable in our society that the man be the taller. Actual size is not as important as the attitude one takes toward it. In youth, the boy often is inclined to feel inferior when he is shorter than average. The sale of "elevator" shoes points up the high value placed on height by men. Even comparatively tall boys want to be still taller. The fat boy and stout girl are much concerned about their appearance. In our society, obesity has become a consideration in mate selection.

In spite of the saying that beauty is only skin-deep, physical attractiveness is an *important factor* in mate selection. A beautiful girl usually has a decided advantage over a less attractive girl. However, physical attractiveness is only one of the considerations in the choice of a mate. In this connection, something should be said concerning the cruel way in which a person with a physical deformity is often treated. It should not be forgotten that a person with a crooked nose, a birthmark, a withered or shorter leg, a twisted arm, or other defect has the same needs as any other person and may have exceptionally fine potentialities for marriage. Intelligent people are fully able to accept such handicaps or overlook them completely.

Physical Health. For various reasons, there is a high correlation between physical health and marital happiness. Prolonged illness is likely to make a person overdependent. Chronic illness undermines general vitality, so that the ill person is unable to perform necessary work or to participate in social and recreational activities. Illness may preclude having children; or, if there are children, they may not receive proper attention. Children are often deprived of normal happiness and enjoyment when they must always keep in mind an ailing parent. And, obviously, chronic illness is a severe strain on the family budget.

Particularly damaging to marital happiness are venereal diseases, tuberculosis, epilepsy, cancer, insanity, heart diseases, rheumatic fever, hemophilia, asthma, diabetes, and some of the allergies. Because some of these diseases tend to run in families, prospective mates, in all fairness to each other, should know the medical backgrounds of the two families. Regarding problems of inheritance of specific diseases, a medical authority should be consulted. Fortunately, many states have legislation which requires a medical examination before marriage; however, in most cases the examination is limited to venereal diseases.

Intelligence. Intelligence is an important factor in marital happiness. As we have stated, when one is very young, physical appearance is the basis for attaining status. Later, intelligence, especially as manifested in educational achievement, becomes increasingly important, determining very largely the standing one has in our society.

Because the question of intelligence may become a major one between mates (may lead to such problems as whose opinion should prevail in a given situation), it is desirable that a couple know, prior to marriage, how each rates on a general intelligence scale. If several forms of tests indicate a wide range of difference in degree and type of intelligence, such findings should be accepted and adequate adjustment made. Since adjustment to a wide discrepancy in intelligence is often impossible, it is wiser for young people to marry persons whose general intellectual endowment is equal to their own. A wide difference in intelligence means less genuine companionship for each mate, less closeness, less sharing of thoughts and experiences, and possibly eventual isolation from each other. And since intelligence is largely a matter of heredity, children may not attain the level of the more intelligent parent and thus further strain marital happiness.

Emotional Maturity. Writers on mate selection have stressed the importance of emotional maturity. For example, Magoun states: "Happiness depends more upon mature emotions than upon any other single factor. Every sociological study has shown this to be true. Talents are only superficial; emotional maturity is fundamental." [8]

Emotional maturity is very difficult either to define or to evaluate. Magoun lists five signs of emotional maturity:

"(1) Confidence in and respect for one's own integrity.
    (a) believing one's self to be important without taking one's self too seriously.
    (b) recognizing and evaluating pressures from other persons; pressures from outside events.
(2) Ability to face reality honestly, no matter how disagreeable.
(3) Self control, even in upsetting situations.
(4) The desire to serve instead of the desire to shine.
(5) Well developed discrimination." [9]

The following approach to the problem of emotional maturity may give additional insight. Viewed genetically, emotional maturity is attained in somewhat the following manner:

Infants and small children can manifest their needs or react to tensions only by means of emotions. When in need of something, they appeal for help by crying; when they are frustrated, they manifest anger; when they meet with a very new and strange situation, they react with fear. They also become conditioned to smiling, laughing, and reaching out to parents, activities which manifest pleasant emotions. Thus, in early life the vegetative (pertaining to nutrition and growth) nervous system is dominant —both the sympathetic and the parasympathetic. As the cerebral cortex develops, it begins to assume dominance, so that a child substitutes more and more rational processes for emotions. He reaches maturity as this type of behavior dominates emotional

[8] F. Alexander Magoun, *Love and Marriage*, New York, Harper & Brothers, 1948, p. 128. Reprinted by permission.
[9] *Ibid.*, p. 129.

behavior. Maturity does not mean that emotions are absent, but rather that they have the secondary function of reinforcing reason when reason alone is inadequate. Emotions in the adult serve auxiliary functions. The adult without any emotion would be a strange and uninteresting creature. If he could not get angry, everyone would impose on him; if he could not experience some fear, contagious disease would destroy him; if he could not love and be happy, he would be a cold automaton.

Emotional maturity means control of emotion by intelligence, not absence of emotion. The criteria for emotional maturity are these:

(1) A person experiences about as many emotions as his particular society approves.

(2) When he experiences an emotion, it is not excessive.

(3) The emotion does not last very long.

(4) He has learned to experience aesthetic emotions.

He can enjoy the true, the good, and the beautiful. It is recognized that these criteria are vague. However, until we can measure emotions accurately, such approximate criteria will have to suffice.

In general, we may say that an emotionally immature person is one who uses emotions, rather than action and reason, to attain his goal.

Temperament. As was pointed out above, temperament depends upon constitutional make-up and is therefore largely hereditary and subject to very little change. In mate selection, persons of extremes in temperament should be avoided. Since behavior is not so much determined by environmental conditions as by internal make-up, the mate may become the helpless victim of an emotional state to which he has not contributed at all.

The ancient Greeks divided temperaments into four types, or "humors." Their theory is no longer considered valid, but the classification is still helpful. Individuals were considered to be predisposed to choleric, sanguine, melancholic, or phlegmatic behavior. This predisposition is considered today to be the result of the functions of endocrine glands. The choleric is predisposed to anger or rage, the melancholic to frequent and protracted depression, the sanguine to pleasant feelings, changeableness and enthusiasm, and the phlegmatic to passivity and indifference.

Habits and Skills. Anyone who has ever tried to "break" a habit, either his own or another person's, knows how difficult the task is.

"I was first attracted to your father by his lovely whistle."

Mary Gibson and The Saturday Evening Post.

Because conflicting habits can be very annoying, prospective mates should determine whether each other's habits are desirable or, if not, whether they can be adjusted to without undue annoyance.

Of course, an endless number of habits make up our individual pattern of everyday living, and when two lives come together, differences are inevitable even in the simplest habits. Eating habits, for example, are typical, if for no other reason than that a couple will eat many meals together—from 700 to 1,000 in one year. One should keep in mind that tastes for certain foods, as well as for ways of preparation, are established early in life and as a rule remain relatively fixed throughout life. How often has a wife, after having prepared a dish of her liking and according to her training, heard her husband's disheartening remark: "Well, I can eat it, but it isn't prepared the way mother used to cook it."

Other habits which are significant in a marital relationship are those having to do with personal cleanliness, orderliness, punctuality, drinking, smoking, and so on.

Attitudes. It is likewise important to be aware of attitudes, which are primary determiners of behavior. Basic are attitudes toward men, women, home, children, religion, politics, recreation, culture, money, social status, divorce, friends, and in-laws. These will be discussed in another connection. Here we need consider only two of them—men's attitude toward women and women's attitude toward men. Some men can think of women only as servants to men and, therefore, can never give their wives full freedom of expression or participation. Others think of women as mother surrogates, who will protect and manage them. Some women think of men only to the extent to which they can depend on them; these women are "clinging-vine" types, who use men primarily as props. Such an attitude prevents women from becoming co-operative mates; instead, they become burdens to their husbands.

Traits. An examination of the qualities listed by Terman and Adams for a happy marriage will reveal that almost all of them are personality traits or, more specifically, character traits. It would seem that persons who possess a fine moral character also make good husbands and wives, since marriage is one of the highly specialized and intense social relationships.

Personality traits are so broad and general that it is practically impossible to find words which will adequately name them. In spite of this difficulty, it still may be helpful if we list traits which we consider to be essential to successful and happy marital adjustment: (1) loyalty, (2) honesty, (3) patience, (4) tolerance, (5) co-operativeness, (6) industriousness, (7) dependability, (8) sociability, (9) friendliness, and (10) sincerity. The meaning of these terms will emerge in later discussion of adjustments between mates.

EVALUATION OF PERSONALITY AS A WHOLE

While evaluation of certain aspects of the personality is important in the selection of a mate, evaluation of personality as a whole is mandatory. Particular aspects of personality determine how a person will act in particular situations from time to time; personality as a whole determines the general trend and direction of his entire life. We have seen that personality is largely a system of drives. The physiological and psychological drives are regulated so that they can be satisfied in a manner acceptable to society. This result is attainable only in a well-integrated system. To the extent that an individual achieves this integration, he is mature. It is enlightening to know and to understand maturity of personality.

We can best appreciate maturity by contrasting it with immaturity, as illustrated in a child. The child may be characterized as dependent, self-centered, autonomous, ignorant, and irresponsible. All of these characteristics he must outgrow to become mature. There are three criteria for maturity which are fairly easy to apply. The first concerns the drives or needs which a person seeks to satisfy; the second, the manner of satisfaction; and the third, the integration of the entire personality.

Maturity in Drives. It is obvious to anyone that a child's early life centers on physiological needs. According to psychoanalysts, the infant's existence depends upon oral, anal, and genital satisfactions. As the child matures, psychological needs manifest themselves: security, attention-getting, curiosity, affection, and so on. Since all experiences are mediated by the nervous system, some knowledge of its growth and development will contribute to an understanding of how maturity is attained. The first system to function is the vegetative system, with its accompanying feelings and emotions. Closely associated with it is the sensory—motor, or peripheral—system. Finally, there is the higher level of the central system—the cortex. These three systems roughly determine three stages of development: emotional, sensory-motor, and intellectual. In maturation, the lower levels are superseded by the next and higher levels. The lower levels are not abolished but come to be regulated by a higher level. A mature person is one who gets emotional and sensory-motor satisfactions, but under the dominance and leadership of reason.

A cursory observation will reveal that many people live almost exclusively on the first two levels. They seek and talk about emotional thrills. The sensory-motor level of pleasures is expressed in numerous conversational remarks beginning with "I saw, I heard, I tasted, I touched, I smelled," and so on. Much of common conversation centers on sensory-motor pleasures.

To the sensory-motor and emotional pleasures, a mature person adds intellectual pleasures. He does not live only in the present, like a child, but also in the future. He satisfies his present needs in a manner that will not preclude greater satisfaction in the future.

Maturity in the Regulation of Drives. A child depends on others for satisfaction of his needs in an autonomous fashion—that is, he cannot and does not want to take into consideration the rights and privileges of others. A mature person takes care of his own needs but, in addition, helps others to satisfy their needs. In other words, he tries to live in some measure by the golden rule. This he does, not because he is told to do so, but because he finds it best in the long run. This maturity of living by the golden rule is attained, roughly again, in three stages: personal authority, self-control, and self-direction.

Personal authority is the only possible form of regulation in early life, when a child, because of ignorance, has to be told from moment to moment what to do. As the child matures, he not only becomes aware of rules which regulate society but also tries to guide his life by them. When he does so, he has attained a stage of self-control. Finally, he is able to see the underlying principles of the rules. When he guides himself by these principles, he has achieved self-direction. Thus a child at first is told not to take certain objects because they belong to someone else. Next, he learns the rule which states that he should not steal. Finally, he sees the reason why, in an ordered society, the rights of others must be respected.

It is clear that immaturity in husband and wife, in the sense that they live on the first or second level instead of on the third, is not conducive to marital happiness.

Integration of Personality. From what has been said above, it is obvious that a well-integrated personality has so well learned to satisfy his lower drives in harmony with the higher (the emotional and sensory-motor with the intellectual) that he has a minimum of conflicts within himself; and his personal needs are so regulated by the consideration of others' needs that there is a minimum degree of conflict between himself and society.

Since most authorities on marriage agree that many marital conflicts are due to immaturity in one or both of the mates, the concept of maturity should be clear to anyone contemplating marriage. According to Allport, a mature personality is characterized by (1) extension of the self, (2) self-objectification, and (3) a unifying philosophy of life.[10]

Extension of self means that the individual does not stop growing at any one point, and that his growth is not haphazard but is planned and has definite direction.

Self-objectification implies that the person has insight and a sense of humor. He knows his own weaknesses and strength. Thus, what he thinks of himself and what others think of him are practically identical. His sense of humor gives him the capacity to laugh at his own foibles, weaknesses, and blunderings and, at the same time, to share and enjoy similar shortcomings of "human nature" in those he loves and respects.

A unifying philosophy of life means that a person has arrived

[10] Gordon W. Allport, *Personality*, New York, Henry Holt & Company, 1937, pp. 213–214.

at a system of values based upon his conception of the nature of the universe. Stated in other words, a person has found an answer, satisfactory to him, about the meaning and purpose of his life and, as a consequence, has arrived at basic principles which guide his life. He has a goal and knows how to reach it.

OTHER FACTORS IN MATE SELECTION

Since personality is a product of heredity and environment, much can be known about a person if the environment in which he has grown up is known.

Parental Happiness. Researches in marital happiness have shown that there is a high correlation between happiness in marriage and happiness in the marriage of parents. Terman and his associates list happiness of parents as the most important factor contributing to marital happiness (see p. 133). Burgess and Cottrell assign numerical values, from 40 down to 0, to the items which contribute to happiness. The only item given a value of 40 is the happiness of parents and the absence of conflict between them.[11]

Parental happiness provides the most favorable atmosphere for the growth of desirable personality characteristics. It also creates a natural expectancy for one's own happiness in marriage. Conversely, children who grow up in unhappy homes are likely to be emotionally tense, insecure, and fearful of a prospective marital relationship.

However, factors other than parental happiness contribute to happy adjustment between husband and wife. One should not conclude, therefore, that young people growing up in other than happy homes cannot be successful in their own marriage. Perhaps the greatest danger such couples face is that they may become overanxious to succeed. Their experience in the parental home may cause them to regard as a danger sign every conflict, no matter how natural and normal in the adjustment between two personalities. The result may be too much tension.

[11] Ernest W. Burgess and Leonard S. Cottrell, Jr., *Predicting Success or Failure in Marriage*, New York, Prentice-Hall, Inc., 1939, pp. 275–283.

The studies mentioned above also stress that affection for parents and for siblings is important. Terman states that strong attachment of either individual to parents is "markedly favorable to happiness, especially in the case of husbands." [12] If a child is loved by his parents, he himself will be able to love and to expect and accept love from a mate.

Religious Differences. Almost all authorities agree that religious differences can be hazardous to a happy adjustment. Some even warn categorically against mixed marriages.[13] In our society, most mixed marriages take place between Catholics and Jews, Protestants and Jews, and Catholics and Protestants. Since there are radically different branches among Protestants and Jews, intermarriage between members of such branches is often as dangerous as between members of the major faiths. The problems presented by religious intermarriage are three in kind.

First, religious differences may involve difficulties in adjustment between the mates themselves. Much depends upon how much religious beliefs and attitudes have become a part of the personalities. Since religious beliefs are emotionally tinged, they are not easy to modify. Often a person cannot give up a religious belief because he feels that he would then be disloyal to those who have influenced him and whom he has respected and loved. The problem of differences is often aggravated by the attempt of one partner to convert the other to his religion. It should be remembered that young people in love tend to withdraw and live in a world of their own. But as time progresses, they return to closer contacts with their friends and relatives, who make them more aware of their religious beliefs and customs. The result of this "return to reality" is to make religious differences between mates stand out in greater relief.

Second, difficulties almost always attend the adjustment to parents and friends. Even when mates are able to reconcile their own differences, others often cannot accept them without some prejudice. Members of a religion often regard marriage outside

---

[12] *Op. cit.*, p. 371.

[13] See, for example, Clifford Adams, *How to Pick a Mate*, New York, E. P. Dutton & Company, 1946, Chapter 8.

their religion as an attack upon their faith, while those of the faith into which an "outsider" has married may be unwilling to accept him as an equal. Many such cases come to the attention of marriage counselors. The authors have become acquainted with several persons who suffered because, in spite of their serious attempts to become a part of their husbands' or wives' religious groups, they were always treated as "outsiders."

Third, children of mixed marriages often face the same problems as their parents; they do not fit into any religious group. This can become crucial when the children are ready for marriage. When they meet with difficulties of this nature, they very often blame their parents. A typical case is that of a Jewish woman who married a Catholic man. When she came to discuss her problem, she was dejected and depressed because, although she and her husband had managed to get along together for twenty-five years, her three daughters, as they reached the marriageable age, blamed the parents for their failure to attract mates. The young girls, reared as Catholics, complained that young Catholic men, very much interested in them at the beginning of a friendship, dropped them immediately upon discovery that their mother was Jewish.

Naturally, Catholics are not the only ones who sometimes react in this manner. Such reactions can be found in any one of the mixed combinations.

The foregoing points should not be interpreted as meaning that religious intermarriages are never successful. In many instances they are successful, but those who enter into mixed marriages invariably have to pay some price. Such a condition will undoubtedly be true until there is a more effective rapprochement among the various religious groups. For the present, it is not surprising that the divorce rate for mixed marriages of the major religious groups is from two to three times that for marriages of couples coming from the same religious background.[14]

Much of what has been said about religious intermarriages applies also to race, nationality, economic status, and other cultural differences.

[14] Judson T. Landis, "Marriages of Mixed and Non-mixed Religious Faith," *American Sociological Review*, June, 1949, 14:401–407.

Education of Mates. Education in mate selection is undoubtedly significant. How should education be evaluated? Formal education does not seem to be a satisfactory criterion. There are highly educated people who have received only limited formal schooling. Nor do graduates from a high school or college all attain the same level of education, because some students have greater capacity and more motivation than do others to profit from formal education. Furthermore, the quality of education available in some high schools and colleges may far excel that in others. It is entirely possible for graduates from a top-ranking high school to be as well educated as graduates from a college where academic standards are less stringent.

It is necessary, therefore, to differentiate between general education and formal education. It stands to reason that for mutual adjustment formal education should be more or less the same. Having approximately the same level of education gives a couple not only a common range of information but also similar interests. Common interests are necessary if husband and wife are to share and participate in many activities. When the educational level differs markedly between mates, it is difficult, and in many cases impossible, for them to have the same circle of close friends. If one mate is not well informed, his judgment is less reliable and his contribution toward making family decisions may be negligible. An educated person (and we mean here either self-educated or formally educated) is also usually more tolerant and understanding, qualities which facilitate smoother social adjustments. As a rule, if there is a wide gap in the educational level between mates and this gap cannot be bridged after a few years of married life, the result will be gradual isolation one from the other.

Chronological Age Differences of Mates. It is difficult to generalize about the importance of age difference in the selection of a mate. A person has not only a chronological age but also a mental age, emotional age, social age, economic age, recreational age, physiological age, and educational age; and these ages are often not highly correlated. Thus, one man may be senile at the age of sixty and another still mentally alert at the age of ninety.

148   *Marriage Adjustment*

Some men are physiologically old (which includes sexual virility) at fifty, while others are still physiologically young at seventy.

When all of these ages in two persons are highly correlated with chronological age, it is obvious that a few years' variation in chronological age does not make much difference. According to the 1950 census, the average age at which women marry in the United States is 21.4, and the average for men is 23.8. Since women mature three to four years sooner than men, a woman of 21 is really the same age as a man of 24. Studies of marriages in which women were five or six years older than their mates have shown that these marriages are frequently happier than the average. Because of public prejudice, however, a couple may face serious difficulties when the wife is considerably older than her husband. When the husband is considerably older than his wife, his sexual vigor may wane before his wife's. With the onset of old age, he may grow physically less active and thus be limited to fewer activities than meet his wife's desires. Also, the couple may have some difficulty in maintaining friendships, because the husband may not be accepted in the younger set, and the wife by the older friends.

POOR MARRIAGE RISKS

Since love will bring the greatest happiness in marriage, one should never marry a person who is unable to experience real love. True love is characterized, as was indicated above, by a feeling of oneness, belonging, sharing, and participation. There are individuals who possess personalities utterly devoid of the capacity to experience these four qualities. In the early stages of falling in love, it may be difficult to detect the specific symptoms in these personalities, but the general symptoms are fairly obvious. When in doubt, the judgment of an expert should be sought.

The Psychopath. The psychopath is essentially a grown-up child who has never learned to regulate his infantile desires in keeping with standards acceptable to society. His problem is fundamentally a difficulty in character. The principles of right and wrong, good and bad, have never been incorporated into his personal make-up. Like a child, he is egocentric; the world exists only to serve him. He is a law unto himself; he is impulsive, uninhibited, carefree, and freely expressive. Living for his own immediate pleasure, he cannot think of the happiness of others, nor is he capable of thinking of the future. Cleckley has made a thorough study of psychopathic behavior and described the typical psychopath. Summarizing his observations, we note the following characteristics of a psychopath: (1) Usually of superior intelligence and showing no intellectual deteriorization. (2) No demonstrable irrationality neurosis, psychosis, or marked nervousness. (3) No sense of social responsibility. (4) Cannot be trusted because of his total disregard for truth. (5) Unable to accept sincere blame for any of his faults. (6) Lacking in a sense of shame. (7) Commits theft, fraud, and other acts without any apparent goal. (8) Lacks ordinary common-sense judgments. (9) Seems unable to learn and to profit from past experience. (10) Unusually egocentric. (11) General poverty of affect. (12) Practically devoid of insight. (13) Cannot appreciate kindness and consideration by others. (14) Frequent overindulgence in alcohol. (15) Behavior while drunk more bizarre than that of the average person. (16) Devoid of suicidal tendencies. (17) As a rule, weak sex drive characterized by promiscuity and sexual deviation. (18) No verified adverse heredity. (19) Psychopathic tendencies may manifest themselves at any period in life. (20) No consistent life plan. (21) Seems to seek failure and social and spiritual self-destruction.[15]

Psychopaths are especially dangerous because on first acquaintance they are usually friendly and flattering. They will do anything to get what they want, but are incapable of giving. Some women are likely to fall in love with them at first and later find breaking away difficult. Consequently, a woman often will marry a psychopath (in spite of obvious psychopathic symptoms) with the intention of reforming him. Such expectations are doomed to

[15] Hervey Cleckley, *The Mask of Sanity: An Attempt to Reinterpret the So-called Psychopathic Personality*, St. Louis, The C. V. Mosby Company, 1941, pp. 238–255. By permission of the author.

failure, because even psychiatrists almost invariably give up such persons as hopeless.

The Narcissist. Like the psychopath, the narcissist is so much in love with himself that he cannot love another person. (The word comes from the story of Narcissus, who fell in love with his own image reflected in a pool.) One might think that a narcissist would not wish to marry. He does, nevertheless, but primarily to attain social status, thereby enhancing his ego. His aim is to use another person for his purposes, or to make another person part of himself. According to Symonds, narcissism manifests itself in the following ways:

"(1) Autoeroticism. (2) Egocentricity. (3) Self-absorption. (4) Self-admiration. (5) Overestimation of the self. (6) Domineering. (7) Demands on another person. (8) Being on guard against another person. (9) Disregard of another person. (10) Jealousy. (11) Using another person. (12) Making other person dependent on self. (13) Becoming dependent on others. (14) Sensitivity to neglect or criticism. (15) Depreciation of others." [16]

The Neurotic. The neurotic is an emotionally unstable person. His emotional responses typically are greater than seems warranted by the situations giving rise to them. He is troubled by so many inner conflicts and suffers from so many frustrations that he invariably makes a poor mate. He is obviously unable to assume his share of responsibility. In many cases, such a person leans too heavily on a mate for constant support.

A person may be neurotic in various degrees. Minor degrees are hard to recognize and may require an expert's judgment. Major degrees can be recognized easily by the average person. Robert W. White lists the following three criteria for judging a neurotic tendency:

"There are three criteria by which defensive overworking can be recognized. (1) The first is indiscriminateness: a given attitude is assumed not only when appropriate but even in the most unsuitable circumstances. A person who craves affection and approval, for instance, must have it from everyone, even from bus drivers and store clerks who are of no real importance in his life. He may even require it from

[16] Percival M. Symonds, *The Dynamics of Human Adjustment*, New York, Appleton-Century-Crofts, Inc., 1946, pp. 542–546. Reprinted by permission.

his children and pet animals. The trend has a compulsive intensity that does not permit it to be adapted to circumstances. (2) Another attribute of neurotic trends is their insatiable character. The person seems never satisfied; he does not reach repose, but always needs a little more of the same kind of satisfaction. The man who moves toward people wishes that even a congenial evening had been a little more congenial. The man who seeks triumphs wishes that even a signal success had been a little more glorious. The person who manages to separate himself from all close ties wishes that he could also be free from minor personal contacts. (3) The blocking of neurotic trends creates disproportionate frustration, probably with signs of anxiety. If aggressive competitiveness, for instance, is serving as a neurotic trend, to be beaten in some competitive enterprise will throw the person into a state of desperation. For him the defeat means vital threat." [17]

A neurotic person "in love" will expect blind, impossible devotion from his mate. He is extremely sensitive. Any attention to another person he interprets as rejection of himself. He constantly makes demands upon his mate and is incapable of giving much in return. One young lady who was at first highly flattered by being so much "needed" by her newly acquired sweetheart later begged to be told how to escape his demands. As she phrased it, she felt like "a squeezed-out lemon," trying to be at once the man's mother, sweetheart, guardian angel, and constant source of emotional comfort.

There are a number of subtypes of neurosis, and their symptoms are legion. For this reason, no attempt will be made to discuss them here.[18]

Sexual Deviant. Special attention is called to the sexual deviant because well-meaning friends, sometimes even people who should know about the consequences, advise marriage as a cure for misdirected sex urges. Cases coming to the attention of marriage counselors have shown that marriage never cures any of the deviations encountered. Such a marriage, instead of curing the deviant, makes many people unhappy—the unfortunate mate, relatives, and friends. Deviation is not merely a habit to be broken; it is a symptom of basic personality structure. Cure is

[17] Robert W. White, *The Abnormal Personality*, New York, The Ronald Press Company, 1948, pp. 255–256. Reprinted by permission.

[18] There are many good popular books on the subject. The reader is referred especially to Karen Horney, *The Neurotic Personality of Our Times*, New York, W. W. Norton & Company, 1945, and *Self Analysis*, 1942.

impossible unless the entire personality is changed, and that is difficult even where there is a sincere motive for a change and an expert is consulted. Change is still more difficult when it is attempted in order to please another person or merely to conform to society.

Undue Attachment to Parents. A young man who is overattached to his mother, or a young woman to her father, tends to make a poor mate; such a person cannot, in complete love, give of himself to husband or wife. This quality of overattachment sometimes is not easy to evaluate before marriage, and yet it is important that it be evaluated. Some signs are easily observable in the young man. He consults his mother about every major decision concerning his "girl friend"; he gives his mother a detailed account of the time spent with the girl; he shares more secrets with his mother than with the girl; in case of differences of opinion, he is inclined to side with his mother. When a man finally marries in spite of such overattachment, his wife and his mother become rivals for his attention and affection, and in too many cases it is the mother who wins out. An illustrative case is that of Mrs. F., who reported the following:

"I recognized before my husband and I were married that he appeared to be overly attached to his mother, but it didn't occur to me that his relationship to her could ever interfere with our happiness. I assumed that after marriage, as his wife, I would certainly come first in his love and attention, but I was mistaken.

"When we married he insisted that we live in the second floor apartment of his widowed mother's house. Apartments were difficult to get and, too, I was led to believe that it was a wise step in economy for us. But now I see that much more than that is involved. He can't bear to live away from her. Although he usually sees her in the morning as he goes to work, he makes a practice of calling her every day on his lunch hour. If he has any message for me he calls her to tell me. He rarely calls me directly. Occasionally, his business takes him on short trips out of town. As usual he calls her and brings her a gift when he comes home. It wouldn't seem so strange if only once in a while he'd bring something to the children and me. And when he gets sick—oh, a touch of cold or any small disturbance—he has to move right downstairs where his mother can take care of him. I hate myself for feeling so upset and jealous, but I can't seem to help it. It looks as if the wife should come first in a husband's love, but I don't."

The situation recounted in the preceding case tends to create unhappiness in the wife and conflict in the husband. It is often the precipitating factor in serious emotional and general personality disturbances. In extreme forms of attachment to the mother, the young man may suffer from what Freud called the Oedipus complex, which is a repressed desire for incestuous relationship with the mother. Such attachment is considered normal by most psychoanalysts in early childhood, but abnormal in adult life.

What has been said about the attachment of a young man for his mother applies equally to overattachment of a daughter for her father. The latter cases are, however, far more rare.

Finally, among types of person who should not marry unless cured are drug addicts, alcoholics, those infected with venereal diseases, and the insane.

INTERPRETATIVE SUMMARY

1. In selecting a mate, a person should begin by self-examination and evaluation. It is especially necessary to analyze one's love ideal, one's capacity to make another person happy in marriage, and one's motives for marriage.

2. Modern research has shown that two people who have a similar background and personality structure are likely to make better adjustment to each other in marriage than two who are different from each other in such respects.

3. One may be considerably more effective in mate evaluation by keeping the structural aspects of personality in mind, as they were outlined in Chapter 3, than by merely looking at personality as a whole.

4. However, the total make-up of personality is also important. In this connection, one must examine the drive system of a person and the manner of satisfaction of drives, as well as the total integration of personality.

5. In the evaluation of personality maturity, one will profit by keeping the three criteria of maturity in mind: (a) extension of self, (b) self-objectification, (c) a unifying philosophy of life.

6. Other special factors to be kept in mind in mate selection are home background, religious affiliation and attitudes, race, nationality, economic and social status, educational level, and age difference.

7. It is doubtful that a psychopath, narcissist, extreme neurotic, sex deviate, overdependent person, drug addict, or alcoholic will ever make a good mate without first having undergone thorough psychotherapy.

THOUGHT QUESTIONS AND PROJECTS

1. Do this project at the blackboard, where all members of the class can observe its progress: Three men take places at the board on one side of the room; three women on the opposite side. They should all write *rapidly*, and *not* in order of importance, ten traits which they would look for in the selection of a mate. No participants should look at the others' work until told to do so. When the lists are finished, make observations such as the following:

 (a) Are the traits listed by the women noticeably similar? Is the rank order similar, despite the fact that they were not told to rank them according to importance?

 (b) Follow the same procedure for the men's lists.

 (c) Now compare the women's lists with those of the men. Note particularly any traits included by one sex but omitted by the opposite sex.

2. (a) If single, do you look for the same qualities in a date which you want eventually to have in a mate?

 (b) If married, did you marry the type of person you used to date?

3. Is there any correlation between *physique* and *temperament* in personality?

4. What social conditions often tend to "set the stage" for an individual to select a mate with traits similar to his own?

5. Do you think it would be wise for all states to require through legislation a thorough medical examination (not merely for venereal diseases) prior to marriage? Do you think it is fair

for a person to request a "clean bill of health" from the prospective mate?

6. Are you acquainted with two or three couples representing mixed marriages which appear to be successful?

    (a) Do you know examples which cannot be called successful?

    (b) What factors seem to be requisites for a happy mixed marriage?

7. What types of personality are considered to be great risks in mate selection?

Suggested Readings for Further Study

Adams, Clifford R., *Preparing for Marriage,* New York, E. P. Dutton & Company, 1951.
    Chapter 2. Your Chances of Getting a Mate.
    Chapter 9. Is the One You Want the One You Need?
    Chapter 10. Crucial Traits for a Happy Marriage.
    Chapter 11. Before You Pick Your Mate.
Baber, Ray E., *Marriage and the Family,* 2nd ed., New York, McGraw-Hill Book Company, 1953.
    Chapter 4. Mate Selection and Courtship.
    Chapter 5. Mate Selection (Cont'd).
Bowman, Henry A., *Marriage for Moderns,* 3rd ed., New York, McGraw-Hill Book Company, 1941.
    Chapter 5. Age for Marriage.
Burgess, Ernest W., and Paul Wallin, *Engagement and Marriage,* New York, J. B. Lippincott Company, 1953.
    Chapter 6. Choosing a Mate.
Burgess, Ernest W., and Harvey J. Locke, *The Family,* 2nd ed., New York, American Book Company, 1953.
    Chapter 13. Mate Selection.
    Appendix B. Schedule for the Prediction and Measurement of Marriage Adjustment.
Christensen, Harold T., *Marriage Analysis,* New York, The Ronald Press Company, 1950.
    Chapter 8. Choosing a Mate.
    Appendix. Schedule for Studying Preference Patterns in Dating and Mate Selection. (Prepared by Harold T. Christensen and Evelyn S. Wigent.)
Cole, Lawrence E., *Human Behavior,* Yonkers-on-Hudson, New York, World Book Company, 1953.
    Chapter 22. The Super-Ego: Social and Psychobiological Considerations. (The Psychopathic Personality: A Self-System with a Weak Super-Ego. Pp. 764–784.)

Conway, J. D., "Whom Shall I Marry?" *Information,* 1953, 67:37–39.

Doherty, J. F., "Interracial Marriage," *Interracial Review,* 1953, 26:101–103.

Duvall, Evelyn Millis, and Reuben Hill, *When You Marry,* rev. ed., Boston, D. C. Heath & Company, 1953.

    Chapter 1. What You Bring to Marriage.

    Chapter 8. Who Gets Married?

Farrier, B., "Do Mixed Marriages Work?" *Sign,* 1952, 31:50.

Himes, Norman E., *Your Marriage,* New York, Rinehart & Company, 1940.

    Chapter 5. Choosing a Mate Wisely.

    Chapter 6 and Appendix A. How to Predict Your Chances of Happiness in Marriage.

Landis, Paul, *Your Family and Family Living,* New York, McGraw-Hill Book Company, 1946.

    Chapter 5. In Selecting a Mate Consider Personality Traits.

Magoun, F. Alexander, *Love and Marriage,* New York, Harper & Brothers, 1948.

    Chapter 5. Criteria for Choosing a Mate.

Skidmore, Rex A., and Anthon S. Cannon, *Building Your Marriage,* New York, Harper & Brothers, 1951.

    Chapter 4. Friendships and Dating.

    Chapter 6. Wisely Choosing a Mate.

    Chapter 8. Biological and Legal Factors in Mate Selection.

Thomas, J. L., "Mixed Marriages," *Social Order,* 1952, 2:155–159.

Waller, Willard, and Reuben Hill, *The Family: A Dynamic Interpretation,* New York, The Dryden Press, 1951.

    Part III, Chapters 6 through 12. Mate Finding: Establishing Relationships.

Winch, Robert F., *The Modern Family,* New York, Henry Holt & Company, 1952.

    Chapter 14. Romantic Love in America.

8

METHODS
FOR THE EVALUATION OF A MATE

So far, we have stressed the fact that successful marriage depends primarily upon harmonious adjustment between two people of opposite sex. We have also pointed out that marital difficulties stem either from personality inadequacy or from personality incompatibility, so that, in order to avoid disappointment and to achieve happiness, one must know both himself and the prospective mate. In striving for this knowledge, it is important to know not only *what* to look for but *how* to look for it.

Methods of obtaining knowledge are of great importance. As evidence of this general fact, one need only consider the tremendous progress science has made within the last century. During that time, man has mastered more of his physical environment than he had been able to master during all preceding centuries. This mastery did not come of increased intelligence; men who lived several thousand years ago were just as intelligent as modern men. The chief reason for the tremendous progress in modern times is the discovery of what is known as the scientific method. This method consists, briefly, of the refinement and mastery of techniques, means, and instruments for gathering data, and the perfection of experiments for the verification of hypotheses. With such progress in the physical world resulting from the use of a more systematic, scientific method, the question arises as to whether some similar method cannot be applied to problems inherent in certain social relationships, such as in the selection of mates.

Adequate methods for mate evaluation have always been important, but never so important as at present. As has been noted, in former years people who married usually had grown up in the same environment and in the same type of home, and they usually were of the same nationality. Thus, husband and wife had learned to know each other over a long period of time and under

"He's the retiring type—$20,000 a year!"

F. Wilkinson and The Saturday Evening Post.

circumstances completely familiar to both mates. Today, for a number of reasons, including greater freedom in mate selection, less time—sometimes as little as a few weeks—is often available for learning to know one's prospective mate. As a result, methods of acquiring such knowledge are today of prime importance.

Modern psychology and sociology have provided at least a few helpful methods, which, while they are not as accurate as those used in physical science, are a great improvement over mere haphazard "getting acquainted." Several of these methods can be applied by any intelligent couple. The more intricate are available through professional counseling.

Before discussing desirable means of mate selection, it may be of some value to examine several unsatisfactory, unscientific methods relied upon by many individuals.

Unreliable Methods of Mate Evaluation

There are a number of reasons why many people use unreliable methods of mate selection. First, many individuals are aware of their inability to evaluate another personality adequately and at the same time are not familiar with acceptable methods. Second, some of the unreliable methods have been used for centuries and thus have acquired a certain prestige. Third, some people regard mate selection as both mysterious and mystical, and are determined to keep it that way, so as not to destroy the "romance" of it. Fourth, others look for short-cut methods which require little if any effort on their part. Fifth, certain specious methods are highly and persuasively advertised.

There are a number of such questionable methods, only a few of which will be discussed briefly here: phrenology, palmistry, fortune telling, astrology, and physiognomy.

Phrenology. The phrenologist pretends to tell character from the shape of the skull, on the assumption that certain character traits are revealed by "bumps" on the head. It has been definitely proved that character traits, such as courage and honesty, are not located in any one section of the brain. Even if they were, they would not show themselves on the surface of the brain, much less on the surface of the skull.

Palmistry and Physiognomy. Palmistry is the belief that personality is revealed in the lines of the hands, and physiognomy that these traits are reflected in the facial features. Both the lines

in the hands and the general pattern of the face are due to heredity and therefore are not indicative of personality traits, which are
almost wholly dependent upon experience. The records of experience are found in neural patterns and not on the surface of the
body.

Fortune Telling. Fortune telling in all forms—crystal gazing,
tea-leaf readings, cards, or what you will—is a survival of ancient
superstitions. Obviously, these forms can be harmless when used
as playful fun and romantic phantasy, but not when they are used
seriously.

Astrology. Astrology claims that human affairs and personality
make-up are determined by the positions of the stars. According
to this theory, there are twelve stars and, consequently, twelve
types of personality of either male or female sex. In order to bring
about a successful marital adjustment, one merely has to look up
the star under which he was born and then find a mate born
under a complementary star. Here is advice given to the *Virgo*
wife—that is, one born between August 24 and September 23:

> "The ruling planet of your sign is Mercury. And since Mercury rules
> the intellect, your husband must help you to live up to the opportuni-
> ties for mental development which the stars have given you.
> "Like most daughters of Virgo, you have a keen eye for detail. You
> love to study a problem and to solve it by some device or system of
> your own. You are great on devices and systems! Your husband
> mustn't let you follow this tendency too far; it will complicate your
> own life and burden his.
> "Most mentalities are not so dexterous as your own. Your husband
> should try to keep you from talking too much about your own ideas.
> They are more important to you than to anyone else, and men don't
> like women who talk about themselves. They reserve that privilege for
> their own sex!
> "The chief faults of your sign with which your husband may have
> to contend are a tendency to be over critical, a failure to express the
> appreciation of others which you often feel, a slowness to forgive
> which is the natural counterpart of your slowness to anger, and a
> tendency to keep too much to yourself.
> "Perhaps a husband born under Capricorn or Taurus would be best
> fitted to bring out your good points. But whatever sign he is born
> under, he should persuade you to present a more 'social' side to the
> world. It will increase your popularity with both sexes, and your
> chance of happiness in your married life.

"Above all, your husband should urge you to be less critical—to remember his good points, and forget his bad!" [1]

The assumptions of astrology are completely at variance with our knowledge of the origin and nature of personality (see Chapter 3). If personality were a product of the influence of a star which was in ascendance when a person was born, differences in intelligence, home environment, education, religion, or culture in general would be of no consequence. Since all persons born under the same star the world over would be alike, a man born and reared in any small community in the United States should be able to marry any woman born under an appropriate star in any part of the world, irrespective of intellectual, educational, religious, or cultural differences, and have perfect harmony! The assumption that the entire population of the earth can be divided into twelve distinct types is in contradiction with what we know about individual differences. (The question of *types* will be considered shortly.)

If there is no scientific truth in astrology, how do so many people get the impression that they possess the characteristics ascribed to them in astrological readings? The characteristics are so generalized that they apply in some degree to everyone, and there is a tendency to minimize the characteristics which do not apply. One can read to a person born under Capricorn the characteristics of a person born under any other sign, and he will believe that these characteristics apply to him—he will see a marked similarity of his own personality to the one described.

RELATIVELY HELPFUL METHODS

Graphology. Professional graphologists almost invariably make excessive claims about their ability to deduce personality characteristics from handwriting. Using a sampling of a person's handwriting in the form of a brief sentence or the signature, they examine it as to regularity, cultural conformity, distribution of spacing, emphasis on initial letters, pressure slant, width, con-

---

[1] Reprinted by permission of Dodd, Mead & Company from *Astrology for Everyone* by Evangeline Adams. Copyright 1931 by Evangeline Adams Jordan. Pp. 234–235.

nectedness, direction, and overlining. On the basis of these observations they claim they can tell to what extent a person possesses certain traits such as punctuality, drive, resourcefulness, initiative, persistence, will power, ambition, honesty, loyalty, and dependability. To be sure, students of human nature would be highly pleased to find such a simple key to unlock the mysteries of personality, but the problem is not that easy. It is true that certain indications regarding personality may be evident from handwriting, since it is one form of expressive behavior. But in order to know what these indications mean, one must be familiar with the intricate, complicated structure of personality and its dynamics, plus many factors which relate to it. An atomistic "sign" approach to handwriting is unscientific and valueless. Until much more is known about handwriting analysis, a person is well advised not to be guided by it in the selection of a mate.[2]

Typology. This term refers to the attempt to classify people into a few basic types, and thus to simplify the process of learning to know one's fellow men. The child begins life by knowing a few people through first-hand experience—father and mother, brothers and sisters, and so on. As the child grows up and becomes acquainted with other persons, he associates them with the few people he has known. At first a boy or girl is likely to associate a teacher with the mother. Later, abstract similarities are noted and people are put into classes. One speaks of a tall type, short type, intellectual type, emotional type, possessive type, dominant type, jealous type, blonde type, brunette type, and so on. In all of these, there is an attempt to find a simple key to unlock the mystery of personality. It is assumed that if people are alike in one respect, they will be alike in other respects. But to say that all blondes or brunettes are alike makes about as much sense as to say that all trees are alike because they have green leaves, or that all cars painted black are otherwise the same.

Throughout the centuries there have been numerous scientific attempts to classify these endless varieties in human personalities. One of the earliest attempts was made by Hippocrates at about

---

[2] One reliable source of information about the scientific significance of handwriting is R. Wolfson's *A Study in Handwriting Analysis,* Ann Arbor, Edwards Brothers, 1949.

400 B.C. He classified all people according to temperament into four groups: the sanguine, melancholic, choleric, and phlegmatic. Little, if any, progress with this approach was made until in 1862 Alexander Bain, an early British psychologist, assumed that every individual possessed a constant amount of "psychic energy." Depending upon the direction of the flow of this energy, a person would belong to either the mental type, the volitional type, or the vital type. In 1923, a Swiss psychoanalyst, C. G. Jung, published a book on the psychology of human types. Depending on the direction the mind takes, Jung said, people fall into two groups— the introvert, who is primarily occupied by what goes on in his own mind; and the extrovert, whose mind is directed primarily to the outside world. This concept has become quite popular. Sigmund Freud, in 1924, posited three types of personality, based on psychosexual development. When the libido (psychoanalytic term referring to "life energy" or basic drive) is fixated upon the anal mechanism, we have the anal-erotic type, characterized by obstinacy, orderliness, and parsimony. When the libido is fixated in the mouth, the oral-erotic type results. Of this there are two subtypes—the passive, who manifests dependency, optimism and general immaturity; and the active or sadistic, who is pessimistic, anticipates malice, and is bitter and sarcastic toward others. The phallic type results when the libido does not express itself in the normal heterosexual manner. This type is characterized by narcissism, ambition, and exhibitionism.

Two attempts have been made to base personality types upon the structure of the body as a whole. (One by Emil Kretschmer in 1925, the other by W. H. Sheldon in 1940, 1942, and 1944.) Sheldon classifies bodies into three types, to which are related three types of temperament. First is the *endomorph*, who has well-developed or even overdeveloped viscera. The temperament related to this type is called "visceratonia" and is characterized by sociability, affection, gluttony, and love of comfort. The second, the *mesomorph*, is the athletic-appearing individual, whose temperament is referred to as "somatotonia." Persons of this type are interested in muscular activity and self-assertiveness. They love power and often are ruthless. The third type, the *ectomorph*, is long and slender and possesses a temperament called "cerebrotonia," which manifests itself in inhibition, restraint, and asocial behavior.[3]

On the basis of the principal roles a person plays in society and the status he achieves, sociologists have formulated a number of typologies. We have already mentioned (in Chapter 4) Spranger's six types: the *theoretical, economic, aesthetic, social, religious,* and *political.* Lasswell recognizes five social types: (1) The *bureaucrat* or *administrator,* who is guided by need for emotional security. He is orderly, precise, rigid, methodical, and punctual. (2) The *boss,* who delights in power over people. He is an opportunist with little respect for principles. (3) The *diplomat,* who uses more indirect means than the boss to achieve power. He is suave, clever, calm, patient, and often not above double-dealing. (4) the *agitator,* who is dissatisfied with the status quo and seeks revolutionary changes. He is usually quite emotional and very much interested in himself. (5) The *theorist,* who is more interested in constructing a logical picture of the world than in bringing about change.[4]

There are quite a number of other types, depending upon the criterion used for classification. As regards their value, the authors agree with Kimball Young who, after a careful and thorough examination of all typologies, has come to this conclusion:

> "Actually, individuals do seem to fall into certain clusters of behavior patterns, and, as obviously inadequate as common-sense typology about this fact is, we must contend that everyday experience gives some foundation for developing general concepts about behavior and for classifying individuals under certain terms. . . . The problem is really one of selecting those criteria of traits, attitudes, values, and habits which will serve as central tendencies of a cluster or class of persons and will set them off from another cluster or class. The heart of our present difficulty lies here. We have not yet hit upon completely satisfactory differentiating criteria of personality make-up." [5]

In view of what has been said so far, we can see that assigning a person to a certain type does not give us a key which will unlock his personality. Being able to perceive that a person belongs to a

[3] W. H. Sheldon, *The Varieties of Temperament,* New York, Harper & Brothers, 1942.

[4] L. D. Lasswell, *Psychopathology and Politics,* Chicago, University of Chicago Press, 1930.

[5] Kimball Young, *Personality and Problems of Adjustment,* 2nd ed., New York, Appleton-Century-Crofts, Inc. 1952, p. 252. Reprinted by permission.

certain type will give us some insight into his personality structure, but this perception leaves us ignorant about other, perhaps
equally important, characteristics. Thus two persons may be alike
in being introverts, but one may be a research specialist and the
other a daydreamer; one may be honest, the other dishonest; one
may be kind and considerate, the other selfish, and so on. We
can visualize this type of contrast and similarity in the following
manner:

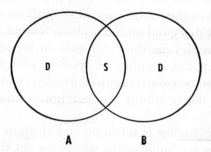

FIGURE 7. Both A and B are introverts. The part of their personalities
represented by S is similar, whereas the remainder of their
personalities, represented by D, is dissimilar.

Since the types mentioned are not mutually exclusive, one individual may belong to several types at the same time. Typing alone
does not lead to a complete and full understanding of an individual.

Response to Subliminal cues

Intuition. Another rather widely accepted short-cut to knowing
another individual is intuition. Intuition is direct knowledge of the
personality of another individual without recourse to perception
and reasoning. Some people consider this method, which has a
long history in philosophy, psychology, and fiction, the only infallible way of judging another personality. At present, we cannot
accept this view. Much intuitive knowledge is far from infallible,
and much of what seems intuitive can be explained as simpler
processes.

Intuition often is *unconscious* typing. We have stereotypes,
"pictures in our head," of races, nationalities, professions, major

trait patterns. When we meet a person who fits into one of our stereotypes, we endow him with all the characteristics of this concept and believe we know him.

Another kind of intuition is nothing more than responding to marginal cues. From the people we know, we have learned to associate certain personality traits with facial expression, tone of voice, manner of speaking, laughing, walking, and the like. On meeting a person who has one of these characteristics, we jump to the conclusion that he possesses all previously associated personality traits. At other times, intuitive judgment is based upon a combination of marginal cues. Intuitive feeling is stronger when one person resembles another, not only in facial expression, but also in tone of voice, manner of speech, and so on. Since the characteristics are transferred automatically (instantaneously and unconsciously), the resultant "knowledge" seems highly reassuring.

Especially convincing is intuition based upon subliminal cues. (Subliminal cues are impressions which we get through our sense organs below the level of awareness.) Subliminal cues are rather common in our everyday experiences. Whatever we look at has a field and a background. When you look at your watch to see the time, you are aware only of a few things on the face of your watch. Ask anyone who has looked thousands of times at his watch to describe in detail the shape of the hands, the color and pattern of the numbers, and other details, and you will find that he is incapable of doing so. Yet if you put side by side two watches which are alike except in these details, he will be able to recognize his watch immediately. There are subliminal cues, not only in vision, but in all the sense organs. We respond to these subliminal cues in others as we respond to marginal cues, and we feel we "know" things intuitively.

In many cases, so-called intuition is merely a form of identification. From early childhood a person learns to put himself in another's place—to perceive and to feel the world as the other perceives and feels it. When he perceives someone in a certain situation, he imagines what he himself would feel and then projects his responses into the other person's mind. Thus he gets the impression that he knows the other person.

All the forms of intuition mentioned operate in every individual's life and are to some degree helpful in understanding others, but they are far from infallible and should be constantly checked and rechecked by more accurate methods.

Something should be said here about sex differences in intuition. It is often claimed that women are more intuitive than men. Insofar as this is true, it can be accounted for in the following manner. We have stressed several times that women are more interested in other persons than are men; consequently, they will pay more attention than do men to anything pertaining to a better understanding of people. Thus women can more readily identify themselves with others than can men. In so doing, they may become more aware of the thoughts, feelings, and moods of others.[6]

Being not only more interested in other people, but also more dependent on them, women find it important to sense another person's true feelings. Feelings can be perceived more through facial expressions, gestures, and tone of voice than through words, because words often are used to disguise as much as to reveal the true state of mind. We have seen that intuition is often based upon marginal and subliminal cues. Since dogs do not understand words, they learn their master's moods from nonverbal cues. Sometimes their responses are so accurate that one gets the impression a dog possesses mystical powers. Children react in the same way at first, but later give less attention to facial expressions and pay more attention to the meaning of spoken words. Perhaps women never get as far away from this first stage as do men.

From what we have said about intuition, we can conclude that the so-called "intuitive judgments" of other people are in no way perfect and reliable. There is no sure short-cut to the knowledge of personality.

There are, however, methods generally recognized as more helpful in gaining knowledge of personality than those described above. These methods are of two types: those that can be used successfully by any individual, and those which are made available to the layman by specialists trained to use them properly.

[6] See K. Koffka, *Principles of Gestalt Psychology*, New York, Harcourt, Brace and Company, 1935.

METHODS OF JUDGING PERSONALITY FOR THE LAYMAN

Stagner states: "The techniques of scientific psychology in the estimation of personality are in some instances merely refinements of those used by everyone in daily life." [7] It follows that the average person might examine the techniques of scientific psychology to see how he himself can utilize them.

Time-Sample Method. This method has been used in recent years to study children's behavior. It consists in observing a child for shorter or longer periods—from approximately three to ten minutes at certain periods during a day. Observed are idleness, activity, leadership, crying, laughter, the handling of toys, and so on. If these short-span observations are continued for some time, a certain consistency in behavior will be noticed. This method is essentially that used informally by a couple during the dating, courtship, and engagement periods. They see each other at stated times and under particular conditions. Basic traits can be discovered by watching types of activity enjoyed, topics of conversation, management of money, behavior toward other people, and so on.

Test Situations. This method was used extensively and perfected by Hartshorne and May. [8] In one test, a child was given the opportunity to be either honest or dishonest in a lifelike situation. He was sent to a store, where, after a purchase, the storekeeper gave back too much change. It was then observed whether the child, having been instructed first to count his change, would pocket some money on his way from the store back to school. Generosity was tested by giving a child more pencils than he needed and then informing him that there were children without pencils, to see how willing he was to share with others.

[7] By permission from *Psychology of Personality*, by Ross Stagner. Copyright, 1948. McGraw-Hill Book Company, Inc. P. 18.

[8] H. Hartshorne and M. A. May, *Character Education Inquiry*, New York, The Macmillan Company, 1930.

This method may seem somewhat unfair, but it is useful when hidden or unconscious motives must be discovered. If it is important to know how a prospective mate will react to former sweethearts, friends, relatives, or parents, test situations should be arranged. All kinds of habits, attitudes, values, traits, and roles can thus be discovered.

Not Too good

✓ **Graphic Rating Scales.** It is desirable for anyone to know what his friends think about a prospective mate, but unfortunately such information is quite often secured in an unsatisfactory way. Frequently the friend is asked simply, "What do you think of _____?" This question is so general and vague that one seldom can get a satisfactory answer. Here one might use the principles of the rating scale. This method involves the following steps: selecting a significant trait, defining it, and asking the rater to mark a place on a percentile line. This mark will indicate, in the opinion of the rater, to what extent a person possesses or does not possess a given trait.

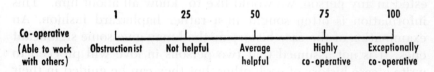

	1	25	50	75	100
Co-operative (Able to work with others)	Obstructionist	Not helpful	Average helpful	Highly co-operative	Exceptionally co-operative

FIGURE 8. Rating Scale of Traits.

Naturally, it is not always appropriate to give one's friends such a scale, but the *idea underlying it* can be used. However, caution should be exercised in several respects. Not everyone is gifted in the art of rating others accurately. A good rater or judge should be experienced and should have some insight into his own personality make-up. Any judge tends to rate a person higher if he likes him. For these and other reasons, it is usually desirable to get the opinions of several persons.

Some people can be rated much more easily than others because they have more accessible personalities. Also, certain traits can be rated more easily than others: traits involving social behavior and self-expression can be rated much more easily than traits pertaining to attitudes toward oneself and one's inner life.

On the whole, ratings are complimentary to the individual rated, perhaps because it seems somewhat cruel and unfair to speak ill of a person when one has oneself been complimented by being asked for an opinion. There is a strong tendency also to rate one's friends too high.

Closely related to this point is the "halo effect." If a person is rated high in one trait, there is a strong tendency to rate him high in every other trait. Thus, if a person is intelligent, we tend to think of him as also very kind, understanding, and sympathetic.

It is important to secure the judgment of others because of one's halo tendency. If a young man likes a young woman for her beautiful figure, he is likely to rate her high in intelligence, sympathy, co-operativeness, economy, and other traits. The rating by friends is necessary also because, in a sense, one marries a mate's friends. One must be accepted by them and must, in turn, accept them.

Case-History Method. Whenever we become seriously interested in any person, we would like to "know all about him." This information is often sought in a rather haphazard fashion. An examination of the case-history method may give some significant cues. It is not assumed that two persons in love will proceed to write a case history of each other, but they can be guided in their efforts to know each other by concentrating on facts such as those used in a case history. The sources for a case history are the person himself, parents, siblings, friends, teachers, and indeed anyone who has known him. One should be aware of the results of forgetting and improvising: all information gathered should be used cautiously and checked carefully.

Information sought should center on family background and history—an important area, since there is a high correlation between happiness in the marriage of parents and success in the marriage of their offspring. Specific items would include relationship to family and friends, history of illness and disease, school adjustment, recreational interest, vocational adjustment, emotional make-up, sex adjustment, and ambitions.

Scales and Tests. The two basic questions raised about any test are: First, is the test reliable, that is, is it self-consistent? Second, is it valid, that is, does it measure what is supposed to be measured? It is difficult to establish standards of reliability and validity for a test, especially a personality test. One therefore should not take too seriously the numerous tests which appear in many of our popular magazines.

Three tests which are among those currently used in connection with professional counseling are suggested below. They are readily available and can be scored and interpreted easily. A couple may find some enlightenment by taking them. However, even these tests must be used with caution, since their reliability and validity have not been fully determined. These tests, like many other personality tests, are not fool-proof, because one can influence the results by not marking questions truthfully and objectively.

The first such instrument is known as "A Marriage Prediction Scale" by Burgess and Cottrell.[9] The authors of the scale suggest that the questions be answered in terms of conditions as they prevail "at the time of marriage." The scale is based upon data derived from a careful and prolonged study of 526 urban, middle-class couples living in Illinois.

The second test recommended is called *The Personal Audit* by Clifford R. Adams and William M. Lepley.[10] On the basis of this test a couple can find out how they rate on: seriousness-impulsiveness, firmness-indecision, tranquility-irritability, frankness-evasion, stability-instability, tolerance-intolerance, steadiness-emotionality, persistence-fluctuation, and contentment-worry.

Since one's system of values strongly determines his behavior, a third instrument for measuring such values is suggested: Allport-Vernon-Lindzey's *Study of Values*.[11] The values measured by this test are mentioned on p. 87.

[9] Ernest W. Burgess and Leonard S. Cottrell, Jr., *Predicting Success or Failure in Marriage*, New York, Prentice-Hall, Inc., 1939, pp. 275–283.

[10] The test is available in two forms. Tests and a manual of directions can be obtained from the publisher, Science Research Associates, 57 West Grand Avenue, Chicago 10, Illinois.

[11] Gordon W. Allport, P. E. Vernon, and Gardner Lindzey, *Study of Values*, rev. ed., Boston, Houghton Mifflin Company, 1951.

METHODS AVAILABLE THROUGH PROFESSIONAL COUNSELORS

While the above methods are often valuable in self-evaluation and in the evaluation of a mate, it is sometimes necessary, and usually desirable, for one contemplating marriage to consult a well-qualified marriage counselor. Such consultation is desirable for a number of reasons. First, human personality is so complex that at best its understanding is limited. Second, in addition to evaluation of a personality as it exists at the moment, a mate somehow must also be able to predict what the individual will be and what he will do in the future. Such prediction requires insight into personality dynamics, a matter which lies beyond the ability of the layman. Third, there is a strong tendency for a person to rationalize about someone with whom he is in love. Undesirable qualities are either overlooked completely or greatly minimized. In other words, it is almost impossible for anyone to consider his own love-involvement objectively. Fourth, more or less serious questions may arise about a mate to which one simply cannot find satisfactory answers. Instead of remaining in a state of uncertainty and tension, the advice of a professional counselor should be sought.

In what ways can a marriage counselor assist a person in obtaining more information about personality maturity and mutual compatibility? Primarily, in two ways: through interview and by the use of a variety of tests. A personal interview is of great value to the counselor because he will know what to look for, how to obtain the information, and how to interpret it. He has also a great variety of tests at his disposal. He can measure intelligence, neurotic tendency, temperament, a variety of skills, attitudes, interests, traits, various types of adjustment, and the integration and stability of personality as a whole. He will not claim that his tests are perfect, but will use them to gain deeper insight and to verify his impressions. He will be able to give information which ordinarily the counselee could otherwise secure only over a long period of time, if ever.

Thus far we have stressed the psychological aspects of the evaluation of a mate. This by no means implies that a thorough knowledge of health and physical make-up is not also important. For such information, a couple should consult a physician. He will examine them not only to determine their physical health but also their adequacy for the reproductive functions. He will give them information about sexual anatomy, the physiological aspects of sexual intimacy, and the methods of birth control, if they are interested in planned parenthood.

INTERPRETATIVE SUMMARY

1. It is not sufficient to know *what* one is looking for in a mate; one must also know *how* to look for it.

2. Social-science methods, though not so accurate as the methods used in physical science, are nevertheless helpful.

3. Because of ignorance and superstition, many persons still turn to phrenology, palmistry, physiognomy, fortune telling, and astrology for help in selecting a mate.

4. Handwriting experts claim that, when used with caution, the analysis of one's writing may help identify a person as belonging to a certain type. Also, certain techniques which fall under the heading of intuition may have some value.

5. The average person will be greatly aided in his evaluation of a mate by using the principles involved in the time-sampling method, test situations, graphic rating scales, and case-history method.

6. Just as persons are willing to take vocational tests to guide them in vocational choice, so individuals should be willing to be rated on rating scales and to take tests that will guide them in mate selection and in marital adjustment.

7. Since no person possesses all the skill and knowledge necessary for the evaluation of a mate, one should not hesitate to consult a person trained in marriage counseling, not only when problems arise, but in order to avoid problems.

8. In addition to a marriage counselor, a couple should also consult a physician to determine physical fitness.

Thought Questions and Projects

1. Members of the class should secure samples of advertisements, personal cards, or notices publicizing the services of fortune tellers, astrologists, phrenologists, and palmists. Students who have had a "personality analysis" from such sources may wish to share their reactions with the class.

2. What is a "stereotype"? Why is stereotyping as applied to mate selection often misleading?

3. What is meant by the term *intuition?*

4. What are "personality rating scales"?

   (a) Members of the class should secure samples of rating scales as used for personnel selection in admission offices. Note traits stressed in each. Is there adequate range of degrees for marking each trait?

   (b) What are the advantages and the disadvantages in the use of rating scales?

5. Traits develop in clusters. With a given trait, other, related traits are expected in a personality. What other traits would you be likely to find with *loyalty?* What traits would be absent? How does knowledge about the clustering of traits help one in evaluating the personality of a prospective mate?

6. Study the following schedule and inventory, which are designed to measure traits and to predict possible marital happiness based upon such traits. Rate yourself on these.

   (a) Schedule for the Prediction and Measurement of Marriage Adjustment, in Ernest W. Burgess and Harvey J. Locke, *The Family,* 2nd ed., New York, American Book Company, 1953, pp. 693–716.

   (b) *An Inventory for Predicting Marital Happiness and Sexual Adjustment,* by Clifford R. Adams, 1951, available from Science Research Associates, Chicago, Illinois.

7. What are the advantages of a personal interview with a marriage counselor for a couple who want to evaluate their compatibility?

SUGGESTED READINGS FOR FURTHER STUDY

Allport, Gordon W., *Personality*, New York, Henry Holt & Company, 1937.
Part IV. Analysis of Personality.
Chapter 14. A Survey of Methods.
Chapter 15. Common Traits: Psychography.
Chapter 16. Analysis by Ratings, Tests, Experiments.
Chapter 17. Expressive Behavior.
Part V. Understanding Personality.
Chapter 18. The Ability to Judge People.
Chapter 19. Inference and Intuition.
McClelland, David C., *Personality*, New York, William Sloane Associates, 1951.
Part I. Methodology: How Personality Is Studied.
Chapter 1. The Scientific Approach to Personality: The History of a Belief.
Chapter 2. Obtaining the Facts.
Chapter 3. Interpreting the Facts.
Chapter 4. Relating the Facts to One Another.
Part II. Trait as a Personality Variable.
Chapter 5. Expressive Traits.
Chapter 6. Performance Traits.
Chapter 7. Trait Theory.
Murphy, Gardner, *Personality*, New York, Harper & Brothers, 1947.
Part V. Wholeness.
Chapter 26. Personality Structure.
Chapter 27. The Recognition of Personality Structure.
Chapter 28. Projective Methods with Adults.
Chapter 30. Continuity.
Chapter 31. Discontinuity and Typology.
Mursell, J. L., and R. B. Cattell, *Personality: A Systematic Theoretical and Factual Study*, New York, McGraw-Hill Book Company, 1950.
Stagner, Ross, *Psychology of Personality*, 2nd ed., New York, McGraw-Hill Book Company, 1948.
Chapter 1. The Scientific Study of Personality.
Chapter 2. Methods in the Study of Personality.
Chapter 3. Methods in the Study of Personality (Cont'd).
Young, Kimball, *Personality and Problems of Adjustment*, 2nd ed., New York, Appleton-Century-Crofts, 1952.
Chapter 9. Typology: Facts and Theories.
Chapter 10. Theories of Personality.
Chapter 11. The Study of Personality.

9

DATING
OR PERIOD OF EXPLORATION

In our society, young people of opposite sex go through three stages of adjustment to each other before marriage: dating, courtship, and engagement. Dating is exploratory—"playing the field"; courtship is selective—"going steady"; and engagement is experimental—"trial adjustment." Dating will be discussed in this chapter; courtship and engagement in the next two chapters.

There are several kinds of dates. The *ordinary* date is with a person one has known more or less for some time as a member of a neighborhood group. A *special* date or *glamour* date is with some relatively new person. The *blind* date is usually arranged by a third person or another couple. A *pick-up* date is with a person one meets by chance.

SIGNIFICANCE OF DATING

Nature of the Adolescent. Since dating is primarily an experience during adolescence, it cannot be understood fully unless one first understands something of the adolescent personality. Adolescence begins with puberty and ends with the attainment of maturity. It is thus a transitional stage between childhood and adulthood. For girls, it is the period from about 12 to about 21, and for boys from about 13 to about 22. The period is often subdivided into early, middle, and later adolescence.

Typically, the young adolescent is self-conscious about his

physical make-up. He is experiencing a period of rapid growth, which often gives him a feeling of awkwardness; his legs and arms seem too long and poorly co-ordinated. The proportions of his body are changing. The secondary sex characteristics—such as bodily hair growth, increased activity of the axillary sweat glands, shifts in shape and contour of the body, a marked change of voice in boys and modified tonal quality of voice in girls—make their appearance. The boy is changing into a young man and the girl into a young woman. New hormones, sex hormones, are poured into the blood stream, and they cause new and unfamiliar sensations. The adolescent feels that he is not the same person he was; often he feels lonely for his old self.

There is a strong attraction to the opposite sex. Only yesterday the girl was not interested in the boy; today she is fascinated by him. Only yesterday the boy "hated" girls and threw pebbles after them as a signal of his dislike; today he feels peculiarly drawn to them and throws stolen glances at them. Yesterday both had their own *status* within their respective groups, in which they felt more or less secure; now they seek a new status in a new world. There is a great concern about physical appearance; freckles or a peculiar nose become sources of great worry. Clothes become all-important; a great deal of time is given to primping and grooming. Up to now, the parents determined the child's status; now, each one seeks his own status from his peers on the basis of appearance and individual achievement. Dependence on parents, in other words, is given up for self-dependence and self-reliance. There is a new orientation and re-examination of values.

Not all this is accomplished in one day, nor is the change in a straight line. The adolescent is characterized by many inconsistencies. G. Stanley Hall's early observations of adolescence still hold today. He discovered eleven inconsistencies: (1) oscillation between activity and idleness, (2) fluctuation between elation and depression, (3) self-confidence versus self-depreciation, (4) oscillation between selfishness and altruism, (5) good conduct and bad conduct, (6) oscillation between society and solitude, (7) nice sensitivity alternating with callousness, (8) enthusiasm for knowledge versus indifference, (9) knowing versus doing, (10) conservatism alternating with radicalism, and (11) proximity of wisdom and folly.[1] The problem is one of giving up a previous role and adopting a new one. The old one cannot be abandoned completely until the new one has been fully acquired.

CHARACTERISTICS OF DATING

Dating is one aspect of learning a new role in life, that of associating temporarily with a person of the opposite sex. It is learning to *know oneself* as much as to know the other person. Let us look at some of its important psychological characteristics.

An Experience of Being on One's Own. Having a date is a first serious attempt to break away from home ties. Up to now, the boy and girl have moved mostly within the family circle. They have occupied a place in the social world determined largely for them by their having been born into a certain social setting. Now each makes an attempt to become a member of a new group of his own choosing. For this reason, they are anxious to arrange their own dates, to make their own selections. When they are on a date, what they do and how they act toward each other is a manifestation of their concept of themselves and of each other. From this viewpoint, dating is a great adventure.

Sampling the Opposite Sex. In general, there is a strong desire, at least in the early period of dating, to have dates with as many different members of the opposite sex as possible. This varies, of course, with self-confidence and self-assurance of individuals. It is motivated not only by curiosity about the opposite sex, but also by a desire to experience one's reactions to different individuals. Some fraternities even have rules that their members have frequent dates, but not too frequently with the same girl, unless the two go steady.

Whether or not a great variety of dates is a good preparation for successful marriage has not been fully established. Terman has not found any significant correlation between variety and suc-

[1] G. Stanley Hall, *Adolescence*, Vol. 2, New York, D. Appleton & Company, 1904, pp. 75–94.

cessful marriage.[2] Hamilton found that 100 men he studied had 681 love affairs and 100 women had 677 love affairs.[3] This attests to variety, certainly, but the author does not come to any definite conclusion about the effect of these affairs on marital adjust-

"I'll remember this evening, Gerald, long after I'm married to Charlie Smith."

Walter Goldstein and The Saturday Evening Post.

ment. Burgess and Cottrell have stated that nearly one half of the men who made a poor adjustment in marriage had had almost no women friends before marriage, whereas those who had had

[2] Lewis M. Terman *et al., Psychological Factors in Marital Happiness,* New York, McGraw-Hill Book Company, 1938, pp. 257–259.

[3] G. V. Hamilton, *Research in Marriage,* New York, Albert and Charles Boni, 1929, pp. 210–211.

several girl friends made the best adjustment. The women who made good adjustments in marriage had a few, or several, or many different dates before marriage.[4] Adams and Packard quote with approval one authority who states that "a girl needs to know twenty or twenty-five young men in order that she may have sufficient range to find someone eligible for her needs."[5]

Insofar as dates serve to make one acquainted with oneself as well as with others, it stands to reason that several different date partners are more desirable than only one. This does not mean that the last person dated is usually selected as a mate. In fact, one may return even to the first person dated and do so with greater knowledge and contentment.

Training in Etiquette. Dating offers young people an opportunity to learn points of etiquette, acts of courtesy, and niceties of manners which make for smoother social interaction. Through the trial-and-error experiences of dating they have a chance to observe the behavior of others, to discover areas in their own behavior which reflect a lack of social grace, and to learn how to enhance personality. By becoming acquainted with basic guiding rules of etiquette young people can develop a sense of personal adequacy, charm, and poise. Dating affords diversified situations for such training.

Dating for Fun. The primary objective of a date is mutual enjoyment for the present. Each date is, therefore, an event in itself, and it does not imply any kind of obligation for the future. The couple seeks a variety of sensory and intellectual pleasures and emotional thrills. They go out to be entertained by others in movies, theaters, at concerts, and at sports. They may engage in a great many activities together, such as eating, dancing, card playing, swimming, hiking, cycling, playing table tennis, golf, or innumerable other games, collecting nature specimens of all kinds, cooking, reading, following each other's hobbies, and doing other things that can be invented by an ingenious couple. Intellectual

[4] Ernest W. Burgess and Leonard S. Cottrell, Jr., *Predicting Success or Failure in Marriage*, New York, Prentice-Hall, 1939, pp. 128–132.

[5] Clifford R. Adams and Vance O. Packard, *How to Pick a Mate*, New York, E. P. Dutton & Company, 1946, p. 28.

discussions are usually motivated by a desire to please the other person; therefore, intense arguments are generally avoided.

Dating as a Training in Proficiencies. When one examines all the diversified activities that young people can pursue on dates, it becomes obvious that dating provides valuable opportunity for the development and use of numerous abilities. A dating couple is highly motivated to learn how to excel in skills which make for a more interesting relationship. Participation in motor skills, such as swimming, horseback riding, dancing, skating, bowling, playing tennis or golf, is especially important to the adolescent, since his status is strongly determined by physical prowess. Learning to play musical instruments together, learning to paint, or participating in any phase of the fine arts will add to his skills. Dating gives opportunity for acquiring skill in the art of conversation. Various discussions, although interspersed with adolescent babblings, double talk, gags, overworked phrases, and coined words usually unintelligible to the adult, represent significant progress on the part of a young dating couple in gaining poise in their acquaintanceship.

Lessons in Co-operation. Co-operation, or joint action for common benefit, is essential for a successful marriage. Since the goal in dating is *mutual* enjoyment, the dating activity becomes a training in co-operation. On a date, one learns to think less of his own wishes. The intelligent person looks on the process of give and take not as a restriction of his enjoyment but as an extension. One important function of dating in mate selection is the elimination of persons whose selfishness would make them poor risks in such a relationship as marriage, the essence of which is co-operation.

Lessons in Emotional Control. The emotions which must be especially controlled during dating are *anger, jealousy,* and *"love."* Since co-operation is learned only slowly and since the adolescent is still quite inconsistent, many frustrating situations occur. Even though interests may be similar, they will not always coincide, so that the results are disappointment and tension. At this time, not to "fly off the handle," to develop tolerance, is a prime necessity. In spite of every effort, quarrels may result. (The nature of these is discussed in the next chapter.) When dating is on a temporary basis, it is natural that the person with whom one went out one night will go out with someone else the next night. This may easily give one a feeling of neglect or even rejection. It may result in ego-hurt. The rule of the game is not to be jealous—a rule hard to learn. But it must be learned, at least to some degree, if one is to remain a respected member of his group.

During dating, "falling in love" is out of place. For a girl not to become emotionally involved is not an easy matter. If she does so before the young man is ready, she is likely to lose him, for he does not want to be "caught." If the young man becomes emotionally involved too soon or too easily, he may be looked upon by the girl as "too easy to get." All in all, dating provides excellent opportunity for learning to be objective about the opposite sex.

The following case illustrates what happens when one person becomes serious about dating and the other dates merely for enjoyment.

No member of Ray D.'s family had gone to college. When he finished high school with an excellent record, he was awarded a scholarship to a top-ranking university. Ray was an attractive young man, who rightfully could be called a "heartbreaker." From the time he entered the university, he followed a consistent pattern: He aimed for the most beautiful girl in the crowd and won her easily with his suave manner, amorous "line," and undivided attention. But when he became aware that she had fallen in love with him, he summarily reviewed for her his one and only goal in college—to complete the five years of basic preparation in journalism. And he had no intention of becoming seriously involved in love or in getting married until he had finished his five years of training. He then broke off his courtship and went on to the next girl. As a result, he left behind him a succession of disillusioned girls who fell in love while he was dating for the experience of dating.

A Source of Recognition or Prestige. Dating is a highly selective process. To "rate a date" is an achievement, especially if the date is with a very desirable partner. The bases of selection sometimes are unconscious, but often as not they are highly conscious. They are frequently used to enhance one's importance. Of great significance for the young man is that the girl be physically attractive, charming in manner, and generally popular. The man should probably be tall, dark, and handsome, and of athletic build. He is expected to show social poise, to be a good conversationalist, good dancer, good "sport," to be liked by others, and to belong to a certain social set. There are other characteristics. Because of the prestige involved, being asked for a date, or being accepted, is a source of joy and pride. It means that one is respected, if not love-worthy. Such experiences make it easier later to believe that one will make a desirable mate.

PROBLEMS CONNECTED WITH DATING

Getting Dates or Proper Dates. Getting the right kind of date quite often is a serious problem for a girl, especially since she has to wait to be asked. She may not get a date for several reasons. She may live in an environment where few men are available, or her work may be of such a nature that she meets few men. The latter is especially true of nurses, social workers, librarians, and teachers. She may not be physically attractive or may have personality problems which keep young men away. Sometimes her expectations limit the number of men whom she would find acceptable.

Young men also may live in an environment where few girls are available, or they may not have enough money, or may be too self-conscious, or so tied to their mothers' apron strings that they cannot break away. At any rate, young people may experience heartaches because for one reason or another they are left on the side lines.

Becoming Emotionally Involved. As was mentioned above, the chief purpose of dating is widening one's experience. However, one person may fall in love and become too "serious" before the other is ready. Such involvement is interpreted by the less interested individual as not playing the game fairly. Consequently, persons who let themselves become too emotionally involved with those they date are usually avoided.

Jealousy. Not to be asked for a date may make a girl jealous of another girl and may break up friendships, especially if one girl feels that the other is encroaching on her territory. A boy may be filled with resentment if a girl refuses him a date but accepts someone else whom he regards as his rival. Such a situation also may result in or aggravate feelings of inferiority.

Convention. Our society has many rules which govern dating, most of which have already been enumerated. All of them deal with the regulation of young people's desire for pleasure. The question that presents itself, therefore, is to what extent a young couple should conform to social mores and to what extent they may seek their pleasures in spite of rules. Such decisions are often of far-reaching consequence, for they may affect the person's reputation, with the accompanying rewards or punishments which society can inflict.

THE PROBLEM OF PETTING

According to Kinsey's study,[6] petting is pre-eminently an activity of high-school and college youth. Ninety-two per cent of these groups engage in petting before marriage. Eighty-four per cent of males of grade-school level engage in petting; however, their petting, as a rule, is not very elaborate.

Petting has increased in modern times for several reasons: (1) Marriages are often delayed because of prolonged educational preparation, especially for people going into professions. (2) There is less chaperonage; young people are more on their own. (3) Modern youth is more exposed to sexual stimuli, such as scantily clad women, suggestive forms of dancing, certain types of entertainment, such as may be seen on television, in movies, and

[6] Alfred C. Kinsey *et al.*, *Sexual Behavior in the Human Male*, Philadelphia, W. B. Saunders Company, 1948.

in stage shows. Cartoons, pulp magazines, and even general advertising tend to capitalize on the sexual theme. (4) Modern youth does not conform as much to religious teaching and mores as did youth in former years. They often believe that the only objection against petting comes from religious and ethical codes and that if those are set aside they are absolutely free to do as they please. Such reasoning is dangerously unsound. A couple should be well informed as to the possible effects which petting may have on them. The pleasurable advantages of petting are balanced by disadvantages which must not be overlooked. Therefore, these effects should be carefully evaluated before petting is engaged in.

Petting is pleasant because it consists of the stimulation of pleasure zones of the body. It is closely linked to the tactile sense, which many consider to be the most primitive sense. Our culture encourages experiencing pleasures from all other senses. For example, we go to a great deal of trouble to prepare foods and liquids in such a fashion that we derive the greatest pleasure from the sense of taste; we create all kinds of odors to get pleasant sensations from our sense of smell; and we compose music to provide pleasant stimulation for our ears. Thus, it may be argued, if we approve of these kinds of pleasure, why not also of the pleasure derived from petting?

Overindulgence. There is danger that petting may be engaged in to excess. Since the pleasure derived from petting may be great and the urge persistent, a couple may resort to it so much and so often that they deprive themselves of the opportunity of participating in other activities which would help them to understand each other better. Petting may reduce the association to the physical level.

Greater Sexual Tension. While it is true that, for some, petting may reduce tension, for others it may serve to increase it. To some, petting is only a preliminary to sexual activity and, when this is ruled out, it may result in frustration and resentment. Such couples may find that the only way they can get along with each other is to abandon petting altogether.

Danger of Sexual Intimacy. A couple, having decided not to engage in sexual intimacy before marriage, may find that in petting they are carried so far along that they engage in intercourse against their better judgment. The result may be pregnancy, with all the serious consequences of forced marriage, an illegitimate child, or an abortion.

Feelings of Guilt and Shame. Whether one feels guilt in connection with petting depends, of course, upon training and background. Since petting is more or less taboo in our society, there are few individuals who can engage in it without some feeling of doing wrong. Young people should be especially aware of the fact that their reasoning about religious and moral precepts may be nothing more than rationalization. Even when they reason objectively, they still may not do away with their feelings. These feelings may lead to serious emotional upsets.

Commonly it is the male who is most aggressive in petting. The girl quite often cannot engage in it without some loss of self-respect. She may give in for fear of being regarded as a prude, or for fear of losing a possible mate. Insofar as she engages in it unwillingly, petting becomes a poor preparation for later marital sex adjustment. For the young man, such petting is apt to lead to selfishness.

Reinforcing Romantic Notions of Marriage. Petting is invariably accompanied by endearing words, which often give rise to much idealization resulting in attitudes and beliefs that cannot be realized in the everyday life of marriage.

INTERPRETATIVE SUMMARY

1. Dating is used primarily for immediate pleasure; it does not imply any commitment for the future.

2. Dating may be regarded as a pleasant method of learning new roles in boy-girl relationship.

3. Persons who date learn to know themselves as well as the

opposite sex. They acquire social skills, learn the expected rules of etiquette and co-operation, and learn emotional control.

4. There are a number of problems connected with dating, among them rating a date, becoming emotionally involved, and petting.

5. Petting is a special problem because there are no general codes pertaining to it. Its effects must be evaluated by each couple as they concern them.

THOUGHT QUESTIONS AND PROJECTS

1. How would you define "dating"?

2. Can you point out specific social skills learned as a direct outgrowth of dating experience?

3. List some socially organized ways whereby young people have the opportunity to become acquainted and to participate in dating.

4. Does social "rating" within your school or circle of friends depend upon whether or not one dates?

5. Would you prefer to marry someone who had dated only a few persons prior to dating you, or someone who had dated several different types of persons? Support your answer.

6. What is the class opinion as to how frequently a dating couple should be together during the exploratory stage?

7. Do you think the woman should help plan the activities for a date as often as does the man?

8. Is "going Dutch" on dates ever practiced by your circle of friends?

9. Try this project if you have several foreign countries represented on your campus. Appoint as many interviewers from the class as there are foreign countries represented in the school. Then ask each to interview a student (or students) from a designated country about dating practices in that country. Students who conduct the interviews may then present an oral report to the class in which they compare and contrast dating practices in the various countries, including their own.

10. What are some common problems connected with "petting"?

11. Have you had "blind" dates? Were they arranged for by a personal friend or by a social chairman for a special event? Did any such date lead to courtship? To marriage?

SUGGESTED READINGS FOR FURTHER STUDY

Adams, Clifford R., *Preparing for Marriage*, New York, E. P. Dutton & Company, 1951.
   Chapter 6. Sex Adventuring.
   Chapter 7. Do Possible Mates Shy Away?
   Chapter 8. Making People Like You.
Baber, Ray E., *Marriage and the Family*, 2nd ed., New York, McGraw-Hill Book Company, 1953.
   Chapter 16. Conflicting Sex Patterns.
   Chapter 17. Irregular Sex Expression: Social Costs.
Burgess, Ernest W., and Harvey J. Locke, *The Family*, 2nd ed., New York, American Book Company, 1953.
   Chapter 12. Love and Courtship.
Christensen, Harold T., *Marriage Analysis*, New York, The Ronald Press Company, 1950.
   Chapter 7. Learning to Love.
Duvall, Evelyn Millis, and Reuben Hill, *When You Marry*, rev. ed., Boston, D. C. Heath & Company, 1953.
   Chapter 3. Dating: Practice Makes Perfect.
Landis, Paul H., *Your Marriage and Family Living*, New York, McGraw-Hill Book Company, 1946.
   Chapter 6. Finding Your Proper Mate Should Not Be Left to Chance.
Lindgren, Henry Clay, *Psychology of Personal and Social Adjustment*, New York, American Book Company, 1953.
   Chapter 17. Building Sound Relationships between the Sexes.
McKinney, Fred, *Psychology of Personal Adjustment*, 2nd ed., New York, John Wiley & Sons, 1949.
   Chapter 10. Social Adjustment.
Merrill, Francis E., *Courtship and Marriage*, New York, The Dryden Press, 1949.
   Chapter 4. Dating and Courtship.
Stroup, H. H., "Economic Aspects of Dating," *Family Life*, 1952, 12:3–6.
Winch, Robert F., *The Modern Family*, New York, Henry Holt & Company, 1952.
   Appendix (pp. 489–493). Dating, Rating and College Fraternities.

10

COURTSHIP

THE MEANING OF COURTSHIP

Courtship begins when two people of opposite sex limit their dating to each other. In courtship, each is taken "out of circulation." The understanding arrived at involves self-imposed limitation on association with others of the opposite sex. It means giving up some freedom. Whereas *dating* has as its primary aim a pleasurable broadening of experience, *courtship*, or "going steady," has in addition definite reference to the future. Courtship implies the possibility of marriage at some future date. It is the tentative selection of a mate.

Courtship may have a "sudden" beginning, as when two people fall in love; or it may be a gradual outgrowth of dating. In the latter case, it is sometimes hard to tell when dating ends and courtship begins. In some instances, the transition from dating into courtship may present serious problems. One partner may fall in love and insist on going steady, while the other may wish to continue the temporary dating arrangement. How to resolve this problem depends upon the two people involved and the general situation in which they find themselves; in any event, the application of pressure is undesirable. For instance, it is unwise for a girl who wants to change a dating relationship into one of restricted courtship to bring pressure to bear on the young man by saying something like this: "You can go out with other girls if you wish, but I'm not interested in other young men—I'd rather just stay at home." It is equally important that friends or relatives not pressure two young people into going steady. Going steady should be a result of mutual understanding not influenced by any outside forces.

SIGNIFICANCE OF COURTSHIP

Status. While two young people going steady should be proud of each other and delight in being seen with each other, some young people occasionally select a boy or girl friend solely for purposes of *showing off* or *impressing* associates. Such behavior implies, not selection for the other's own sake, but a conquest, using the other as a tool, treating him or her like a piece of property—a car, a fur coat, or a diamond ring. Naturally, the desirable motive for going steady is mutual respect. When this motive is operative, both persons experience a satisfying enhancement of their ego.

Getting Acquainted. Going steady should have as its aim getting better acquainted. Getting acquainted implies learning more about the other person, as well as about oneself. In this connection, each can use information gained from the study of personality, differences between the sexes, methods used in the evaluation of personality, and the basic qualities to look for in a mate. Some of the observable aspects (discussed in Chapter 8) are mentioned here in brief review: (Cultural and family background, education, health, emotional control, intellectual endowment, range and type of experiences, habits and skills, attitudes, interests, values, significant traits, roles an individual can play, and one's concept of himself.)

Getting to know each other better during courtship than during dating will succeed provided the following conditions prevail: Having dated a sufficient number of persons of the opposite sex so as to have arrived at a comparative basis for judging qualities in another individual; being seriously interested to the point where every effort is put forth to know each other's qualities; being frank and truthful with each other; and having opportunity to associate with each other under a variety of circumstances such as alone, at home, with different groups of friends, with strangers, in every season of the year, in good and bad moods, sick and well, angry and calm, tired and full of energy, depressed or jovial, and so on.

Obstacles to Getting Acquainted. A person in love is prone to overvalue his love object. In his phantasy thinking, a man will

"They haven't seen each other since last night."

Reginald Hider and The Saturday Evening Post.

idealize his sweetheart: She is the most beautiful, intelligent, noble, considerate, and the like. He will endow her with all that he regards as desirable. In other words, he will *project* into her characteristics from his own mind and by doing so will blind himself to seeing her as she actually is or as she is perceived through less biased eyes. The difficulty will be aggravated by her constant attempt to find out what he wishes to see in her and then to act accordingly. Of course, the girl will also idealize and project. A major function of a protracted association is to afford ample opportunity for the gradual removal of the blinders.

A New "We" Feeling. Up to the stage of going steady, each partner is a member of a group, composed of a family and friends. The family group is not of an individual's own choice—he is born into it. Friendships are only more or less the product of choice or selection. But going steady definitely is a matter of the individual's own decision. It implies relinquishing ties with the past and establishing new ties. A new feeling of belonging emerges. The couple evolve their own common interests; they delineate their own value system. They begin to have secrets. Communication between them will have features and elements known only to them. They speak a language all their own. In brief, they become a new social unit.

Co-operation. Going steady is an excellent lesson in co-operation. The couple set their own goals, and that process involves an adjustment to each other's interests. They must be aware of these goals, clearly define them, and help each other to accept them. They must learn how to agree. Having done so, each is expected to use his skills and resources in order to attain the common goal. In many cases, so doing will involve some degree of denial for the sake of common action.

Role Playing. Young people soon discover that the society in which they live expects them to conform to certain rules. Just as an author of a play prescribes to his actors words and actions, so society has gradually evolved roles for all its members, whether they are acting as individuals, married mates, or in groups. These roles are not very clearly defined, but they are nevertheless rigorously enforced. Those who conform are rewarded by praise and many privileges, and those who do not conform are punished by loss of respect, deprivation of normal privileges, and infliction of pain. In going steady, a couple gradually becomes more and more aware of the man-woman role and has opportunity to learn it.

Conformity or Nonconformity. A couple sooner or later discover that their particular interests may conflict with the role prescribed by society for couples going steady. A couple may want to go by themselves on extended trips to some distant place, or they may want to engage in premarital sexual intercourse. If they do either, they will meet with disapproval. In this way, they are faced with the important decision as to what extent they will be bound by society. Whatever they do becomes a training in living as a new unit in a larger society.

COURTSHIP PROBLEMS

Premarital Sex Experience. The question of premarital intercourse may come up during the dating period, but it is much more likely to arise during courtship, when two people see each other regularly and under a variety of circumstances. The problem is a serious one, because at this stage the sex urge is strong and our society is determined to enforce the taboo against sexual intercourse outside of marriage. It will depend upon the individuals concerned whether or not they conform to the mores of our society. Since they are to make the ultimate decision, they should be well informed about the implications of premarital intercourse and the reasons for and against it.

A few preliminary statements are in order. First, it is still a question as to what extent reason can control the sex urge. It is well known that many young people, in spite of strong convictions against any premarital sex intercourse, still on occasion engage in it. No amount of reasoning will ever stop the physiological urge. At most, as many studies by clinical psychologists and psychiatrists have shown, reason can only aid toward repression of the urge and stop it from ever coming into consciousness. When the urge becomes conscious, it quite often will induce rationalization, which makes the satisfaction of the urge possible. Many engage in forbidden sexual activity only to regret it afterwards.

The problem is not the same for everybody. In the first place, there is a great difference in the degree of the sex urge from person to person, as to both its frequency and its intensity. There are some individuals who have a sex urge daily or several times daily, while others experience it rarely—once a month, or only several times a year. Some can banish the urge from consciousness with ease; for others, this is impossible. The difference may be in part due to intellectual endowment, but it certainly is also a result of training.

Reasoning does not take place in a vacuum. In order to produce results, mental processes need content, just as a mill needs wheat in order to produce flour. The better a person is informed, other things being equal, the better his judgment is. It is for this reason that every person should have all the available information pertaining to sex.

Sex Mores Relative to Culture. Every person should be well informed about the sex mores of his society. It should never come as a shock to anyone that other cultures may have different, often opposite, sex norms. Our Anglo-Saxon culture taboos premarital sex experiences. In other societies, they may be permitted or even encouraged. Any textbook on anthropology contains information about this topic. An anthropologist, George Peter Murdock, stated recently that 70 per cent of the 250 human societies he had studied permit "sexual experimentation" before marriage.[1]

Nor is our Anglo-Saxon culture unanimous in its condemnation of premarital intercourse. The experience in England reported by Himes will illustrate this point:

> "When I went to England in 1927 as a Fellow of the Social Science Research Council to make a study of the birth control clinics in that country, I was surprised to find in analyzing the figures of a Scottish birth control clinic that a large proportion of the women were pregnant prior to marriage; and that some had already given birth to one child and were pregnant a second time before they married. I confess that I was somewhat shocked, and wondered about the morality of the Scotch working classes. Then I was informed that it was the custom among many unskilled laborers in Scotland not to marry until fertility had been demonstrated. . . . Since reproduction is one of the primary purposes of marriage, this situation is not half so shocking as it first appears. Shock subsides when we understand the reason for

[1] *Time*, February 13, 1950, p. 57.

the custom. 'Handfasting,' as the practice is known, is institutionalized in certain Scotch classes and no one thinks much about it." [2]

Incidence of Premarital Intercourse. Several investigators have found that not all persons in our society conform to our mores regarding premarital intercourse. While studying their data one must keep certain points in mind. First, each investigator deals with a small sample of our total population, and many authorities have rightfully warned against the conclusion that any of these limited samples give a true or representative picture of what actually happens in our country. Second, the mere fact that some or many deviate from our mores is in no sense a justification for further deviation. Third, it cannot be assumed that such deviations have been beneficial to everyone concerned.

Reasons For and Against Premarital Intercourse. Some individuals will be surprised that reasons for premarital intercourse are even mentioned in view of the fact that religious teaching and mores definitely oppose it. Certainly all the religious organizations in our country, Catholic, Protestant, and Jewish, are agreed on this point. Our mores are equally explicit. To millions of young people who take their religion seriously, or those who accept our mores wholeheartedly, premarital sex experience is not a matter of personal choice, however strongly they may be tempted to engage in it.

In stating possible reasons for and against such experiences, we have in mind those persons who are lukewarm in their adherence to religious teaching and to the acceptance of mores. There are also those who do not belong to any religious organization and those who view our mores as antiquated precepts. No matter what may be the attitudes of a person concerning premarital intercourse, before indulging he must consider the consequences on himself, on the partner involved, and on society in general. For he must realize that the prime motive of a mature person is not the selfish pleasure of the individual but the interest and welfare of society as a whole.

[2] Norman E. Himes, *Your Marriage*, New York, Rinehart & Company, Inc., 1940, p. 105. Reprinted by permission.

REASONS FOR PREMARITAL SEXUAL INTERCOURSE

Relief from Physiological Tension. Since the male reaches the peak of his sexual capacity in the later teen age, his mind may be frequently preoccupied with sexual matters. Therefore, actual experience will bring him relief from sexual tension.

Removal of Sex as a Central or Important Factor in Marriage. Since mores do not permit a couple to engage in sexual activity before marriage, desire for such activity frequently becomes the chief reason for marriage. The sex urge, if repressed, may be so strong that it displaces important psychological reasons for not getting married.

Removal of Many Frustrations. One important cause for quarrels between a couple is sexual frustration. If by intimacy this frustration is removed, it may be possible that the couple will have fewer quarrels and get along more harmoniously.

Greater Objectivity. Once two people have been sexually intimate, they feel freer and more objective in their discussion of the problem of sex, as well as of any other intimate personal subject.

Removal of Barrier for Love. Some feel that a couple really in love with each other must share each other completely. Any barrier is considered an indication of incomplete love. Girls quite often feel that love is sufficient reason for entering into an intimate relationship. As an excuse for it, one often hears: "I loved him so."

Better Indication of Sexual Compatibility. Insofar as intercourse can occur under favorable circumstances—physical as well as psychological—it may be a good test of sexual compatibility.

Learning Proper Sexual Techniques. It is claimed that, since man is not born with a sex instinct, he must learn to perform the sex act adequately. Premarital intercourse, it is felt, provides the necessary experience.

Confidence on the Part of the Wife. Some wives who enter marriage as virgins are afraid of the sex act. Premarital intercourse will give the wife confidence, and that confidence will help greatly in bringing about adequate sexual adjustment between mates.

REASONS AGAINST PREMARITAL SEXUAL INTERCOURSE

Against Religious Teaching. The person who is in favor of premarital intercourse sets himself up as an authority against religion. How and where does he get his evidence that he is right in this matter and religion is wrong?

Against Mores. A person who rejects the mores of his group quite often looks upon them as being merely capricious notions rather than the outgrowth of experiences of a society over a long period of time. Is he alone qualified from his limited experience to set up new mores?

May Encourage Infidelity. A person who ignores religious teaching and mores concerning premarital intercourse may lay the foundation for equal disregard for marital fidelity.

Defeats Mastery of Sex Drive. By learning to control the sex drive, a person may gain mastery not only over it but over other drives, such as hostility, anger, aggression. He may be able to control any type of behavior which may be called excessive, such as drinking, overeating, or smoking. Learning to control the sex drive will be beneficial to a person after marriage, for, even in marriage, control is necessary because of differences in the degree of sexuality of the mates, necessary separation of mates over a period of time, or religious convictions regarding overindulgence.

Psychological Tension. While premarital intercourse may remove physical tension, it may produce psychological tensions.

These may be due to feelings of guilt, shame, and fear of discovery by society.

Courtship Degraded to Physical Level. Premarital intercourse, once engaged in, may easily become excessive, particularly among adolescents with strong sex urge. It may be engaged in to the exclusion of many other activities which might better enable a couple to get acquainted with each other.

Forced Marriage. Having sex experience with a girl may make a man feel that he should marry her, even though he may not really want to do so. The girl may have similar feelings.

Mistrust and Suspicion. A young man, having used all his persuasive powers to induce a girl into sexual intimacy, afterwards may believe that, since she had relationships with him, she would be willing to have similar intimacies with others.

Loss of Reputation. As long as the double standard of morality persists, a girl may live in constant fear—and often with good reason—that a young man with whom she has been intimate will reveal their secret to other men. She thus may undermine her chances of getting married at all.

Fear of Its Effect on Future Mate. Because of the double standard of morality, a girl may also fear that if she becomes intimate with a man she believes might marry her, this fact will be discovered later by her husband, who then may lose respect for her.

Loss of Respect. It often happens that a young man may lose respect for the very girl who was intimate with him. This is especially true where a man thinks of sex as something degrading and cannot harmonize it with his idealistic conception of women.

Danger of Pregnancy. In spite of modern means of prevention, unwanted pregnancies do occur. According to some researches, 4 per cent of all children born in our country are illegitimate. Premarital pregnancy may lead to illegal abortion, with all its undesirable consequences.

Unfavorable Conditioning. Too often premarital sexual intercourse takes place under unfavorable physical and psychological circumstances and thus results in unsatisfactory sexual experience. Since first experiences are very impressive, premarital intercourse may lead to faulty sex adjustments later. The act may be extremely painful for the girl, may leave her unsatisfied, and may give the young man a feeling that he is sexually inadequate.

Danger of Venereal Disease. The danger of venereal disease is especially great when one or both partners have been or are promiscuous.

Premarital Relations and Marital Happiness. The discussion of the effects of premarital intercourse would not be complete without reference to some authorities who have directed researches on this controversial topic. Many writers have expressed definite opinions, only some of which have been based on the findings of scientific research. Perhaps the two most notable researches dealing with the question of premarital relations are those of Kinsey and associates[3] and those of Terman and associates. Their conclusions are cautious if not equivocal.

Kinsey discusses at length the various effects of premarital intercourse on those who engage in it. His findings indicate that there may be some desirable effects and some undesirable effects. With regard to the effects of premarital sex intercourse on marriage he states: "It is impossible at this point to attempt an over-all evaluation of the effects of premarital coitus on marriage." [4]

Terman states on the basis of his research of 792 married couples: "Data merely show that in general those husbands and wives who were virgins at marriage or had intercourse only with each other tend to have higher mean happiness scores than do the other groups." [5] On the basis of this conclusion one can argue for or against virginity before marriage. One must remember, however, that these conclusions were reached only by statistical

[3] Alfred C. Kinsey *et al.*, *Sexual Behavior in the Human Female*, Philadephia, W. B. Saunders Company, 1953, pp. 307–330.

[4] *Ibid.*, p. 228. Reprinted by permission.

[5] By permission from *Psychological Factors in Marital Happiness*, by Lewis M. Terman *et al.* Copyright, 1938. McGraw-Hill Book Company, Inc. P. 329.

analysis. One is justified in asking how many other factors besides sex may have contributed to the greater happiness of those studied.

LOVERS' SPATS

An old proverb states: "The course of true love seldom runs smooth." It is certainly true that whenever two individuals associate with each other intimately over some period of time, some friction may develop, even though the motive for association is love. This friction may be called a misunderstanding, conflict, quarrel. We call it a spat.

Causes for Spats. Though specific causes for spats are many, most of them can be classified in one of the following four groups: (1) personality make-up, (2) temporary conflict of interest, (3) situational limitations, and (4) projections.

Personality make-up. Since no two personalities are identical, either in the elements that enter into their structure or in their total integration, there are likely to be frictions in closer or intimate association. The causes for friction may be on any level, involving experience, habits, skills, attitudes, interests, values, traits, selves, or the ego or self. This last factor is especially important during adolescence, for, as we have seen above, the adolescent personality is still more or less inconsistent.

Conflict of interests. No matter how similar the interests of two people are, they probably will not coincide all the time. For example, think of two persons who are both interested in symphony orchestras. On any one evening, the man may be set to attend a concert, while the girl may not be in the proper mood for it. Since one must give in to the other, some irritation is inevitable. An isolated experience such as the one described need not result in a spat, but if the conflict of interest occurs repeatedly one is likely to say: "Whenever I want one thing, you want another." To which the other is likely to reply: "How about you? You never want what I want."

Situational limitations. Even though two people find it pleasant to be in each other's company, some resentment may remain because of this restriction. Although one enjoys being selected as a "steady," some desire may remain for "being in circulation." Occasionally, the latter desire may break into consciousness, especially when the "real person" breaks through one's idealization. It has been stated above that two persons in love idealize each other—do not see each other as they actually are. But on occasion, actual characteristics manifest themselves in such force that awareness of them comes as a shock or disillusionment and is experienced as a frustration. There may also be sexual frustration. Becoming sexually aroused by each other and yet finding oneself restricted may lead to tension and anger, even though the couple has decided to abide by society's moral code.

Projection. A number of spats are due to the mechanism of projection—that is, attributing to someone else tendencies, motives, ideas, feelings, and beliefs of one's self. When certain characteristics are thought to be undesirable, a person is often unwilling to acknowledge them as his own and, therefore, is likely to ascribe them to someone else. As long as two people who go steady do not know each other sufficiently well, projection is likely to operate. It will underlie many of their "misunderstandings." For example, John, before going steady with Joan, dated Harriet frequently. Sometimes his thoughts go back to Harriet. He remembers the good times they used to have together. He would like to date her again, but he knows that his doing so would displease Joan, and so he suppresses his desire. One day he sees Joan talk to a former boy friend and immediately accuses her of disloyalty. She resents his remarks, and a quarrel is on.

Attitude toward Spats. Young people looking upon quarrels as inevitable are not seriously disturbed when quarrels occur. In a sense, these spats are desirable, for they indicate areas of conflict which should receive attention if a more harmonious association is to prevail. Most young couples, while perhaps not aware of this function of spats, react unconsciously to the need for adjustment. For instance, a couple may have had a severe quarrel. They break up in a great huff and she bids him good night saying, "I will never speak to you again." But any household that has watched a distressed young daughter go through the resulting crisis knows that afterwards she will usually stay within inches of the telephone and forbid any member of the family to tie up the line. And that family can estimate the lapse of time before the call comes in by taking into account the distance from their house to the nearest drugstore with a telephone booth.

How Spats Should Be Handled. Since the ultimate result of lovers' spats should be to make closer association between the lovers possible, certain rules should be kept in mind:

(1) If possible, the point of friction should be discussed only after anger has subsided, especially where it is intense, for in extreme anger a person may do or say things which may "cut too deep."

(2) The reason for expression should not be merely personal relief from tension without regard for its effect on the other person. To get relief, a person often will be brutal in his remarks and afterwards will say: "Now I feel better." But how about the other person?

(3) In quarrels, a person should not seek out weak spots or painful areas of the other person. Such an approach smacks of sadism.

(4) The areas of conflict should be discovered first and remarks confined to those areas. If the friction is in the periphery of personality, the center should not be attacked. If the cause is an undesirable habit, for instance, the *total* character should not be criticized. If it is a faulty opinion, the person should not be called a fool. If he is ill-informed about *one* matter, he is not therefore a "stupid peasant." If he cannot appreciate the motive for one act, he is not therefore totally lacking in insight. If he acts once without considering the interests of the other, he is not therefore totally selfish.

(5) Other persons should be left out. Seldom is a problem solved by telling a person that he is just like his father or that she is just like her mother. Comparison with anyone else is likely to lead away from the problem at hand and raise unrelated issues.

(6) Issues should be settled permanently. Once a problem has been thoroughly aired and accepted by both as settled, it should

never be reintroduced into a new quarrel. Doing so is frustrating and invariably leads to more serious and prolonged conflicts.

(7) Time should be given for "cooling off," especially to the person who feels he has been wronged. In a quarrel, physiological conditions are brought about by the dominance of the sympathetic nervous system. It will take some time for tension to reduce sufficiently to let the parasympathetic nervous system function. These processes are beyond the control of the individual.

(8) Waiting until the first tensions have been relaxed does not mean that frustrations should be permitted to accumulate. Tensions not periodically released have a tendency to become integrated into larger and larger systems of frustration and tension and may ultimately lead to deep-seated hate.

It should be remembered that spats are symptoms of friction, that they are inevitable, and that they should be resolved in such a manner as to bring about more harmonious adjustment in the future.

The Financial Problem in Courtship

In our society, the man is expected to defray the expenses of courtship, which, depending on the length of the courtship and the frequency with which two people see each other, may represent a considerable amount of money. For those who have a sizeable allowance or an independent income, no problem exists; but for others it is a serious one.

In many cases, a desirable solution may be an *entertainment fund,* to which both contribute, not on a fifty-fifty basis, but on the basis of their respective incomes. The only serious objection to such an arrangement is that it is not in accordance with custom. Its advantages, however, are many. (1) It is a step toward greater equality between men and women. Through it a woman can assume responsibilities in keeping with the equal privileges she seeks. (2) It provides opportunity for each to see how the other will manage money and thus will reveal his or her attitude toward money. (3) Each is free to make suggestions as to how to spend the money budgeted for a month. For when the girl does not know how much money is available, she may feel hesitant about making suggestions for fear of being looked upon as extravagant. The man thus is better able to learn her real interests. (4) Since the couple has more money available, they can do more things together. (5) A joint fund will make it unnecessary for the girl occasionally to contribute money under the table or to buy tickets for the theater or a concert. This practice, often looked upon by the girl as a special contribution for which she should have special credit, may result in embarrassment for the young man. (6) The young man who spends only his money on the girl may regard it as an investment, from which he expects some kind of return. And the girl in turn may believe that she owes such favors to him. (7) When a man has spent considerable sums of money on her, a girl may feel obligated to continue the relationship into marriage, even though she may not want to marry the man.

To the authors' knowledge, almost all couples who have had experience with a joint entertainment fund have found the arrangement highly satisfactory. Because of prevailing custom, it is usually up to the girl to suggest such an arrangement. If she is seriously interested in a young man and cherishes her dignity, she will profit most from it.

PROBLEMS IN TERMINATION OF COURTSHIP

Courtship is a transition period; it will end either in engagement or in separation. In some cases, one party may be ready for engagement while the other is not, often resulting in a serious problem, especially if there is outside pressure. There is no general solution to such a problem. But pressure exerted on the person who is not ready for engagement rarely helps. Any decision must be arrived at by mutual agreement. The young man who is not ready for engagement should bear in mind that if the courtship is unduly prolonged and ends in separation, any resulting disadvantage is usually greater for the girl. She may have reached an age when it is harder to meet another prospective husband; and by custom, her initiative in looking for another mate is severely restricted.

The ultimate aim of courtship is marriage; the function of courtship is to discover mutual compatibility. If incompatibility is discovered, courtship should be terminated. A couple that is incompatible before marriage almost invariably will be incompatible after marriage. Incompatibility is indicated when a couple constantly, or more often than not, frustrate each other. Quarrels and loss of interest in each other are symptoms of incompatibility. Breaking up may be painful, but not so painful as forced association. In most cases, it is advisable to make a clean break and thus avoid constant hurting and being hurt. The couple may well remain on good terms one with the other, realizing that neither one of them may be to blame. Both may possess fine personalities which somehow are not compatible.

Another problem arises when one partner is convinced that courtship should be terminated short of engagement and the other wants it to continue. In such cases, the relationship must also be broken off, even though the experience is painful for one of the two. It is better for one to suffer temporarily than for both to spend a lifetime of misery and unhappiness. In cases where one, usually the young man, threatens suicide if the courtship is ended, termination is all the more necessary; continuing the relationship would only mean enslavement for the girl. Threats of suicide seldom result in suicidal action; if they do, the real cause lies in the maladjustment of the person who took his life.

The following case illustrates how a prolonged courtship was dissolved, to the benefit of each person involved:

> Janice H. finished high school at the age of 17 and went to work as a secretary in a small firm. It was there that she met and started dating Mel, age 19, whose background was similar to her own. They had many common interests, attended a young people's Sunday evening club at a church, and took a course together at a nearby evening school. For a year their courtship went along steadily and smoothly, until Mel began to talk about becoming formally engaged. At first, Janice seemed to be happy about the idea; then she became depressed. This change in her disturbed Mel. Finally they agreed to talk to a marriage counselor. They were both sincere persons, each eager not to hurt the other through any change in their relationship. At the interview Janice said:

"I've had a wonderful year dating Mel. We've been good for each other; we've learned to do many things together, to co-operate and to share; yet, when we reached the point of actually becoming engaged, which, of course, should lead to marriage, I was frightened. I guess I'm too young yet, or at least I feel as if I haven't had enough experience to feel sure. Maybe I need to date other fellows more, so that I'll be certain. The same is true for Mel. We've dated so steadily —maybe he needs to know other girls too."

Mel added the following during his part of the conference:

"I feel I really love Janice, and yet it is true that we've been more or less 'growing up' together. It sounds cruel to say it, but maybe we've been preparing each other to make good mates for someone else. I know I'll make a better husband as a result of this year of courtship with Jan. Even if I should lose her, I can't lose all the wonderful things we've done for each other."

Since their company had been wanting Mel to replace its field representative for two months, the opportunity of a trial separation was pointed out to them. Mel accepted the offer and consequently was out of town for most of that period. Janice tried to go out more; she joined two clubs, which made new contacts for her. At the end of the two months, both knew the answer. They had served each other well in the ways that the period of courtship can help toward preparation for marriage. They were able to ease out of their relationship without hurting each other. Janice married another man; Mel, another girl. Today the two couples make a congenial foursome at bridge and are the best of friends.

INTERPRETATIVE SUMMARY

1. In courtship, two persons limit their dating to each other. Courtship does not center on immediate pleasurable activities but looks toward possible marriage.

2. Courtship enhances the ego because it gives both persons the feeling of having been selected; it promotes the "we" feeling and provides opportunity for more intimate acquaintanceship.

3. In addition to the problem of petting, a couple going steady is likely to face the problem of premarital sexual intercourse. Aside from the mores, a couple must consider objectively the effect of premarital intercourse upon their personalities, as well as upon their relationship.

4. Lovers' spats are almost inevitable. If they are properly handled, a couple invariably profits from them, because such quarrels may indicate areas of conflict.

5. A joint recreational fund may be the answer to financial problems which are likely to arise in a prolonged courtship where resources are limited.

6. Termination of courtship by breaking the relationship is advisable in some cases, in spite of its accompanying unpleasantness.

THOUGHT QUESTIONS AND PROJECTS

1. What are the fundamental differences between the casual dating relationship and one of "going steady"?

2. What are the advantages and disadvantages of "going steady"? On your campus, approximately how many dates do couples have before they are considered to be "going steady"?

3. If members of your class represent both rural and urban areas, inquire to see whether there are marked differences by localities in the kinds of social activities engaged in during the process of courtship.

4. Is there merit in continuing the experience of courtship with one's mate even after marriage?

5. What do you consider the major problems of the period of courtship?

6. Point out specific techniques and attitudes of co-operation learned during the period of courtship which help prepare a couple for marriage.

SUGGESTED READINGS FOR FURTHER STUDY

Baber, Ray E., *Marriage and the Family*, 2nd ed., New York, McGraw-Hill Book Company, 1953.
　　Chapter 4. Mate Selection and Courtship.
　　Chapter 5. Mate Selection and Courtship (Cont'd).
Bowman, Henry A., *Marriage for Moderns*, 3rd ed., New York, McGraw-Hill Book Company, 1954.
　　Chapter 6. Courtship and Engagement.
Koos, Earl Lomon, *Marriage*, New York, Henry Holt & Company, 1953.
　　Chapter 6. Before Marriage: Courtship.

Landis, Judson T., and Mary G. Landis, *Building a Successful Marriage*, 2nd ed., New York, Prentice-Hall, 1953.
  Chapter 8. Premarital Sexual Relations.
  Chapter 9. Mixed Marriages.
Magoun, F. Alexander, *Love and Marriage*, New York, Harper & Brothers, 1948.
  Chapter 6. Courtship.
Merrill, Francis E., *Courtship and Marriage*, New York, The Dryden Press, 1949.
  Chapter 1. Courtship as a Social Relationship.
Skidmore, Rex A., and Anthon S. Cannon, *Building Your Marriage*, New York, Harper & Brothers, 1951.
  Chapter 5. Courtship and the Growth of Love.
Smith, E., and J. H. G. Monane, "Courtship Values in a Youth Sample," *American Sociological Review*, 1953, 32:76–81.
Stokes, Walter R., and David R. Mace, "Premarital Sexual Behavior," *Marriage and Family Living*, 1953, 15:234–249.

11

ENGAGEMENT

A couple is considered engaged as soon as they have reached a definite decision to marry. Most couples seal this decision by some token, usually a diamond ring, and make a public announcement. It is for both a happy occasion in the conviction of having

"Oh, George! It's smaller than I'd hoped for, but larger than I'd expected!"

Ben Roth and The Saturday Evening Post.

attained an important goal in their lives. It enhances their prestige in their own eyes, as well as in the eyes of their friends. They feel greater security in each other because more than previously they move together toward a definite goal. People around them are aware of their new status, a fact which in itself reinforces their attempt to become better adjusted to each other. All the factors mentioned in connection with courtship operating to bring about greater harmony between the two are now intensified. There is a stronger "we" feeling and more co-operation.

Engagement serves two useful functions: (1) It permits more intensive and extensive personal adjustment. (2) It permits planning for marriage.

A More Intensive and Extensive Personal Adjustment

Revealing Secrets. In establishing a new unit, a couple faces the problem of how to create this new whole and yet maintain individuality, or uniqueness. Each individual must "open up" to the other, and yet must be left an individual core; otherwise, one or the other personality will be "absorbed" by the partner and thus lose its capacity and ability to enrich the union. We deal here with intangibles which are nevertheless real to everyone who has ever entered into an intimate fellowship with an individual or a group. An illustration may help us understand the situation. In a democratic organization, over-all interests are paramount, yet the rights of the individual are always safeguarded. In a totalitarian organization, the individual does not count; he is merely an instrument or a tool to be used by the state. If marriage is to provide the greatest happiness for both partners, it must be democratic. A person must somehow remain a distinct individual and, at the same time, must sufficiently reveal himself to his prospective mate so that together they can function as a real unit.

The immediate question concerns the extent to which a person shall share his intimate thoughts and experiences with his partner. This revelation is especially important when it involves secrets which, when known, may have the effect of lessening the partner's

esteem for the one who confides. Only a general guiding principle
can be given: Tell everything which, if concealed, might have a
detrimental effect on the new union. The individual, of course, is
still left with the difficult task of determining what is and what is
not detrimental. Since each case is unique, and since decisions
cannot be made without a thorough knowledge of both personalities, only a few general suggestions are offered here.

Each partner has a right to know if there is some weak hereditary strain in the other's family background, such as the prevalence of physical or mental illness. Such knowledge, while it may
not prevent marriage, may influence the couple's decision about
having or not having children. If either party has had some serious
illness of which the other is not aware, this fact should be revealed. Such illnesses include venereal disease, heart disease, tuberculosis, or any infectious disease which has subsided temporarily but may flare up later. A criminal record, flagrant previous
immorality, serious mental disturbance, alcoholism, and drug addiction also belong in this group. Financial obligations or indebt-
edness which may encumber the union should be made known
during engagement.

Because of our moral code, or, more precisely, because of
our double standard of morality, revealing previous sex experiences presents a special problem. Should such experiences be
revealed? The answer will depend upon the motive behind such
revelation. If the motive is to bring about better adjustment to
each other, then such revelations are justified. It is unwise and
unfair for a man to talk about his previous sex experience in
terms of conquest, as a means of enhancing his ego, while expecting his fiancée to talk about her own in terms of confession, as if
admitting that she did something of which she should be ashamed.

Whether the woman should tell her fiancé about previous
intimacies cannot be answered without qualification. The following factors, however, should be taken into consideration. What
effect will it have on him? Some men are mature enough to
regard whatever the fiancée has done in the past as her own
affair. If such a man respects a woman enough to become engaged
to her, he trusts her to have conducted her personal life on a
mature basis. She may or may not mention her previous sex

experiences, but if she does, her telling should merely aim to complete the couple's information about each other. As a rule, a gentleman does not ask such personal questions of his fiancée. The man who does ask is very likely oversensitive about such matters, in which case such information will hurt his ego, for he wants to be the "one and only." He pictures his fiancée as a girl who has had no life of her own before she met him.

What if the man should discover the lack of virginity at the couple's first intercourse after marriage? Many a woman is troubled by the question of whether a man can tell. We may note that the presence or absence of the hymen is no indication of previous sex experiences. A woman who has reason to believe that her fiancé would be upset by knowing of her previous sex experience, and who fears that such information might come to him after marriage, will be wise to tell him about it beforehand; otherwise, their marriage may suffer. If he is told and cannot accept the fact, he should be free to withdraw from the engagement.

Some women have guilt feelings about previous sex experiences and believe they need confession to get relief. Many people, if not most, are brought up with the attitude that a wrongdoing must be confessed. A child breaking a rule learns that, if he confesses, the consequences of his infraction are somehow lighter. A woman might confess to someone, other than her husband, whose confidence and judgment she respects. This confession does not risk giving her fiancé the feeling that she is a moral weakling; nor does she expose herself to consequences which might far outweigh the significance of the act confessed. Depending upon her background, she might confess to the family physician, a priest, rabbi, minister, psychiatrist, clinical psychologist, or marriage counselor. In most cases, such confession will give relief from tensions produced by guilt feelings.

Bringing in Family and Friends. No person lives in a social vacuum before marriage; everyone but a hermit belongs all his life to some social unit or units. After engagement, however, even more than during courtship, a couple forms its own center. Friends and relatives who were in the immediate center now move to the periphery, but they exercise some pull on the new unit and, therefore, must be taken into consideration by an engaged couple.

Each fiancé ordinarily marries also the other's family. The characters and attitudes of its members are of great importance, especially if the couple plans to live in close proximity to them. The affianced is entitled to know them well in order to facilitate the best possible adjustments. A "family skeleton" should be

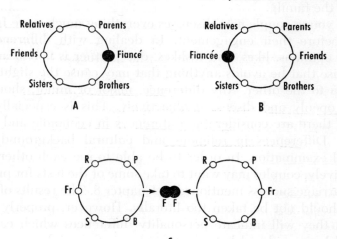

FIGURE 9. In A and B, social life of fiancé and fiancée is linked to that of family, relatives, and friends. In C, their social life centers on each other and others move to the periphery.

made known. Every attempt should be made to get the approval of close members of the family for the engagement. How much trouble nonacceptance of a fiancé can cause will be discussed later. We should note here that many a happy marriage has been ruined by in-laws.

Personal friends also must be taken into consideration, for they should now become the friends of both partners and enrich their united life. Future happiness is already in jeopardy if one partner says, "After we are married, you must give up your old friends, because I do not like them."

Once the engaged couple is accepted by the respective relatives and friends, general adjustment is facilitated. There is less acting and more naturalness. When the young man calls at his fiancée's home, her father is not immediately chased out of the living room, nor is he made to change from sport shirt to dress shirt. The mother may not even change her dress. Little brothers and sisters do not have to force a smile at each other, but may go on with their quarreling. The household is not rearranged before the fiancé steps in—he is well acquainted and is already feeling like one of the family.

The young couple now discusses everything much more frankly than before their engagement. In dealing with differences in tastes, opinions, likes, and dislikes, one partner is not so anxious to please that he avoids anything that may cause the slightest irritation to the other. Any difference, major or minor, should be faced openly and discussed objectively. This is especially true where there are considerable differences in economic and social status. Differences in religious and cultural background need careful examination. In order to be able to see each other more objectively, couples may want to take some of the tests for predicting marriage success mentioned in Chapter 8. The results of these tests should not be taken too literally. However, properly interpreted they will indicate personality differences which can and should be considered before marriage.

Sexual Intimacy. Since the fiancés will see each other more now and are likely to be often by themselves, the question of sexual intimacy will be more pressing. Some may take the attitude that they are "just as good as married" and engage in sexual intercourse. It certainly is not true that they are "as good as married." Engagement should and must be considered a preliminary step to marriage and cannot exclude the possibility of its eventual termination. For this reason, all the points for and against premarital intercourse still hold true. Whatever a couple decides should be based on the fact that they are not married.

Motives for Marriage. The couple should consider seriously what they expect to get out of their marriage (see Chapter 5). They may wish to list all their motives and arrange them in the order of their importance. These lists should be compared and major differences thoroughly discussed.

Parental Home as a Model. Suppose a young man who comes from a fine and happy home plans to be married. His ideal is to model his future home after that of his parents. On the surface, this goal seems to be commendable, but in reality it is undesirable. Even though he knows much about his parental home, he probably knows little about the intimate adjustments between his parents, certainly not enough to guide him in solving problems that will be unique to his own home. For this reason, he is likely to be tense and uncertain. Inclined to cast himself in the role of his wife's mentor, he automatically would give her a position inferior to him. His wife, in turn, would feel uncertain and insecure in her actions. Her husband could not give her clear and definite instruction. She constantly would imagine what someone else might do in a given situation. She would soon come to feel that she is not herself but her mother-in-law. Such conditions result only in resentment and bitterness.

It is equally undesirable to try to create a new home opposite in kind to that of parents whose homes were unhappy. All that was said above applies here, too, in a negative sense. In addition, there is a constant feeling of being watched for errors and an oversensibility to any mistakes. As an example, one may cite a young man who came from a home broken by his mother's infidelity. As a result, he doubted his wife's loyalty. He was constantly on the alert to find out whether or not she was overfriendly to other men. In his state of anxiety, he interpreted any kindly gesture toward them as a real threat to the security of his home.

No one can enter marriage without having been somewhat molded by the atmosphere of his parental house. This influence may serve to enrich the concept of the home and family, but it should never restrain a couple from establishing their own individual pattern. Partners in marriage should have the privilege of expressing themselves freely in the creation of a new familial unit. Just as every personality is unique, so every new family created by two individuals must also be unique.

PLANNING FOR MARRIAGE

After marriage, several definite changes will take place in a young couple's mode of living. Typical changes which should be anticipated and planned for involve economic support, sexual relations, and children.

Economic Support. Perhaps the first important economic decision concerns the standard of living. A couple can be happy on any standard of living. The problem becomes serious when either or both must adjust to a lower standard than that to which they are accustomed. The question to be answered is: Will the satisfaction gained from being married outweigh the privation to be incurred? The standard can be decided upon when satisfactory information is obtained from a reliable source as to how much it will cost the couple to live together in keeping with their income and savings.

Working Wives. In order to maintain a satisfactory living standard, it may be necessary for the wife to work, at least for some time. Here the financial aspect is not the only one to be considered. First, will the wife's working mean a loss of status for the husband? The belief that a man should not marry until he can afford to support a wife and family is still widespread. If either partner so believes, the wife's working may mean lowering of self-respect. The opinions of friends and relatives are also to be considered here. Furthermore, work after marriage involves additional responsibilities for the wife; it is not easy to be in a full-time job and do the necessary housework at home. She may soon become so exhausted that she may not have energy for companionship with her husband. To lighten her burden, a husband must be willing to co-operate in household duties, for which he may often have to acquire many new skills.

It is important, too, for the fiancé to remember that a woman may dislike housekeeping and household management and favor, instead, work outside the home while delegating household responsibilities to employed help. She also may possess talents and ambitions which she feels must be realized or attained. Such pursuits will of course limit the time available for housework. The prospective husband should know his future wife's vocational needs in order to void later conflicts over the subject. To insist that the wife give up her self-expression in some career may dampen her initiative and crush her spirit. Some satisfactory solution can usually be found, but the problem must be faced frankly *before* marriage.

Information about Sexual Relation. Marriage counselors are frequently impressed by the appalling number of couples who have been married for some time (and even have had several children) and yet remain ignorant about essential sexual information. Every prospective husband and wife should become familiar with the detailed structure and function of his own and the mate's sexual apparatus. Such information can be gained by reading one or several books specifically written for this purpose.[1] A list of such books will be found in Appendix A.

Prevention of Conception. It is important for any couple planning marriage to decide whether they wish to practice birth control. To decide properly, they must know the meaning of birth control and must be informed about the reasons for and against its practice. For a detailed discussion of birth control see Chapter 17.

Number of Children. It is desirable for a couple to agree before marriage on the approximate number of children they wish to have. Sometimes one person is set on having no children at all, or at most one or two, while the mate may want many children. On the surface, this may not appear to be a serious problem, and yet misunderstandings and conflicts frequently grow out of such disagreement.

---

[1] Especially valuable is Abraham Stone and Hannah Stone, *A Marriage Manual,* New York, Simon & Schuster, 1952. In this book the authors visualize a young couple about to be married, who come to them with specific questions normally asked by any prospective bride and groom. The answers are based on scientific knowledge and are given in a simple, straightforward manner.

Planning for the Wedding

The cost and size of the wedding, as well as the matter of who should officiate, naturally should be agreed upon by the prospective bride and groom. Wise parents leave these decisions to the couple. But in all too many cases the beauty of a wedding is marred by conflicting parental tastes and opinions. Should there be differences of opinion about these matters, it is wise for the bridegroom to accede as much as possible to the wishes of the bride. It is almost invariably true that the wedding has greater emotional and sentimental significance for the bride than for the groom. In the ensuing years she will relive this experience innumerable times, especially when she attends the wedding of a friend and that of her own daughter. *Her* wedding should give her the maximum of joy and happiness. The groom should remember that, during the nuptial planning and the wedding, his bride is the center of attention and that soon after the wedding she will move to the periphery and he to the center.

Immediate Preparations for Marriage

Physical Examination. By physical examination is meant not merely a blood test for venereal disease (which test is required in most states before a license is issued), but a thorough physical checkup. Ideally, such an examination should take place even before engagement, but since this is seldom feasible, it should be arranged soon after engagement. The man should be examined for sterility. One out of ten married couples cannot have children. Contrary to popular belief, inability to have children may be due to the husband's sterility. The bride's examination should include pelvic measurements to determine ease or difficulty of childbirth. It may be possible to learn whether the woman can have children by normal delivery or whether Caesarean section will be needed. Such information may determine how many children, if any, a couple may decide upon.

A good medical examination will inspire confidence and remove many worries and fears. It may call attention to deficiencies which prospective mates must consider before marriage or have treated.

If birth control is favored by the couple, the bride should go either to a qualified physician or to a birth-control clinic to be instructed fully in the proper use of contraceptives.

Seeing a Marriage Counselor. Since marriage involves not only physical but also psychological or personal adjustment between two people, many questions to which the couple cannot find satisfactory answers in books on marriage may arise. As a rule, the couple will have discussed special questions with older or younger married people, whose answers, while sometimes helpful, are ordinarily not authoritative enough to give satisfaction. It is often wise, therefore, to consult a qualified marriage counselor. In Appendix C, the reader will find listed agencies through which he can get the proper information. In some cases, seeing a counselor may require a trip to a larger city, but such a trip is well worth the expense.

The problems taken up with the marriage counselor will depend, of course, upon the individual couple. Attitudes and relationship to in-laws are among the most important ones. Often one or the other partner has questions which cannot be discussed frankly and objectively with the mate. The marriage counselor is in a position to give unbiased suggestions. The young man who has a life insurance policy with his mother as beneficiary is an example. His fiancée may intimate that the policy should be changed to make her the beneficiary after marriage. He may find it difficult to discuss with her this and similar matters in which his mother represents a possible opposition. His divided sense of loyalty hampers his ability to view fairly all factors involved. In such cases he may need an unbiased person to help him make the decision. (Other problems with in-laws will be discussed in a later chapter.)

The marriage counselor is interested in the *personality make-up* of the couple. He may want to give them personality tests, or refer them to a specialist. In some cases, the counselor may discover serious emotional immaturity, which may require prolonged therapy and consequently a postponement of marriage.

The counselor will discuss *attitudes toward sex*. All too many people are brought up with the feeling that sex is inherently bad. It is not an easy matter to overcome such an attitude in marriage; advice given by a marriage counselor usually helps.

On the whole, the marriage counselor can help prevent many problems in marriage before they arise. The greatest obstacle to consulting a counselor is not so much the fact that there are few of them, but that people somehow consider it humiliating to take their problems to him. They take pride in solving their own problems. This is, of course, false pride. Too often, a couple will go to a marriage counselor only if they run into serious difficulty *after* marriage. But one should remember that "an ounce of prevention is better than a pound of cure."

In some cases, a couple may need to consult a specialist in addition to a marriage counselor—a specialist on human heredity, gynecology, psychiatry, or law. Such consultation may save money and worry in the future.

LENGTH OF ENGAGEMENT

Terman and his associates found little relationship between length of premarital acquaintance and marital happiness; however, they found a significant relationship between length of engagement and marital happiness. The happiness score for husbands who were engaged from 0 to 2 months was 64.7; for those who were engaged 5 years or more, 73.4. The score for women engaged from 0 to 2 months was 66.5; for those engaged from 1 to 2 years, 71.8. The difference is not great, and yet it is one of the largest differences found by Terman. Terman also states: "Right judgments are about as likely to be made within the first year of acquaintance as thereafter, the evidence for this being somewhat stronger for the wives than for the husbands. . . . Women can size up a prospective mate about as successfully in one year as the man is able to in three years." [2]

[2] By permission from *Psychological Factors in Marital Happiness*, by Lewis M. Terman *et al.* Copyright, 1938. McGraw-Hill Book Company, Inc. P. 198.

Burgess and Cottrell found a consistent relationship between both length of acquaintance and length of engagement and marital adjustment. It is interesting to note that the percentages for those engaged 3 to 8 months and those not engaged at all are just about the same. Of the former, 32 per cent made a poor adjustment, 27 per cent, a fair adjustment, and 41 per cent, a good adjustment. For the latter, the respective percentages were 36 per cent, 26 per cent, and 38 per cent. The percentages for those engaged 2 years or more were 12 per cent poor, 24 per cent fair, and 64 per cent good adjustment.[3]

Probably the mere length of engagement is not so important for successful adjustment in marriage as is the qualitative relationship between the engaged persons. That time is required to achieve such a relationship is obvious; how much time depends upon a number of factors, such as (1) the length of time the prospective mates have known each other before engagement; (2) how often and under what varied circumstances they have seen each other during engagement; (3) similarities and differences in their personalities; (4) number and kinds of conflicts encountered; (5) how well they are qualified to judge each other's personality and, in general, to what extent their philosophies of life coincide.

The engagement should last as long, and only as long, as the couple need to accomplish the purposes of engagement discussed above. Apparently this should be a matter of months up to about a year. But it is important to note that the above studies were made some years ago, and that since then young people associate with each other on a more realistic basis and without many of the old inhibitions.

Prolonging an engagement entails some disadvantages. Breaking an engagement which has continued over a long period of time works a great hardship on the woman, because her opportunity for finding another mate will have lessened considerably. A long engagement will invariably be a strain on both persons if they have decided not to engage in intercourse before marriage. Furthermore, both may come to take their engagement as a matter-of-fact association causing tension because of unsettled

[3] Ernest W. Burgess and Leonard S. Cottrell, Jr., *Predicting Success or Failure in Marriage*, New York, Prentice-Hall, Inc., 1939, pp. 164–168.

conditions. It becomes a transition period which seems endless. The couple have an uncertain status, neither single nor married. Finally, their association may be marred by recurrent periods of doubt.

Some adverse effects of a long engagement are well illustrated in the following case:

> Miss T., age 26, came into a counselor's office, displayed a beautiful diamond ring, and opened the conversation: "Do you see this ring? I've been wearing it for two years. I've decided an engagement ring can become a symbol of isolation. When I took it two years ago, I never dreamed I'd be wearing it forever without a wedding ring. Following a rather brief courtship, Charles and I were madly in love, and so he insisted that I take his ring. I was hesitant even then, because he didn't want to discuss any possible plans for marriage. He said that he only wanted to be formally engaged. At that time, he was in government work which moved him from place to place, and so he claimed he didn't want to marry until he could locate permanently—which he thought would be a matter of only two or three months from then. But we've gone on and on like this. He is away most of the time, and I see him only rarely, so that socially I'm left out of everything for lack of an escort. I resent the fact that I've been forced to assume so much responsibility for his widowed mother, who lives a few blocks from me. I do shopping for her, chauffeur her around, and handle many business details for her. I have a feeling that she watches every move I make to be sure I'm loyal to Charles.
>
> "Every time he comes home he insists that it won't be much longer until we can be married. He gets angry if I try to talk about our future and says: 'What difference does it make? We are *definitely* engaged; everybody knows it and that's as sure as being married.'
>
> "I've reached the point where I feel that I'm just being used for his convenience. I'm already 26 years old and anyone knows a girl's chances to meet a desirable husband decrease every year at my age. My love for him is cooling off; I feel that I'm losing out in every respect. As long as I wear this ring, I am tied—all chances are closed to me. I don't even have Charles, because he is away so much of the time. I don't see why we should call ourselves engaged. My friends think we should break up for my sake."

THE BREAKING OF AN ENGAGEMENT

It must always be possible for either partner to break off an engagement; otherwise, its function as an experimental adjustment to marriage would not be served. General principles that should govern the breaking of an engagement are difficult to state. Mere feelings of doubt on the part of one or the other person do not seem to be a sufficient reason for breaking an engagement, for such feelings are almost invariably to be expected when people are confronted by serious decisions. The more conscientious a person is, the more likely he is to have doubts; only the lighthearted do not experience any. However, if these doubts are persistent and are due to important changes in one or the other person, they could lead to the breaking of an engagement. Loss of affection, crippling accidents, ill health, drastic economic loss, and discovery of basic character defects are changes that may cause such a break. (Here we should emphasize what was said before: *never marry another out of a sense of duty* or because of sympathy.) Each case naturally must be decided on its own merits. This is especially true when parents are unalterably opposed to the marriage. Before breaking an engagement for any reason, a couple may want to discuss their problem with a marriage counselor.

If an engagement is to be broken, it is wise to let the woman announce it. In this manner, less stigma will be attached to her, and she will find it easier to secure another mate.

Interpretative Summary

1. Engagement between two persons is a more or less public declaration of intention to marry.

2. During engagement a couple should reveal to each other anything and everything which might have an adverse effect on their marital happiness.

3. Whether to reveal sex experiences with anyone other than the one engaged to is a problem. Because of differences in attitude about the matter, no general rule can be laid down, except that whatever is related should not take the form of a confession.

4. During engagement, a couple not only must learn to know each other better but also must have an opportunity to get acquainted with each other's friends and relatives.

5. During this period, a couple must also reach an agreement about anything pertaining to their future standard of living, re-

lationship to in-laws, spacing of children, and type of wedding.

6. Any couple will profit not only from a thorough premarital medical examination but also from consultation with a qualified marriage counselor.

7. Engagement is a transition stage and therefore should not last too long.

8. If during engagement serious obstacles to a happy union are discovered, the engagement should be broken.

Thought Questions and Projects

1. What do you consider to be some typical problems or areas of differences which should be discussed and agreed upon by an engaged couple?

2. Do you think long separations during engagement defeat the real purpose of the engagement period?

3. Ask several married couples of your acquaintance the following questions:

    (a) How long were they engaged before marriage?

    (b) If they could relive this period, would they choose to shorten it, extend it, or keep it the same length? If any change one way or the other is suggested, reasons for such may be helpful to know.

4. Do you think the engagement period justifies more intimacy between couples than does the period of courtship?

5. Interview several individuals who are or have been married to find out if they had any premarital counseling. If so, in what areas? If not, is it their opinion that marital adjustment would have been smoother for them if they had had premarital counseling?

6. What reasons do you hear given most frequently for the breaking of engagements? How can an engagement be broken so as to cause the least hurt to all concerned?

7. Observe class reactions, especially noting any differences between male and female responses to the question, whether engaged couples should confess all to each other concerning

(a) their past experiences—especially with persons of the opposite sex.

(b) known physical and hereditary defects.

(c) "skeletons" in the family closet, etc.

8. Compare answers from several engaged couples as to what they *expect* out of marriage.

9. Select one or two controversial topics related to the engagement period as reported by Burgess and Wallin (see Suggested Readings for Further Study). Get class reaction to these studies.

SUGGESTED READINGS FOR FURTHER STUDY

Adams, Clifford R., *Preparing for Marriage,* New York, E. P. Dutton & Company, 1951.
Chapter 12. Before and During Engagement.
Burgess, Ernest W., and Paul Wallin, *Engagement and Marriage,* New York, E. B. Lippincott Company, 1953.
Chapter 8. Disagreements and Stresses in Engagement.
Chapter 9. Broken Engagements.
Chapter 10. Measuring Success in Engagement.
Chapter 11. Sex and Engagement.
Chapter 12. Assessing Premarital Intercourse.
Christensen, Harold T., *Marriage Analysis,* New York, The Ronald Press Company, 1950.
Chapter 9. The Transition into Marriage.
Duvall, Evelyn Millis, and Reuben Hill, *When You Marry,* rev. ed., Boston, D. C. Heath & Company, 1953.
Chapter 5. The Meaning of an Engagement.
Fishbein, Morris, and Ernest Burgess, eds., *Successful Marriage,* rev. ed., Garden City, New York, Doubleday & Company, 1955.
Chapter 4. Premarital Sex Relationships, by Anna O. Stephens, M.D.
Chapter 5. Premarital Physical Examination, by Lovett Dewess, M.D.
Himes, Norman E., *Your Marriage,* New York, Rinehart & Company, 1940.
Chapter 2. Sex Problems of Modern Youth.
Chapter 3. Premarital Sex Relations.
Chapter 7. Engagement: Personality Testing.
Chapter 8. Engagement: Its Planning Opportunities.
Koos, Earl Lomon, *Marriage,* New York, Henry Holt & Company, 1953.
Chapter 7. Before Marriage: The Engagement.
Landis, Paul H., *Your Marriage and Family Living,* New York, McGraw-Hill Book Company, 1946.
Chapter 12. The Question of Having Children Should Be Discussed before Marriage,

Locke, Harvey J., *Predicting Adjustment in Marriage*, New York, Henry Holt & Company, 1951.

    Chapter 5. Courtship and Engagement.

Magoun, Alexander F., *Love and Marriage*, New York, Harper & Brothers, 1948.

    Chapter 7. The Period of Engagement.

Stone, Hannah M., and Abraham Stone, *A Marriage Manual*, rev. ed., New York, Simon & Schuster, 1952.

    Chapter 1. Fitness for Marriage.

12

WEDDING AND HONEYMOON

THE WEDDING

Meaning. A wedding is a symbol through which the bride and groom declare before a legally authorized official and witnesses that they have accepted each other as husband and wife. It is an event of significance for (1) the couple, (2) the parents, (3) the civil authority, (4) the church, and (5) society.

For the Bride and Groom. The wedding ceremony does not mean the same thing, of course, for every couple. Much depends upon the personalities of the couple and upon circumstances surrounding the marriage. What is said here, therefore, applies in varying degrees to various couples.

First of all, the wedding signifies a great change in a couple's life: They are leaving the single state and entering into married life. Henceforth they will be thought of as belonging together. It is the end of one period in their life and the beginning of a new one. Each will play a new role with the other and in the eyes of society. It means, too, the end of a long period of waiting, a period characterized by hopes and aspirations, but also by some uncertainty, some hesitation, some doubt, and possibly some fear. As the time of the wedding approaches, tensions usually develop. The giving and receiving of vows serves to release this tension and, for this reason, is a thrilling experience. The experience is fatiguing and yet at the same time relaxing and comforting. It is followed by a feeling of accomplishment and a new sense of security. The bride and groom may experience elation, but as well some anxiety because of the newness and uniqueness of the event. For both, it is a fulfillment. There is in each a feeling of self-realization and a sense of really being a person who counts, a person who is somehow important, whose being genuinely matters.

The wedding also means complete union, without any reservations or feelings of guilt. Sex urges can be released now without any fear of disapproval—in fact with approval and (in the case of religious persons) with the church's blessing. Marriage is the achievement of genuine union, with mutual enjoyment and happiness as the principal goal.

For Parents. If the parents approve of the marriage, they not only accept a son-in-law or daughter-in-law but recognize that their children have become sufficiently mature to live their own lives. This recognition means relinquishing certain rights and responsibilities. The bride's parents, who are normally quite concerned with protecting their daughter, now entrust her to someone else. In our society, marriage is usually considered as "giving the bride away." Fortunate is the couple whose parents fully believe and practice this old saying! The daughter should be given completely to her husband; the son, to his wife.

It is to the great advantage of the couple that the parents fully approve of the union, since such approval gives them a good beginning in their adjustment to each other. Parents who do not approve frequently hope that the marriage will fail, in order to demonstrate that they were "right." Some parents even go so far as to use reprehensible means to break the union. Studies by Burgess and Cottrell indicate that when both sets of parents approve of the union, newlyweds attain a better than average adjustment in marriage.[1]

For the Civil Authority. In Western society, the wedding ceremony was originally performed by the father. Such was the practice of the ancient Hebrews, Greeks, and Romans. Later, when the Christian Church became powerful, the blessings of the priest

[1] Ernest W. Burgess and Leonard S. Cottrell, Jr., *Predicting Success or Failure in Marriage,* New York, Prentice-Hall, Inc., 1939, p. 169.

were added, and still later the ceremony was taken over completely by the Church. With the Reformation, marriage came to be regarded as a civil contract, and the state either supervised the ceremony or, in some cases, took over complete responsibility. In certain European countries (for example, in Catholic France), the marriage in every case must be performed by a civil authority, with a religious ceremony optional. In our country, the state must issue the license, but the marriage may be performed by either civil or religious authority.

The state recognizes marriage as a contract between a man and a woman. The contract provides certain privileges but also imposes various responsibilities. The state protects the property rights of the couple, as well as the property rights of each individual. In case of divorce, the property rights of either party are approved or regulated by the state. The state also regulates the inheritance of property and holds parents responsible for the proper care of their offspring. The state regulates, to some degree, even the selection of a marriage mate. Through the marriage ceremony, a couple attains legal status. About half our states, however, permit common-law marriages, which they legalize when a couple has lived together as husband and wife without the formality of a wedding ceremony. (The length of time required to establish the status of common-law marriage varies from state to state.)

For the Church. The principal religious organizations in our country consider marriage as either a sacrament or a holy estate. When a couple is married by a representative of a religious organization, either at home or in a church, the couple is presumed to partake of divine blessings. Their wedding has, in addition, the approval of organized religion. For religious people, this element in the ceremony is a highly valued experience, one which helps the couple realize that their act has spiritual significance reaching far beyond the mere satisfaction of their personal desires.

For Society in General. The public ceremony calls attention to the fact that the couple now belong to each other. It is a warning to others not to interfere with them in any way. It gives the couple the protection of society against any attempt to break up their marriage. Society as a whole feels keenly about preserving marriage as an institution, and a new couple is welcomed as a further reinforcement of that institution.

All in all, a couple has a great deal to gain by conforming to the cultural customs of a marriage ceremony, and a great deal to lose by not conforming. It is no wonder, then, that the marriage ceremony has a rich symbolic meaning.

Type of Wedding. Since the wedding ceremony is a climax to all that had preceded, each couple will select the type of wedding most suited to their taste. The wedding can be either a small or a large home wedding, a formal or informal wedding in a hotel or similar public place, a simple or large church wedding, a secret wedding, or an elopement. There are advantages and disadvantages in all types.

The importance of allowing the prospective bride and groom to make the decision concerning their own wedding cannot be overemphasized. Parental help is desirable, but parental dictation in such matters can be most frustrating for a bride and groom. The following case, in which both families took over all details of the wedding plans, illustrates extreme dominance; only an unusual sense of humor helped the bride and groom endure their ordeal. The first part of Marion's story runs as follows:

> "Alf and I both want a simple wedding, a home wedding with just our families and a few close friends. But the other evening, when we told my mother, she flew into a rage, declaring that no daughter of hers would marry like that. She had had that kind of wedding because her parents couldn't afford any other, but she says she and Dad can afford a big affair. So she's busy making plans for an elaborate church wedding, followed by a reception at an expensive hotel. I think she has invited everyone she ever knew. Now she has set out to arrange all the details. I have no choice in anything. She has selected all my wardrobe, the invitations, and even my bridesmaids. It has reached a point where it is ludicrous. It isn't *our* wedding; it's *her* wedding. To make matters still worse, Alf's mother and father defy the usual custom of allowing the bride's parents and the bride to make the plans—now even *they* want in on the arrangements."

After a lapse of a few days, Marion made a progress report:

> "If Alf and I didn't really love each other and if we weren't able to

laugh at the whole situation, our marriage would have been doomed long ago. Now his parents and my parents are quarreling with each other over details of the plans. Alf's parents want the wedding at their church; my parents want theirs; Alf's parents demand that their minister perform the entire ceremony; mine say no, that their minister should be completely in charge. They have even disagreed over the time for the wedding. Our invitations were ready to be mailed and now they are actually going to change them and, as a result, delay our wedding another week."

The counselor later learned that additional compromises were made. At last came the evening for rehearsal, at which time both ministers arrived. This was one point yet unsettled. Justly embarrassed by the awkward situation, the ministers sensed the problem and obviated further tension by suggesting sufficient modification in the ritual to allow their equal participation in the ceremony.

While Marion and Alf were on their honeymoon, they wrote the counselor the following letter:

"Today we had our second wedding. As we were driving along, we came upon a lovely little chapel. When we went in to see the rose windows and carved figures, we seemed to have the same desire—to repeat our vows in the sanctity of that chapel. When we expressed our desire to the minister next door, he said he'd be glad to oblige. You'll never know how much we enjoyed *our* wedding; you know the extent to which the first one belonged to our parents."

It is claimed by Burgess and Cottrell that marriages performed by a religious representative are happier than others. Insofar as this is true, it most certainly is not because of the religious ceremony itself, but because of character traits and attitudes of a couple who seek such a ceremony.

Secret Weddings and Elopements. Neither secret weddings nor elopements are recommended as the best possible beginning for married life. They should be resorted to only if they are the one way out. The most common cause of elopement is some kind of parental disapproval. In some cases, it may be a means of circumventing certain state laws. It certainly is thoroughly undesirable, however, for a couple to elope to another state because of health laws. In other cases, eloping may have the purpose of eliminating the expenses of a wedding. But on the whole, a secret wedding or elopement means temporary escape from an unpleasant situation which has to be faced sooner or later. Where there is parental disapproval, it is an attempt to force a change. Occasionally, parents will accept the inevitable with little resistance, but often the antagonism is strengthened. This means beginning marriage with a serious handicap.

Either a secret wedding or elopement deprives the couple of the satisfaction which normally accompanies a regular wedding. In addition, they are invariably under emotional strain because their action has to be hidden from others. Fears and guilt feelings may be strong and may have a detrimental effect on their intimate adjustment. Furthermore, a couple gets great satisfaction later

"But, Ethel—all I can remember saying is that I had nothing particular against marriage!"

Salo and the Chicago Tribune–New York News Syndicate, Inc.

from reliving the wedding; this is especially true for the wife. If the wedding is not pleasant, this source of pleasure will always be lacking. Quite often, also, the couple may be embarrassed later in life when they cannot talk freely to friends and children about their wedding ceremony.

Date for the Wedding. The couple usually comes to some agreement about the month for the wedding, but the specific date

Menstrual cycle

usually is left to the bride, so that her menstrual cycle can be taken into consideration. A wedding should be planned to take place after the cycle. However, the date should not be set too soon after the expected end of the cycle, since overexcitement and other psychological factors connected with the wedding often delay the period.

THE HONEYMOON

Meaning. The word honeymoon has a twofold meaning. First, it signifies the trip which most couples take immediately after the wedding. Second, it implies a special attitude, namely that of wanting to please the mate in every possible way. The trip soon ends, but the honeymoon attitude need not end. In fact, in a well-adjusted couple, it is dominant throughout their married life. Some couples become tired of pleasing the mate soon after marriage; their honeymoon is at an end. The honeymoon attitude is lacking in a mate who says, "I have been doing everything I can to please you. It is about time for you to think about me."

Conditions Which Promote the Honeymoon Attitude. It is essential for a couple to begin marriage alone, away from relatives and friends. No one should accompany the young couple on their honeymoon; nor should anyone "drop in" to surprise them. Cases are known where a relative, sometimes the mother of the groom or bride, has taken advantage of a honeymoon automobile trip to visit a place he or she has always wished to see.

The couple needs to be alone for several reasons. If minor problems arise between them, they must have an opportunity to discuss them without interference and without the possibility that one or the other will consult a third person. This experience will help the newlyweds learn from the start to rely on each other rather than to seek the help of outsiders.

By being where no one knows them, the couple is free to live as it pleases. Their intimate life may make them somewhat self-conscious and shy. For this reason, friends and relatives may serve only to embarrass them. There is often a certain degree of awkwardness at first in being husband and wife. It is well for the two persons to try out their new roles alone, where no critic is near to observe these initial attempts.

Where to Go and What to Do. Where newlyweds spend a honeymoon is determined in large measure by their economic condition. Cost will determine the distance they can travel and how long they can stay away from their responsibilities. Of equal, if not greater, importance is the fact that they should go to a new place which is of interest to them. No matter how much they may be in love, to be continually with each other over a period of time, without any distractions, may prove to be too strenuous. Seeing and doing new things together not only will be stimulating for the time being, but also will serve them later as a background for pleasantly shared memories. Whatever is undertaken should not be too fatiguing, of course; nor should it appeal to the interest or skill of one only. Such an activity will tend to dampen the spirit of the other and stress differences rather than similarities.

Engaging in interesting activities will remove the possibility of excessive self-analysis or of prying too soon into each other's innermost thoughts and feelings and will avoid the danger of doubting one's adequacy in pleasing the partner. The honeymoon is not the time for showing fears and doubts which had better be left for later and more gradual sharing.

The following case as related by Mrs. L. illustrates that the honeymoon can be too long, too expensive, and too fatiguing:

"I think some of our present problems could have been less serious, if not avoided completely, if we had taken a shorter honeymoon. A honeymoon of three and one half months is too long, as I now see it. Oh, of course, it was a wonderful trip, especially since I'd never been abroad. We visited nine different countries. As I look back, however, I think we would have enjoyed it even more after we'd been married a year or two. Maybe if we had taken off two or three weeks for a honeymoon and then gone back to settle in our own house, we would have adjusted more easily, in a typical, natural setting. As it was, we spent far too much money—all that our parents gave us for the trip and almost all of our savings. This entire first year has been one of debts and more debts. We are constantly under tension, trying to "save face" with our families and friends.

"I also found that by the time we got into the second month of the honeymoon, I was exhausted from being constantly on the move. I felt as if I were suspended in mid-air, without roots and constantly surrounded by strangers. For a while I enjoyed it, but in time even my husband seemed like a stranger to me. I had never been away from my family for longer than a few weeks at a time—and even then I was near enough to telephone them or to receive mail regularly. So I was actually homesick. The change was too great, too sudden for me. We both became tired and, as a result, were irritable with each other. It seemed as if we were constantly trying to adjust to new places and strange people rather than to each other. To see some new places is all right, but we had too much. I think we chose an unnatural method of becoming better adjusted to each other. I'm inclined to believe that drawn-out honeymoons delay that period of adjustment between husband and wife when they should be concentrating on their home. There is where a couple really learns how to live together. Maybe it would be wiser to take long trips, such as ours, after adjustment has had a chance to take place."

It is apparent, whether the honeymoon trip is long or short, that two persons starting to live side by side, day after day, will need to make various adjustments. The innumerable expressive habits of the one must be adjusted to those of the other. Difference of opinion concerning the management of joint finances may show up soon after marriage. Newly married couples may suddenly realize that they are away from home, away from parental care and protection, and that their future security must be found in the new interdependency which should exist between mates.

Sex and Honeymoon. The reader will find further discussion of sexual adjustment in marriage in Chapter 16. Here we shall stress only a few points that apply especially to the honeymoon.

While it is always desirable to engage in sexual intercourse under favorable circumstances, this is especially true for the first coitus between husband and wife because of the factor of primacy—the first impressions we get of anything are likely to be retained more vividly and longer than later ones. In many cases, the first experience sets the pattern for later ones. Numerous cases are known where the first sex experiences were so unpleasant that they affected adversely the couple's sexual adjustment throughout life. In order to avoid such consequences, the couple should keep in mind the following suggestions.

The first act is likely to be somewhat painful for the virgin wife. Marriage counselors can give examples of wives indicating definite conditioning against coitus because of excessive pain on the honeymoon. Sometimes the bride will develop strong resentment against the groom because she feels that he is brutal and thinking only of his own pleasure.

It is sometimes advisable, in spite of custom, not to engage in intercourse on the wedding night, because the bride is likely to be tense, even exhausted, from the physical strain and the excitement of the wedding. Psychologically, she may be ready, but physiologically, she may not be.

A further factor to be taken into consideration is inhibition against the sex act. A lifelong training in the feeling that the act is immoral and indecent cannot be overcome by a mere realization that now, after marriage, it is "right." Mentally, this "rightness" may be accepted, but emotionally, it may not be. As a result, the wife may appear to be frigid, or the husband may discover that he has become impotent. Such conditions are invariably due to emotional factors. A number of studies have revealed sexual difficulties in both husband and wife. According to Hamilton's study, 15 out of 100 husbands questioned were impotent in their first attempt at sexual intercourse, and 93 out of 100 wives studied reported failure to achieve orgasm in their initial experience.[2] The exact percentage is not so important as the general fact that newly married couples may not find their first sex experiences satisfactory. Such failure should not cause disappointment or alarm for the future.

Even when the first experiences are successful, some couples are disillusioned because too much was expected from the sex act. When it is realized how often couples are sexually aroused before marriage without the experience of satisfaction, such disillusionment may not seem strange. There is, of course, always the expectation that, after marriage, the act will be overwhelming and completely satisfying.

Frequency of coitus on the honeymoon is largely determined by individual differences in the potency of the sex drive and by

[2] G. V. Hamilton, *A Research in Marriage*, New York, Boni, 1929.

the degree of mutual satisfaction. What may be too frequent intercourse for one couple may not be sufficient for another. It is known that coitus is much more frequent soon after marriage than in later years.

In most cases, the urge is more frequent in the male, since the male reaches his greatest sexual potency in his teens and the female at about the age of twenty-eight to thirty. However, it can also happen that the bride has more frequent urges than the groom. Where there is such a discrepancy, understanding should be reached by frank discussion. Knowledge about the physiology of sex in the male and in the female will be of great help.

Provided they have proper knowledge, in no case should a feeling develop in either the bride or groom that they cannot satisfy each other's needs. The danger is that when the bride's urges are more frequent than those of the groom he may develop feelings of inferiority. Since the bride can enter into the sex act even though she may not be physiologically ready, she can engage in it whenever the groom has such an urge; therefore, she seldom develops feelings of inferiority. If the groom's urges are more frequent than hers, her reaction may express itself in one of two ways: "This is all he wanted me for," or "I am happy that I can please my husband although I do not have as frequent an urge as he has." Fortunate is the bride who can take the latter view. This does not mean that the groom should disregard the bride's feelings. With frankness and good sense, a successful sexual adjustment can be attained.

INTERPRETATIVE SUMMARY

1. A wedding is a ceremony presided over by a legally authorized official to signify the entrance of a couple into marriage.

2. For most couples, the wedding is the fulfillment of many cherished wishes and desires.

3. By this ceremony, parents relinquish their rights in, and responsibilities for, their son or daughter and entrust them to a husband or a wife.

4. The state accepts the married couple as a legal unit.

5. In a church wedding, the couple receives the church's approval.

6. Secret weddings and elopements deprive a couple of many satisfactions derived from a formal wedding.

7. The honeymoon signifies not only a trip away from home but also an attitude of pleasing each other as much as possible.

8. A couple must be well informed about sexual adjustment before the wedding and honeymoon in order to have a good beginning for their marital sex life.

Thought Questions and Projects

1. Are there justifiable reasons for a "secret wedding"? What are possible difficulties arising from such a wedding?

2. What circumstances tend to make couples elope?

    (a) Do you know couples, now apparently happy, who eloped for their wedding?

    (b) Do you know of elopements which did not end happily?

3. Would you rather be married by a clergyman or by a justice of the peace? Support your answers with reasons.

4. State laws vary as to the required length of time between date of application for license and the date of the wedding. Poll the opinions of the class on this statement: After securing a marriage license, a couple should be allowed to marry

    (a) immediately.

    (b) after a delay of one day.

    (c) after a delay of three days.

    (d) after a delay of five days.

    (e) after a delay of _____ days.

5. Some marriage counselors share the opinion that if more time, thought, and preparation were spent in education for married life and less emphasis on overly elaborate weddings more marriages would be successful. What is your point of view?

6. What is meant by the "honeymoon year"?

7. What conditions determine the effectiveness of the honeymoon?

8. If there are students of foreign nationalities and societies in your class, compare their wedding customs with those of your own social group.

9. What services are available in your community for helping young couples to plan and prepare for their wedding and honeymoon?

SUGGESTED READINGS FOR FURTHER STUDY

Adams, Clifford R., *Preparing for Marriage,* New York, E. P. Dutton & Company, 1951.
  Chapter 13. The Wedding Day and the Honeymoon.
Bowman, Henry A., *Marriage for Moderns,* 3rd ed., New York, McGraw-Hill Book Company, 1954.
  Chapter 9. Wedding and Honeymoon.
Harper, Robert A., *Marriage,* New York, Appleton-Century-Crofts, 1949.
  Chapter 6, pp. 109–118. Planning the Wedding.
Himes, Norman E., *Your Marriage,* New York, Rinehart & Company, 1940.
  Chapter 10. The Premarital Examination.
  Chapter 11. The Wedding and Honeymoon.
Koos, Earl Lomon, *Marriage,* New York, Henry Holt & Company, 1953.
  Chapter 8. The Wedding and the Honeymoon.
Magoun, F. Alexander, *Love and Marriage,* New York, Harper & Brothers, 1948.
  Chapter 8. The Honeymoon.
Post, Emily, *Emily Post's Etiquette,* New York, Funk & Wagnalls Company, 1950.
Skidmore, Rex A., and Anthon S. Cannon, *Building Your Marriage,* New York, Harper & Brothers, 1951.
  Chapter 13. The Wedding and the Honeymoon.
Woods, Marjorie Binford, *Your Wedding: How to Plan and Enjoy It,* rev. ed., Indianapolis, The Bobbs-Merrill Company, 1949.

13

STRUCTURE
OF A PSYCHOSOCIAL UNIT

After marriage, a couple concentrates more seriously and more intensively on efforts to create conditions conducive to the full realization of their union. In most cases, this means attainment of mutual happiness. To what extent they will attain their goal depends upon three basic factors: their culture, their motives for marriage, and their respective personalities.

CULTURE AND A PSYCHOSOCIAL UNIT

Stages in Development of the Unit. Culture provides the frame of reference within which any marriage is shaped. Culture is often divided into material and nonmaterial elements. The former includes such physical objects as houses, implements, machines, tools, and vehicles. The latter comprises bodies of knowledge, skills, patterns of thoughts, attitudes, values, and beliefs. This division into material and nonmaterial is only relative, for physical objects apart from thought have no meaning or usefulness. Perhaps one should speak of material and nonmaterial features only as aspects of culture, both of which have a tremendous influence on the patterning of a marital union.

The material features have had a significant effect on the woman's place in marriage. She has been freed very largely from the production of goods outside the home, and modern improvements in the home have removed much of the drudgery from housekeeping. She therefore has more time and energy left for the enhancement of the psychological atmosphere of the home.

Nonmaterial culture is equally significant in molding a new unit. It gives content and form to the relationship of its members. It stresses what should bind individuals together, and prescribes the framework of the unit's operation. Our culture outlines four stages in the development of a marital union and defines the roles for each. These four stages can be represented graphically in the following manner:

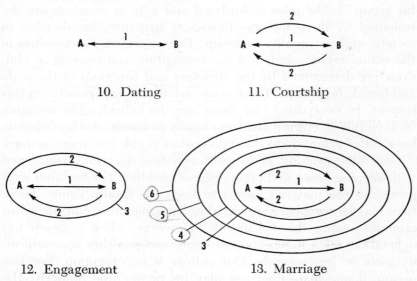

10. Dating   11. Courtship

12. Engagement   13. Marriage

FIGURES 10–13. A male, B female; 1 attraction, 2 love, 3 opinion of relatives and friends, 4 public opinion, 5 law, 6 religion.

In all four of the above figures, A represents man and B represents woman. Number 1 indicates the attraction existing between them. It should be noted that this attraction is present in all four stages. It may grow more intense and meaningful from one stage to another. Number 2 stands for love, which is added to mere attraction and is the reason why the two persons now tend to make their relationship permanent and exclusive. Number 3 signifies the opinions of friends and relatives. Their opinions operate as outside forces to hold A and B together. Numbers 4, 5, and 6 represent public opinion, law, and religion, all three of which are powerful supporting forces. They are brought to bear upon A and B to facilitate, protect, and perpetuate their union.

Definition of Roles. Culture delineates the roles of man and woman at any one of the four stages, but especially at the stage of marriage. A role is defined by Sargent as "a pattern or type of social behavior which seems situationally appropriate to the individual in terms of the demands and expectations of those in his group." [1] The roles of husband and wife in marriage are determined by three factors—biological structure, membership in society, and personality make-up. The respective functionings in the sexual relationship, and the conception and bearing of children, are determined by the structure and functions of the male and female organisms. There is no variation in role possible in this respect. In everything else there may be considerable variation from culture to culture and from family to family. Anthropologists have called attention to these diversities in role in various groups.

Generally speaking, in our culture system the wife is concerned with keeping house and taking care of children, the husband with providing the material means to keep the family going. These roles may be completely reversed under some other culture, as for example among the Tchambuli.[2] However, when a group has defined the roles, it expects conformity and punishes nonconformity more or less severely. Our culture is no exception. For this reason, if one mate does not play his or her role properly, the other may hide it from society or may not even be willing to recognize it. Punishment by society affects the innocent as well as the guilty.

> "If the marriage is a failure and the husband does not play the part that would be necessary for maintaining the role, the wife may continue to pretend in public that all is well, that she is happily married and has a pleasant home. She must keep the recognition of the true state of affairs from the public because she is keeping it from herself. She is still playing that she is happily married and doing her best to disregard the unpleasant interludes with the husband's non-coopera-

[1] S. S. Sargent, *Social Psychology*, New York, The Ronald Press Company, 1950, p. 279.
[2] See Margaret Mead, *Sex and Temperament in Three Primitive Societies*, New York, William Morrow Company, 1935.

tion. If the public becomes aware of the failure of the marriage it will be necessary for her also to recognize that failure or to withdraw from the public. Only in retreat or in an asylum can we be successful in maintaining a role against a public rejection of that role. Disgrace, which is often so intolerable as to lead to suicide, always consists in the public rejection of a character part which we have adopted. Disgrace seldom threatens physical harm or serious physical discomfort. An astonishing number of men in public life have failed to survive a public rejection of their role." [3]

"He has his good faults."

Chon Day and The Saturday Evening Post.

Inasmuch as our mores regulate the roles of husband and wife, both should make an effort to familiarize themselves with these mores and should agree on the extent to which they wish to conform or deviate. The roles of husband and wife should be as much as possible complementary to each other. Where one is weak, the other may be strong. This type of relationship is de-

[3] E. R. Guthrie, *The Psychology of Human Conflict*, New York, Harper & Brothers, 1938, pp. 141–142. Reprinted by permission.

termined largely by the personality make-up of each mate at the time of their marriage. It is at this time that they set the pattern of their relationship, which under ordinary conditions endures throughout life. The first pattern of their behavior with each other is almost as basic for later behavior as childhood experiences are for later personality development. Since all roles are learned, roles may be changed after marriage. But changing roles requires a great deal of effort, as was indicated in connection with personality changes. Growth of personality during maturity consists largely in learning to play roles more efficiently, to perceive these roles ever more clearly. Gradually one learns to perceive himself in the light of the part one plays. In this sense, marriage fosters personality growth.

Dominance and Submission. Dominance and submission are closely related to role taking. Who assumes the role of leadership? Dominance is controlling the actions and attitudes of others. (It should be differentiated from domineering, which means the act of controlling another's behavior in one's own interest.) Dominance, in any democratic society, is equivalent to leadership. A leader is not concerned primarily with his own interest but with the interests of those he leads.

Dominance (or ascendance) and submission characterize every social relationship, from the lowest to the highest. Animals have been studied in this connection, especially with reference to their organizations. As a rule, the male is the dominant member of the group. If there are several males in one group, a hierarchy of relationships is soon evolved on the basis of physical strength and skill. The female leads only at the period of heat and then only for a brief time. Summarizing the observations of several researches of animal behavior, Kimball Young says of apes:

"The more experienced male is quick to detect the decline of the female's sexual aggressiveness and soon resumes his dominance. As a rule, the male behavior is marked by impulsiveness, directness, immediacy, and insistency, all expressed by forcible means if necessary. The female, on the other hand, uses cajolry, begging, indirection, and sexual allure, especially during periods of heightened sexual activity." [4]

[4] Kimball Young, *Social Psychology*, 2nd ed., New York, Appleton-Century-Crofts, Inc., 1944, p. 26. Reprinted by permission.

Wherever pairs of birds have been studied, one manifested aggressive and attacking behavior and the other manifested fear, avoidance, and submission. Even domestic fowl establish a pecking order. A pecks B; B never pecks back, but pecks C and so on down. Human society also manifests a kind of "pecking order," and this applies to the smallest unit, the family. According to our culture norms, the male is to be the dominant member of the social unit. When the wife is the dominant member, the husband is said to be "henpecked."

Ascendance and submission are due not only to strength or skill but also to the fact that this type of arrangement facilitates unified action. Where there is no such organization, much time and effort are wasted in bringing about action. Even in the most democratic organization, leaders are elected. In time of danger—as in war—these leaders are given great power in the supervision of those below them. The question in marriage is not whether there should be dominance and submission, but only how they should be determined and to what degrees they should be observed. The so-called 50–50 relationship means merely that husband and wife have divided their areas of dominance or ascendance. It is accepted that decisions are arrived at by mutual agreement, but with the understanding that the final word should be had by the one into whose area the problem belongs.

The question of relationship between marital happiness and type of organization has been studied by Paul Popenoe and by Leonard S. Cottrell, Jr. In the former's study,[5] which dealt with 3,000 married couples, 87 per cent of couples with a 50–50 relationship were declared to be happy by people who knew them. Forty-seven per cent were declared to be happy where the wife dominated and 61 per cent where the husband dominated. Each group comprised approximately a third of the total.

Cottrell's study (see Table 6, p. 246) gives the percentage distribution of happiness ratings of strong and weak personalities.[6] As will be seen from this table, the best arrangement seems to

---

[5] "Can the Family Have Two Heads?" *Sociology and Social Research*, September, 1933, 18:12-17.

[6] Ernest W. Burgess and Leonard S. Cottrell, Jr., *Predicting Success and Failure in Marriage*, New York, Prentice-Hall, Inc., 1939, p. 333. Reprinted by permission.

be that in which the husband and wife are about equal or in which the husband is somewhat more dominant than the wife.

middle class
Democratic Society

TABLE 6

Personality Combinations	Very Happy	Happy	Average	Unhappy or Very Unhappy	No. of Cases
Husband much stronger	23.6	21.4	24.7	30.3	89
Husband somewhat stronger	34.6	28.8	17.3	19.2	104
Husband and wife equal	34.4	24.5	23.2	17.9	151
Husband somewhat weaker	20.8	25.0	29.2	25.0	120
Husband much weaker	4.4	24.4	32.2	38.9	90
Whole sample	24.9	24.9	25.1	25.1	554

It should be kept in mind that these conclusions have been reached in a certain frame of reference—that is, in a middle-class sample of a larger democratic society. The results might be different in some other society. Nor is it possible to conclude definitely that these couples were happiest because they conformed to our democratic ideal or that this type of organization gave to each mate greater freedom of self-expression based upon personality make-up. Since the happiness of any individual ultimately depends upon his ability to satisfy his needs, if would seem that a marital adjustment where this can take place is the most desirable. In any particular case, the important point is not a 50–50, 60–40 relationship, but rather one in which each person can be himself and can be accepted fully by the other. Where one is definitely weaker than the other, that person would be most happy if he did not have to accept a 50–50 responsibility. Many mates are happy when one of the two can freely assume a greater load of responsibility without any coercion or conceit. Such understanding enhances both partners' security without devaluating their personal contribution.

LEVELS OF PSYCHOSOCIAL UNITS

The level of any marital union is indicated by the meaning, significance, or value which each mate has for the other. These, in turn, are revealed by the motives each has for entering marriage and for growth which takes place after marriage. When we examined the motives for marriage in Chapters 5 and 6, we discovered that they are based upon four concepts of marriage—possession, partnership, companionship, and the merging of two personalities.

Possession. Not only in primitive but also in modern societies, there are marriages which are consummated primarily for the purpose of possessing a mate. The wife may want to possess a husband for economic reasons; the husband may want to possess a wife for self-perpetuation in children, for economic reasons, as a symbol of his success in life.

The case of Mrs. H. illustrates well what is meant by the possession of a person as a means to an end. Mrs. H. came for advice on how to handle the conflict between her husband and their fourth child, George, then 18 years of age. The precipitating cause for the violent conflict between George and his father came when the son flatly refused to go into his father's business following graduation from high school. His two older brothers and a sister were already in the firm as a result of pressure from the father. According to George, they were afraid to go against the father's wishes. Everyone in the family jumped when Mr. H. issued a command. George had made up his mind that it would not happen to him. When Mrs. H. was asked further about George's earlier relationship with his father and about her own relationship to her husband, she said:

"Mr. H. has a very domineering personality. He has always treated members of his family as if they were instruments or tools in his hands, to be used in any way to bring profit, gain, or satisfaction to him. He literally wants to possess one, just as he owns the machines in his factory; in fact, I think he expects to push buttons and have people around him go into action. He has always been very impersonal in his relationship with people—that includes me, too. You see, about a year after our marriage, I found out about something through a close friend that made me realize just how he manipulated people to get what he wanted. I learned why he was so eager to rush our 'whirlwind' romance, why he even wanted to set an earlier wedding date than was originally planned. It came out that the manufacturing firm which he now owns had a top position open which he wanted badly. He qualified in all ways except that he was single; they preferred a married man. Furthermore, the president of the firm was eager to negotiate a merger with my father's company—a competitor. So the matchmaking became a business deal, and Mr. H. got his position shortly after we were married. Within a year, the firms were reorganized into one. And, of course, he owns all of it today.

"I soon learned, too, why he wanted children. It was certainly not as objects of attention and affection, because he has given little of his time to them. He told me shortly after our first son was born that he wanted at least six children—that he hoped they would be boys, but that if they were girls he would give them a business education. His sole ambition was to have enough children to fill the controlling positions in his manufacturing company. It is inconceivable to my husband that any one of our seven children should have a mind of his own, that he could possibly want to do anything other than work for him. George says he sees what has happened to his brothers and sister— they are completely dominated by their father. I see it, too. I have seen it through the years, and for that reason I have no desire to urge George to follow his father's wishes. I think he should be allowed to make his own decision. He likes the sciences and has done well in them, so much so that his teachers are encouraging him to go on for advanced study. It's enough that the older children and I have been and are forced to be my husband's chattel as long as he lives."

Partnership. Sometimes marriage is merely a partnership—a relation into which two people enter for mutual profit. Such a marriage is maintained only so long as each member receives some benefit—physical, physiological, or psychological. In any case, it is for purposes of self-enrichment.

Companionship. The level of companionship is somewhat higher, since it stresses primarily psychological satisfactions— intellectual and emotional. It is based to some extent on "give and take," but the giving is predicated on the expectation of receiving something in return. Each individual in a companionship benefits from the skills, knowledge, viewpoints, attitudes, and philosophy of life possessed by another personality. Thus the opportunity is provided for mutual enrichment.

The Merging of Two Personalities. This is the highest, and possibly the most difficult, form of social relationship. While self-interest is still a strong motive, it is tempered by a sincere interest in the mate for his own sake. The interests of both are so common that no differentiation is made between the rights or privileges of the individuals. Needs that arise are considered to be completely mutual. There is no "sacrificing" for the other, just as there is none for oneself—each does what is done because it must be done. The following criteria of merging should make this type of association clear. There is a feeling of *oneness*. In ordinary social relationships, one is always aware of protecting his own rights, as well as those of other individuals. A certain amount of acting is necessary in order not to reveal socially disapproved motives. In the merging of personalities, this aspect is reduced to a minimum. Each feels that he is *understood*—that is, he knows that he is being judged by motives accepted by the other, and not by overt action or behavior. When he makes errors, his mate does not misinterpret his fundamental motives.

Another criterion is a feeling of *belonging*, the reverse of possession. Each feels that he belongs because of his value. He counts as an individual, as someone who is needed, so that he can voluntarily submerge himself in the union without fear of losing his individuality. He feels secure in his importance for the other person.

A third criterion of merging is *sharing*. This sharing is without cautious calculation as to the exact amount each contributes or receives. Each gives according to his capacity and general personality. The factor of significance is that each mate is *willing* to share with the other all that he has, regardless of the proportionate ratio of his and his mate's contributions. Such sharing occurs at the intellectual, the emotional, and the physical levels. Responsibilities are mutual, and gain from such sharing is reciprocal.

A fourth criterion is *participation*—doing things with each other to attain individual and common goals. The areas of participation include maintenance of a home, rearing of children, recreation, friendships, and work.

Distinguishing Features of Marriage as a Psychosocial Unit

In our society, there are a great number of psychosocial units—groups of people who are drawn or held together by some psycho-

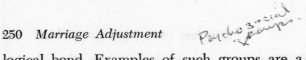

logical bond. Examples of such groups are a club, a lodge, a fraternity, a sorority, a union, a church, and a nation. A better understanding and appreciation of marriage as a psychosocial unit is facilitated if we single out the distinctive psychosocial features of this unit as compared with others. We shall not attempt to compare marriage in each instance with these other units; however, the reader is asked to keep them in mind.

Marriage centers in a *home*. There is no other institution or organization which compares with marriage in the fact that it creates and centers in a home. The meaning and value of a home do not depend upon its exchange or market value, but rather upon a number of psychological factors: the sentimental value which comes from the collection of meaningful items assembled by a husband and wife—little gifts between mates; interesting souvenirs representing pleasant vacation trips together; gifts from friends; heirlooms; and articles obtained as the result of considerable sacrifice, saving, extra work, and creative skills on the part of both husband and wife. Therefore, the real value of a home or of any part of it depends upon what the couple has put into it and the experiences which have enriched their lives. As a rule, a home —whether large or small, elaborately furnished or poorly equipped—is the result of joint effort, planning, and sacrifice. It is symbolic of working together. In a sense, every part of a home and its appointments are an expression of the couple's personality, for it reveals their tastes, skills, values, and interests.

The home serves as a means of ego-building, for one of the roots of the ego concept is possession. A home also serves to point out a couple's distinct place in a community; it puts them on a par with others and is a tangible manifestation of their rights in society as a whole. All of these factors enhance the feeling of what is called "pride of ownership."

The home is indeed a castle. In it, the couple reigns supreme. No one has the right of intrusion, not even, without special authorization, officers of the law. While no couple is completely free to regulate their lives within the home, yet they are freer there than in any other place. In a home, both feel that they are their own masters.

As time goes on, a home becomes increasingly more meaningful because of day-to-day experiences and the accumulation of memories—both painful and pleasant—all of which serve to bring the couple closer together and to bring about many emotional and ideational attachments to the home as a whole and to the various parts of it.

A home becomes especially precious as a place where parents feel they perpetuate themselves in begetting children and rearing them according to their best skills and highest ideals. It is a place where their life becomes enriched by the entertainment of relatives and friends.

The home is a base of operations from which people go forth to engage in numerous activities. It is always a place of refuge to which they can retreat and gather strength for new efforts. All of this reminds one of the well-known expression "the sanctity of the home." In the sense that a home is set aside for the exclusive use of a couple, it begins to have an aura of sanctity.

Range of Needs Satisfied. In the course of history, man has created many institutions which serve to satisfy his needs. Among them are the school, the church, industry, business, and the state. None of these satisfies as many of his needs as marriage. An examination of the motives for marriage will impress anyone with their range. A person may enter marriage for one or several reasons, but if his marriage works out successfully, all the desirable goals will be attained—at least to some degree. He will find satisfactions ranging from the simplest physical needs to the highest and deepest psychological desires. He will find food, physical comfort, sexual expression, self-perpetuation in children, security, recognition, adventure, companionship, affection, and love.

Degree of Intimacy. Each individual is, in a sense, a microcosm —a small world within himself. His needs and interests often conflict with those of society; yet he must constantly seek his satisfactions in such a fashion as to be acceptable to others. What others think of him is extremely important to him, for it means success or failure in his life. For this reason, he must be constantly aware of the rules laid down by his society. To many of these rules he can conform easily and freely. To others he cannot conform, but he must give the impression that he does. This conflict results in frustration and tension from which he constantly seeks relief. He can secure partial release by revealing his private thoughts and feelings to his friends, but there are limitations to this possibility: He may not have close friends and close friends can become enemies. There is also the constant fear of loss of respect.

A successful marital adjustment is extremely helpful here, because each mate can reveal without reservation to the other any secret which might bring condemnation by society. Because of their mutuality of interests, each one realizes that what may be harmful to one may be harmful to the other. Such realization brings with it a shared sense of protection.

Within the four walls of a home, artificiality can be replaced by naturalness, and the couple can associate with each other without many of the restraining devices of our civilization. In marriage, by sharing each other's personal likes and dislikes, innermost thoughts, secret ambitions, and personal beliefs, there results an intimacy found nowhere else in any social grouping.

Interdependence. No man is complete within himself. For self-preservation and self-realization, he depends upon others. Various other persons serve him to satisfy these needs, but none so well as a mate in marriage. The only other relationship which comes close to it is the relationship between parent and child, and this is to a great extent a one-sided relationship: The child depends upon the parent, but the parent does not depend upon the child to the same degree. In marriage, there is a mutual dependence; and the greater this mutuality, the more satisfying the union. It serves the needs of receiving no less than of giving. The latter is especially ego-building.

How important interdependence in marriage can be may be surmised from an examination of the great number of needs which a couple seeks to satisfy in marriage. It is in connection with this interdependence that personality inadequacy and incompatibility become vitally important. It will be remembered that these two factors underlie unhappiness and divorce. In a sense, interdependency is the crucial element in a successful marriage.

Ease of Communication. One great obstacle to harmony between individuals, groups, or nations is the difficulty of communication between them. There are at least three causes for this condition. First is the fact that man experiences many emotions and tensions that lend themselves only with great effort to verbalization. Anyone will experience fear, anxiety, joy, elation, and ecstasy which he cannot express in words. The same inability applies to a great variety of sensations which come from various parts of his body. Second is the fact that there are thoughts, ideas, and beliefs which are so abstract or complex that it is difficult to find the exact words to express them. Or it may require too much time to explain them to others, as is true in the case of two individuals who have radically different philosophies of life. Third are the limited means of communication. The basic means are gestures and words, both of which depend upon the meanings they arouse in another person. These, in turn, rest upon the existence of a common background and training.

All three of these obstacles are greatly reduced, in many cases to a minimum, in a well-adjusted couple. Two people begin marital adjustment with some degree of similarity in their personality make-up. This fact, plus the fact that they live intimately with each other for many years, tends to make them perceive alike, think alike, feel alike, and act alike. We know that perception depends not only upon external stimulation but also upon the content of the mind. Exposed to a new environment, people will see the same things in the same way if they have a common background and interests. A couple marry partly because of similar capacities and similar values. The experience of living together increases these initial similarities.

Because of these similarities and identities of personality and experience, a husband and wife can communicate with increasingly greater ease as time goes on. They can sense each other's feelings and sensations almost instantaneously and, in most cases, unconsciously, so much so that they cannot explain how and why they do sense them. They need only a few words to communicate to each other complex and rich meanings. In many cases, only a minor gesture, such as a glance, a wink, a smile, a frown, or a touch, is required to convey complex meaning. For all of these have the same meaning for both of them.

INTERPRETATIVE SUMMARY

1. Marriage creates a psychosocial unit which is held together not only by physical attraction and love but also by forces coming from the outside of the two persons, such as the opinions of friends, public opinion, law, and religion. Later, children create an additional bond between parents.

2. Although they are not clearly defined, the roles for a husband and wife serve as a useful guide in their adjustment to each other.

3. The dominance-submission relationship between husband and wife should be based upon the talents of each.

4. On the basis of values assigned to a mate, marriages may be classified as representing possession, partnership, companionship, and the merging of two personalities.

5. In the possession type of marriage, one mate is used by the other as a means to an end; in partnership, both are interested in mutual profit; in companionship, the emphasis is on intellectual and emotional sharing and participation; in merging, both seek unification of their personalities.

6. The distinctive features of marriage as a psychosocial unit are its home-centered pattern, the wide range of needs satisfied, the degree of intimacy, interdependence, and the ease of communication between the mates.

THOUGHT QUESTIONS AND PROJECTS

1. What does the word *role* mean as used in a sociological-psychological context?

2. What factors may contribute to a clash in roles between husband and wife?

3. Distinguish between dominance and the act of domineering.

4. Would you prefer a mate who in relation to you is submissive, equal, or dominant in personality? Explain your answer.

5. In what respect does partnership differ from companionship in marriage?

6. Discuss as freely as conditions permit:
   (a) What does the word *home* connote to you?
   (b) Do you want your own home to be like the one in which you grew up *or* do you want an entirely different type of home? Explain.

7. Give reasons to support the view that "newlyweds should live apart from relatives or friends no matter how meager their dwelling may be—it's their first home together."

8. Think of several illustrations which help to clarify the term *interdependency* in marriage.

9. What conditions are necessary to create a permissive climate in which communication between husband and wife may be strengthened?

Suggested Readings for Further Study

Allport, Gordon W., "The Mature Personality," *Pastoral Psychology*, 1952, 2:19–24.

Burgess, Ernest W., and Harvey J. Locke, *The Family*, 2nd ed., New York, American Book Company, 1953.
   Chapter 9. Expectations and Roles.

Carroll, Herbert A., *Mental Hygiene—The Dynamics of Adjustment*, 2nd ed., New York, Prentice-Hall, 1952.
   Chapter 4. Need for Emotional Security.
   Chapter 5. Need for Mastery.
   Chapter 6. Need for Status.

Harper, Robert A., *Marriage*, New York, Appleton-Century-Crofts, 1949.
   Chapter 7. Learning to Live Together.

Jacobson, A. H., "Conflict of Attitudes toward the Roles of the Husband and Wife in Marriage," *American Sociological Review*, 1952, 17:146–150.

Levy, John, and Ruth Munroe, *The Happy Family*, New York, Alfred A. Knopf, 1938.
   Chapter 5. Living Together.

Mace, D. R., "Personality as an Expression and Subordination in Marriage," *Marriage and Family Living*, 1953, 15:205–207.

Stone, A., and L. Levine, "The Dynamics of the Marital Relationship," *Mental Hygiene*, 1953, 37:606–614.

Strodtbeck, F. L., "The Interaction of a 'Henpecked' Husband with His Wife," *Marriage and Family Living*, 1952, 14:305–308.

Waller, Willard, and Reuben Hill, *The Family*, rev. ed., New York, The Dryden Press, 1951.

Chapter 16. Bases for Marriage Solidarity.

14

UNIFICATION OF TWO
PERSONALITIES

One of the characteristics of the honeymoon is the conscious attempt of each partner to adapt himself to, so as to please, the mate. The honeymoon begins to wane just as soon as either mate expects modification of the other without changing himself. The shift of emphasis from adaptation to attempting to change the other is ordinarily a gradual one. Probably most couples reach a sort of balance between these two attitudes during the second year of their marriage. Then there is likely to be an attempt by either to bring about changes in the mate so as to please himself. One often hears words like these: "You always expect me to give in to you. It's about time you considered *my wishes*."

Such changes in attitude may cause serious conflicts. If a couple is able at this time to resolve their conflicts to their mutual satisfaction, their happiness for the future is assured. If the conflicts remain, husband and wife may grow farther and farther apart. The result for many couples is divorce, or at best life beside each other rather than with each other for the rest of the marriage. Both partners may believe themselves in bondage, in some cases seeming like "cell mates" rather than husband and wife. What can be done to avoid this state of affairs? We shall examine the problem in this and the following chapters.

Degree of Unification

Type of Harmony to Be Expected. The intimate life of husband and wife requires that the two be able to function harmoniously. Too much disharmony may cause friction which may disturb their peace of mind and, at the same time, greatly limit their united

"You're so unfair! Every time we disagree you want to compromise!"

Bill King and the Chicago Tribune–New York News Syndicate, Inc.

efforts. But absolute harmony is undesirable, for it may deprive them of necessary interstimulation and make their union monotonous. The word *harmony* is associated, of course, with music. The richness and pleasantness of any musical composition does not mean absolute harmony, but rather a proper blending of harmony with a "dash" of disharmony, or consonance and dissonance. In the same manner, genuine harmony between a couple, plus a bit of disharmony now and then, makes their relationship interesting and fascinating.

It must be remembered that no personality is so completely unified and integrated that inconsistencies cannot be found in it. Every sincere person will discover such inconsistencies within himself—in attitudes, interests, and values. It happens frequently that before a particular decision is made an individual may have a debate with himself. Similar disagreements must be expected in marriage between two unique and distinct personalities.

Preservation of Personal Identity. No couple should ever seek to merge or unite their personalities to such a degree that the identity of either is lost. In order to bring about an effective union, they both must be able to submerge their individualities into a larger whole—their marital union. To what extent their personalities merge will depend, in addition to their intentions, upon the fluidity or rigidity of their respective personality structures. Since each personality entering into this union is unique, it is obvious that each resulting union must also be unique. Only the individuals involved can determine to what extent the "I" can be supplanted by the "we." It is an extremely difficult and delicate problem to find the proper balance between this "I" and "we." In most marriages, the problem arises again and again, since it seems impossible to find one general principle which can be applied automatically to each and every concrete experience.

An analogy, imperfect though it is, may throw some light on the nature of the problem. Water is composed of oxygen and hydrogen, two elements which separately are gases. When they combine in the ratio of two parts of hydrogen and one part of oxygen, they become a liquid. Both are modified and, consequently, possess qualities they did not have as separate elements. But their identity is not destroyed, for they can be separated into gases again. In a similar manner, marriage demands that both mates be modified. Neither can be exactly as he was before marriage. The change that takes place, however, must be only a modification and not a destruction of his personality. Any attempt to remake a mate in one's own image is a threat to marital happiness.

OBSTACLES TO UNIFICATION

It has been sufficiently established that both a husband and wife, in order to live harmoniously with each other, must modify their behavior as well as their personality structure. Just what must they modify? Terman's research into the psychological factors of marital happiness has given a comprehensive answer to this question. This research involved a study of 792 couples, who answered a long list of questions about marital happiness and, in addition, were given a battery of tests, including the Strong Vocational Interest Test and the Bernreuter Personality Inventory. What interests us especially at this point are the grievances listed by husbands and wives, and the personality characteristics of happy and unhappy husbands and wives.

Grievances of Husbands and Wives. The husbands listed 57 grievances and complaints, and the wives, 53. The following table enumerates these complaints and indicates the rank of seriousness.

TABLE 7[1]

Order for Husbands	Rank for Seriousness	Order for Wives
W. nags me	1	H. selfish and inconsiderate
W. not affectionate	2	H. unsuccessful in business
W. selfish and inconsiderate	3	H. untruthful
W. complains too much	4	H. complains too much
W. interferes with hobbies	5	H. does not show his affection
W. slovenly in appearance	6	H. does not talk things over
W. quick-tempered	7	H. harsh with children
W. interferes with my discipline	8	H. touchy
W. conceited	9	H. has no interest in children
W. insincere	10	H. not interested in home
W.'s feelings too easily hurt	11	H. not affectionate
W. criticizes me	12	H. rude
W. narrow-minded	13	H. lacks ambition

[1] By permission from *Psychological Factors in Marital Happiness*, by Lewis M. Terman *et al.* Copyright, 1938. McGraw-Hill Book Company, Inc. Pp. 99–100.

Order for Husbands	Rank for Seriousness	Order for Wives
W. neglects the children	14	H. nervous or impatient
W. a poor housekeeper	15	H. criticizes me
W. argumentative	16	Poor management of income
W. has annoying habits	17	H. narrow-minded
W. untruthful	18	H. not faithful to me
W. interferes in my business	19	H. lazy
W. spoils the children	20	H. bored with my small talk
Poor management of income	21	In-laws
In-laws	22	H. easily influenced by others
Insufficient income	23	H. tight with money
W. nervous or emotional	24	H. argumentative
W. easily influenced by others	25	Insufficient income
W. jealous	26	H. has no backbone
W. lazy	27	H. dislikes to go out with me
W. gossips indiscreetly	28	H. pays attention to other women
W. has much poor health	29	H. has poor table manners
W. has too many social affairs	30	Preference for amusements
Preference for amusements	31	H. quick-tempered
W. too talkative	32	Attitude toward drinking
W. no interest in my business	33	H. untidy
W. extravagant	34	H. too wrapped up in business
W. too interested in clothes	35	Intellectual interests
Choice of friends	36	H. has vulgar habits
W. tries to improve me	37	Respect for conventions
W. interested in other men	38	H. conceited
Lack of freedom	39	Choice of friends
Respect for conventions	40	H. gambles
W. late with meals	41	H. spoils the children
Intellectual interests	42	Lack of freedom
W. fussy about neatness	43	H. too talkative
Attitude toward drinking	44	Religious beliefs
W. visits, entertains a lot	45	H. jealous
W. not faithful to me	46	H. late to meals
Religious beliefs	47	H. swears
W. a poor cook	48	H. drinks
Educations	49	Educations
W. swears	50	H. considerably younger
W. works outside home	51	Tastes in food

Order for Husbands	Rank for Seriousness	Order for Wives
W. a social climber	52	H. smokes
Tastes in food	53	H. considerably older
W. considerably older	54	
W. smokes	55	
W. drinks	56	
W. considerably younger	57	

Outstanding Features of Happy and Unhappy Wives and Husbands.

"Happily married women, as a group, are characterized by kindly attitudes toward others and by the expectation of kindly attitudes in return. They do not easily take offense, and are not unduly concerned about the impressions they make upon others. They do not look upon social relationships as rivalry situations. They are cooperative, do not object to subordinate roles, and are not annoyed by advice from others. Missionary and ministering attitudes are frequently evidenced in their responses. They enjoy activities that bring educational or pleasurable opportunities to others and like to do things for the dependent or underprivileged. They are methodical and painstaking in their work, attentive to detail, and careful in regard to money. In religion, morals, and politics they tend to be conservative and conventional. Their expressed attitudes imply a quiet self-assurance and a decidedly optimistic outlook upon life.

"Unhappily married women, on the other hand, are characterized by emotional tenseness and by ups and downs of moods. They give evidence of deep-seated inferiority feelings to which they react by aggressive attitudes rather than by timidity. They are inclined to be irritable and dictatorial. Compensatory mechanisms resulting in restive striving are common. These are seen in the tendency of the unhappy wives to be active "joiners," aggressive in business, and overanxious in social life. They strive for wide circles of acquaintances but are more concerned with being important than with being liked. They are egocentric and little interested in benevolent and welfare activities, except in so far as these offer opportunities for personal recognition. They also like activities that are fraught with opportunities for romance. They are more inclined to be conciliatory in their attitudes toward men than toward women and show little of the sex antagonism that unhappily married men exhibit. They are impatient and fitful workers, dislike cautious or methodical people, and dislike types of work that require methodical and painstaking effort. In politics, religion, and social ethics they are more often radical than happily married women. . . .

"Happily married men show evidence of an even and stable emotional tone. Their most characteristic reaction to others is that of cooperation. This is reflected in their attitudes toward business superiors, with whom they work well; in their attitudes toward women, which reflects equalitarian ideals; and in their benevolent attitudes toward inferiors and underprivileged. In a gathering of people they tend to be unself-conscious and somewhat extroverted. As compared with unhappy husbands, they show superior initiative, a greater tendency to take responsibility, and greater willingness to give close attention to detail in their daily work. They like methodical procedures and methodical people. In money matters they are saving and cautious. Conservative attitudes are strongly characteristic of them. They usually have a favorable attitude toward religion and strongly uphold the sex mores and other social conventions.

"Unhappy husbands, on the other hand, are inclined to be moody and somewhat neurotic. They are prone to feelings of social inferiority, dislike being conspicuous in public, and are highly reactive to social opinion. This sense of social insecurity is often compensated by domineering attitudes in relationships where they feel superior. They take pleasure in the commanding roles over business dependents and women, but they withdraw from a situation which would require them to play an inferior role or to compete with superiors. They often compensate this withdrawal by daydreams and power fantasies. More often than happy husbands, they are sporadic and irregular in their habits of work, dislike detail and the methodical attitude, dislike saving money, and like to wager. They more often express irreligious attitudes and are more inclined to radicalism in sex morals and politics." [2]

General Characteristics of Unhappy Mates.

"It is especially characteristic of unhappy subjects to be touchy or grouchy; to lose their tempers easily; to fight to get their own way; to be critical of others; to be careless of others' feelings; to chafe under discipline or to rebel against orders; to show any dislike that they may happen to feel; to be easily affected by praise or blame; to lack self-confidence; to be dominating in their relations with the opposite sex; to be little interested in old people, children, teaching, charity, or uplift activities; to be unconventional in their attitudes toward religion, drinking, and sexual ethics; to be bothered by useless thoughts; to be often in a state of excitement; and to alternate between happiness and sadness without apparent cause." [3]

Inferences for a Married Couple. Any couple seriously interested in achieving a successful marriage can profit from an examination of both the grievances and outstanding personality features of other couples. Such an examination will call attention to the nature of problems which can arise in their own marriage. Other people's problems indeed may indicate some already exist-

[2] *Ibid.*, pp. 145–146, 155.
[3] *Ibid.*, p. 369.

ing irritations which, if not removed, may threaten the couple's happiness. Looking at each grievance, they must evaluate it on the basis of the significance it may have for either of them. They may find some grievances superficial, others of moderate importance, and still others of great consequence. To know the feelings of a mate about these matters is extremely helpful. Outstanding personality features of both happy and unhappy mates were quoted for the purpose of giving each mate an opportunity to compare his own personality make-up with that of persons successful or unsuccessful in the establishment of a happy marriage. There are two possible attitudes toward obstacles to happy marriage: One may either accept them or remove them. It is not an easy matter to decide which alternative to follow, nor is it easy to put one or the other of these alternatives into practice.

SURMOUNTING OBSTACLES TO UNIFICATION

Man has a strong tendency to change his environment to suit himself. This tendency includes other human beings. When he meets a person with different personality characteristics from his own, or different beliefs, different attitudes, different values, he immediately sets out to "improve" him—to reform him, to "convert the heathen." The question that concerns us is not why he tries to change other people, but how it is possible for him to set aside this tendency at all, as he does for some time after selecting a mate. The answer is love. As long as the emotional and sexual elements in his love are strong and the mental element is characterized by phantasy thinking, he idealizes his mate. During this period, everything about the other person seems wonderful and fascinating. (One is reminded of a wife who said to her husband: "Before we were married, I was just as unreasonable as I am now, but then you thought I was cute.") But when, in the course of time, the idealized person is replaced by the real person, an intelligent decision must be made as to what to accept in the mate and what to try to change.

Reasons for Adapting Oneself to a Mate. One reason for the differences in personality structure between husband and wife is the fact that one is a man and the other a woman (see Chapter 4). A man should never try to change a woman into a person with the characteristics of a man; nor should a woman try to change a man into a person with the characteristics of a woman. Since many psychological differences between men and women are due to our culture, some mates feel that the other should and can change. Such change is not likely for several reasons. Once culture has become a part of one's personality, it may be as difficult to change as a part of the body. Also, every man and woman has a social role to play, and gets satisfactions from doing so. To be regarded as feminine when you are a man, or masculine when you are a woman, may become annoying, to say the least. One can appreciate the Frenchman's reaction to the statement that there is little difference between men and women: *"Vive la différence!"* (Long live the difference.)

An important consideration for adapting oneself to a mate, rather than attempting to change him completely, is respect for the uniqueness of the mate's personality. Before any attempt is made to change or modify a personality, it must be clearly recognized that every individual is unique. Variation is a fundamental law of nature. Microscopy and mathematics have demonstrated that even every snowflake differs from every other. No two animals of the same species are alike, nor are two plants. For example, not only trees differ from one another, but also any two leaves on the same tree. The more complex the organisms, the greater the differences. No two human beings look exactly alike, not even identical twins. All human beings have the same basic structure— that is, bones, muscles, skin, hair, heart, lungs, stomach, intestines, etc., but uniqueness shows itself in differences between the parts and the way in which they are integrated into one organism.

In a similar way, personalities, being made up of almost innumerable units, are distinct from each other and yet basically alike. They are distinct in that each unit differs from individual to individual (even two habits dealing with the same objective situation are not identical); nor are the units integrated in the same fashion in two people. Because the heredity and environment which produce a personality can never be duplicated, each person is unique. There could never have been another individual exactly like him; nor can there ever be one in the future. Recognizing this fact of uniqueness should stop any intelligent person from looking for an exact replica of himself and, much more, from the foolish attempt to shape his mate in his own image.

The fact that some aspects of personality cannot be changed at all and others only with extreme difficulty is reason enough why mates must adapt to each other. They will find it wise to adapt to the other's intelligence, temperament, ego concept, philosophy of life, traits, many attitudes, and basic habits.

Having accepted the idea of adaptation, the question arises as to how adaptation can be achieved.

Methods of Surmounting Obstacles to Unification

Accommodation. Accommodation means a peaceful and satisfying co-operation between groups or individuals in spite of any conflicts between them. For example, employer and employees work together even though they may have conflicting views about the distribution of profits. Two or several political parties sometimes join their forces, although they conflict in their desire for power. In the same manner, a husband and wife may get along with each other quite well in spite of some areas of conflict—politics, religion, friends, and others. In order to facilitate closer union and harmonious functioning, each party makes a sincere effort to stress points of agreement and to minimize and perhaps avoid areas of conflict. Such an effort, if successful, may lead to tolerance or even to introception, both of which are discussed in the following paragraphs; if it is not successful, it invariably will lead to antagonism or dissolution of the union.

Tolerance. Tolerance here means the complete and wholehearted acceptance of differences between husband and wife. Such acceptance is not based upon a sense of superiority—"I am big, I am broad-minded"—nor is it based upon a belief that the mate is still immature and in due time will be able to outgrow certain characteristics. Real tolerance is based upon respect for differences in personality, a respect which comes from the full realization that a mate has a "right" to be as he is constituted. In other words, it is intelligent acceptance of differences without annoyance at these differences. Persistence of annoyance is a sign of immaturity. In fact, one may say that tolerance is a sign of personality maturity.

Introception. This term, popularized by two noted psychologists (Wilhelm Stern and Gordon W. Allport), is explained as "the adoption by an individual of cultural standards (conventions, morals, ideals) into his own personal system of motives and desires, or the incorporation of the interests and values of other human beings into his own life. . . . What one loves becomes a part of him. Anything one can admire, feel sympathy for, appreciate, revere, deliberately imitate, or become unconsciously identified with, may be introcepted into the personality and remain ever after a vital part of it."[4]

Because of possible differences between mates in home environment, education, work experience, social contacts, travel, and so on, one mate may find much in the other which he might well introcept. Many aspects of personality, such as habits, skills, attitudes, interests, values, and traits, may be introcepted. For example, one mate may be more affectionate than the other as a result of having grown up in a home where there was much overt expression of affection. The mate who is not so affectionate may acquire this trait. One mate may acquire by introception interests in the fine arts or may learn new skills.

The process of introception is desirable for at least three reasons. First, it builds up the self-respect of an individual when he feels that he possesses qualities worthy of introception by another. Second, it serves to enrich the personality of the one who introcepts. Third, it reduces possible areas of friction and increases the number of mutual enjoyments.

[4] Gordon W. Allport, *Personality, A Psychological Interpretation,* New York, Henry Holt & Company, 1937, p. 217. Reprinted by permission.

REMOVING SOME OBSTACLES TO UNIFICATION

An examination of the obstacles to a happy marriage will reveal that they are of two more or less distinct types. Some problems are based primarily upon momentary conditions of the organism; others have their roots in the very structure of personality. The former give rise to grievances such as the following: nags me, complains too much, interferes with hobbies, interferes with my discipline, criticizes me, neglects the children, does not talk things over, is late to meals, and gossips indiscreetly. True, some of these grievances may have deeper roots than appear at first sight, but on the whole they are due to lack of information, unwillingness to think, and certain temporary moods. What can be done about them will be considered presently.

Obstacles having their roots in personality structure account for the following grievances: feelings too easily hurt, not interested in children, fussy about neatness, slovenly in appearance, quick-tempered, harsh with children, nervous and impatient, has annoying habits, stingy with money, too interested in clothes, swears, drinks, and is jealous.

Units of personality structure are not equally basic. Although every unit of personality is related to every other, some units are superficial, while others are more central. It is important to recall here that units or aspects of personality become increasingly more complex as one moves from records of individual experiences to the center of personality, the ego, or the self (see Chapter 2). As a rule, the more central a personality aspect is, the more difficult it is to modify. A study by Darley shows the following degrees of resistance to change, from the least to the most resistant: (1) recently acquired attitudes toward objects remote from the self, (2) opinions based on ignorance or misinformation, (3) superstitions, (4) deep-seated prejudices, (5) opinions or systematic stereotypes based on early childhood training, and (6) opinions about the self.[5]

[5] J. G. Darley, "Changes in Measured Attitudes and Adjustments," *Journal of Social Psychology*, 1938, 9:189–199.

Having decided that an undesirable kind of behavior or personality aspect is subject to change, the next step is to discover the most effective motive for this change.

Motives for Changing. There are three basic motives for changing or modifying one's behavior or personality. The least effective of these is desire to please a mate. As a rule, when this motive is effective at all, it is so only for a short time. Since it is not easy to bring about any such change, resentment often develops against the person for whose sake the effort is being made. The resulting attitude often may be summed up as follows: "Why should I change? Why can't he change? He is not perfect either!" About the most annoying statement one mate can make to another is, "If you love me, you will do it for me."

A more acceptable motive for changing one's behavior or personality is to attain greater mutual happiness. Thus motivated, the person who changes can expect some reward for his effort.

The most effective motive is self-improvement. When an individual realizes that by bringing about a change he will profit himself, self-interest will stimulate him to put forth his greatest effort, and he will succeed, at least to some degree.

Means of Self-improvement. Assuming that a mate has discovered the nature of obstacles to happiness in marriage, has recognized the need for a change, and is properly motivated to bring about such a change, what is he to do next? Probably the best procedure is to see a qualified counselor, just as it is advisable to see a doctor when one is ill. A counselor is able to diagnose the problem and suggest methods of solving it. The counselor discovers whether or not an annoyance is deep-seated or superficial; he can differentiate between causes and symptoms; and he can suggest proper techniques and methods.

If, however, an individual for valid reasons cannot avail himself of the services of a counselor, he should put forth every effort to remove the difficulties himself. Having decided that the source of his problem is some type of obnoxious behavior, he should ask himself the question, "What satisfaction do I get from this type of behavior?"

All behavior is motivated, especially persistent behavior. As a rule, there are several motives for any type of behavior. Let us illustrate this fact by examining the motives which underlie gossiping. Why does a person gossip? He may belong to a group in which gossiping is a common practice and, therefore, may gossip to achieve or maintain status. Gossiping may be caused by a desire for revenge. A person who has been hurt by another may try to get even by gossiping about him. Envy is another cause for gossip, with the intention of degrading the other person and, incidentally, elevating oneself. Gossip may be due to a desire for vicarious satisfaction. The particular subject of gossip often indicates the individual's need for the kind of experience he gossips about. For this reason, gossip usually reveals more about the gossiper than about the person who is the object of gossip. The latter may have done something (or may merely be charged with having done something) which the gossiper himself wanted to do but did not dare. Sometimes a gossiper commits an act or contemplates one which is not in harmony with our mores. Gossiping about such an act is then motivated by the desire to discover other people's attitude toward it. People gossip also to impress others with the secrets someone else has confided in them. Finally, gossip may be motivated by a desire to unmask hypocrisy in general, as if one were to say: "People are hypocrites. They act as though they conform to our mores, when in fact nobody does."

It quite often happens that finding out the reason or reasons for one's behavior is sufficient to eliminate it. Some people will stop gossiping just as soon as they understand what has prompted them to engage in it. In other cases, discovering the motive behind an action may lead to other, more constructive ways of achieving the same goal. Let us assume that a person has discovered the cause for his gossiping to be a desire for more recognition. It is then much better for him to concentrate on finding other means for attaining this end.

Methods of Changing Habits. In order to modify an undesirable unit of personality, mere awareness of the underlying motives is often not sufficient. In most cases, modification also requires knowledge of methods or techniques necessary to bring about a change. These will differ with the complexity of the unit concerned. Since bad habits can obstruct good adjustment and since they belong to the more overt levels of personality structure, we list some basic rules for changing habits.

First, make it a source of pride to overcome the habit, so that not to persist in overcoming it would lead to loss of self-respect. Next, find one good reason for changing and, whenever an occasion arises for using the habit, think of this specific reason. Thinking of a specific reason again and again is much better than *smoking* alternating between several reasons. Thus, if the habit of smoking is to be eliminated for reasons of health, think of this reason and not of how you will save money or please other people by not smoking. Third, arrange things in such a manner that carrying out the habit will be followed by unpleasant consequences— physical pain, humiliation, or shame. Fourth, overdoing certain habits, especially motor habits, will make them repulsive. Fifth, perform an act voluntarily which is performed involuntarily. *stuttering* Voluntary stuttering in some cases helps one learn control of the vocal apparatus. Sixth, tell at least one or two close friends of your decision to break the habit. Fear and shame of what they might think, should you not succeed, may serve as reinforcement to your own decision.

Assisting a Mate in Changing Modes of Behavior or Personality Aspects. The decision of one mate to modify his behavior or some personality aspect will vitally affect the other mate, who cannot remain neutral: There is a strong desire to be of some help. And much help, indeed, is what is needed. However, it must be the right kind of help, for the wrong kind is worse than none at all. Overanxiety to be of assistance may be a hindrance rather than a help. What the mate can do and should not do in such circumstances can be presented by stressing the "don'ts." In order to make these "don'ts" more meaningful, let us assume a situation where the husband realizes that he should be more affectionate. To help him, the wife might keep in mind the following rules: (1) Don't create the feeling in him that he should change for your sake. Remember that genuine motivation must come from within him. (2) Don't use the threat, "If you love me, you will change." Love never demands, but freely gives and freely receives. His love can be a strong motivation, but it must originate within him. (3) Don't give him the feeling that he must improve himself in order to be a "normal" husband. (4) Don't compare him unfavorably with any other man. A wife should never say, "Why don't you act like Mary's husband?" Nor should she hold up a former sweetheart or husband as an example for him to follow. This approach can lead only to resentment and jealousy. It may also serve to increase any feeling of inadequacy he may already possess. (However, the husband himself may profit by watching the behavior of another man, provided he holds this man in high respect.) (5) Don't tell him that he should take *you* as an example to follow. Self-praise is seldom desirable, and it may cause such resentment that the mate may look for weaknesses in your personality, if only for self-defense. (6) Don't feel sorry for him in a motherly sort of way. You'll hurt his pride. (7) Don't prod and nag him into putting forth greater effort. He will resent being pushed too fast and constantly bossed in his trial-and-error efforts to change. (8) Don't become impatient at his slow progress. Expect some relapses and disappointments. Such changes as he is trying to bring about require time; therefore, be patient without being condescending. (9) Don't give him advice on how to master his problem. Let him discover the best methods for himself. Make suggestions if he solicits them, but never do so with the idea that they must be carried out, for at that point they cease to be suggestions and become commands. Such suggestions and advice may throw responsibility on you. You may be blamed if he is not successful. (10) Don't feel that you have to reward him for any success. He should not be treated like a little boy who needs praise or some other recognition. He should not be "mothered." Show sincere appreciation for his efforts by your general attitude toward him. (11) Don't use his willingness to improve in one thing as a lever to force change in other respects. He will feel that he is being taken advantage of. (12) Don't analyze him. Because of popular writings on psychoanalysis and psychotherapy in general, too many people feel that they are equipped to solve all human problems. It will help you to understand that his difficulty may have its origin in his early home environment. But he can and should discover this fact for himself. (13) Don't expect that when your husband becomes more affectionate all your marital problems will be solved. There is a tendency to take *one* problem in marital adjustment as the cardinal one. As a rule, this is not true. The problem may be only symbolic of more deep-seated difficulties.

MECHANISMS OF UNIFICATION

In the preceding chapter it was pointed out that mates are attracted to each other and then held together by love, and that relatives, friends, public opinion, law, and religion exercise pressure to make their union permanent. It was stated also that within this framework a couple will create a psychosocial unit possessing unique features. In the present chapter, we have stressed that creating such a union requires a process of adjustment between mates, demanding the acceptance of some personality characteristics and the modification of others. Now we should note some psychological mechanisms which operate between two mates. These mechanisms may tend either to draw them closer together or to produce a distance between them. Since all of these mechanisms function largely on the unconscious level, it is desirable to bring them more to consciousness in order to facilitate the good they may do or to decrease the harm they may cause.

The following mechanisms will be considered briefly here: identification, introjection, projection, sympathy, and empathy. The first three center more in mental processes; the latter two, in feelings and emotions.

Identification. Identification means putting oneself in the place of another person—seeing oneself as one sees the other person, or behaving as if he were the other person. The motive for identification may be either enrichment of one's life or the desire to understand another person better. In marriage, the latter motive is especially desirable. While marriage brings many satisfactions to mates, it also requires certain sacrifices of them. Either may be so impressed by his own sacrifices that he feels the other has too easy a life. One corrective for such a viewpoint may be to act out intentionally the role of the mate. Such an experience will often make the husband aware for the first time of problems the wife faces and ordinarily lead to greater respect for her. A wife's identification with her husband's role will have similar results. Provided each mate is sincere in making marriage a success, periodic mutual identifications will serve to bring them closer together.

Introjection. As previously stated, introjection is experiencing within oneself or ascribing to oneself what actually belongs to other persons, objects, or conditions. The motive is usually self-aggrandizement—seeking greater importance. In introjection, one seeks to belong to an exclusive club, fraternity or sorority, or to align himself with a great leader. By introjection, a husband takes pride in his wife's beauty, charm, skills, and various accomplishments; and a wife, in her husband's strength, power, leadership, and professional success. Insofar as introjection is possible, each mate feels flattered and enriched.

Introjection is also a strong counteragent for competition. Instead of competing with each other for certain achievements, each person delights in the success of the other.

Projection. The word *projection* has many meanings. It is used here in the sense of ascribing one's own personality characteristics to others. Naturally, one mate can attribute to the other his good or bad, noble or base qualities. Which type he projects will make a vast difference in the couple's happiness. Each mate must be especially on guard against a tendency to attribute to another his own base qualities which he is unwilling to acknowledge in himself—in other words, to make the other into his scapegoat. Unfortunately, such a process often operates between husband and wife. Its effect is usually irritation, anger, and even hate. But projection of one's fine qualities and noble motives is also possible. When this occurs, the one who projects is convinced that he has a fine and worthy mate; and the one who is the object of such projection feels himself to be accepted and wanted.

Sympathy. Sympathy is sharing feelings and emotions. In a marriage in which there is mutual respect, there is also a strong and sincere attempt by one partner to reproduce within himself any feeling or emotion experienced by the other. This is done for the benefit and satisfaction of the one who originally experienced the feeling or emotion. If the emotion has been painful and unpleasant, sharing it serves as a great source of comfort and strength, for such sharing gives the sufferer a feeling of not being alone at a time when he feels rejected or "singled out for punishment." If the emotion is pleasant and exhilarating, there results the feeling of being worthy of such an experience when it is shared by the mate. A mate's failure to accept the offer of a shared emotion has a great tendency to "dampen" it. A husband or wife may then say, "Whenever I feel happy, you pour cold water over me."

Empathy. Empathy is closely related to sympathy. Here also, the feelings and emotions of another are reproduced within oneself, not, however, in the interest of another but for one's own purposes. As introjection produces vicarious intellectual experiences, empathy produces vicarious emotional experiences. Through empathy a wife may participate in her husband's feelings of triumph, joys, elations, and also in his embarrassment and discouragement. It is not difficult to perceive why she may participate in his happiness. But why must she participate in his unhappiness? The answer may be that she feels so much oneness with him that his moods are reflected in her. Or she has derived so much pleasure from participating in his joys that not to participate in his sorrows seems like disloyalty. The greater the number of experiences which can be shared through empathy, the more the two mates will be unified. In addition, empathy may contribute to the enrichment of one's own life.

INTERPRETATIVE SUMMARY

1. While harmony between husband and wife is desirable, it should never be sought at the expense of individual uniqueness.

2. Terman and associates directed a research study in which they discovered obstacles to unification. Results of the study are quoted extensively.

3. A careful examination of this analysis points to the necessity of self-modification, as well as to the desirability of changes in the mate.

4. Some of the obstacles to unification can be surmounted by accommodation, tolerance, and introception.

5. In order to modify oneself in the interest of harmony, a person must have not only the desire to change himself but also some knowledge of the techniques for making such changes.

6. A mate can be a help or a hindrance in bringing about changes.

7. Five mechanisms of unification were examined briefly: identification, introjection, projection, sympathy, and empathy.

Thought Questions and Projects

1. Where would couples in your community go to seek professional help if their marital difficulties were such that they could not solve their own problems?

2. Ask ten married persons what each considers to be the most common causes for conflicts between mates. Note the extent to which there is duplication of differences in the answers. Would you say that the factors of age, education, sex, and cultural background affect the answers of those interviewed?

3. Do you think that if a person, prior to marriage, learns the art of getting along with friends in general, adjusts well to roommates, and works smoothly with others, he is likely to be adequately prepared to face marital differences? Justify your opinion.

4. Observe a happily married couple whom you have known well for several years. Can you detect little acts of behavior and gestures on their part which reflect a close relationship between them?

5. Could you offer a few words of advice and caution to a husband or wife who is intent upon effecting personality changes in his or her mate?

6. It has been stated that often the most severe quarrels start from small, insignificant misunderstandings. Can you give illustrations to support this statement?

7. Think of examples from your own experience or from observation of others to illustrate each of the five mechanisms of unification: identification, introjection, projection, sympathy, and empathy.

Suggested Readings for Further Study

Adams, Clifford R., *Preparing for Marriage*, New York, E. P. Dutton & Company, 1951.
  Chapter 19. Making Your Marriage Work.
Allport, Gordon W., *Personality*, New York, Henry Holt & Company, 1937.
  Chapter 18. The Ability to Judge People.
  Chapter 19. Inference and Intuition.
Baber, Ray E., *Marriage and the Family*, 2nd ed., New York, McGraw-Hill Book Company, 1953.
  Chapter 6. The Husband-Wife Relationship.
  Chapter 7. The Husband-Wife Relationship (Cont'd).
Bowman, Henry A., *Marriage for Moderns*, 3rd ed., New York, McGraw-Hill Book Company, 1954.
  Chapter 10. Personality Adjustment in Marriage.
  Chapter 11. Personality Adjustment in Marriage (Cont'd).
Cuber, John F., *Marriage Counseling Practice*, New York, Appleton-Century-Crofts, 1948.
Duvall, Evelyn Millis, and Reuben Hill, *When You Marry*, rev. ed., Boston, D. C. Heath & Company, 1953.
  Chapter 15. What Holds a Marriage Together?
Goldstein, Sidney E., *Marriage and Family Counseling*, New York, McGraw-Hill Book Company, 1945.
Harper, Robert A., *Marriage*, New York, Appleton-Century-Crofts, 1949.
  Chapter 7. Learning to Live Together.
Jung, Moses, ed., *Modern Marriage*, New York, Appleton-Century-Crofts, 1947.
  Chapter 4. The Background of Conflict in Marriage, by Kurt Lewin.
Koos, Earl Lomon, *Marriage*, New York, Henry Holt & Company, 1953.
  Chapter 12. Roles in Marriage.
Merrill, Francis E., *Courtship and Marriage*, New York, The Dryden Press, 1949.
  Chapter 15. Frustrated Roles.
Mudd, Emily Hartshore, *The Practice of Marriage Counseling*, New York, Appleton-Century-Crofts, 1951.
Waller, Willard, and Reuben Hill, *The Family*, rev. ed., New York, The Dryden Press, 1951.

Chapter 16. Bases for Marriage Solidarity.
Chapter 17. Marital Success.

Winch, Robert F., *The Modern Family*, New York, Henry Holt & Company, 1952.

Chapter 15. Companionship, Love and Marriage: The Theory of Complementary Needs.

15

EMOTIONAL ADJUSTMENT

Pleasant emotions cause a person to move toward the source of stimulation while unpleasant emotions drive him away from it or against it. We are drawn closer to a person who is the source of pleasant experiences for us, and we move against or away from a person who arouses unpleasant emotions in us. A marital union is no exception to this fact. In order to be successful, marriage must provide pleasant stimulation between husband and wife and should be characterized by as few unpleasant experiences as possible. An intelligent husband or wife will therefore endeavor to be the cause of numerous pleasant experiences for the mate and will try to avoid those conditions which may result in annoyances. To attain this kind of relationship, both husband and wife must have achieved a definite level of emotional maturity; they must be familiar with and aware of conditions and situations which may engender emotions.

Emotional Immaturity

Emotional maturity does not mean the absence of any emotions, but rather *conformity of the emotional life of any individual to the norms laid down by the group or society to which he belongs*. Emotional maturity is therefore a relative matter—relative to the chronological age of the person and relative to the time and place of his existence. The criteria for emotional maturity therefore are not well defined, and this is especially so because emotions are difficult to measure. In spite of these limitations, some broad characteristics of emotional maturity can be delineated.

(1) A person is immature if there are *too many* situations in his life to which he responds emotionally. As the person matures, he substitutes reason and action for emotion in more and more situations. Thus it seems perfectly proper for a child to cry when he is denied a nickel, but it is ridiculous for a grownup to cry when his needs are not met. There will be fewer situations to which a maturing individual responds with unpleasant emotions such as excitement, agitation, anxiety, dread, fear, terror, horror, worry, disgust, anger, rage, fury, and hate. He will learn, at the same time, to react to many situations with pleasant emotions—joy, delight, amusement, love, and the like. In our society, a positive sign of emotional maturity is the ability to enjoy life in general; to respond with feelings of appreciation for the creative efforts of mankind as expressed in the fine arts of painting, sculpture, music, architectural design, and literature.

(2) The internal changes involved in attaining maturity are primarily those resulting from the dominance of the parasympathetic or sympathetic nervous systems, or from an admixture of these two. The specific changes were discussed in connection with falling in love (Chapter 6). Maturity or immaturity is partly a matter of the *intensity* of these emotions. A child experiences the emotions "all over"; there is very little gradation. A mature person never is completely overwhelmed by any emotion. He may not have learned to substitute reason completely, but reason at least reduces emotional intensity. He may get angry, but he will overcome his anger and not fly into a rage or fury; he may be frightened, but he will not experience terror or panic. Maturity also shows itself in the *duration* of emotions. The unpleasant emotions are aroused, but they are overcome after a short period. The mature person may show grief or sorrow at the loss of a dear one, but after a reasonable time he will come back to his normal self. Furthermore, his emotions do not fluctuate from moment to moment. He does not cry one moment and laugh the next—there is some persistence, since his emotions are aroused by situations that have meaning. Nor does the mature person shift his pleasant emotions too rapidly from one person to another. Thus, if he loves a person,

there is some degree of permanency. He does not fall in and out of love in quick succession. In fact the more mature he is, the more permanent his emotions are.

(3) The overt responses related to emotions involve the striped muscles—or voluntary muscles—and some duct glands. In general, attaining maturity in emotional responses consists of substituting the finer muscles for gross muscles. Childish responses are striking, kicking, scratching, biting, screaming, shouting, jumping up and down, stamping, and crying. The emotionally mature person channelizes emotional energy from the gross muscles of his body to the finer muscles of speech. The emotionally immature will direct his emotional responses to the objective stimulus of the emotion—to the person or object which aroused the emotion. Thus, he must injure a person to get relief, or he must kick a frustrating object. The mature person realizes that the real need for emotional release is to get rid of tension, and he therefore will sublimate his energy—that is, express it in a socially approved manner.

(4) The emotionally mature person is aware of the emergency nature of emotions. He realizes their auxiliary function and tries to limit them accordingly. The immature person uses emotions for his own satisfaction. He seeks thrills of one kind or another. He either creates emotional situations or seeks them. And he uses his emotions to control his environment, to bend other people to his whims. A child soon learns from experience that emotional behavior such as crying and manifesting fear and anger calls attention to his needs. The immature person persists in using forms of these means to get what he wants. He has not learned to differentiate between "thing-technique" and "person-technique." As Griffith says, "The phrase 'thing-techniques' refers to the fact that the objects and events around the child may be taken as simply impersonal or physical in nature. They may, for example, be pushed, pulled, or otherwise manipulated, but in no sense of the word invited, persuaded, or cajoled. This means the person-techniques do involve invitation or persuasion." [1] In other words, the immature person does not realize that people around him also

---

[1] Coleman R. Griffith, *Introduction to Educational Psychology,* New York, Rinehart & Company, Inc., 1935, p. 609. Reprinted by permission.

have needs and wants which must be satisfied. He can think of other people only as tools for his own satisfactions.

From what has been said about emotional immaturity, it is obvious that an immature person makes a very poor partner. Not only will he be unable to share responsibility, but also he will actually become a burden to the other mate.

Let us now examine the various specific emotions involved in marital adjustment.

MARRIED LOVE

In Chapter 6 we stressed that emotion is one element in love, which is a quality of experience resulting from the integration of mental, emotional, and sexual responses to a person of the opposite sex. Love is a quality which makes two persons merge into one and gives them a feeling of oneness and belongingness, of sharing and participation. It is a state in which each one of two people realizes that his happiness can be attained only when the other also is happy. As a consequence, each one lives not only for himself, but for the other, sometimes even more for the other than for himself.

(Since love in marriage may grow, may die out, or may turn into its opposite—hate, the foundation on which love rests must be examined further. Love ultimately rests upon the satisfactions one can get from another person. In other words, a man's love for a woman will rest upon her ability to satisfy his needs or desires. Likewise, a woman's love for a man will depend upon his ability to satisfy her needs. In other words, complementary abilities are important. Since these needs differ from individual to individual, people love or are loved for various reasons. Any person is happy or is in love to the extent that his need or needs have been met. Since many of the needs to be met are unconscious, it is often true that an individual may not know what makes him love another person. And for the same reason, a mate may not know how to make the other person happy.

(A more satisfactory way of isolating the factors entering into a love relationship can be derived from the objective considerations of the needs and desires of a mature personality. What are the satisfactions that a mature person seeks in marriage?

The criteria of a mature personality were discussed in Chapter 8. Here it may be stated briefly that a mature person in our society is one who derives pleasure not only from the satisfaction of his own needs and desires but also from the satisfaction he can

"Okay, Helen. You are mine and I am yours. Now let's drop the subject."

Hank Ketcham and The Saturday Evening Post.

give by meeting the needs and desires of other people. Hence, a mature husband derives pleasure when he can satisfy not only his own needs, but those of his wife as well.

We have said that love is a quality which results from the integration of ideational or mental, emotional, and sexual responses to a person of the opposite sex. A mature man is in love with his

Love

LOVE AND A MATURE MAN

wife when he derives intellectual, emotional, and sexual (and other physical) pleasures from her *and* when he is able to give his wife the same pleasures. If the pleasures are not mutual, he is selfish or brutish. These conditions, of course, are also true for the wife. In other words, love is based upon giving and receiving. One can never demand in the name of love. What is given is given freely; it springs from the very nature of love. *Demanding* changes the whole basis of a marital relationship. A love relationship is the free and unhampered self-expression of two mature personalities toward each other.

Growth of Love. In a marriage, love usually cannot remain static. It must either grow or wane. If it grows, it will do so for three reasons. First, each mate grows. Each will become more and more aware of his own needs and desires. He will learn which needs can be satisfied and which cannot be satisfied and thus will acquire a more realistic attitude toward marriage. He will acquire greater skill in the satisfaction of needs. The second reason for growth is a more thorough knowledge of the mate—knowing his needs and the means of satisfying them. The third reason is the accumulation of many memories of mutual satisfactions of needs. These center on the thousands of things which the couple experienced together. Painful experiences, as well as pleasant experiences, weld them together. Success in meeting many situations together inspires confidence and hope in the future. The feeling grows that each was meant for the other and that life without the other would be empty and meaningless. The "we" supplants the "I" almost completely.

Waning of Love. Just as it can grow, love can wane and ultimately die. This situation happens to many married couples. They begin their married life by being very much in love and then gradually begin to "cool off," and many grow entirely "cold" toward each other. They merely live side by side, without any special attachment to each other. What has happened?

Love subsists and grows on the foundation of mutual satisfactions. If these are removed, love gradually disappears. How this takes place between any two people can be determined only by a careful examination of all the factors which enter into their marital relationship. The problem is complicated; often it involves unconscious factors which the partners themselves are unable to discover. Any marriage counselor has heard the questions, "What is happening to our love?" "What is happening to us?" The general cause is, of course, the absence of giving and receiving satisfactions.

Failure to *give* satisfactions is probably the more frequent cause. The cares and worries of daily life often displace interest in the happiness a couple can give each other. More specifically, there is first a lessening of intellectual companionship. The husband becomes so interested in his work or profession that he has little time to discuss current topics with his wife; he soon lives in a world by himself. The wife is so engrossed in the routine of housework and in taking care of the children that she cannot keep alive her intellectual interests in anything outside of the house. Husband and wife, in these circumstances, soon have very little to share; they live in two different worlds. In addition, they neglect experiences which might give common emotional satisfactions, such as participation in creative work, the cultivation of mutual friends, enjoyment of the fine arts, and various types of recreation. Often the sexual life becomes a matter of routine— limited to physiological needs; in many cases, it becomes even burdensome. For wives it may become merely a matter of duty.

Although the couple may do nothing in particular about the state of their relationship, love may disappear from their married life simply through gradual neglect of each other. They do not realize, of course, that everything has its price, even love. Not realizing this, one mate may tend to blame the other—may try to make him feel that maintaining love is his duty, that, once having married, the other *must* continue to love, no matter what the mate does or does not do.

HATE

The following are samples of thousands of items appearing in the public press as reasons for divorce requests:

(1) Charged that his wife hit him with a milk bottle, smashed a tumbler on his hand, knocked out one of his teeth with a plate, battered him with a shovel, yanked him downstairs by one leg, scratched him, pushed a lighted cigarette in his face.

(2) Charged that every time she was near her husband she would "break out in a rash from head to toe."

(3) Wife had deceived him by allowing him to go on thinking that he was her fifth husband when in reality he was her seventh.

(4) Husband refused to be kissed because he was afraid of germs.

(5) Husband spent five nights a week playing bridge, the rest of the time talking bridge.

(6) Husband threw knives and a flatiron at her, pushed her down a stairway, struck her across the chest with an ironing board, tried to toss her out a window.

(7) Caused her to become deaf by beating her, and then broke her hearing aid when she refused to listen to his talk.

(8) Complained that, among other things, her husband told friends she was dead.

(9) Wife not only served pea soup for breakfast and dinner but also put pea soup sandwiches in his lunch box.

(10) Had helped her husband write four songs, which he had then dedicated to four other women.

(11) Husband insisted on having photographs of his four ex-wives in the couple's bedroom.

Not only will some mates injure, annoy, and harass each other, but also attempts at murder have been proved in court. Sentences are pronounced each year on husbands and wives who killed their mates. Naturally, some of these people were not in love with each other when they married, but some were. The question naturally arises as to how it is possible for love to change into hate. In the cases cited, hate is not only implied but also very frankly and freely expressed.

Hate is the opposite of love, but both involve strong emotions. In love, one endeavors to bring about as much happiness in the other person as possible; in hate, one seeks to hurt, to injure, or to avoid the other as much as possible. Love is not changed into hate suddenly, for hate is just as much a matter of growth as is love. In some cases hate may appear to be of sudden onset, but even in such cases it is due to transfer of hate from one person to another. Thus, a husband may transfer hate for his mother to his wife, and a wife may transfer her hate from one man or from men in general to her husband.

Hate, which in most cases develops gradually, results from frustrations; and frustrations in marriage are inevitable. The in- *FRUSTRATions* terests of husbands and wives are not identical, even though they may be very much alike; there are bound to be some conflicts. Even though husband and wife usually are alike in basic interests, the desire to satisfy these interests may not coincide. Every time one or the other is thus frustrated, there is some degree of resentment. Because of love, this resentment usually is repressed. If resentments are not expressed periodically, they accumulate. As time goes on, one mate will gradually develop an ambivalent feeling toward the other—that is, will like him for some things and dislike him for others. Accumulated bad feelings are now and then expressed with some intensity, causing considerable anger in the mate.

What has been said so far applies in greater or lesser degree to every married couple. The conflicts and resentments described may eventuate in hate, depending upon (1) the personality make-up of each mate, (2) the amount of insight each possesses, (3) the type of interests which are frustrated, and (4) the extent of repression or suppression.

Some individuals are so constituted that every frustration, no matter how minor, involves their ego—that is, affects their self-respect. Such persons react violently to frustration, a reaction which is resented by others who feel that the reaction is out of proportion to its cause. Some couples have enough insight to take frustrations in their "stride." Knowing that some frustrations are inevitable, they do not doubt the mate's love because of every minor misunderstanding. They recognize that intimate relationships are bound to lead to conflicts. They know that no matter how fine and noble their ideal of love may be, they both still possess some imperfections in their personality make-up.

Some frustrations arouse more resentment than others. Two are mentioned only as examples. First, there is certainly a need for respect of the other person's sense of good judgment. If the other's judgment is constantly belittled or ridiculed, the reaction is likely to be violent. Second, repeated or constant frustration of the sex drive may engender anger in one partner who feels that an important basis for marriage is repudiated by the mate. This anger is much aggravated if the sex drive happens to be especially strong. Hate will grow exceptionally if there are frequent and prolonged repressions of anger. Since these repressions accumulate in the mate's unconscious, the time may come when the stored anger will surge into consciousness and completely displace love. This phenomenon may be illustrated diagrammatically in the following manner:

Hate grows

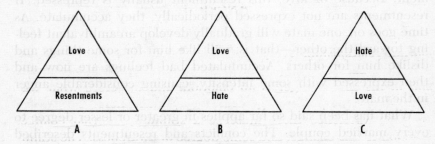

FIGURE 14. A, B, and C represent conscious and unconscious levels of behavior. In A, love is dominant, and various resentments are repressed. In B, the resentments have developed into hate. In C, hate has become conscious and dominant, and love has been repressed.

This development also may explain why it is possible for some couples, after having experienced hate, to return to love. When hate is expressed, it serves as a catharsis—that is, purifies the unconscious thoughts and feelings, and enables the mates to love each other again. Such a change may happen when a couple is contemplating divorce. They may express all their hate to other people, sometimes to the court, and then become reconciled. This fact alone indicates something of the service which can be rendered to an estranged couple by a marriage counselor with psychological insight.

Hate' Cathartic Effect

Finally, it should be stressed that, while resentment and anger may be inevitable in a marital relationship, hate is not inevitable. If a couple is unable to stop the stream of anger which leads to hate, they should seek the help of some capable person to assist them. Hate destroys marriage and damages both partners. The one who hates not only inflicts irreparable damage to the mate's person or personality, but also inevitably does a great deal of harm to himself. His personality is often so warped by hate that he becomes a social and vocational misfit, and his physical and mental health may be affected.

ANGER - is inevitable

Because anger in marriage is inevitable and can damage the marital relationship, everyone entering marriage should understand the nature of anger and know how to handle it in himself and in the mate. Anger is an emotion, and therefore what was said about emotions in general is pertinent here. For every "anger" experience there must be a stimulus, internal change, reaction to this change, and some degree of awareness. The stimulus for anger is usually some form of frustration. How such a stimulus functions can be seen in the infant. A six-month-old infant whose arms are held tightly for a few minutes will pull his arms, kick his feet, squirm, and scream; his face will grow red, and great tension can be observed in his entire body. This behavior is a manifestation of anger. In the adult, psychological frustrations produce the same result. Any restraint of what we in our culture consider freedom brings about a violent reaction. We become "fighting mad." If a person has been subjected to repeated frustrations, his anger will increase, by conditioning, with every repeated stimulation. Moreover, any part of an earlier anger-inducing situation may call forth an intense response in the future. For instance, a person may make us angry by what he says, and we may at the same time be struck by the tone of voice, the facial expression, and so on. At a later date, seeing in this person a similar facial expression, though unrelated to the

Frustration

Freedom

Frustration — Aggression

original anger-causing situation, may tend to make us angry. This point is especially important in marriage, where two people associate intimately with each other.

Controlling Anger. As a first step in the mastery of anger, one must realize that aggression is only one way of getting rid of emotional tension; it is not an absolutely necessary outlet for anger. The main function of anger is release from tension, and release may be accomplished by other muscular activity than attack on the source of irritation. Only through prolonged and strongly motivated training can one learn to release emotion in other forms of muscular exercise. Nor are all re-directions wholesome. Kicking the dog when angry at one's wife, instead of kicking the wife, is a re-direction of energy, but certainly not a desirable one. Going for a walk, playing tennis, golf, and so on, are more desirable re-directions. Wanting to injure the other person in order to get rid of emotional tension certainly is a sign of emotional immaturity and even may be a manifestation of sadistic tendencies. The one who has learned to disassociate aggression from anger has gone far in controlling it.

Another, even better method of controlling anger is to decrease the number of situations which cause anger. The fact that frustrations are inevitable in marriage does not mean that their number cannot be decreased. It is utopian to believe that one will ever get rid of all of them, of course, but the better one knows a marriage partner, the fewer the irritations that will arise. A sincere study of possible frustrations should be undertaken by every couple as soon as possible. The list of grievances mentioned in the previous chapter should be helpful.

Two rather common causes of anger in marriages are *criticism* and *nagging*. *Criticism* is the careful examination of the meaning, implication, or merit of anything. Criticism in this sense certainly can be and is helpful in a good marital relationship. Some mates have the attitude, however, that criticism should be avoided, no matter how justifiable. The wife may be completely wrong when she reacts to constructive criticism by saying: "Before we were married you never criticized me. Now you criticize me. You don't love me any more." Constructive criticism is never dictatorial; it calls attention to something which can be improved. If justified and accepted, it improves the relationship.

It is true, however, that sometimes criticism is unjustified, especially when the critic merely wants to assert his mastery or superiority and is so conceited that he cannot believe he might be mistaken. A good rule in criticism—for it almost invariably hurts—is to cushion it by calling attention to the many good qualities the mate possesses and by emphasizing that the point in question is mentioned merely to help further growth. Thus used, criticism is absolutely necessary; otherwise the attitude may soon develop that "I don't care how you are or what you do."

Nagging is chronic criticism. In nagging, the same criticism is repeated over and over again without constructive suggestions, or merely to express a general dissatisfaction. Such a state of affairs can only irritate and will do neither person any good.

Frustration tolerance is a measure of the intensity or amount of frustration a person can take before getting angry and of the degree to which his anger is aroused. There are great individual differences in frustration tolerance, due in part to hereditary factors and in part to environment. For the latter reason, an individual can do a great deal to overcome excessive irritability. To be an adequate mate, he must learn to master irritability. If he cannot do so himself, the need for psychotherapy is definitely indicated.

Quarrels. Quarrels are a means of getting relief from emotional tension induced by anger. Their primary function, therefore, is not so much to solve a problem as to discharge tension by the use of words highly charged with emotion. The words used are those which the individual has found by past experience capable of relieving tension and, at the same time, of inflicting ego-hurt on the mate. Because of their irrelevance to the problem at hand and because of the pain they bring about, quarrels should be resorted to only as a last means, and even then with moderation. The ideal marital relationship is, of course, one in which there are no quarrels. But the most important thing in marriage is not to realize ideals but to get personal satisfaction, and doing so sometimes may lead to quarrels. It is much better to get rid of individual tension, even at some pain, than constantly to repress all anger and thus let it develop into hate. If tension is released properly, husband and wife will feel closer to each other after the quarrel than before.

As was pointed out above, a quarrel is indicative of personality aspects which do not harmonize. As these personality clashes are removed, greater harmony and unity result. Perhaps that is what the poet meant when he said:

> Ah, blessings of the falling out
> That all the more endears
> When we fall out with those we love
> And kiss again with tears.

Of course, it is not the "falling out" which endears, but the removing of the obstacle between people who love each other.

How may both the number and intensity of quarrels be reduced?

When a person is angry he may use offensive words merely as a means of getting rid of emotional tension. If a husband and wife are aware of this fact, neither will take the other's harsh words at their literal meaning but will recognize that he or she resorts to angry words just as if crying out in pain. In most instances, if the emotionally disturbed person is not answered with the same irate tones, his anger is brought more quickly under control. On the other hand, in some cases a strong response addressed to a disturbed person may actually help to break his spell of anger and thereby contribute to his relief from tension.

At all times, both mates should be aware of the fact that a quarrel is only *one means* of getting relief from tension. It certainly is foolish to believe that it is "manly" to fight. "Stand up and fight like a man" implies that a "man" will resolve a quarrel by using gross muscles. Nothing is farther from the truth. Animals resolve their differences in this manner. Children know only this method, as do uncivilized and many uneducated persons. It requires more manhood not to fight than to fight or use severe words. To analyze a frustration situation rationally at the time of frustration requires great mastery of oneself. To channelize an intense stimulus to thought rather than to muscular action is an important step in mastering oneself and one's environment.

A comparison between discussion, debate, and argument should clarify the point. In the following diagram, let X represent the problem which two people face.

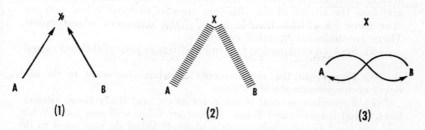

FIGURE 15. (1) Discussion. (2) Debate. (3) Quarrel.

In *discussion*, whatever A and B say applies directly to the problem. What each one says is important insofar as each throws further light on X.

In *debate*, X is used merely to win a point—to show superiority of one over the other. In a debate, A and B might even exchange roles—that is, take the negative rather than the affirmative side. In some cases, one actually may find mates arguing one day on one side of the problem and the next on the other side.

In *quarrel*, X merely serves to get both aroused. They forget all about X as such, and start to fight each other. This we find among couples who have acquired the habit of quarreling—any problem serves as a means of setting them against each other.

Another means of reducing the number of quarrels and their intensity might be summarized in the words: Think before you act. Magoun has given ten rules of action to forego an impending quarrel.

"(1) First, recognize that you are now getting angry. Go off by yourself (take a walk, sit in the park, or in an empty church).

"(2) Wait until your fantasies have stopped imagining what you would like to do, or say, to the other person.

"(3) Ask yourself what is going on inside you and inside the other person. What is the disagreement really about? Her changing the furniture around, or a struggle for domination? Most of us perceive only an expurgated edition of what goes on in our minds.

"(4) Carefully distinguish between your interpretation of the situation and the actual situation. Each of us must realize and accept his lack of complete knowledge in every situation. Any good mind knows that all ideas are relative and only partial truth is possible for anyone. Then why make personal opinions a matter to be defended against attack? How much better to endeavor to see the other person's facts, and how the reality of the situation appears to him? When you say, 'The cause of all this trouble is. . . .' the statement is incomplete. There are undoubtedly other causes.

"(5) Seek an explanation for your feelings in your childhood experience.

"(6) Figure out the requirements of what you want to do and never underestimate the difficulties.

"(7) Formulate several possible solutions, and study these alternatives. What is inevitable? What is possible? What will you gain? What will you lose? Is the result worth a quarrel? What do you want to do about it? Never overestimate your abilities. Beware of hope pretending to be judgment.

"(8) Put your plan into action at the right time.

"(9) Evaluate the results after the issues are clarified and passions have cooled.

"(10) Think through what further to expect in the future as a result of what has happened. Where is this going and how fast?" [2]

When an argument or a quarrel is unavoidable, certain rules are observed by intelligent people. Nations try to observe rules, even in a war; why not husband and wife in a quarrel? The rules are the same as those mentioned in our discussion of lovers' spats in Chapter 10, which should be reread at this point.

JEALOUSY

Jealousy is so often experienced by persons who are in love that many regard it as a sign of love. The fact is that there can be love without jealousy and jealousy without love. Jealousy is an unpleasant feeling or attitude which arises whenever a person is afraid of losing something to someone else, or when he has lost something which he values. Analyzing this statement

---

[2] F. Alexander Magoun, *Love and Marriage*, New York, Harper & Brothers, 1948, pp. 268–269. Reprinted by permission.

further, we find that the element of fear predominates—the fear of loss, the fear of losing, and the fear that what we lose will become another's gain. Fear is an expression of insecurity. One who is secure within himself and secure in what he possesses does not experience jealousy.

Jealousy should be distinguished from envy. Envy is an unpleasant feeling or attitude aroused in a person when he perceives in someone else's possession something which he lacks or desires. Thus, when he sees a man who has a beautiful wife, a fine job, or an attractive home, he is envious. Had he had the opportunity to get these for himself and had someone taken them away from him, he would be jealous. In other words, there must be some degree of possession or ownership before there can be jealousy. A young man is in love with a girl. If another man shows interest in her and there is danger that she may turn to him, the first man will become jealous. Furthermore, to be jealous, that which one is about to lose must be valued. If the young man truly values her love, her expressions of affections, her time devoted to him and to his interests, he will be jealous.

Jealousy differs in intensity, depending upon how much the object is valued, the degree of insecurity, and the presence of envy. A girl who wishes to try to test the love of a young man may expose him to a jealousy-inducing situation. Should he become jealous, she feels sure of his love. Such a test is only partially effective. It is true that he could not become jealous had she no value for him, but his jealousy may be due also to a feeling of insecurity which might be aroused in him whenever he is in danger of losing *anything*. His reaction actually may be envy of the person to whom the girl turns.

Perhaps the most intense jealousy is aroused when there is danger of losing something valuable to a person of whom one is already envious. Jealousy then may become pathological. An example of such jealousy was brought to the authors' attention recently. A man of fifty-five who had never been sexually fully potent became aware of his waning sexual powers. This condition made him envious of younger men, a feeling which he expressed freely. When he noticed what he believed to be undue friendliness between his wife and a certain young man, he

[margin note: Envy]

immediately responded with violent jealousy, which resulted in delusions about the relationship between his wife and the young man. He accused them of repeated intimacy and even stated that his wife had had two abortions. He would never let her out of sight; he believed she flirted with any and every man on the street, in theaters, and elsewhere.

The effects of jealousy are so unpleasant that every attempt should be made to avoid it. Jealousy does to love what a disease germ does to a healthy body— makes it sick and even destroys it. Continuous jealousy is bound to destroy the finest of love relationships. One example is that of a young woman who came to the authors to tell about her wonderful love for a young man. She was delighted that he loved her so much; he became violently jealous if she merely smiled at another man! Within a matter of weeks, however, she became so frustrated with the young man that she felt like a "nervous wreck." She screamed when his name was mentioned.

Few emotions will make people more wretched than jealousy —either the one who is jealous or the object of the jealousy. Since no one is completely secure, no one is completely immune from jealousy, so that to make anyone jealous intentionally is "playing with fire." A jealous idea, once implanted, may take root and grow. An intelligent person will find other means of being reassured of love.

Jealousy after marriage often stems from feelings of inadequacy. For instance, a husband who is not successful in his business or profession, or enjoys little status among his own sex, may seek to bolster his ego within his home. He wants to be accepted by his wife as being superior and masterful. Thus the slightest sign of attention his wife may pay to other men or the remotest possibility that she may compare him with other men arouses feelings of jealousy. In order to avoid such unpleasant feelings, he may plead with her not to make him jealous. He may go so far as to dictate how his wife should behave when with other men. He may excuse his domination on the basis that he wants to protect her from other men. Actually he is protecting himself from further aroused feelings of inadequacy. He should of course recognize his weaknesses, strive to do everything possible to overcome or at least reduce them, rather than try to build up his ego by regulating his wife's behavior.

Since jealousy between mates is fairly common, a few words on how to handle a jealous mate are in order. However, once jealousy has become pathological, the services of a psychotherapist should be secured. In less serious cases, the following hints may be helpful.

(1) Build up the self-confidence of the jealous mate. The cause or causes for inadequacy must be discovered, and the proper methods must be used to eradicate them.

(2) Within reason, avoid situations which may induce jealousy.

(3) If you have acted properly and your mate still objects, do not admit to a false accusation merely to appease the mate. Such admission will only reinforce his jealousy and arouse further suspicion that the whole truth has not yet been told.

(4) Do not try to convince the jealous mate by reasoning. Jealousy is a feeling or emotion and cannot be reasoned away. In such situations, an expression of real love accomplishes more than hours of reasoning. A sincere smile, a tender kiss, or an embrace usually give the assurance the mate needs.

SENSE OF HUMOR

To "laugh it off" is an excellent method of ridding oneself of tensions, no matter what frustrations produce them or how one feels them—as anger, hate, fear, or jealousy. Laughter exercises muscles. The heartier the laughter, the more muscles involved. If tears flow, so much the better. The whole exercise drains irritating tensions. To laugh in this manner requires a sense of humor. A sense of humor is considered by psychologists to be one of the main criteria of a mature personality. To laugh because of a sense of humor is not the same as to laugh at a joke. Allport says: "True humor has been defined by the novelist Meredith as the ability to laugh at the things one loves (including, of course, oneself and all that pertains to it), and still love them. The real humorist perceives behind the solemn event, himself for instance, the contrast between pretension and performance. That which he values becomes, for the time being, vain show. There is a sudden shift of emphasis; for the moment all the world's a stage where nothing really matters, and where the actors, including oneself, can be viewed with the detachment of Olympus." [3]

A sense of humor is an important factor in marital happiness. Since a sense of humor is not innate but acquired, a married couple has the responsibility of developing it. Through sincere effort they can do so by acknowledging not only their points of strength but also their weaknesses. When one hears husband and wife tell humorous stories at their own expense, one can be sure they are happy with each other. They have reached that point of understanding in their relationship where they can laugh at and with each other.

INTERPRETATIVE SUMMARY

1. Emotions are extremely important in marriage. Pleasant emotions hold a marriage together and are conducive to happiness; unpleasant emotions are not only a hindrance to good adjustment but may actually disrupt the marriage.

2. Effective marital adjustment demands emotional maturity.

3. A person is emotionally mature when his emotions conform to the criteria laid down by the group to which he belongs. The criteria described are the frequency of the emotional states, the degree of their intensity, their duration, and the appropriateness of the emotion with reference to the situations.

4. Married mature love ultimately depends upon the capacity of each mate to give and to receive needed satisfactions.

5. When two persons are well adjusted to each other in marriage, love invariably will grow; conversely, if they are not well adjusted, love will wane.

6. If satisfactions are decreased and frustrations increased in marriage, love may be displaced by hate.

[3] Gordon W. Allport, *Personality,* New York, Henry Holt & Company, 1937, p. 223. Reprinted by permission.

7. No matter how well adjusted a husband and wife may be to each other, they still may arouse anger in each other on some occasions. Two common causes for anger—negative criticism and nagging—can and should be eliminated in marriage.

8. Since discussions can lead to arguments, a couple must learn the art of discussion, in which differences of opinion can and should be expressed.

9. Instead of conceiving jealousy and love as intimately related, one must realize that there can be love without jealousy and jealousy without genuine love.

10. A sense of humor—the ability to laugh at or with someone we love, *including* ourselves, is an invaluable aid to good adjustment in marriage.

THOUGHT QUESTIONS AND PROJECTS

1. Can you mention specific symptoms of emotional immaturity displayed by your unmarried friends which, if carried over into married life, could cause dissension between mates?

2. In what ways is health sometimes impaired by emotional disturbances?

3. What are commonly known physiological changes resulting from an intense emotional experience?

4. Mention some typical overt signs of an emotional state.

5. What factors appear to be significant in a marriage if love is to continue to grow?

6. What would you recommend as a mature approach to solving conflicts between mates?

7. State specific conditions which may cause love to be turned into hate.

8. What circumstances may predispose a person to chronic jealousy toward a mate?

9. Keep a record of your emotional experiences over a set period of time—three days or a week. Record each time you are aware of sensing fear, anger, love, hate, jealousy, etc. On your report write:

(a) Time of occurrence (hour of day and day of week).
(b) The situation which evoked the emotion.
(c) How you felt during the disturbed state.
(d) Length of duration.
(e) What you did about it.

You may find it interesting to compare your record with that of a friend, or you may like to submit an anonymous report, along with other members of the class, for comparison and further discussion.

Suggested Readings for Further Study

Cameron, Norman, and Ann Magaret, *Behavior Pathology*, Boston, Houghton Mifflin Company, 1951.
  Chapter 4. Symbolization, Role-Taking and Emotional Reactions.
Carroll, Herbert A., *Mental Hygiene*, 2nd ed., New York, Prentice-Hall, 1952.
  Chapter 4. The Need for Emotional Security.
Clark, Le Mon, *Emotional Adjustment in Marriage*, St. Louis, The C. V. Mosby Company, 1937.
  Chapter 1. Sex and Love.
  Chapter 5. Love as a Human Attribute.
Dreikurs, Rudolf, *The Challenge of Marriage*, New York, Duell, Sloan and Pearce, 1946.
  Chapter 1. What Is Love?
  Chapter 5. Living Together.
  Chapter 6. Jealousy.
English, O. Spurgeon, and Gerald H. J. Pearson, *Emotional Problems*, New York, W. W. Norton & Company, 1945.
Locke, Harvey J., *Predicting Adjustment in Marriage*, New York, Henry Holt & Company, 1951.
  Chapter 9. Personality Traits (1).
  Chapter 10. Personality Traits (2).
Magoun, F. Alexander, *Love and Marriage*, New York, Harper & Brothers, 1948.
  Chapter 10. Emotional Adjustments.
Munn, Norman L., *Psychology*, 2nd ed., Boston, Houghton Mifflin Company, 1951.
  Chapter 14. Emotional Behavior.
  Chapter 15. Feeling and Emotion in Everyday Life.
Ruch, Floyd L., *Psychology and Life*, 4th ed., Chicago, Scott, Foresman and Company, 1953.
  Chapter 6. Emotions—Inner Springs of Action.
  Part V. Reference Manual—Brain and Nervous System, pp. 399–427.

Stagner, Ross, and T. F. Karwoski, *Psychology*, New York, McGraw-Hill Book Company, 1952.
    Chapter 3. Emotions.
Vaughan, Wayland F., *Personal and Social Adjustment*, New York, The Odyssey Press, 1952.
    Chapter 4. Growing Up: Becoming a Mature Person.

16

SEXUAL ADJUSTMENT IN MARRIAGE

LEARNING TO CONTROL THE SEX DRIVE

One important fact for husband and wife to remember is that, on the human level, at least in our society, the sex act can never be confined merely to the physical or physiological level. By the time man is able to engage in sex expression, many habits, attitudes, ideas, beliefs, and values about sex have been integrated with the sex drive, so that whenever this drive is present, it is accompanied by psychological elements. Bergler expresses this idea in the following words:

> "It is incorrect to present the sex act itself as quite as simple and commonplace as the satisfaction of any other structural, that is, biologically determined, need. For we know that even in the case of biologically determined instinct satisfactions, there is present a complex psychic superstructure, or at least there can be, and one cannot properly understand the phenomenon without knowledge of the superstructure. Nevertheless it is at least half true when the biological factor in sex is over-emphasized, and the psychological superstructure is neglected." [1]

Since the satisfaction of the sex drive is so significant in marriage, and since no other biological drive is as much subject to regulation in our society, it is important to understand this "psychic superstructure" if adequate sexual satisfaction is to be achieved.

Let us consider first a simpler drive, that of voiding the bladder. In infancy, this is a reflexive function. When the bladder

---

[1] Edmund Bergler, *Unhappy Marriage and Divorce*, New York, International University Press, Inc., 1946, p. 16. Reprinted by permission.

is ready to be emptied, sensory nerves carry an impulse to a reflex center that leads to efferent fibers which activate the muscles, releasing the urine. Only later in life, when the higher centers are mature, can this function be regulated mentally. The nervous system is equipped with a series of arcs or loops, from the lower to the higher, or from the peripheral to the central. Whenever a higher arc is ready to function, it takes control of the lower arc. Thus, at first, voiding of the bladder is controlled by arcs in the pelvic region, and later by the brain. A simplified diagram may help to visualize what actually takes place.

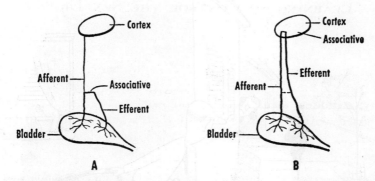

FIGURE 16. A. Voiding of bladder controlled by lower centers of the nervous system because neurons in cortical center are not mature.
B. Voiding controlled in cortex.

The sex function is regulated in a similar fashion, except that it is much more complex. During infancy and childhood, before the sexual apparatus is mature, it functions more reflexively. When the penis of an infant is stimulated, erection follows. An infant must be aware of this stimulation. According to psychoanalysts, similar pleasure is derived from stimulation of other erogenous zones—the mouth and the anus. The psychoanalysts have proved that sexual pleasure is experienced by a child before the sex apparatus is mature. This pleasant sensation connected with the stimulation of erogenous zones makes it possible for a child to receive some sex training before sexual maturation.

At maturation, the internal and external sex organs reach their full size; ova and spermatozoa are produced, and the various endocrine glands connected with sex give off hormones It is at this time that the sex drive becomes potent. It is now aroused not only by external stimulation, but also by internal

Al Johns and The Saturday Evening Post.

stimulation in the sex apparatus and by psychic processes. It is now that the psychic processes become so important; they are interposed between sexual stimulation and sexual response. Just as voiding of the bladder cannot take place in the adult without psychic control, so sexual functions cannot take place without such control.

PSYCHIC SUPERSTRUCTURE OF SEX

The core or essence of the psychic superstructure or control of sex in our society is the belief that sex pleasure is to be sought only between husband and wife. Any form of sexual satisfaction before marriage or outside of marriage is taboo. The effect of this belief is to make the psychic superstructure inhibit the sex drive and to turn it into a system of restrictions. Since seeking pleasure through sexual stimulation is present throughout childhood and becomes especially strong during adolescence, more and more potent inhibitions must be inculcated into the growing person to keep the sex drive restrained. Whatever he learns becomes a part of his personality.

A large part of human personality centers in the sex drive. While the sex drive is important in personality, the degree of its importance and one's general attitude toward it depend upon the individual's psychological make-up. In turn, an individual's psychological make-up depends upon the influence of his social-cultural environment; upon whether the person is masculine or feminine; upon the educational training attained—whether of elementary, high-school, or college level—and upon his particular combination of experiences. With these points in mind, let us consider some of the prevalent attitudes toward sex, as derived from general observation, from answers given on questionnaires, and from clinical studies.

Attitudes toward Sex in Our Society. In our society there is considerable fear of the sex impulse. English has the following to say about this feeling of fear:

> "Why is the sexual situation so faulty at present? The difficulty seems to begin in childhood when the mind is being formed. Adults have so much fear of the sexual impulse—far more fear than is warranted. There are two basic urges in mankind—sensual gratification and aggression. The former is no more dangerous to society than the latter; in fact, less so. Yet aggressive impulses are not feared as the sexual impulses are. Fighting is discouraged among children, but it is not taboo. In fact, sports and games are encouraged and even open fistic encounters among boys are regarded as desirable to the child's development. Even murder, while condemned, can be discussed with children and they are allowed to see it in the movies and the comics

and hear about it on the radio, but that same child must not hear of sex. Is sex more powerful or more malicious to man's welfare than aggression? We think not. Yet sexual activity—the only means of complete physical expression of love—is tabooed and punished from the earliest days onward. It is assumed we have the power to control aggression but that we cannot control our sexual desires!" [2]

Many children are taught that anything pertaining to sex is low, dirty, indecent, animal-like, and brutal. The close proximity of the sex organs to the organs of elimination has the effect of reinforcing the idea that sex is dirty. Stories told about brutal attacks of males on women and girls strengthen the idea of sex as a bestial thing.

Sex is regarded by many as immoral and sinful. This attitude is sometimes carried so far that sex and sin are taken to be synonymous. There are some who hold that sex is sinful even after marriage. Intercourse, they maintain, is permissible only for purposes of procreation. Even bearing of children may be viewed as sinful, an attitude perhaps related to the religious doctrine that children are conceived in sin. Most people who believe that sexual activity outside of marriage is sinful think that after marriage sex is "proper"; however, some still cannot really enjoy sexual pleasure, because they have been taught that such pleasure is evil. According to them, a refined person does not seek this kind of physiological pleasure.

Many married people cannot eradicate the deeply ingrained attitude that sex *per se* is "wrong." For the male, the sex act becomes a means of relief from tension. He may enjoy the act of relief, but somehow he cannot enjoy it as an end in itself. Often coupled with this attitude is the notion that a wife should not enjoy the act. Some men are shocked if their wives show passion. Such an attitude naturally soon forces the wife to hide her passion. Many girls are brought up by their mothers never to think of sex as a source of pleasure, but only as a duty, as something to satisfy the brutal nature of man.

Each individual has a definite biological urge for sex satisfaction, but the conflict of this desire with psychological con-

[2] From *Successful Marriage*, by Morris Fishbein, M.D. and Ernest W. Burgess, Ph.D. Copyright 1947, 1955 by Morris Fishbein, reprinted by permission of Doubleday & Company, Inc. P. 99.

ditioning against sex results in ambivalent feelings toward sexual expression; it is both wanted and not wanted. In some cases, this contradiction has serious results—serious in the sense that they produce neurotic tendencies.

There are, of course, many people who accept sex as a source of pleasure to be enjoyed. However, since it is an act which involves two people, the problem arises as to what extent the act can be made mutually enjoyable. It may involve the very ego. In both sexes, there is often a worry about the ability to satisfy a mate. Some couples will harbor this concern only before marriage, but for others it may be a problem throughout life. Because of their inhibitions, some can never discuss the matter openly and objectively. Others, because of ignorance, do not know that proper sexual adjustment to each other is invariably a matter of learning.

The psychic superstructure pertaining to sex contains other aspects of personality. Previous sex experiences, either with the present mate or with others, habits, values, traits, role conception, and self-esteem—all somehow enter into the sex act. On the human level, the sex act is at any time much more than merely a physical union. It is a most complex interpersonal relationship.

UNDERSTANDING THE OPPOSITE SEX

Because of the complexity of the human sex relationship, some understanding of the sex function of both male and female is necessary for both men and women. In addition to what was said about differences between men and women in general, therefore, it is appropriate that more be said about their differences in sex function. We understand people best who are like ourselves, because we are able to put ourselves in their place. Since there are definite differences between men and women, identification causes some problems which can be solved only to the extent to which one knows the other person. To be aware of these differences should aid in proper sex adjustment.

In the male, the physiological sex urge may occur, on the

average, about two or three times per week. The spermatozoa mature at a rapid rate after puberty. Whenever several hundred million have accumulated—at a rate of about 100 million a day— hormones are poured into the blood stream and the individual usually experiences an urge for sex expression. This condition does not require conscious thinking about sex. The production of sperms goes on whether the individual wants it or not. The female, too, has cycles, but they are not so uniform. In animals, the cycle is definite and intense. Any female animal at the period of heat, which occurs during the time of ovulation, manifests great sexual activity. Many women experience greater sex urges shortly before and after the menstrual period. Whether or not this is wholly physiological, we do not know. Certainly the feeling of being wanted or needed by the mate is important for women. Perhaps the primary drive is to be close to the male, a drive which *may* express itself in sexual intercourse.

In men, the sex urge is more localized than in women. Man's primary sex zone is in the genital organ and the secondary sex zone in the lips. Women derive sex pleasure from more areas of the body and may have a sex urge without actually recognizing it. Because of the complexity and extensity of the female sexual apparatus, it normally takes a woman longer than it does a man to become sexually aroused. This complexity may also be the reason why it takes her longer to achieve an orgasm. Psychological factors are important, because training can considerably alter an established form of response. A favorable attitude toward sex will help a woman become aroused more quickly and attain orgasm in a shorter time.

For the male, the achieving of sexual union is not only a means of sexual release but also a means of dominance. Women, as a rule, experience the sex act as one of submission. To what extent this fact is due to innate structure or to culture it is impossible to say at present. The very fact that man has something to give in the sex act and the female something to receive may make one more dominant and the other more submissive.

The manner in which men and women become acquainted with sex satisfaction may account for the indifferent attitudes of some toward the sex act. For the male, the first heterosexual experience is associated with a great deal of pleasure, and pleasure only, unless he suffers from some inadequacy. For women, the first sex experience is almost invariably connected with pain, and sometimes there is pain even with later experiences. Even the first awareness of sexual maturity is different for the two sexes. For the male, ejaculation is always pleasant. For the female, menstruation, if not painful and a source of fear or shock, is at least unhygienic. For the male, the sex act is a complete event; for the female, it may be merely the beginning of a pregnancy—and there are many occasions after marriage when intimate relationship is desired but pregnancy is not.

All in all, the sex act means much more to a woman physiologically and psychologically than it does to a man. Probably for this reason she never can enter the sex act as lightly as a male. She invariably feels that she must be loved, or at least very much needed as a person and not as a means toward an end. Before she can enter into the sex act, she must either love or respect her partner. After marriage, she may seek coitus more as a means of reassurance of her husband's love than as a source of physical satisfaction.

SEXUAL UNION OF HUSBAND AND WIFE

The Place of Sex in Marriage. A great deal has been written about the relationship between happy or successful marriages and sex satisfaction. The consensus is that the sexual relationship between husband and wife is one important factor in marriage. Just how important it is depends upon the personalities of the two persons involved. However, when there is no sex satisfaction in marriage, one very important factor in marital happiness is lacking. Most authorities would agree with the following statement by Seward: "Sex as such is not solely responsible for happiness or unhappiness, but happiness or unhappiness is immediately reflected in the sexual sphere. In other words, sex may be regarded as a sensitive though not infallible marital barometer." [3]

[3] By permission from *Sex and the Social Order,* by Georgene H. Seward. Copyright, 1946. McGraw-Hill Book Company, Inc. P. 210.

Terman and Kinsey base their opinions about this matter on research. Terman states:

"Our data do not confirm the view so often heard that the key to happiness in marriage is nearly always to be found in sexual compatibility. They indicate, instead, that the influence of the sexual factor is at most no greater than that of the combined personality and background factors, and that it is probably less. The problem is complicated by the fact that the testimony of husband and wife regarding their sexual compatibility is influenced by their psychological compatibility. Couples who are psychologically well mated are likely to show a surprising tolerance for the things that are not satisfactory in their sexual relationships. The psychologically ill-mated show no such tolerance but instead are prone to exaggerate in their report on sexual maladjustments. The two sexual factors of genuine importance are the wife's orgasm adequacy and relative strength of sex drive in the two spouses." [4]

Kinsey, after examining six thousand marital and three thousand divorce histories, concludes:

"Sexual maladjustments contribute in perhaps three quarters of the upper level marriages that end in separation or divorce, and in some smaller percentage of the lower level marriages that break up. Where the sexual adjustments are poor, marriages are maintained with difficulty. It takes a considerable amount of idealism and determination to keep a marriage together when the sexual adjustments are not right. Sexual factors are, in consequence, very important in a marriage." [5]

We may say that while marriage may persist with some degree of happiness when sexual union is absent or is unsatisfactory the happiness is not so complete as it might be. For many couples, such a condition is unacceptable. Unsatisfactory sex relationship may be a cause or an effect of difficulties of adjustment to each other. Sexual union between husband and wife is not only a physical but also a psychological phenomenon. Nothing, therefore, should be neglected to make the sex act a mutually pleasant relationship.

Frequency of Intercourse. The question of frequency of intercourse is raised both by couples who find the experience

---

[4] By permission from *Psychological Factors in Marital Happiness,* by Lewis M. Terman *et al.* Copyright, 1938. McGraw-Hill Book Company, Inc. P. 376.

[5] Alfred C. Kinsey *et al., Sexual Behavior in the Human Male,* Philadelphia, W. B. Saunders Company, 1948, p. 544. Reprinted by permission.

mutually pleasant and by those with some sex problems. The reasons given by the former are usually based upon some fear— fear that they might "lower" their union by overindulgence in sex, or fear that too frequent intercourse might affect their health, or fear that the male might deplete his reservoir of sexual energy. None of these fears is warranted. A couple should enjoy their sex life to the extent that it remains mutually satisfying. Their health will not be undermined so long as they use common sense. In no case can a male exhaust his sex potential at any time, since only a limited number of spermatozoa reach their maturity each day.

Factors that affect the frequency of the sex urge include general conditions of health, age, length of marriage, mode of life, occupation, religion, moral concepts, and degree of harmony between the individuals. Quite often it is found that persons who do not have many psychological satisfactions will resort more often to physiological satisfactions.

In passing, something should be said here about nymphomania and satyriasis. Nymphomania is an exaggerated degree of sexual desire in the human female, and is a symptom of a personality or mental disorder. Satyriasis is a similar disorder in the male. Both of these disorders as a rule require a specialist— a psychiatrist—for diagnosis and treatment.

No better answer can be given to the question about frequency of sexual intercourse than to state the practice of married couples in our society. Perhaps the most reliable information about the matter has come from the Kinsey studies.

> "In the population as a whole, and in all of its subdivisions, the highest frequencies of marital intercourse occur in the youngest age groups. Males who are married between 16 and 20 start with frequencies which average 3.9 for the population as a whole, and many individuals that age have intercourse on an average of 5, 7, 10 or more times per week. There is considerable individual variation, and the 15 per cent group who are capable of multiple orgasm may regularly secure 14, 21, or more climaxes per week from intercourse with their wives. Frequencies drop steadily from the teens to about 2.9 at age 30, to 1.8 at age 50, and to 0.9 at age 60." [6]

[6] *Ibid.,* p. 569.

Intercourse during Menstruation and Pregnancy. Most couples in our society avoid intercourse during menstruation; however, there is no sound scientific reason why a couple may not engage in it at this time, provided it is mutually desired. There may, of course, be aesthetic or religious reasons. Some couples abstain from coitus during pregnancy for aesthetic reasons or because of taboos which have been handed down from earlier periods.

There is no danger whatsoever in intercourse during pregnancy if several precautions are taken. First, coitus should be avoided during the time when menstruation would normally occur the second or third time after conception. Second, intercourse should not occur during the last two months of pregnancy. At other periods of pregnancy, intercourse may be engaged in freely, except that as pregnancy progresses, vigorous activity should be modified considerably. After childbirth, there should be no intercourse for six to eight weeks.

As to desire for intercourse on the part of pregnant women, there is marked difference. Some women are unusually passionate during this time, perhaps because before they were afraid of pregnancy and, now that it has taken place, they can enter more unreservedly into the act. Pregnancy also makes husband and wife especially precious to each other. On the other hand, there are women who lose all interest in sex just as soon as they realize they are pregnant.

There is perhaps no other period when husband and wife must show each other greater consideration than during pregnancy. Neither should put the other under undue strain.

PROBLEMS IN SEXUAL ADJUSTMENT

Almost all couples at some time or other meet with difficulties in sexual adjustment. Some of these difficulties present only minor problems, while others are of such a complicated nature as to require more skill in handling and more information than the average couple possesses. Two rather common mistakes are often made—namely, casting all blame on the partner and/

or trying to "cure" him or her without viewing the problem as one of co-operation. By understanding the nature of their problems, their causes and their effects, a husband and wife may be sufficiently motivated to do their best to handle their difficulties intelligently. If, however, they find that they are unable to solve their problems alone, they should not hesitate to consult a physician, psychiatrist, clinical psychologist, or marriage counselor.

Inability to Achieve Orgasm. While inability to achieve orgasm is primarily the problem of women, there are a few men who cannot achieve orgasm during intercourse but can do so through masturbation. Because these men are able to achieve orgasm at some times and not at others, organic causation must be ruled out and replaced by psychological factors, some of which are mentioned below.

Some homosexual men can enter into a heterosexual relationship, but the sex act seems so unnatural for them that they cannot complete it. Some men look upon the wife as a mother substitute and consider coitus with her to be indecent. They become sufficiently aroused sometimes to enter into the sex act, but to complete it would seem like violating their mother relationship. There are some men who regard sex as so low and indecent that they cannot enter fully into the act.

There has been much speculation about the percentage of women who do not achieve orgasm in coitus. Estimates have ranged from 75 per cent down to 8 per cent. Many such estimates are based upon clinical studies. However, since the clinician is likely to deal with women who have such problems, his estimate is possibly too high.

There are a number of causes for women's inability to attain an orgasm. All of them are more or less speculative; because of the nature of the problem, one cannot get scientific evidence. The causes are either physical or psychological. The difficulty may be with the husband or with the wife. Undoubtedly in some cases several factors work together to produce this undesirable result.

Frigidity. There is no general agreement among authorities on sex as to the *meaning* of frigidity. For some, frigidity means the absence of vaginal orgasm. Other authorities contend just as strongly that a woman is not frigid unless she has no desire for the sex act. Between these extremes are still other authorities who say that a woman is frigid when she does not derive any pleasure from coitus, or when she enters the sex act from a sense of duty. We will use the term to mean that a woman has either no desire for the sex act or is cool toward it and tolerates it merely as a responsibility. When she engages in it, she may experience some pleasure, but without orgasm of any kind.

It is doubtful whether absolute and permanent frigidity exists. If it does, it probably is due to glandular disorders.

Since there is no agreement about the meaning of frigidity, it is impossible to give exact percentages as to its *prevalence*. From information available, the best we can say is that from about one fourth to about one third of all married women (or 10 to 15 million) in the United States are sexually unresponsive. The *effect* of this condition upon marital adjustment can be surmised by anyone. It causes one of the conventional aspects of a marital relationship to be removed. To what extent it will affect marital happiness will depend upon the couple.

The *causes* of frigidity are physical, organic, or psychological, or a combination of these. Physiologically, there may be lack of or inadequate hormones, especially sex hormones. There may be sensory anesthesia (absence of sensation). Sexual anesthesia may also be functional, the result of mental and emotional conditions.

By far the majority of cases of frigidity are due to psychological factors. If, as is often the case, orgasm inadequacy leads to frigidity, the causes for such inadequacy apply here. The reader is reminded that all the inhibitions built into the psychic superstructure of sex may apply. Unhealthy attitudes toward sex, ignorance, fears, and guilt may result in frigidity. In some cases frigidity is merely one symptom of a neurotic personality.

Impotence. A man is said to be impotent when he is incapable of participating in the sex act. Impotence may be due to physiological or psychological factors. It is in many cases a source of great humiliation for the husband. Unfortunately, husband and wife often seek help only after years of attempted self-cure. Whatever may be the causal condition of impotence, the effect is usually the same—unsatisfactory sex life. There are, of course, degrees of dissatisfaction depending upon the persons involved. The couple may accept the condition and stress the aspects of companionship in their marriage.

INTERPRETATIVE SUMMARY

1. Because of the direct or indirect training a person receives in our society, the sex act can never be merely a physical union; it involves also a psychic superstructure.

2. This psychic superstructure consists of many ideas, beliefs, and attitudes.

3. Frequently a man or woman, prior to marriage, has received negative teaching about the sex act which interferes with normal sex life after marriage.

4. A good sexual adjustment between a husband and wife requires full and thorough familiarity with the differences in structure and function of their bodies, as well as with differences in their background and training about sex.

5. There is a marked variation of opinion about the importance of sex in marriage. Probably the least that can be said is that if sex life is absent or is not satisfactory, a marriage is not as complete as it might otherwise be.

6. In view of the complexity of the sex act, it is not surprising that there are numerous problems connected with it.

7. Sometimes the husband, but more frequently the wife, cannot attain an orgasm in the sex act. The causes of this condition are rarely physical. In most cases they are psychological in nature. Information and changes in attitude often can remedy this type of difficulty. In severe cases, psychotherapy may be necessary.

8. It is estimated that from one fourth to one third of the married women in the United States are relatively or com-

pletely frigid. The causes are seldom organic. Most often they are psychological factors and lack of proper skill on the part of the husband. Treatment will attempt to discover the causes and to remove them.

9. Impotence in men can in most cases be overcome by proper treatment if it is due to psychological factors.

THOUGHT QUESTIONS AND PROJECTS

1. Do you think children in elementary grades are given more helpful sex education today than you received while at that level? Account for your answer.

2. Point out specifically how one's attitudes toward sex are influenced through personal experience and training in early life.

3. Which courses studied in high school and in college have helped you most toward a better understanding of the part that sex plays in personality development? In your opinion, does the college you now attend offer adequate sex education and guidance for those who need it?

4. Why are husband and wife sometimes reluctant to discuss aspects of their sexual adjustment to each other? Has the level of their education any bearing on this situation?

5. How important is the function of the autonomic nervous system in sexual adjustment?

6. If you were asked to suggest the titles of three reliable books which present helpful guides in the area of sexual adjustment, which ones would you mention?

SUGGESTED READINGS FOR FURTHER STUDY

Bowman, Henry A., *Marriage for Moderns*, 3rd ed., New York, McGraw-Hill Book Company, 1954.
  Chapter 12. Personality Adjustment in Marriage (Sex in Marriage).
Durand-Wever, A., "The Influence of the Nervous System on the Structure and Functions of the Human Genital Organs," *International Journal of Sexology*, 1952, 5:250–253.

Everett, Millard S., *Hygiene of Marriage,* rev. ed., Cleveland, World Publishing Company, 1948.

Knepp, T. H., "Need for Sex Education in the High School," *Journal of Social Hygiene,* 1952, 38: 49–55.

Landis, Judson T., and Mary G. Landis, *Building a Successful Marriage,* 2nd ed., New York, Prentice-Hall, 1953.
  Chapter 13. Sex Adjustment in Marriage.

Magoun, F. Alexander, *Love and Marriage,* New York, Harper & Brothers, 1948.
  Chapter 9. The Sex Relation.

Stone, Hannah M., and Abraham Stone, *A Marriage Manual,* rev. ed., New York, Simon & Schuster, 1952.
  Chapter 7. The Art of Marriage.
  Chapter 9. Health in Marriage.

Sweeney, E. E., "Partners in Sex Education," *Journal of Social Hygiene,* 1952, 38:49–55.

Wood, R., "Reason and Tabu in Sexual Behavior," *Journal of Sex Education,* 1952, 4:250–253.

17

REPRODUCTION

When two individuals marry, their plans for the future usually include having a family. As a rule, they consider their home incomplete until they have added children. For most couples it is not a question of whether they shall have children but whether they will be fortunate enough to have them. They are more likely to be concerned with the problem of how soon to start having a family. Are there sometimes obstacles to be overcome in trying to have a family? At what intervals should children be born? How many children should they plan to have? What factors should be considered before starting a family? What should they know about pregnancy and the birth process? What problems of adjustment must they face in connection with the new experience?

We shall try to answer these questions in the following discussion of sterility, birth control, and pregnancy.

STERILITY

Sterility is primarily a medical problem. It is discussed in this book because of the psychological factors involved.

Sterility is the inability to have children after a prolonged period of normal sex relations, usually a period of approximately three years. Since accurate information is not available as to the incidence of sterility, only an estimate can be made. It is usually assumed by authorities that 10 per cent of married couples in the United States are sterile and 15 per cent relatively sterile.

Causes. The causes of sterility may be either physical or psychological, and they may lie within either the male or the female. (Until recent times, it was believed that sterility was restricted to the female.) Some authorities estimate that in 30 to 50 per cent of the cases of sterility, the difficulty lies with the husband. Cary, a leading medical authority on sterility, is more conservative in his estimate: "My statistics disclose that in approximately ten per cent of infertile marriages, the husband is found sterile, that in an additional sixteen per cent his fertility is sufficiently impaired to make pregnancy improbable, and that in seven per cent more, reproductive vigor is sufficiently subnormal to warrant consideration as a contributory factor." [1] The fact of sterility can be determined by an examination of male semen, which may reveal either the absence of any spermatozoa, an insufficient quantity, or a poor quality.

In the female, the following causes of sterility have been established: First, she may have a deficiency of egg formations in the ovary. Second, there may be some obstruction to the passage of the spermatozoa to and through the Fallopian tubes because of an abnormal position of the uterus, inflammation of the neck or other parts of the uterus, infection of the Fallopian tubes, or malformation of the genital organs. Third, in some cases when fertilization does occur, it is impossible for the egg to implant itself in the uterus. Fairly adequate tests have been discovered to determine the fertility of the spermatozoa, but comparable tests for the ova have not been found.

We are not too certain about the psychological factors in sterility. Most authorities who have concerned themselves with these factors have discovered a definite correlation between sterility and the emotional stability of husband or wife. The evidence comes from clinical experience of psychiatrists and psychologists. Magoun says:

[1] William H. Cary, "Sterility. What the Public Should Know," *Birth Control Review*, 1938, 22:50. Reprinted by permission.

"Frigidity, or fear of having a baby before there is opportunity to get adjusted to each other or financially prepared, may lead to childlessness, for the sympathetic nervous system controls the sex functions. A woman's emotions have a great deal to do with her impregnation. Her nervous system affects the pituitary and hypothalamus glands which control the production of sex hormones, and these influence fecundity. On the husband's side, deep or prolonged anxiety will sometimes result in the manufacture of sperm with no life in them." [2]

A case in point is the fact that intense and prolonged emotional excitement causes many menstrual irregularities in women. Neurotic and certain psychotic women may not menstruate for months and even for years. Such cases indicate that the linings of the uterus are affected, and the healthy condition of these linings is necessary for the implantation of the fertilized ovum.

Effects of and Adjustment to Sterility. When a couple is eager to have children, the discovery of the barrenness of their union quite often causes a great emotional shock and disappointment. In due time, there comes serious questioning as to who is to blame for the condition. The first and most intelligent step any couple can take, when convinced of their inability to have children, is for both of them to have a medical examination. This step should be taken before they have strong feelings about their problem, for otherwise one partner may cause the other to suffer. In most cases, the medical examination will establish the cause for sterility. If the cause can be removed, such action should be taken immediately. If it cannot be removed, the whole problem should be discussed frankly.

Any decision will be based upon what the partners consider preferable, their marriage without children of their own creation or the dissolution of their marriage. If the couple decides against separation, they must be willing to accept the implications. The fertile member must accept the sterile one wholeheartedly and without reservations; otherwise, the marriage will be not only childless but also without love and true companionship. If the fertile member is set on having children, he should

[2] F. Alexander Magoun, *Love and Marriage*, New York, Harper & Brothers, 1948, p. 227. Reprinted by permission.

not stay with the mate because of pity. Such an arrangement, in time, would become too heavy a burden to bear for both of them. It undermines the self-respect of the sterile person to be merely tolerated, and the fertile mate may feel unduly noble. Marriage, then, becomes bondage.

When the fertile member fully accepts the sterile one, at least three ways are open to them to enrich their marriage. They can concentrate on making each other happy by devoting to each other the time and energy they might otherwise have expended on the rearing of children. Developing a wide area of common interests will give them opportunity to make their marriage meaningful. In cases where the husband is sterile, they may resort to artificial insemination of the wife. Another solution is to adopt a child, or better yet, several children. Adoption should never be considered because parents want to *possess* a child, or for humanitarian reasons; they should consider it because of a desire to enrich both their own lives and those of the adopted children.[3]

PREVENTION OF CONCEPTION

It is not our purpose to discuss all aspects of birth control, nor do we aim to instruct married couples in the use of contraceptives. Instead, we refer them to Appendix C of this book for a list of reliable agencies, including the Planned Parenthood Federation of America, which, upon request, will furnish information as to the nearest location of the more than seven hundred birth-control clinics in our country. We are primarily concerned with prevention of conception insofar as it affects sexual adjustment between husband and wife. Prevention of conception may affect the sex relationship adversely if one or more of the following conditions prevail: guilt, fear, nervous tension, and decrease of satisfaction.

Guilt feelings about prevention of conception (birth control) are

[3] Couples who contemplate adopting a child can profit a great deal by reading first a number of books available on the topic, especially Lee M. Brooks and Evelyn C. Brooks, *Adventuring in Adoption,* Chapel Hill, University of North Carolina Press, 1939.

due primarily to lack of understanding, especially understanding of what it means. For some, birth control is synonymous with murder. But modern birth control is the prevention of the *beginning* of a new life, rather than its destruction. Prevention is achieved by keeping the male sperm from entering the uterus and thus reaching an ovum in the Fallopian tubes.

Some also believe that birth control means the waste of spermatozoa and ova. But nature is so profuse in the production of these that waste is unavoidable in any case. If conception takes place, only one sperm is "used." Since there are 200 million to 500 million present in each ejaculation, one healthy man produces more spermatozoa in one month than the entire population of our globe. A normal woman has from 50 to 60 thousand ova in her ovaries. Not all of these ova ripen in her lifetime. If one ripens in her every twenty-eight days she can produce approximately 390 mature eggs from the age of 15 to 45. Even if she has 20 children, 370 mature eggs still could not be utilized, not to speak of the thousands which never ripen. In other words, when a couple does not practice birth control, they still "waste" billions of spermatozoa and thousands of ova.

We can see some reason for guilt feeling about birth control only when a couple is healthy and economically and otherwise well capable of having children and yet will not have any. But even this is a matter to be decided by each couple; ultimately it is their and only their affair.

There are a number of valid reasons for practicing birth control, reasons which may contribute to better adjustment between husband and wife, better health for the mother, and more adequate care of a child. Most authorities on marriage agree that a couple should be married at least two years before having a child. This period will give them an opportunity to become adjusted to each other and thus create a proper home atmosphere for a child. When children arrive in rapid succession, they will need the mother's time and energy so much that she cannot be a real companion to her husband; and all his time and energy, furthermore, will be consumed in the effort to earn enough money to support the family. Thus, one of the important functions of marriage, pleasant companionship, will be much limited.

The mother's health will almost invariably be impaired by too-frequent pregnancies. It is the consensus of medical men that, in order to guard the mother's health, children should be spaced at least two years apart. It is true, too, that the psychological effect of being considered primarily a wife for "breeding" purposes often has a devastating effect on a woman's morale.

Birth control may be practiced in the interest of the child's welfare. When a family is too large, the attention any one child can receive from parents becomes limited. The income of the average family is not sufficient to give every child in a large family proper food, medical care, and education, especially in today's economy. Children in our country used to be an economic asset; now they are a liability. The argument here is not for an only child but for limitation of the number of children to what a given family can afford. Ideally, from this viewpoint, rich parents should have many children, and poor families only a few.

Parents who may have guilt feelings about birth control because of religion should know that church leaders, with very few exceptions, are in favor of it. This is true even for the Catholic Church which is not against birth control but only against certain methods used for contraception.[4]

Women often do not get full enjoyment out of coitus because of fear of pregnancy. This fear can be diminished or completely removed in two ways. One is the co-operation of the husband in preventing conception. All too often a husband feels that birth control is entirely the wife's responsibility. He can use certain methods of birth control himself; and he can greatly alleviate his wife's fears by co-operating with her in the methods she may use. The second means of counteracting fears is the use of the best contraceptive techniques. Some of these techniques are still in the experimental stage, some are ineffective, and others even harmful. Actually, there is no ideal method of birth con-

[4] See Encyclical of Pope Pius XI, "Cathi Cormulis," *Christian Marriage,* New York, The America Press, 1936, pp. 17–18.

trol—ideal in the sense of being completely reliable, simple, practical, and in no way interfering with mutual sex pleasure.

The use of any contraceptive method may produce some degree of nervous tension because the concern about its effectiveness is likely to prevent the freedom necessary to achieve full release and pleasure. For example, the rhythm method demands abstinence from intercourse on certain days each month. This abstinence in itself may be felt as a frustration. Even when a "safe" period arrives, there is always some uncertainty about it. Because the menstrual cycle is influenced by emotions, the woman's fears actually may cause her to be irregular. The very fact that whenever intercourse is contemplated one has to think about the use of some contraceptive method has an inhibiting effect upon the sex urge. In some cases, a couple may forego coitus rather than resort to contraception. The whole process of contraception appears to many somewhat unaesthetic. While birth control gives married couples great benefit, they must pay some price for it. The great majority of couples are willing to pay this price, especially if they are concerned about their social status. For birth control has become so widely accepted that a couple with too many children is sometimes looked upon as being either uninformed or selfish.

PREGNANCY

Pregnancy entails specific adjustments for the husband and wife. The majority of couples, when planning to start a family, feel an increased sense of responsibility. They may wonder whether they are ready to have children, or whether certain circumstances and conditions merit consideration before starting pregnancy. We believe there are significant points to be weighed; therefore, we present the following questions.

(1) *Are husband and wife adequately adjusted to each other?* When two individuals marry, they must make innumerable adjustments to each other. This adjustment requires time. They need enough undivided time together to allow their love and

affection to become firmly established. If pregnancy is started immediately after marriage, the couple has less opportunity to adjust as husband and wife.

(2) *Would possible change of plans mean disappointment?* Early pregnancy may result in feelings of disappointment for one or even both mates if it results in the sacrifice of a much coveted career, or a serious interruption in the preparation for life work, or if in any way it blocks an immediate goal which, if not achieved, could have adverse effects on the couple's future.

(3) *Are mates emotionally mature enough to take on parenthood?* A husband and wife need to have attained emotional maturity to the point where they are freed from overdependency on their parents or on each other. They should feel reasonably stable emotionally and self-reliant before assuming the role of parenthood.

(4) *Are mates socially adjusted in their new marital roles?* Prior to the couple's marriage, their friends are predominantly single. After marriage, a couple, in their new role, begin to establish social relationships with married couples. They need a period of time in which to make the transition to a new group, to form new friendships, and to become a part of a somewhat different pattern of social and recreational life. If a young married couple becomes immediately engrossed in matters pertaining to pregnancy, they tend to overlook necessary social adjustments which, if left until later, become difficult to make.

(5) *Are they financially ready for a child?* A couple is ready to start a family when economically able to offer a reasonable degree of security toward the proper care of the mother and child. However, the question of financial status must not be overemphasized, and thus delay parenthood too long. Sometimes planning for and having a child motivates parents to budget their finances more wisely.

(6) *Do the medical records of mates show any indications which would make childbearing inadvisable?* Usually the wife has had a premarital examination, but she should check further to see if there were any conditions in her medical history or any recent developments which might jeopardize the health or life of the mother and child. It is wise to review the medical

history of the husband to determine if complications of a hereditary nature could appear in the offspring.

(7) *Do they want a child for the child's sake?* A couple is
ready to start a family when both husband and wife sincerely
want a child for the child's own sake—not because they think
people expect them to have a child, nor because other couples
are having children. It contributes greatly to the happiness of
an offspring to know he was wanted by his parents for no other
sake but his own.

The preceding points emphasize how to judge readiness for
starting a family. When not to start a family is discussed in Chapter 19. Here we point out only that a couple whose union is on
the verge of breaking up and who decide to have a child as a
means of saving their marriage run great risk of harmful consequences for themselves as well as for their child.

Psychological Effects of Pregnancy. Pregnancy is a normal
condition. A pregnant woman is not an ill person and should
not be treated as such unless, of course, irregularities in her
case are judged by her physician to be unusual and hazardous.
It is fortunate when pregnancy can be regarded by all persons
concerned as a natural process and the pregnant woman can
be granted reasonable considerations without being treated as
a semi-invalid.

Effects on the prospective mother. For the wife who is in
love with her husband and who wants to bear a child, pregnancy
means the realization of her potentiality; perhaps the fulfillment
of her dream as to what marriage actually should be. If it is
the first child she may look forward to the experience as a real
adventure. It is understandable why a woman during the months
of pregnancy enjoys thinking about and discussing minute details concerning the coming child. It is a reality for her from the
moment she knows she is pregnant. She derives satisfaction from
anticipation. Mixed with pleasant feelings, however, may come
less pleasant ones. If she is as yet inexperienced with childbirth
and unfamiliar with its processes, she may have feelings of fear
and anxiety.

Further unpleasant effects may result in cases where the wife does not want the child and is not sincerely in love with her husband. Under these circumstances she may bear resentment toward him and may regard her pregnancy as virtually a kind of punishment. Physical discomforts experienced by her during pregnancy are likely to be grossly exaggerated. Some women, despite the fact that they want children, become frustrated because the period of pregnancy necessitates certain changes in household routine. It may limit some forms of social and recreational activities and may modify intimate relations with the husband. Where there is close co-operation and understanding between husband and wife, bad feelings about such effects seldom arise.

Effects on the prospective father. The happily married husband who wants a family shares his wife's pleasant anticipations. Of course, his feelings cannot be the same as hers. Her awareness of the developing child is ever present, while his realization of what is taking place is primarily on the cognitive level. He cannot sense the child physically; he cannot react with maternal emotions as does his wife. Because of this difference, he may appear serene, unconcerned, and even indifferent about her pregnancy. He may experience what could be called "delayed excitement." The actual thrill of being a parent he can fully experience and appreciate only after the birth of the baby. It is then that he can catch up with his wife's state of happiness, which she has been enjoying for the past several months.

If the husband is an emotionally mature person, he will accept the months of his wife's pregnancy as a period of common endeavor and closest co-operation. He will find satisfaction in an increased responsibility. On the other hand, if he is overly dependent on his wife in that she is more of a mother-protector for him, he may react to her pregnancy as a threat to his emotional security—especially in the later months when she becomes more and more preoccupied with preparations for the birth of the child. Being immature, he cannot bear to have his wife's love and attention divided between himself and the coming child. Such jealousy shows up before the child arrives and increases afterwards. The husband may suffer disappointment because their regular social life and recreational activities have been modified

or curtailed. He may feel deprived because of less frequent intimate relations with his wife.

Effects on siblings. The effects of pregnancy on other children
in the family will depend upon the manner in which the new
situation is handled. When parents tell their children about the
coming baby and give them a chance to share in anticipating
and preparing for the event, they usually find them to be en-
thusiastic. It is their baby, too. On the contrary, when children
are not taken into confidence, not given information and assurance, they may reject the baby. They are likely to view the new
arrival as cause for keen competition for parental love and attention. (The period of pregnancy can offer an excellent opportunity for parents to give their children helpful information about
how a baby begins, grows, and is born.)

Effects on general household. Pregnancy may bring about
physical changes which may have psychological effects on the
family. An addition to the family may necessitate moving to
larger living quarters, a change which in itself requires adjustment to new surroundings, perhaps to new friends, and to a different community. The husband may have to put in longer hours
at work or add an "odd" job to increase the family income. In
some cases he may have to change jobs completely and go into
new work. There is hardly a household that does not suffer
some change in routine to adjust to the coming of a new baby.

Conception. A detailed description of the female and male
reproductive organs as to structure and functions was given in
Chapter 4 (Comparing Men and Women). For our purpose here,
let us review briefly what is meant by conception. During coitus,
millions of spermatozoa, ejaculated in the semen from the male
organ, enter the vaginal tract, pass through the cervix into the
uterus, and on into the Fallopian tube. In this passage, a sperm
may meet an ovum which has been released from the ovary and
ejected into the Fallopian tube. If the sperm penetrates the wall
of the ovum and fuses with its nucleus, conception or fertilization
takes place. The fertilized ovum then continues its journey
through the Fallopian tube to the uterus where it attaches itself
to the uterine wall. The journey of the ovum from the time it

leaves the ovary until it reaches the uterus takes approximately from three to seven days.

Period of Fertility. Pregnancy can occur during the time of ovulation, which refers to the process by which the egg is expelled from the ovary into the Fallopian tube (where, if it meets with the sperm, it can be fertilized). However, there is no agreement and certainty as to how to estimate precisely when the ovum will be released. Ovulation usually occurs approximately fourteen days prior to the beginning of menstruation—that is, during the middle of a regular twenty-eight-day menstrual cycle. Of course, women who have irregular cycles would need to figure accordingly. For them the fourteen-day point may or may not be the middle of the cycle. There is some evidence that ovulation takes place two weeks before the beginning of the menstrual cycle regardless of the irregularity of the cycle. The span of time during which fertilization can take place is relatively brief. Research data do not fully agree as to exactly how long ova and spermatozoa can live. However, it is generally believed that after leaving the ovary, the life of the ovum, if not fertilized, is short, lasting possibly about twenty-four to forty-eight hours. The life of the sperm is comparatively the same, but frequently spermatozoa have been found to live longer than forty-eight hours.

There are three stages of growth and development through which the new form of life passes: first, the germinal stages—from conception until the end of two weeks—during which the new life may be referred to technically as an ovum; second, the embryonic stage—from the end of the second week until the end of the second month—when it is called an embryo; and third, the fetal stage—from the end of the second month until birth —during which time it is known as the fetus.

Presumptive Signs of Pregnancy. Presumptive signs refer to those conditions which ordinarily occur in the early stages of pregnancy. They are recognized as only possible indicators until pregnancy tests and the doctor's diagnosis verify them. Some of the earliest symptoms are temporary cessation of menstruation, early morning nausea, and perhaps vomiting, commonly referred to as "morning sickness"; changes in the breasts, such as coloration, enlargement, and a tingling sensation; increased frequency of urination; discoloration of the vulva and increased discharge from the vaginal tract; change in temperature of the body; changes in skin tone, and increased appetite for certain foods, often of bizarre combination.

Obviously, pregnancy is not easily determined from the foregoing signs, any one of which may be symptomatic of other bodily disorders or psychological disturbances. Temporary cessation of menstruation is fairly common among women suffering from emotional upset. Furthermore, there are women who continue slight menstruation even after the beginning of pregnancy. Early-morning nausea and vomiting can be misleading. Many cases have been reported in which overeagerness in women to become pregnant (or just the opposite, fear of becoming pregnant) produces morning sickness. Thus presumptive signs of pregnancy are not wholly reliable. It is wise to seek a doctor's verification when pregnancy is suspected so that he can observe positive signs when they appear.

A doctor can make a satisfactory examination of the uterine cavity about six to eight weeks after the beginning of the last menstrual period. Such signs as discoloration of the vagina and the enlargement and softening of the cervix may indicate to him further evidence of pregnancy.

Medical Tests for Pregnancy. If there are reasons for wanting still earlier proof of pregnancy, a doctor may recommend the use of one of the urine tests which have proved to be highly successful, yielding about 98 per cent accuracy. These tests are commonly referred to as the Friedman test, which uses rabbits, or the Ascheim-Zondek test, which uses rats or mice. A still more recent test uses a certain toad and is referred to as the "frog test." These tests are based upon the fact that the early morning urine from a pregnant woman contains certain hormones in large quantities which have the capacity of stimulating and speeding up sexual maturation in immature virgin animals. The procedure in such tests is to inject a virgin female rabbit, mouse, or toad with a small amount of the woman's urine. If the woman is pregnant the hormones speed up the development of the animal's egg cells. If a rabbit or mouse is used, it is killed after about two or three days in order to examine the ovaries and genital tract. In the "frog test," effects can be noted within twenty-four hours, when mature eggs are expelled by the frog.

Further Positive Signs of Pregnancy. Pregnancy can also be confirmed at the end of the fourth month when the doctor, with the aid of a stethoscope, is able to detect the beating of the fetal heart. Additional evidence may be had from X-ray examination, which shows the skeleton. Fetal movements of the infant may be felt within the uterus from sixteen to twenty weeks after conception.

Duration of Pregnancy. The simplified way of stating the duration of pregnancy is to say that it lasts for nine months. A nine-month baby is considered full-term; a child delivered after seven or eight months of prenatal development is considered premature. A child is said to have been aborted (miscarried) if it is delivered prior to the end of the seventh month.

Concerning the exact duration of pregnancy, Stone and Stone say the following:

> "The average duration of pregnancy, from the time of conception until birth, is about 266 days. In figuring the expected day of childbirth, however, the calculations are made from the first day of the last menstruation, since this date is known, while the exact time of conception can only be approximated. Accordingly, childbirth should be expected 280 days, which is ten lunar months or about nine calendar months, from the first day of last menstrual flow. There are, however, wide individual variations, and only about one pregnancy in ten ends exactly 280 days from the start of the last menstruation. Hence it is seldom possible to predict accurately the date of an expected childbirth." [5]

Approximating Date of Birth. It is indeed difficult to determine the exact date of delivery, but close approximation can be made. A difference of a few days earlier or later is not unusual. In fact, the same mother may vary considerably from child to child

[5] Hannah M. Stone and Abraham Stone, *A Marriage Manual*, New York, Simon and Schuster, 1952, pp. 84–85. Reprinted by permission.

in delivery on the predicted date. An easy method of calculating the probable date of birth is as follows: Add seven days to the first day of the last period of menstruation, then count back three months. As an illustration, if a woman's first day of her last menstruation was November 18, add seven days to November 25 and count back three months to August 25. The child is likely to be born on or near that date the following year.

Determination of Sex of Offspring. There is no method for determining the sex of a child prior to birth. Nature makes that decision at the time of conception and guards the secret until birth. For centuries there have been suggested techniques, signs, and superstitions as to how to predetermine and predict the sex of a child. At present science is continuing its efforts to devise tests which may indicate the sex of a child before birth but, thus far, no reliable method has been found.

Importance of a Physician's Care. Proper prenatal care is important for both prospective mother and child; therefore, the services of a competent physician or obstetrician (specialist dealing with pregnancy and the birth process) should be sought as soon as there is an indication of pregnancy. This early step offers assurance to the mother and protection against avoidable complications. Ordinarily, a couple are already acquainted with a family doctor, but in cases where they are new in the community and do not know a physician, they can always obtain names of qualified doctors from nearby hospitals or from the office of the county medical association. If near a public library, they may consult the Directory of Medical Specialists, which lists names and addresses of specialists who are certified by the American Board of Obstetrics and Gynecology. They can then determine whether the immediate community has a person who meets their needs and their expectancy in terms of qualifications.

Early visits. At the first visit, the physician makes a thorough examination of the woman's general health. He will want a record of past health indicating serious diseases, especially those affecting the lungs, heart, kidneys, and menstrual cycle; operations, injuries, and obstetrical history of miscarriages and births. Included among many tests will be those for anemia, venereal diseases, and possible signs of infection as shown by urinalysis. He will record weight and blood pressure and note the condition of teeth and the general area of the throat. He will measure the pelvis in order to prejudge conditions at delivery. He will advise her to eat plenty of nourishing food but, if necessary, instruct her on how to control weight. She will be told about safe exercise and modifications in clothing. She is usually cautioned that coitus should be avoided during the early months at times when menstrual periods would be due and during the last two months of pregnancy altogether. If the doctor has reason to suspect that the patient is fearful of pregnancy, or is a believer of "old wives tales," he will take advantage of these early visits to enlighten her. He is able to guide her through the normal life function of pregnancy if she will co-operate with him by following his directions. Good rapport between doctor and patient is important in alleviating anxiety.

Later visits. Ordinarily, a pregnant woman is expected to make routine visits to her doctor. He may request a visit once a month until the end of the seventh month, after which he may expect more frequent visits, such as every two weeks or even once a week. Of course, as the woman nears time of delivery, unusual conditions may require still more frequent visits.

Throughout prenatal care, the doctor will check regularly on weight, urine, and blood pressure. He will note any unusual discomforts reported or conditions such as bloody discharge from the vagina, swelling of the feet, hands, or face, abdominal pain, shortness of breath, headaches, cramps, visual disturbance, and so on, all of which might have an adverse effect on the normal development and delivery of the child.

Preparation for Delivery. The doctor at the appropriate time will discuss plans for delivery with the parents, especially whether confinement in a hospital or at home is preferred. The majority of physicians and obstetricians prefer delivery in a hospital when possible because of available personnel for assistance, sterilized surroundings, and emergency apparatus. On the other hand, delivery at home may be less expensive and to some couples sentimentally satisfying in spite of the fact that it entails greater risk.

Training Courses for "New Parents." Courses of instruction for parents expecting the first child are increasing in popularity. Almost all sizeable communities now offer courses in which husband and wife can learn together, in a practical way, how to care for the new-born. They not only learn together, but also have an opportunity to be with other couples who share a common interest.

BIRTH OF THE BABY

Labor refers to the three successive stages involved in the delivery of the fetus. The first stage begins with the contraction of the uterine muscles, starting with feeble, infrequent movements but increasing in intensity and frequency as the cervix dilates. It is then usually that the "bag of water" (amniotic fluid surrounding the fetus) breaks and passes through the dilated cervix. The second stage, ordinarily lasting about two hours, begins when the head of the fetus pushes through the dilated cervix and works its way through the birth canal to the outside. The third stage begins with the birth of the child and lasts until the expulsion of the placenta which is commonly called the afterbirth. The average duration of labor is approximately sixteen hours for the first baby and ten or eleven hours for subsequent births. Actually there is no complete agreement among authorities as to what forces or conditions of nature initiate the process of birth. For some women labor may be painful, perhaps intensified by their fear of pain as much as by the experience itself. Other women describe labor pains as no more severe than a minor attack of menstrual cramps.

"False labor" is not uncommon, especially among women who are bearing the first child. They may feel slight contractions of the uterus as early as two weeks before actual labor begins. Such contractions are usually felt when the fetus progresses into the lower section of the pelvis and approaches the entrance to the birth canal.

Anesthesias or Natural Birth. Some women prefer the use of anesthetics during childbirth; others prefer natural birth. To follow a specialist's judgment in the matter is usually best. There are conditions in a patient which determine whether she should have an anesthetic, at what stage of labor it should be administered, and what type it should be.

Natural childbirth, that is childbirth without the aid of anesthetics, is being revived and used by some physicians. In this method the woman receives training early in pregnancy as to how to relax, how to become freed from fear and tension, how to breathe properly, and how to anticipate the birth process as a pleasant experience. She is prepared emotionally to look forward to the act of birth.

Lactation. The mother's breasts begin producing milk two to five days following childbirth. The secretion prior to the milk is called *colostrum,* a substance which apparently is quite beneficial to the intestinal tract of the child and serves to aid him in learning to nurse. The majority of physicians prefer breast feeding for babies if the health of the mother permits and if the milk agrees with the child. If the child is breast-fed, milk will continue for many months; if he is not, the breasts soon dry up.

Postnatal Care of the Mother. Postnatal or postpartum care refers to the special care given the mother from the birth of her infant until she has recovered from the usual effects of pregnancy. This care lasts from six to eight weeks.

For the first few days she remains in bed as a precautionary measure, while the pelvic organs—uterus, cervix, and vagina—having undergone physiological changes, begin their gradual return to normalcy. During this time it is essential that she have complete rest, sleep, quiet, and nourishing food. She and the baby are examined daily to safeguard against complications.

By the end of the sixth week following childbirth, she will need a careful checkup to determine the general condition of the reproductive organs. If the report from the examination is favorable, she can return gradually to former work and activities, and abstinence from coitus is no longer necessary.

The New Baby Is Brought Home. A household undergoes a certain amount of change when the new baby is brought home; in spite of preliminary preparation for the occasion, some further adjustments will be necessary.

There is usually need for extra help with household chores until the mother is able to resume such duties and has had time to reorganize her work to allow for the care of the baby. The new mother may need to be cautioned against trying to do too much.

"It must be time to get up. The baby's asleep!"

James Gibson and The Saturday Evening Post.

It is important for her sake and the baby's that she not become overly fatigued.

Relatives and friends with the best of intentions may present a problem. In their enthusiasm, they may want to visit the mother and baby too often and too long. Sometimes they confuse the young mother by offering her conflicting bits of advice from their background of experience. She will be wise to follow only the instructions of her attending physician.

Household routine may be disrupted. Schedules may be interrupted while all efforts are concentrated on establishing a schedule for the new baby. Meals and hours of sleep are irregular; getting to work on time becomes difficult; social life and control of leisure time is uncertain.

If there is already a child in the family, and even if he has been prepared as far as possible for the coming of the new baby, he faces a crucial test when what he considers to be his rival is brought home. More than ever he will need assurance of his parents' affection at a time when the new infant is likely to become the center of attention. He must not be forgotten in the midst of all the excitement.

The husband-wife relationship may be endangered, especially during the first weeks after the arrival of the baby. When messages of congratulations have all been received, when the novelty of becoming parents has passed and husband and wife have once again returned to a normal pattern of living, there is great danger that the new father will be forced into the background. It is easy for the mother to become so engrossed in the care of the newborn that she unintentionally neglects her husband. She must not let the baby supplant the husband as the center of her emotional life.

INTERPRETATIVE SUMMARY

1. The three major topics discussed with reference to reproduction are: sterility, birth control, and pregnancy.

2. Certain deficiencies in either husband or wife may result in sterility.

3. Faced with sterility, a couple may decide either on a childless marriage, dissolution of the marriage, or an artificial insemination (in cases where the husband is sterile).

4. Modern birth control consists in the prevention of conception.

5. Birth control is usually practical for the purpose of limiting the size of families and for better spacing of children.

6. In the United States, birth control is a generally accepted

practice. There are, however, differences of belief in regard to techniques and methods used.

7. Intelligent couples will time the arrival of the first baby on consideration of the effects it will have on them as well as on the child.

8. The general welfare of the family should be given consideration when spacing children.

9. Pregnancy demands new and distinctive types of adjustment by both husband and wife.

10. Possibility of conception is limited to a brief period at the time of ovulation.

11. The only sure way of determining pregnancy in the first few weeks is by medical tests.

12. Because of variation in the duration of pregnancy, prediction of the exact date of birth is impossible, even though date of conception has been fairly well established.

13. At present, there is no scientific method of determining the sex of a child prior to birth.

14. Wise parents will want to consult a physician not only at the time of delivery but also throughout the period of pregnancy.

15. Continued co-operation with a physician is important during the postnatal period of recovery.

Thought Questions and Projects

1. Is there a correlation between sterility and emotional instability of the husband or wife?

2. Secure class opinion on the following question, noting any difference between answers from men and those from women: If a couple found that the husband was sterile, should they

    (a) adopt a child (or children)?

    (b) use artificial insemination?

    (c) resign themselves to childlessness?

3. What arguments can be advanced for or against large families? For or against small families?

4. Find out which states legalize sterilization. What conditions

justify legalized sterilization? What is your opinion concerning the practice?

.5. Secure information concerning the *Birth Control Movement* and the organization of the *Birth Control Leagues*.

(a) Is there a branch in your community?

(b) Is the name *Planned Parenthood Association* a more desirable term?

6. Find out all you can about the life and work of Margaret Sanger.

7. What are some of the reasons offered in favor of planned parenthood?

8. Are there courses conducted in your community for expectant mothers and fathers? If so, who sponsors them? Can you interview one or two couples who have had such classes to find out in what way they benefited from them?

9. What are frequently offered reasons in favor of waiting two years or so before starting a family? What is your opinion?

10. "Baby sitting" is a popular form of employment among young people today. Do you think such experience is rewarding from the standpoint of learning how to care for children, to understand and appreciate them?

11. Mention several "old wives tales" which you have heard concerning the prenatal development and birth of a child. See if you can offer scientific evidence to refute such stories.

SUGGESTED READINGS FOR FURTHER STUDY

Becker, Howard, and Reuben Hill, eds., *Family, Marriage, and Parenthood,* Boston, D. C. Heath & Company, 1948.

Bowman, Henry A., *Marriage for Moderns,* New York, McGraw-Hill Book Company, 1954.
  Chapter 14. Reproduction.

Brooks, Lee, and Evelyn Brooks, *Adventuring in Adoption,* Chapel Hill, University of North Carolina Press, 1939.

Corbin, Hazel, *Getting Ready to Be a Father,* New York, The Macmillan Company, 1946.

Eastman, Nicholson J., *Expectant Motherhood,* rev. ed., Boston, Little, Brown and Company, 1950.
  (All chapters devoted to pregnancy.)

Goodrich, Frederick W., *Natural Childbirth,* New York, Prentice-Hall, 1950.

Jung, Moses, ed., *Modern Marriage,* New York, Appleton-Century-Crofts, 1947.

Chapter 11. The Physical Aspects of Marriage, by E. D. Plass, M.D.

Landis, Paul H., *Your Marriage and Family Living,* New York, McGraw-Hill Book Company, 1946.

Chapter 12. The Question of Having Children Should Be Discussed before Marriage.

Chapter 13. Parenthood Is the Last Important Step in Growing Up.

Parshley, H. M., *The Science of Human Reproduction,* London, George Allen and Unwin, 1933.

Potter, Edith L., *Fundamentals of Human Reproduction,* New York, McGraw-Hill Book Company, 1948.

Stone, Hannah M., and Abraham Stone, *A Marriage Manual,* New York, Simon and Schuster, 1952.

Chapter 4. Reproduction: Childbearing and Childbirth.

Chapter 5. Family Planning.

Chapter 6. Fertility and Infertility.

Van Blarcom, Carolyn Conant, *Getting Ready to Be a Mother,* 4th ed. (rev. by Helen Corbin), New York, The Macmillan Company, 1948.

Zabriskie, Louise, *Mother and Baby Care in Pictures,* 3rd ed., Philadelphia, J. B. Lippincott Company, 1946.

18

INABILITY TO ADJUST IN MARRIAGE CAUSES

If we take happiness as the criterion, marriage can be arranged on a continuum from great happiness to extreme unhappiness. Graphically it can be visualized in the following manner:

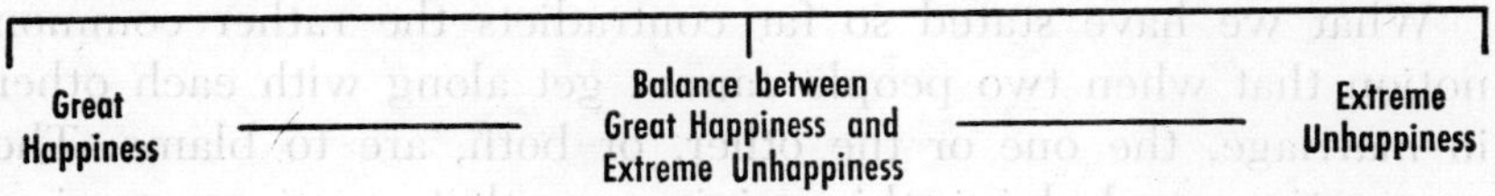

Great Happiness	Balance between Great Happiness and Extreme Unhappiness	Extreme Unhappiness

FIGURE 17. Happiness-Unhappiness Continuum.

If satisfaction is taken as the criterion, the continuum can be plotted from great satisfaction to extreme dissatisfaction. Or we could place love at one end and hate at the other.

There is, of course, no doubt about failure when a marriage must be placed to the right on the line. And there is reason to consider a failure that marriage which has to be rated at the center. In order to avoid disagreement, let us consider any marriage a failure which falls definitely to the right of center on the line. This approach suggests that there are varying degrees of failure. We believe that inability to adjust in a marriage inevitably leads to its failure.

While not all failures in marriage can be prevented, the number can be decreased in proportion to the number of married couples who become aware of the factors which contribute to success and those which contribute to failure. In previous chapters, our emphasis was primarily on factors which contribute to successful adjustment. Now we need to discuss forces which operate against happiness in marriage.

First, however, we point out that there are relative as well as complete failures in marriage. Man fails completely or relatively in many of his endeavors—getting an education, teaching, practicing law or medicine, managing a business, running an industry, participating in politics, government, or sports, and even in the making of friendships. Why should marriage be an exception? Personality is an important factor contributing to the success or failure in the above-mentioned endeavors; in marriage it becomes even more significant in the intimate adjustment between a man and a woman. They must not only work together to achieve common ends but also adjust to each other, often despite fundamental differences in personality make-up. It stands to reason, therefore, that in marriage, too, failure can be either relative or complete.

What we have stated so far contradicts the rather common notion that when two people cannot get along with each other in marriage, the one or the other, or both, are to blame. The assumptions underlying this opinion are that marriage requires only simple adjustment; that anyone who enters marriage and wishes to succeed in it can do so; that if he does not succeed, he somehow did not want the marriage to work or did not do his best to make it a successful one. The stigma of blame is attached especially to a couple whose inability to adjust manifests itself overtly in separation, desertion, or divorce. In such cases, public opinion, the church, and the law attempt to fix blame on one or both of the mates.

While this attitude is being modified at present, it is still quite prevalent. Divorce laws are perhaps the most rigid in attempting to fix blame. Practically all marriage laws imply that when a couple come to a divorce court one partner is at fault, one is guilty. This assumption of guilt is implicit in the terms *plaintiff* and *defendant*. Should a couple agree between themselves to get a divorce, the court usually will accuse them of collusion and throw out their case. For this reason, evidence in many cases is manufactured, and the real reasons are suppressed. One mate assumes guilt. In approximately three out of four divorce cases, the husband assumes the blame, since in our society he can more easily face the public, and he is in a better position than his wife to find a new mate.

Religious faiths formerly refused to recognize any cause for divorce. When certain faiths finally tolerated divorce, they did so by making an attempt to single out the "innocent" party, who alone of the two was permitted to remarry with religious blessing. Public opinion in general has become more liberal in apportioning blame, perhaps because the increase in divorce has brought the problem closer to many more people.

One would expect that the last persons to apply the concept of blame to inability to adjust in marriage would be the individuals involved. But, as every marriage counselor knows, frequently the mates blame each other. Perhaps they cannot be expected to escape the general atmosphere of blame. At any rate, the counselor usually finds it difficult to have the couple consider the problems and their causes rather than fix blame and guilt. It is true, of course, that in some instances a degree of justifiable blame is involved. But only when a couple are willing to look for the real causes of their difficulties and to forego blame-fixing can a workable reconciliation be achieved. When mates insist upon placing blame and guilt on each other, reconciliation is seldom effective, even where repentance has been accepted.

In individual psychotherapy, insight is all-important. It is equally important in marital adjustment. In order to achieve health and happiness, a couple must have insight into the basic nature of their problems.

CAUSES OF INABILITY TO ADJUST

There is sometimes confusion about what are causes and what are effects of inability to adjust. In one marital situation, a certain condition may be the "cause" of the problem; in another marriage, the same condition may be the "effect." In one marriage, for example, alcoholism on the part of the husband or wife may be the product of cumulative, serious conflicts. Here excessive drinking may serve as an escape mechanism. In other cases, alcoholism may be the central cause, from which other marital difficulties arise. There is similar possible confusion between causes and effects in problems of adultery, cruelty, violence, or impotence.

One must be on guard against looking for a single, isolated cause of marital difficulties. As a rule, couples are not ready to try to solve a problem until they can reduce it to a simple cause. On the level of physical phenomena, there may be only one cause. But there is seldom, if ever, one single cause for difficulty in such a complex relationship as marriage. It is true, of course, that often one can easily point to a central or cardinal cause, but even in such cases a number of factors probably contribute to it. Frequently the major cause is actually a combination of many seemingly minor factors. One often meets the following situation in marriage counseling. A couple may emphatically state that they have reached the limit of their endurance. When asked to state their problem, they may say that there are numerous little things which annoy them no end. They admit that the acts referred to are in themselves petty and unimportant, so much so that they feel embarrassed to mention them. Nevertheless, the cumulative effect has become unendurable. Just as love may be the product of many small satisfactions, so hate may result from the combination of an increasing number of "inner" annoyances.

Some couples frankly admit that they do not know why they cannot get along with each other. They claim to have made an attempt to discover the causes of their difficulties, only to realize that they cannot get to the root of their problem. What they offer as causes may be symptoms. This state of confusion is not at all surprising to anyone who is aware of the many unconscious factors involved in marital adjustment. By examining the causes discussed below, a couple may be helped toward gaining sufficient insight so as to direct themselves toward effective action.

The First Year. Many authorities stress the first year as the most crucial in marital adjustment. Foster expresses the following point of view:

"The first year of marriage is one of the greatest adjustment and perhaps the most crucial of any of the years that follow. It is significant that approximately 40 per cent of all marriages which occur in any one year end in separation or divorce by the end of the first five years. The causes of these broken marriages usually have their basis, first, in bad mating and, second, in the inability of the individuals to establish a satisfactory basis for meeting life's problems during the first year." [1]

The first year is critical for a number of reasons. First, the couple must make all the adjustments in marriage discussed in the last seven chapters—that is, they must establish the pattern of their marriage, they must harmonize their personalities, they must adjust to each other sexually, emotionally, and intellectually, and they must learn how to function as one in many areas of life. Second, they must make all these important adjustments when their status as husband and wife is quite new, when they still have not learned their roles adequately and when they do not yet know each other very well. Third, by the end of the first year, the "honeymoon attitude" may either disappear or at least change considerably. It should be remembered that the honeymoon attitude means that each party will think of the other first and do everything possible to please the other. Beautiful and laudable as this attitude may be, it cannot and will not last indefinitely, at least not without modification. Sooner or later both mates feel strained. It is then that one or the other may say, or at least imply in behavior, "I have done everything I could to please you. Why don't you change? Why don't you give in to me once in a while?" Such modification should be considered natural and normal, because each partner must be himself in order to feel at ease, even with his mate. The question should not be whether the honeymoon attitude should be changed but rather how and to what extent it should be changed.

In view of the seriousness and importance of marriage, a wise couple will put forth every effort to understand and tolerate each other and to face life together realistically. If they find that the problems they face are beyond their own ability to solve, they will not hesitate to seek help from persons who can view their

---

[1] R. G. Foster, *Marriage and Family Relationships*, rev. ed., New York, The Macmillan Company, 1950, p. 107. Reprinted by permission.

case objectively, who are qualified to recognize marital difficulties and recommend possible remedies.

SOCIAL AND CULTURAL CAUSES OF INABILITY TO ADJUST

Every couple must realize that they are not completely free to pattern their marital union as they desire. They do not live in a vacuum. Society and culture have created a climate in which their marriage must function. While many factors in this climate are conducive to a happy and successful marriage, others produce stress and strain. And the couple's reactions to these adverse conditions become far more significant than the conditions themselves. It is all important, therefore, that a couple be aware of the possible hazards to their happy union. Some of the hazards to be mentioned will be applicable to all couples, while others apply only to certain groups or types of individuals.

Uncertain Roles. In the past, the roles of each mate were fairly well defined and as a rule were strictly enforced. After marriage, the young man began to play the roles of husband, provider, homemaker, and, in due time, father; the young woman, that of wife, homemaker, and mother. Today the wife may share the role of provider. She may forego the role of mother until after some years of married life.

Such modification cannot take place without causing frustration and tension. But more serious is the fact that every role which each mate has to play is at present only vaguely defined. Burgess and Locke have expressed this change of familial roles as follows:

"In a changing and cultural heterogeneous society, the roles and activities of the family are almost inevitably in a state of flux. Instead of common definitions of family roles entrenched in tradition and crushing all variations by sheer weight of universal conformity, our modern American society presents what at first glance seems to be a chaotic conglomeration of every conceivable pattern of family organization and roles ranging from the patriarchal to the matriarchal family organization and from strict monogamy to a legally sanctioned succession of spouses. Present familial roles reflect changed social situations which have made many time-honored roles obsolete." [2]

The result of the whole situation is that a young couple not only face the problem of adjusting to each other's needs but also lack a clear concept of the kind of union they can create. One wonders if such a couple does not feel as helpless as a person trying to work an intricate jigsaw puzzle without having seen the original pattern intact.

A Way Out. Married couples expect relatives, friends, public opinion, the law, and religion to help preserve the permanency of their union. These forces are not so powerful today, however, as they were in the past (see Chapter 1, pp. 11–13). Consequently, added responsibility rests with the mates to make a success of their union. When the burden of this responsibility becomes heavy, one or the other, or both, may look for a way out of their marriage through annulment, desertion, separation, or divorce. Instead of concentrating on effective ways of adjustment, all attention may be given to the quickest method of escape from the union. The burden of trying to bring about adjustment of course falls on the mate who wants to adjust and not on the one who would resort to escape. This divided approach to the problem has a detrimental effect upon adjustment. Fear that a mate may escape the union if he does not get what he wants at all times may prevail. Out of this atmosphere may come a sense of insecurity which may force one mate to make unjustifiable sacrifices. The case of Mrs. C. is an example.

> "Harold and I have been married for six years. We have two attractive children, a boy of four and a girl of two. We have a nice home, which we own except for a mortgage of $5,000. The first three years of our marriage were very happy. The next two were perhaps less happy. Then about a year ago Harold began to pay less attention to me and the children. At present, he acts as though he were a single man again. He goes out two or three nights a week; he comes home at all hours of

[2] Ernest W. Burgess and Harvey J. Locke, *The Family*, 2nd ed., New York, American Book Company, 1953, pp. 474–475. Reprinted by permission.

the night. He refuses to tell me where he is going and what he is
doing; he says it is none of my business. I don't know how much he
earns or what he does with his money. He gives me so little that I
have hardly enough for food and clothing. Sometimes he even fails to
pay the monthly installments on our home. When he is at home, he
just sits around; he refuses to talk to me and he no longer plays with
the children as he used to. Whenever I express the slightest complaint,
he threatens to leave me. And I know he means it. I don't know what
would happen to me and the children if he should leave. I also hate to
think what my parents and our friends would say if we separated. As
it is, I try to keep all this conflict to myself, but I have reached the
end—I feel I can't take any more."

In this case, the wife was forced to suffer hardship and anxiety
by the very fact that their marriage could be dissolved, perhaps
easily so, if the husband carried out his threats. The case is not
meant to imply that there should be no way out of marriage, but
that the way out should not be too easy.

To make the way out of marriage easy is certainly undesirable,
because too many persons would take advantage of such leniency
at the slightest sign of a marital problem. If every person were
mature when he married, perhaps the way out of marriage could
be made as easy as the way into it. Maturity, in this context,
means that a mate would assume his full share of the responsibility—whatever this might involve—for making marriage a
success. Many mates, however, need some kind of outside pressure to aid them in achieving success in marriage. If a husband
and wife are "required" to stay with each other, at least for
some time, they may be induced into making concessions and
effecting modifications necessary to the success of their marriage.
It is not uncommon to hear a couple relate that, at some time in
their past, their marriage appeared to be "on the rocks," so to
speak, and that they thought about divorce but managed to
get through their crisis. Now, they may say, they feel closer
together than ever and are happier than they were before the
conflict.

We conclude that an easy way out of marriage is no solution
to the problem, that an easy way out merely puts added strain
on the entire process of marriage adjustment and works against
the best interests of both husband and wife.

Mobility. The word *mobility* has many connotations.[3] In our discussion, we confine ourselves to only one kind of mobility—from a small town to a large city—and to show what effects this change may have on marital adjustment problems. The case of Mr. and Mrs. M. is representative of what can happen. Mrs. M. states:

"Our problem seems to have begun when we moved from L—— to this city. L——, where Herb and I grew up, is a small rural town of about 1,500 population. We knew everybody and the entire community knew us. We were active in the Methodist Church, where we were married, attended church regularly, taught in the Sunday School, and sang in the choir. We owned our home, a small one, but nice and comfortable. My husband had a job in the office of a respectable, well-known business. His salary was modest, but we had enough to live on and were really very happy together. We shared many things and had a wonderful group of friends who had interests similar to our own.

"Three years ago, my husband was transferred to this city. We hunted for a small house here but could not afford any we found. Finally, we moved into an apartment building, which was quite a change for us. We found it difficult to make friends. After several months, I met the wife of a man who worked in the same department as my husband. She soon introduced me to her friends, and from then on we started leading a quite different social life. In L——, our crowd of friends didn't drink, smoke, or play cards for money. But I soon found that our new friends did these things and although I had guilt feelings I also began indulging, because I felt left out if I didn't. Our new friends seemed to be nice in every respect.

"We didn't join a church here when we came because there wasn't a Methodist church in our neighborhood. We went at first to a Methodist church about three miles from us but felt some degree of conflict there because when we attended the Young Married Couples' Club in the recreation parlors of the church, there was dancing. Back in L——, we had been taught that dancing and religion don't mix, and here there was dancing sponsored by an organization within the church. Nevertheless, I finally gave in and we attended a few of the church affairs also. Somehow we managed to get through this year of drastic changes, but as time went on I began to feel uneasy. I began to dislike our new mode of life. I stopped writing regularly to our parents; I knew our parents would disapprove of our new social life if they knew about it. I suggested to Herb that we give up our new manner of living and buy a home near a small church of a less progressive type, where we would feel at ease if we joined. He told me that I was plain old-fashioned and that he liked his new way of life.

[3] For an excellent, detailed exposition of mobility and its effects on the family, the reader is referred to Chapter 17 of Ernest W. Burgess and Harvey J. Locke, *The Family*, 2nd ed., New York, American Book Company, 1953.

"After that, I began to withdraw from our friends, using all kinds of excuses for not going out with them as often as previously. At the same time, Herb drew closer and closer to his buddies at the office and to our new friends. Now it is quite apparent that he is withdrawing more and more from me. We have many petty misunderstandings; we quarrel over nothing; he seems to have no patience with me in anything, and recently one of my friends told me that Herb is in love with another woman. I feel helpless and miserable. I don't know what to do."

An analysis of this case brings out several ways in which mobility can affect a marriage. First, controls may be removed, controls such as the conventional expectations of the community, opinions of parents, relatives, and friends, the rules of the church, and even policies at the place of employment. When a husband and wife move into a new community, they are on their own. It is they who must make the decisions and evaluations; their opinions must determine the regulations which govern the actions of their new life. They may or may not be ready to face the challenge. In some cases, change may be taken in stride and welcomed; in others, change may produce frustration. A couple may not be able to relinquish completely the old controls nor yet be able to set up new ones more in harmony with a changed pattern of living. Second, new ideas and concepts about life may affect marriage adjustment, especially if such ideas are not acceptable to both mates. Third, a new environment may accentuate personality differences between the mates. Characteristics heretofore unnoticed may become evident. Lack of flexibility and adaptability may become apparent. Fourth, new friendships may create a breach between mates. If the new friends are not generally acceptable to both mates, social relationships may become strained and, in turn, the closeness between mates may be lessened.

Keeping up With the Joneses. An important characteristic of our society is that we admire a person who "gets ahead,"— "ahead" meaning usually to outdistance the other fellow. Our national hero is the man who started at the bottom of the ladder and climbed to the top. Success stories tell how a man started as a day laborer in his company and became president, or began by selling shoe strings and small notions and later became the owner of several large department stores, or began entertaining on the street corners of the Bowery and sang his way to the top as a famous Broadway theatrical star. Our classic story of success is still the one about the man who was born in a log cabin and grew up to be the President of his country.

Our open class system, which permits vertical mobility, means that one can ascend from a lower to a higher class. Many persons still believe that all one needs to reach the top is initiative and drive. As a consequence, our society is highly competitive. The effect of such competition is anxiety and tension and in some cases even a "nervous breakdown."

Married couples are naturally influenced by this atmosphere. Either they strive together to outdo other couples or one of the mates is highly ambitious while the other mate holds back. If a couple's chief concern becomes that of striving to reach higher and higher levels, they may never create a union which would be the natural and normal one for them. They must "keep up with the Joneses" or, better yet, outdo them with an expensive home, cars, a yacht, clothing, jewelry, and other external evidences of success. If one mate is ambitious to move ahead and the other is not, there may be dissension and conflict. The lagging mate then becomes a "ball and chain." If the husband achieves success and his wife does not, he may find her unsuitable as a wife and may wish to discard her for another. Obviously the reverse may be true; what is said of the overambitious husband is equally true of an overambitious wife. In short, our society has tended to create an atmosphere which is not conducive to happy and peaceful adjustment in marriage.

Family Ties. In order to establish an effective and successful union, a husband and wife must be able to emancipate themselves from their respective families. While most couples find this comparatively easy to do, others find it so difficult that it becomes a serious hindrance to their marital adjustment. The causes for these difficulties may lie (1) in the vagueness of what is expected in emancipation, (2) in inability to take this step, and (3) in the problems created by the parents.

Emancipation is often called a "breaking away" from the parents. The connotation of this phrase jars the finer feelings of respect, love, and admiration for parents, and implies something painful and unfair. In contrast to the negative side of the term, there is also the positive. Viewed positively, emancipation means

"I'm going home to mother—but we'll be back!"

Gustav Lundberg and The Saturday Evening Post.

that the couple must now "stand on their own feet." But what does this imply? A better way of looking at emancipation is to consider it as a change of role. Before marriage, son and daughter had more or less dependent roles in their relation to parents. After marriage, they should assume roles of equality with their parents. Parents now become good friends, perhaps their wisest friends, but still just friends. As a rule, parents are the best friends a couple may have. But it should be recognized that "real friends" do not dictate and demand, but advise and suggest; and one can accept or reject their suggestions after thoughtful consideration without jeopardy to the relationship.

While such a change of roles may present many problems for the husband and wife, as a rule the husband faces the greater difficulty. To emancipate himself from his mother is not easy. Especially is this true for middle-class sons in our American society. Winch found evidence in support of the following three hypotheses: that the mother is the preferred parent; that the son is the preferred child; and that the mother-son relationship is the strongest of the four parent-child relationships. He adds: "In general, to achieve emancipation and independence in the American middle class, the boy has a stronger tie to sever than has the girl. In this task, he is, of course, abetted by the cultural expectation of greater independence, and, correspondingly, failure to achieve it is more conspicuous for the boy than for the girl." [4]

Mother-son ties have their natural beginnings in infancy; they involve strong emotions and they are based upon countless needs satisfied by the mother. Such experiences become a part of the very structure of personality. The mother-son relationship may offer more difficulty under any one of the following set of circumstances: if the mother is unhappily married; if she is a widow or divorcee; if she has no other children; and if she has few friends and outside interests. In cases such as these, emancipation involves more than mere will power; it requires change of personality and the overcoming of guilt feelings on the part of the son, who may find the task beyond his ability. As a consequence, he may become unduly tense, restless, and irritable. The result is unpleasant and distasteful for the wife. She realizes that she married not only a husband but also a mother-in-law of the undesirable type. If the wife protests, she is accused of selfishness and cruelty; if she accepts the situation, she loses self-respect, and often the respect of her friends. Moreover, she may suffer inwardly from guilt feelings and from fear of punishment or retaliation.

Our culture has created an idealized concept of mother which

---

[4] Robert F. Winch, *The Modern Family*, New York, Henry Holt & Company, 1952, p. 299. Reprinted by permission.

approximates perfection. Mother's Day has been used to build up this paragon of virtue. She is pictured only as a fine, kind, noble, self-sacrificing individual, whom only a "heel" would not respect. Perhaps no real mother corresponds to this idealized picture. (As a matter of fact, the more a mother measures up to these qualities, the less she cares to wear the halo of perfection.) Yet there are mothers who have consciously or unconsciously used this concept as a means of controlling their children in such matters as mate selection and general problems of marital adjustment.

What has been said about the husband's inability to achieve independence can likewise be said about the wife's. The consequences are similar, if not the same.

Sometimes a husband or wife cannot accept what may be called a normal, natural relationship with a spouse's family. He or she may be so bound by family ties that it is impossible to admit a second family. There may be strong feelings of loyalty to one's own family, general hostility toward outsiders, and a lack of social skill in making friends or admitting new personalities into one's life.

Further problems concerning in-laws are discussed in Chapter 20, Functioning as a Unit.

PERSONAL CAUSES FOR INABILITY TO ADJUST

In the preceding section, we discussed some environmental factors which may have adverse effects on marriage. Now we consider factors residing largely within the couples themselves.

Thus far in this book, an effort has been made to stress basic principles and suggestions which, if followed, may aid in the promotion of effective marital adjustment. We do not wish to be repetitious; nevertheless, at this point, it seems wise by way of summary and emphasis to call special attention to common pitfalls and danger areas in order that they may stand out in vivid relief.

Incompatibility. Magoun stresses the importance of incompatibility: "The only reason marriages fail is incompatibility. All else —cruelty, adultery, drunkenness—is merely rebellion against frustration of compatibility itself. Divorce is the result, not the cause of failure."[5]

Magoun uses the word *incompatibility* to denote any or all irreconcilable conflicts between two mates. We are limiting the term to mean an irreconcilable conflict between two persons who are normal and mature but who do not suit each other. Either mate might have married some other person more suited to himself and therefore have made a good spouse. Evidence for this statement lies in the fact that there are couples who get a divorce, marry someone else and become perfectly happy in the new union. Sometimes incompatibility shows up only after marriage. A couple may marry on the strength of one or more common factors in their personalities, only to find in the intimate life after marriage that there are insurmountable obstacles to a complete and harmonious union. Sometimes one or the other is aware of the obstacle prior to marriage, but believes it can be mastered. There are cases in which couples are fully aware of the hazard but for one reason or another feel themselves forced into the marriage.

A couple may be incompatible in one or several areas of adjustment; the nature of the difference may affect surface layers of the personality or it may center in its very core. How important the conflicts are cannot be judged objectively by a third person; the essential matter is how important it is to the two individuals concerned. For an observer, the difference in intelligence between a husband and wife may seem highly significant, but to the couple concerned it may not be important at all. However, if there is incompatibility in one area, it may spread to other areas.

For the sake of simplification, let us assume that adjustment can be divided into physical, emotional, and intellectual. A conflict originating in one aspect of the physical level may affect all physical adjustment, as well as emotional and intellectual adjustment. The resulting conflict can be expected on the basis of the unity of the organism and can also be verified from the study of many incompatible couples. For this reason, it is sometimes difficult to determine what is cause and what is effect. A case in

[5] F. Alexander Magoun, *Love and Marriage*, New York, Harper & Brothers, 1948, p. 171. Reprinted by permission.

point is a couple that is sexually incompatible for any of the reasons listed on pages 312–315. Love, in time, may change into hate, and respect for intellectual skill may turn into disdain. This process is reflected in the following report given by Mrs. M.:

"I was divorced from my husband one year ago, after five years of marriage. At the time I got the divorce, I hated him with a blind hatred. I had lost all respect for him—somehow he seemed to be effeminate to me. He was irritable and that made me sarcastic and irritable with him. We would quarrel over anything. I believed at the time that he wasn't doing very well in his business; and he seemed to make friends with the kind of people I didn't like. When we would go out with my friends or even some of our former mutual friends, he never would carry on a conversation. No matter what topic was brought up, he didn't appear to have much to say. He gave the impression of not being very intelligent. Finally we got a divorce. Now, after a year, I have cooled off, and I can see him quite differently. In the meantime, I have had opportunity to compare him with other men whom I have dated. Frankly, I think I must have been blind; and now it is too late because he is remarried—and to a very attractive and intelligent person. I really think he is a good and able person. As I look at our marriage, I am convinced it all began about one year after our marriage. Ray appeared to lose all sexual interest in me and even refused to discuss the matter with me. I got a feeling that he was not normal. From then on, our relationship became worse and worse, so we got a divorce."

The divorce was granted on grounds of cruelty. At that time, Mrs. M. believed it to be the true reason for not getting along with her husband.

Another pertinent illustration of the ramification of a conflict concerns differences in philosophy of life. The nature of such a philosophy was explained elsewhere (pp. 143–144) as a system of values or as the meaning and purpose of one's life. Such a philosophy is slow in emerging and crystallizing; therefore, young people may not be totally aware of their particular basic orientation toward life until they have reached adulthood. Mrs. K., aged thirty, needed help with this kind of problem. Her report was as follows:

"My chief complaint is money, but not the way you may think. I have too much. It is literally the only thing I get from my husband. Whenever I express any kind of dissatisfaction to him, he reaches for his billfold and says, 'Oh, go buy yourself a new hat and dress so you'll feel better. And if that's not enough, you can have more.' He is absolutely fanatical about money—he believes you can buy anything, even a marriage, with it. Except for his money, we have nothing to share with each other. I like music very much; I've begged him to go to concerts with me but he refuses. Some of our friends are interested in the theater, but he won't go with me to see a play. He won't go to any kind of educational program, whether it's about politics, the arts, or even travel. When we invite friends to our home, he dominates the scene with his talk about money-making schemes, stock, bonds, and real estate deals. When we try to bring in other topics for discussion, he throws up his hands, calls us a bunch of intellectuals with our heads in the clouds, and leaves the room. I know you wonder why I didn't see this quality in him before marriage. It was different then. I was so flattered by his incessant flow of expensive gifts and presents that it never dawned on me that there would be a time when I would hate the sight of them. Of course, I used to be disappointed when he claimed he couldn't go with me to certain places because of business obligations. His excuse was that he wanted to be financially secure at the time of our wedding. After we were married, he continued to buy the best of everything for me but, at the same time, refused more and more to go anywhere with me.

"Gradually I have come to realize that I have nothing in my marriage but money. Our relationship has reached a stage where I cannot stand for him to touch me. I yearn to be with people, to help persons in trouble, to live less selfishly. He doesn't care for anyone except as a means of making more money. I have reasons to believe that he is even dishonest in his business deals, but when I confronted him about the matter he flatly denied being dishonest."

Later, in an interview, Mr. K. said:

"It's true that money is important to me. Look at people and you will see that anyone with money counts. You see plenty of poor guys, smart enough and educated, but they don't know how to make a dollar. They don't get anywhere without money. When you have plenty of money, people look up to you. If you'd been brought up the way I was in the slums, you could understand how I feel. My folks were poor and with six kids we didn't have much to eat; we wore our clothes 'till they fell off. I used to want nice things to wear; I was ashamed of the way I looked. I swore then that when I grew up I would do nothing but make money and more money. Now I have it; I am able to help my brothers and sisters and support my parents. They all appreciate what I do for them. Only my wife is dissatisfied. I wish she'd get some sense into her head. I thought any woman would be glad to know she could have money when she wanted it."

The Allport-Vernon-Lindzey "Profile of Values" (see p. 358) gives a graphic picture of their differences.

Mr. and Mrs. K. were not able to reconcile their differences and, consequently, got a divorce. Mr. K. refused to make an adequate financial settlement because, he claimed, "she doesn't care about money." Mrs. K. agreed to take any amount, so long as she obtained freedom from him.

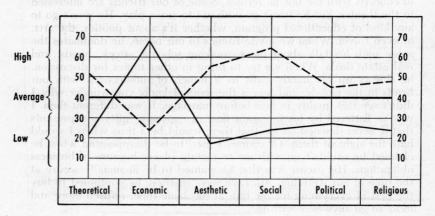

FIGURE 18. Value scales for Mr. and Mrs. K. Heavy line indicates scores for husband; dotted line, scores for wife.[6]

As a person grows older, his philosophy of life or his sense of values may undergo some change. And such modification may give rise to conflict between mates if they fail to understand justifiable reasons for the change. The following case illustrates this point:

Mr. and Mrs. W. had been happily married for thirty-five years. Financially, they started with nothing and had struggled and worked together during this time. They had reared and educated three children, who now were married and doing well. During the thirty-five years, they had accumulated considerable wealth, so that now they had ample means and leisure time to enjoy what they had saved. Mrs. W. became distressed over Mr. W.'s change of attitude—he had turned into a "playboy" according to her. He wanted to do nothing but play cards and golf and travel. She was worn out from a succession of trips all over the world. Mr. W.'s explanation of the situation was that he had worked hard all his life, and that they had had no time to play. Now that they had both time and money, he wanted to enjoy life. Basically, his sense of values had not changed, but circumstances had made possible a difference in emphasis.

There are additional reasons for incompatibility, many of which have been mentioned in other sections of this book. Those treated

[6] Adapted by permission from Gordon W. Allport, P. E. Vernon, Gardner Lindzey, *Study of Values*, rev. ed., Boston, Houghton Mifflin Company, 1951.

elsewhere are differences in intelligence, manifestations of affection, and age disparity.

Personal Inadequacy. By personal inadequacy, we mean any incapacity of structure or function of personality which is a handicap to successful adjustment in marriage. Unfortunately, there are many such inadequacies. (They were listed in Chapter 14.) It must be noted that they may inhere in either husband or wife or both. An incapacity may affect the adjustment in various degrees; it may make adjustment merely difficult or it may make it completely impossible. A mate may help toward adjustment in some degree or may not offer any help. In some cases, one mate actually becomes an additional burden to the other. The significance of any incapacity will depend not only upon its nature but also upon how the more normal mate is affected by it. Thus the same incapacity may be considered by one a burden which he or she is "predestined" to bear in marriage, while by another it may be considered absolutely intolerable. This fact is often overlooked by friends and relatives whose advice is sought in some particular marital problem. They often put themselves in the troubled mate's place, saying: "If I were in your place, I would not live with him (her) for another day." All too often a husband or wife who followed such advice is later convinced of having made a mistake.

Note this cardinal point in effective marriage counseling: A successful counselor does not give specific advice; he tries to help each mate become aware of unconscious, as well as conscious, factors involved in the issue and thus to guide them to a more intelligent resolution of their problem. One effective way of dealing with specific personality inadequacies in a case where mates otherwise are well adjusted to each other is to have them look at the difficulty as a common problem. Thus the wife can say to the husband who is given to gambling away his income: "I love you in every way except for your gambling. Your gambling is wrecking our happy marriage. Let's face it together." This does not mean that they necessarily face the problem alone; they may have to enlist the help of a marriage counselor, a clinical psychologist, or a psychiatrist. But it is still regarded as their joint problem. The husband feels accepted and the wife works with him. This procedure is far more effective than the one in which the wife makes the husband feel that in all respects he is "no good" and that he must change by himself.

Wrong Motives for Marriage. Many marriages fail because the persons entering them expect to get out of marriage the very things which can destroy any happy union. Such people regard marriage (1) as a cure for personal handicaps, (2) as a means to gain selfish satisfactions, or (3) as an ideal or utopian state from which one should expect nothing short of absolute perfection.

It is amazing how many well-meaning but uninformed persons prescribe marriage as a cure-all for (1) sexual problems such as homosexuality, exhibitionism, voyerism (sexual satisfaction derived by secretly viewing nude persons), impotence, frigidity, and excessive masturbation; (2) character defects or vices, such as shiftlessness, drunkenness, and gambling; and (3) personality abnormalties, such as neuroses and even incipient psychoses. It is often believed that drastic changes and new opportunities and responsibilities will "bring a person to his senses." Naturally, all of these disorders exist in varying degrees, and it is conceivable that marriage may have a therapeutic effect on a person suffering from any of them in a mild degree. But even here, great risk is involved if marriage is used as the remedial measure. Indeed, it is safe to say that marriage itself is never a cure for these disorders. The following case may give some brief indication as to the reason for this point of view:

Marge T. met Harry L. while she was employed as secretary in an advertising agency. They had much in common—educational background, interests, and business ambitions. Marge was attracted to Harry because of his keen intelligence and his gay, happy-go-lucky personality. He was everybody's friend—generous, always ready to go out for the evening or to invite the crowd over to his apartment. In fact, they first met at one of his cocktail parties, to which he had invited some of the new employees. After they had dated rather steadily for several weeks, she began to recognize that his drinking involved far more than occasional social cocktails. Finally she asked him if he did not think he was drinking too much. He claimed that he had to; he had to entertain many clients of the firm, and they expected it. Besides, he insisted, he could stop anytime he wanted to. He continued to drink more and more, to the point of becoming obnoxious in his all-too-frequent drunken states. He asked Marge to marry him. She wanted to marry him, because she loved him and had faith in her capacity to help him change. His parents also begged her to marry him, in the hope that he would settle down, become interested in his home, and consequently have less time and interest for drink. An agreement was reached; she would marry him provided he promised to stop drinking excessively. But in only about two weeks after the wedding, he went back to heavy drinking. Soon he was asked to resign from his position in the company, and eventually he had to be institutionalized for treatment. He left a disillusioned, heart-broken wife, who had hoped to create a happy marriage by reforming the husband.

Selfishness. Everyone who marries manifests self-interest in that he seeks greater happiness; however, one must understand that self-interest is not synonymous with selfishness. Self-interest means that a person wants his own share; selfishness means that a person wants not only his share but also the share of another. A selfish person can think of marriage only as something from which he himself wants to derive benefit. He considers marriage good as long as it proves to be beneficial for *him*, but as soon as the relationship does not provide *his* satisfactions, he wants to get out of it. It is this motive which usually underlies the statement, "We will get married and stay married as long as it works." With this attitude, naturally, there is not the proper drive to do one's utmost to make marriage a success. As mentioned above, a "way out" soon becomes uppermost in the mind.

We consider it selfish when a person in selecting a mate thinks only, "What can he or she give me?", or "Can he or she make *me* happy?" Such a person is too selfish to say, "Can I make him or her happy?"

Selfishness after marriage is manifested in innumerable ways. A selfish person uses love as a threat. His central theme becomes, "If you love me, you'll do this or that; if you really care for me, you'll do what I ask you to do." Marriages based upon such attitudes are failures, regardless of whether or not mates stay together. If a couple remain married under these circumstances, one soon becomes the master and the other the slave.

Utopian Idea of Marriage. There is no state of existence in this world where a person can get everything he wants, yet occasionally one encounters individuals who look forward to marriage as a state of absolute perfection. Our American optimism, the Pollyanna idea of life, contributes to this belief. For us, as a rule, stories in popular literature and on the movie or television screen must have a happy ending; we can suffer through a gloomy story, but we expect it to end happily. Tragedies are as unpopular in our country as they are popular in some other countries. If the story is a love story, it must end in line with the idea that the couple will live happily ever after.

One would expect young people to be more influenced by the many tragedies of broken marriages around them than by love stories in magazines, novels, the movies, and on radio and television. But two powerful forces operate against the influence of real experience: the romantic nature of love, and a sort of omnipotent feeling which gives most people the conviction that they can do better than anyone else.

Couples with such an extremely Utopian orientation toward marriage become disillusioned by any marriage, no matter how normal it might be. They are like the woman, about forty-five years of age and of fervent spiritualistic faith, who made the following statement. "I am very much disappointed in marriage. I have been married four times, and not once have I found happiness. I have given up all hope that I will ever be happy on this planet, since I have a definite promise that my soul mate is waiting for me in the next world." Such faith in happiness to be found only in the next world would make it impossible to be satisfied here with anything less than perfection.

Lack of Proper Information. In view of the changing nature of modern marriage and its complexity, it is not surprising that many couples fail to make a successful marital adjustment; for they lack proper information and adequate skills. Favorable environmental conditions, well-integrated personality, and good intentions are not enough. In addition, a couple needs insight, which can come only from formal as well as informal training.

Informal training alone is becoming increasingly insufficient, not only because it is difficult to train oneself for a complex skill, but also because by the time such skill is acquired much harm may already have been done. Not infrequently one can hear statements such as, "If I only had known this or that before, I think my marriage would not have failed." It is true that as yet we do not have tabulated, statistical proof of the value of formal training in marriage adjustment. But the testimony of many couples who have had such training, and of marriage counselors and others who deal with marital problems, seems to indicate that, in today's world, formal training for marriage is becoming more and more a necessity, not merely to avoid failure, but also to achieve greater happiness.

INTERPRETATIVE SUMMARY

1. Marriages can be classified, on the basis of mutual happiness, on a continuum from complete success to complete failure, with varying degrees of success or failure between these two extremes.

2. This chapter concerns itself with marriages which are either relatively or completely unsuccessful.

3. Instead of stressing "blame" for failures in marital adjustment, an attempt is made to point out causes for such failures.

4. What are causes in one marital failure may be effects in another. Causes and effects are often confused.

5. Adjustments during the first years of marriage are, in most cases, crucial for success or failure in later years.

6. Causes for inability to adjust in marriage are found either in the social and cultural conditions in which a couple lives or in the personality make-up of the mates.

7. The social and cultural conditions which may affect a marriage adversely include these: poorly defined roles of husband or wife; ease of escape from marital responsibility; excessive mobility of couple; overzealous desire "to keep up with the Joneses"; and inability to break family ties.

8. Causes which may be attributed to either or both mates for failure include these: incompatibility; personality inadequacies; undesirable motives for marriage; selfishness; Utopian ideas of marriage; and a lack of proper information about marital adjustment.

THOUGHT QUESTIONS AND PROJECTS

1. In your opinion, what are the important environmental and personality factors which adversely affect marital adjustment?

2. Check recent statistical data giving legal grounds for divorce in each state. Which grounds are mentioned most frequently? Which ones least? Compare Eastern states with Western, Northern with Southern. Do you think there should be uniform divorce laws for all states?

3. Examine several newspaper clippings illustrating reports of divorces granted. Note the grounds for each. Do they sound like the "real" reasons or reasons which follow "the letter of the law"?

4. Are marital roles clearly defined in our present society?

5. What is the meaning of the term *mobility*? Is mobility an important factor in marital problems involving men in the armed forces and their wives?

6. Can you mention well-known novels in which "vertical mobility" is unsuccessfully resolved in marital adjustment? Successfully resolved?

7. Do you know cases in which either the wife or the husband is overattached to a parent? What are the causes of such attachment?

8. What influences in our society encourage Utopian ideas of marriage in young people? Why do the frequency of divorce and the knowledge of unhappy marriages fail to alter this concept?

9. Why is there not full agreement as to the causes underlying successful and unsuccessful marriage? Why does opinion differ considerably about the relative significance of these factors?

10. Returns from the following project can be enlightening.

Objective: To find out the reasons most commonly given by persons seeking divorce.

Procedure: Appoint four committees. Assign a committee to each of the following persons to be interviewed: a professional marriage counselor; a representative of a religious organization, such as a minister, rabbi, or chaplain in the armed forces; a judge of the domestic relations court; and a representative of the Family Welfare Association.

Bring together all findings in the form of a panel presentation or special committee reports.

SUGGESTED READINGS FOR FURTHER STUDY

Burgess, Ernest W., and Harvey J. Locke, *The Family,* 2nd ed., New York, American Book Company, 1953.
  Chapter 20. Family Disruption.
Harper, Robert A., *Marriage,* New York, Appleton-Century-Crofts, 1949.
  Chapter 12. Divorce.
Howard, Sidney, *The Silver Cord,* in *The Theatre Guild Anthology,* New York, Random House, 1936.
  (A play in which sons struggle to escape an overdominant mother in order to have mature marital relations.)
Komarovsky, Mirra, "Cultural Contradictions and Sex Roles," *American Journal of Sociology,* 1946, 52:184–189.
Lewin, Kurt, "The Background of Conflict in Marriage," in Moses Jung, ed., *Modern Marriage,* New York, Appleton-Century-Crofts, 1947.
  Chapter 4.
Lockwood, Lemo D., and Mary E. N. Ford, *Youth, Marriage and Parenthood,* New York, John Wiley & Sons, 1945.
  Chapter 9. Attitudes toward Separation and Divorce.
McClelland, David C., *Personality,* New York, William Sloane Associates, 1951.
  Chapter 9. Roles and Role Models.
Merrill, Francis E., *Courtship and Marriage,* New York, The Dryden Press, 1949.
  Chapter 15. Frustrated Roles.
  Chapter 17. Broken Roles: Divorce.
Monahan, Thomas P., "Does Age at Marriage Matter in Divorce?" *Social Forces,* 1953, 32:31–37.
Palmer, W. J., "Fact against Fiction in Divorce," *American Bar Association Journal,* 1952, 38:653-656.
Turner, Bernadette F., "Common Characteristics among Persons Seeking Professional Marriage Counseling," *Marriage and Family Living,* 1954, 16:143–144.

19

INABILITY TO ADJUST IN MARRIAGE

EFFECTS

In view of the intimacy, complexity, and significance of a marital union, it is not difficult to surmise that inability to adjust in marriage will have serious and far-reaching consequences affecting the marriage relationship as such, the personalities of the mates, and the lives of the children.

Effects on Marriage Relationship. When a marriage fails, a couple may continue to live with each other by maintaining a formal marital status, or they may dissolve the marriage. In the former case, they will live with each other in disharmony; in the latter, they will resort to annulment, separation, or divorce.

Living in Disharmony. Referring to the figures or graphs in Chapter 13, we can visualize a state of marital disharmony in the manner shown in Figure 19.

There is a definite break in the attraction between husband and wife; love has disappeared, and in many cases has been displaced by hate. The essence of marriage has vanished and all that remains is the form; in other words, the kernel is dead and is surrounded by a mere shell.

Since such a relationship is unpleasant, the question may be raised as to why the couple continue to live together. The reasons obviously differ from couple to couple. The most common reasons are the following: (1) The couple may still have a glimmering hope that they may change or that something will happen to bring them together again. (2) Their sense of duty may be so strong that they disregard their personal feelings. They have given their word of honor and will stick to it. This sense of duty was very strong and practically universal in former years. While it is somewhat less influential at present, nevertheless it remains paramount for many couples. (3) There may be children involved for whose sake a couple will remain married. This factor appears to be important in holding many marriages together, if we can judge by the reasons given to marriage counselors for not getting a divorce. In some cases, the common desire to do what is

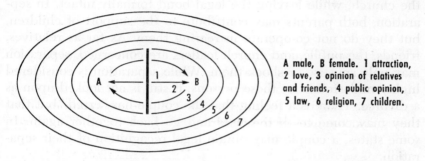

A male, B female. 1 attraction, 2 love, 3 opinion of relatives and friends, 4 public opinion, 5 law, 6 religion, 7 children.

FIGURE 19. Living in Disharmony.

best for the children may bring the parents closer together again. Other couples definitely wait until their children are grown before they proceed with a divorce. (4) There is also the fear of hurting or shocking parents. This factor may be a strong deterrent when parents are old and set in their views or when a parent is ill. Such statements as the following are not uncommon: "I cannot think of bringing shame to my family; no one in our family ever got a divorce." "My mother has such a weak heart; if she ever heard about my divorce, it would kill her, and I would rather suffer than have to think I may have hastened her death." (5) Public opinion about divorce, though greatly modified from what it once was, is still an important force in keeping marriages together. This is especially true in smaller communities or when the husband holds a position which could be adversely affected by popular opinion. (6) Membership in a church or personal religious beliefs may make an overt dissolution of marriage impossible. (7) Legal restrictions still stand in the way of many couples. They may not have legal grounds for divorce; they may be unable to "manufacture" some or would feel guilty when doing so; they may not have the money for necessary legal fees; or they may not have sufficient financial security for separate maintenance, support, or alimony.

Separation. Whether voluntary or forced by either mate, separation also breaks the bond established by the couple's children, "stretches" the bonds of opinion of friends, of the public, and of the church, while leaving the legal bond formally intact. In separation, both parents may contribute to the support of children, but they do not co-operate in rearing them. As far as relatives, friends, the public, and church leaders are concerned, separation may only surprise or shock them. While separation is considered highly undesirable by these persons, it still is not looked upon as a divorce. There is a feeling that the couple has "erred" but that they may come to their senses and go back together again. In some states, a couple may obtain legal recognition of their separation.

It is impossible to tell how many persons are involved in such separation. Statistics of separation refer to all couples living apart, regardless of the reason. As stated in the first chapter of this book, the number probably runs into many hundreds of thousands.

A similar and still more deplorable way of dissolving marriage is desertion, which is an action taken by one member of the union with or without the knowledge of the other. Usually it is the husband who takes this way out. It is the method used commonly among the poorer classes of our society; hence it is often called "the poor man's divorce." Worthy of note also are the facts that more urban than rural, more Negro than white, and more mixed than unmixed marriages are dissolved in this manner. Baber estimates the desertions per year to be one fourth as many as divorces.[1] All but three of our states (Louisiana, New York, and

---

[1] Ray E. Baber, *Marriage and the Family,* New York, McGraw-Hill Book Company, 1953, p. 494.

North Carolina) regard it as legal grounds for a divorce. It is possible that in time these states also will recognize desertion as a legal ground for divorce.

Annulment. In annulment, the court considers a marriage never to have existed and declares the ceremony null and void. After annulment, it is assumed that the individuals are regarded as never having been married. Annulments are usually granted when the couple did not conform to marriage law; for example, as to age or blood relationship. In addition, there are grounds for annulment which may be the cause or result of a couple's inability to adjust to each other. Among such grounds are fraud, duress or force, insanity, idiocy, impotence, habitual intoxication, or a discovery that a previous marriage still exists. Some few states will annul a marriage for concealment of pregnancy (Arizona and West Virginia), unchastity (West Virginia), failure to have the marriage ceremony performed by a proper authority (Connecticut and Kentucky), and other similar grounds. The Catholic Church will not grant a divorce under any circumstances but may annul a marriage for such reasons as consanguinity, clandestineness, defective consent, terrorism, and disparity of worship. For further and more detailed discussion of this topic, the reader is referred to Catholic authorities, especially to Edgar Schmiedeler, who is Director of the Family Life Bureau, National Catholic Welfare Conference.[2]

Divorce. The most common and most drastic method of dissolving a marriage is divorce. In divorce, not only is there a break between the couple but they shake off or break through all bonds that held them together. We may visualize the pattern of this result in the manner shown in Figure 20, page 370.

Under "living in disharmony" we mentioned seven reasons why people live together in marriage in spite of their problems. In a divorce, the drive to get away from each other is so strong that all these reasons and any others are pushed aside. The desire to be free from each other has become paramount.

---

[2] See his *Marriage and the Family,* New York, McGraw-Hill Book Company, 1946.

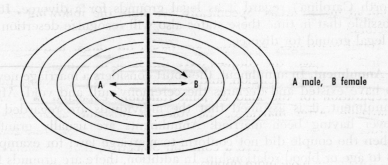

A male, B female

FIGURE 20. Divorce.

There are, however, factors other than this personal urge which determine whether or not a couple will resort to divorce. The general social climate in which they live may influence their decision. Their community and region, their occupation, their education, and their religion all affect it more or less.

"(1) *Community and regional differences:* Divorce is about twice as common in urban as in rural areas. Also the rates are highest in the Pacific and Mountain states, and lowest in the Northeastern region.

(2) *Occupational difference:* It is much more common among the semiskilled than among any other occupational group, being about double that of the professional group.

(3) *Education:* There is some evidence that the higher the educational attainment, the higher the ratio of divorce.

(4) *Religion:* The chances of being divorced are higher for those married by a civil official than for those married by a clergyman. One study by H. Ashley Weeks in Spokane showed that divorce rates in families of school population were three times as frequent in non-Catholic as in Catholic families; four times as great in mixed Catholic-Protestant marriages as in Catholic and for families of no religious affiliations the rate was six times the Catholic." [3]

It would be interesting to discuss all possible reasons for these differences in divorce rate provided we had reliable research data from which to determine the causes. Present research is inconclusive and lacking in agreement. Therefore we confine ourselves to the question which has received more extensive study and attention—namely, why there are fewer divorces in rural

[3] Kimball Young, *Sociology*, 2nd ed., New York, American Book Company, 1949, p. 344. Reprinted by permission.

than in urban areas. Specifically, we note the following causal factors.

Rural marriages, as a rule, are based on longer acquaintance before marriage; the couples have the same or similar economic and social status, religion, and education. There is usually more preparation for the kind of joint functions expected in a rural marriage. After marriage, the roles of husband and wife are rather definite. Each may have specific work duties, but, generally speaking, they have a common objective, that of managing a farm. They have more opportunity to share work interests. They are likely to find that when there is leisure and recreation to be enjoyed, their free time coincides and therefore can be spent together. A rural couple finds that their life centers largely on common friendships. Everybody in the community knows them; hence they take what people will think about them more seriously than do their city cousins. Rural couples who consider divorce as the way to dissolve an unhappy marriage find more obstacles to getting one than do urban couples. Additional complications come from the fact that religion, of a more conservative type, usually plays an important part in the lives of rural people. The church is often the center of their social life; therefore, to take a step which does not receive the sanction of the church automatically costs them their social contacts. Legal services for obtaining a divorce are not easily secured in a rural area, and the divorce trial is likely to be a public affair. There may be a deep-seated emotional attachment to the farm property, and financial settlements become difficult and involved. Finally, the rural divorcée usually finds it far more difficult to remarry than does the divorcée in the city.

When one considers all of these conditions, one is impressed by the fact that there are still half as many divorces in the country as in the city. This fact underscores the importance of mutual adjustment in any marriage.

Remarriage. Another consequence of the inability to adjust is remarriage of a husband or wife while the first mate is still living. Not only may divorced persons marry once, but Hollywood has accustomed us to reading notices like this one: "Mrs. X married Mr. Y; this makes her fourth marriage and his third." (Of course, it is much more common in conservative circles for persons to remarry only once.) Thus while our culture disapproves of contemporary polygamy, it is beginning to condone "successive polygamy." In other words, we are beginning to believe it "right" for a person to have as many mates as he pleases, so long as he does not have more than one at a time.

In recent years there has been a high rate of remarriages. According to the Bureau of the Census, about five and one half million persons obtained divorces from 1940 to 1946, and during the same period the number of divorced persons who had not married increased by only about 500,000.[4] William Carlson Smith, after reviewing all the available literature on remarriage, states: "We may conclude that about one-half of divorced persons remarry."[5] This statement becomes more meaningful when the remarriage rate of divorced persons is compared with that for widowed persons. From information supplied by the Metropolitan Life Insurance Company it can be estimated that a divorced woman of thirty has ninety-four chances in a hundred of eventual remarriage, while the chances of a widow of the same age to remarry are ninety-six in a hundred, and for a widower of the same age, ninety-two in a hundred.

It is also significant that there is a strong tendency for divorced persons to marry other divorced persons. On the basis of information supplied by the Bureau of the Census, it can be estimated that nearly 60 per cent of all husbands and wives who have been married more than once have mates of more than one marriage.[6] One may gather from these statistics that while divorced persons have been disappointed in their particular marriage, they are not disappointed with marriage itself.

Research regarding the degree of success in remarriage by divorced persons is limited. One study worthy of note is that made by Paul Popenoe. Of his sample of 1,058 remarriages, 62 per cent of the couples considered themselves happy in their new

---

[4] *Current Population Reports*, Series P–20, No. 10, Washington, D.C., Bureau of the Census, February 6, 1948.

[5] From *Successful Marriage* by Morris Fishbein, M.D. and Ernest W. Burgess, Ph.D. Copyright 1947 by Morris Fishbein, reprinted by permission of Doubleday & Company, Inc. P. 339.

[6] *Current Population Reports*, Series P–20, 21, December 19, 1948.

marriage as compared with 70 per cent in first marriages.[7] This is a fairly high percentage of success when one considers the many handicaps of divorced persons, such as those listed below under effects of divorce, and, in addition, the presence of children from the first marriage. A second husband may find it difficult to accept such children as his own. They may be an additional burden financially, or he may be jealous of the wife's attention to the children by another man. If children are already in the newly made family, there may be reluctance to add more. Sometimes stepchildren intentionally try to come between the parents.

There may be a number of reasons for the relatively great success of remarriages. Probably those who have been married before have a more realistic attitude toward marriage. One would assume that they had learned something about the problems of adjustment from their first marriage. Added to this is the fact that often a person obtains a divorce in order to marry someone better suited to his own personality and general pattern of life.

SPECIFIC EFFECTS OF INABILITY TO ADJUST IN MARRIAGE

Let us now consider fourteen effects of inability to adjust in marriage and see what happens when a couple decide to live together even though they are miserable in their union. It is obvious that the effects will vary with the intensity of the conflict and with the personalities involved. What is stated here, therefore, does not apply to every couple in the same degree. In the following enumeration, we have in mind couples who have completely failed in their marriage and yet cannot or will not dissolve it. The effects listed have been observed in marriage counseling and reported in the literature and research on the subject.

(1) Inability to adjust, as an admission of defeat in one of the major areas of life, carries with it feelings of humiliation and hurt. This ego-hurt is even more painful because of the prevailing belief that marital adjustment is easy and that anyone can

[7] Paul Popenoe, "Divorce and Remarriage from a Eugenic Point of View," *Social Forces*, 1933, 12:48–50.

accomplish it. The intensity of the pain varies, of course, with the degree of happiness anticipated in marriage.

(2) There may be an attempt to compensate for failure in marriage by being a perfectionist in another area. The husband may try to excel in work; the wife may compensate by engaging

"Am now waiting for the bus at Jefferson and Cherry. Darn it, Edith, I still say you watch me too closely!"

Jeff Keate and the Chicago Tribune–New York News Syndicate, Inc.

excessively in social life, or she may become unduly concerned with the petty details of housekeeping or overattached to the children.

(3) Often there is withdrawal from any form of shared activities, such as contacts with friends, enjoying together the usual forms of recreation, or attending public affairs together. Still

further withdrawal may take the form of excessive daydreaming.

(4) Husband and wife may regard each other as cell mates; a feeling of imprisonment may easily lead to general rebellion against anything and any person who is instrumental in keeping them in this unhappy state. They may rebel, therefore, against the whole social order, religion, parents, and even children. It is not too uncommon to hear the wife say to her child, "If it were not for you, I would have left your father long ago." (Obviously, the husband could say the same about the wife.)

(5) The mates are likely to attempt to play a dual role. While living in disharmony, they may try to give the impression that they live harmoniously. Such a relationship breeds a feeling of hypocrisy, a constant fear that the dual role will be discovered or that one or the other may expose the whole truth to outsiders. Now and then one finds a couple exceptionally capable of deceiving the outside world. A case in point is the following:

> The husband was a prominent member of a university faculty. His wife was an attractive, well-educated person. They had been married for twenty years, of which the last thirteen had been spent in serious, continuous conflicts with each other. The antagonism between them was so great that they could not associate with each other intimately on any level. They decided not to get a divorce for two reasons: they wanted to wait until the children were grown and independent, and the husband was in danger of losing his position if he obtained a divorce. They succeeded so well in hiding their difficulties that not even their closest friends became aware of their strained relationship. How well they succeeded may be gathered from the following reaction. When a new president was appointed to the university, his wife, for some reason or other, made an evaluation of the marital happiness of the couples on the faculty, and, in her opinion, this couple rated highest. One can imagine her surprise when the couple later obtained a divorce.

(6) Many efforts are made to seek escape from the unpleasant situation. Either mate may stay away from home as much as possible; the husband may seek out a position requiring extensive travel. The husband may resort to excessive gambling and the wife to overeating, especially sweets. Both may try to drown their sorrow in alcohol. In extreme cases there are secret wishes for the mate's death, attempts at murder, and sometimes actual murder. Our daily papers report such cases. Occasionally, a mate may turn upon himself and commit suicide.

(7) _Attitudes and sentiments are changed._ Trust is displaced by mistrust; respect by disrespect; sympathy by actually wishing the mate to suffer; moral support by undermining of self-confidence. Former faith in the mate can now become constant suspicion, and love may turn into hate.

(8) The urge to punish the mate is ever present. It may express itself in a variety of forms such as negative criticism, refusal to speak (which may be carried on for days and even weeks or months), refusal to provide adequate money for housekeeping expenses, and enslavement of the mate by threatening desertion or suicide or feigning heart attacks.

(9) It is not surprising that under such conditions sex life is unsatisfactory. It may not be attempted at all or, if attempted, the wife may feel herself "raped." In order to avoid this experience, she often resents anything which may lead to the sex act. In extreme cases, she may say, "I can't stand to have him touch me." Lack of such sexual satisfaction may lead to various forms of sublimation, masturbation, or extramarital affairs. As added punishment, the extramarital affairs may be flaunted openly before the mate.

(10) Persons who have failed to adjust in marriage may develop a feeling of envy toward anyone happily married and may actually go so far as to interfere with the marital happiness of others.

(11) Cynicism about love and marriage may grow out of experienced failure. There may be a feeling that nothing is sacred or important in this world. Embittered persons tend to find fault with everything and everybody.

(12) Usually there are tensions, uneasiness, restlessness, irritability, "flying off the handle," and numerous quarrels, quarrels which unfortunately seldom if ever solve the problem. As one woman put it, "We never have a clean fight." What she meant was that the quarrel never had a cathartic effect—never seemed to end.

(13) There is a loss of strength which came from a feeling of solidarity or oneness with reference to the outside world. If husband and wife have made normal adjustments to each other, they may have disagreements; but let an outside enemy appear

and they unite, close ranks, and draw together. On the other hand, when adequate basic adjustment has not been reached, there is no such unity. There is not the comfort of sharing problems with someone who understands. There is the empty feeling of being alone, regardless of how many persons may be around.

(14) Living in an incessant state of disharmony can affect physical and mental health. There may be premature aging. An atmosphere of conflict can precipitate any one of several disorders referred to as psychosomatic, such as peptic ulcer, forms of bronchial asthma, allergies, migraine, and essential hypertension. In still more severe situations, persons become outright neurotics, developing fears, anxieties, obsessions, compulsions, hysteria, and hypochondria. And in extreme cases the result of trying to spend one's life in a perpetually aggravated relationship may be a psychosis.

Many of these harmful effects can be observed in the following case:

When Mrs. B. came for her first interview, she found talking to a counselor unusually difficult. She frequently interrupted herself by making such remarks as the following:

"It frightens me to talk about myself and my husband like this. Even my thoughts frighten me. To hear myself saying these things out loud to another person gives me quite a shock. I really feel terrible."

After a few interviews, Mrs. B. became more fluent in discussing her problem. Finally, she confided that she was miserably unhappy in her marriage, and had been unhappy for the last eleven of the fourteen years she had been married. However, she had tried desperately hard to hide from relatives and friends the truth concerning her marital relationship. In reference to her early background, she related the following story:

"My husband and I met at the university, where he was completing his Master's degree in business administration the same year I was finishing my bachelor of music degree. We were very much in love during the entire year. Following graduation, Jack had an excellent opportunity offered him with a firm in my home town—it's where we still live. It is a small place of about five or six thousand population. His parents have always lived in a rural community about twenty miles from us. In fact, Jack and I first became interested in each other because when we were introduced we discovered that we came from the same county. Consequently, we had many acquaintances in common, and we had heard of each other's families. My parents and his parents are quite active citizens in their respective towns. I guess you might call them somewhat conservative but, nevertheless, good substantial people. I remember that some of our friends told us at our wedding that it would be hard to find two families more suited than ours to join together.

"And I suppose today the casual observer would view Jack and me and our children as an ideal family. Jack has done very well in business. He's now vice president of his company, in line for the presidency; we own a nice home with just about everything money can buy. We have three children, ages 13, 11½, and 9 and, of course, we belong to the organizations and clubs found in a town such as ours. Our circle of friends includes people from his home town, as well as from the town where we live. I know that most of our friends see us as the so-called 'ideal couple.' I feel so hypocritical because behind this front of false happiness lies plenty of conflict and continuous quarreling. I often think of how happy we were during the first two or two and a half years of our marriage. I don't believe anyone could be happier than we were. Then something began to happen to us—we quarreled over nothing. We started to drift apart. I'll never forget the day we celebrated our third wedding anniversary—or rather our parents did it for us. I felt so terrible because I knew down deep in my heart that I didn't feel close to Jack any more. And I doubted his love for me. I could see that he had changed too.

"About a year after the birth of our second child, I had periods when I became so depressed I didn't care what happened. I guess you could say I even neglected the children, because I did leave them with my mother many times when it wasn't necessary at all. I felt so tied down by them. I think I wouldn't have objected to being tied down if Jack and I hadn't been quarreling so much. I was desperately alone.

"Jack and I were so far apart and yet we dared not let anyone know how we felt. You know what it's like to live in a small town, where everyone knows you and knows everything you think or do. So we kept our differences very much to ourselves. Finally, we agreed to see what a trial separation would do for us. My sister, living in New York, had been wanting me to be her accompanist in a series of club programs on which she was to appear as soloist. So that opening gave me a good excuse to be away for six weeks without arousing the suspicion of our relatives and friends. My trip to New York was wonderful; it gave me a tremendous lift in spirits to be back again in professional music circles. And I had a really gay time in the city with my sister's crowd—I felt so free—I could be myself again. But when I returned home, I soon found I had to go back to acting—pretending that I was really glad to be back home with Jack. I felt so guilty about my feelings toward him and yet I couldn't change them. It was such a strain to be on guard all the time so as not to let our families or friends get the slightest inkling of our relationship. If only I could have talked to someone about our problems, but I didn't dare. There was absolutely no one in whom I could confide. I couldn't even tell my sister while I was East with her. I didn't think she'd understand; she's several years older than I and she has never married. Also, I feared that she might unintentionally say something to our parents which would arouse their suspicions. So I kept my feelings very much buried within myself. We went along like that for about three years.

"Finally, we decided to have another child, or rather Jack wanted another one—he wanted a boy so badly. I can't honestly say I wanted another child; I really didn't, yet I had one glimmer of hope, that maybe the child would help to bring us to a better understanding. I guess I also thought that if I were only lucky enough to give Jack a boy, it would somehow pay back what I couldn't give him in love. After the birth of our third child, who, fortunately, was a boy, Jack seemed to show more enthusiasm for the children. We began to spend more time together, and on the whole, I believe, we reached a better understanding than we had had for years. When the baby was about nine months old, we left the children with my parents and took a vacation trip—we flew to Mexico for three weeks. The trip was wonderful—it took us completely away from our families, friends, and work. We were just together, enjoying everything. Somehow we seemed to capture some of the old romance of college days."

Mrs. B. later continued her story by adding that shortly after their trip, the United States entered World War II. Her husband's firm was converted into a war plant, supplying parts for a larger firm in Chicago, and Mrs. B. and the children were moved to Chicago for what turned out to be a period of fourteen months. This experience brought about another crisis in the life of Mrs. B.

"While living in Chicago, we had an opportunity to make new friends—and in many cases they were much more liberal than our friends back home. I also had a chance to use my music more, because through it I was eligible to join two clubs—one professional and the other primarily social, but music was the hobby of the groups. I also did volunteer work at the service men's clubs. I soon found that I was easily attracted to the men I met at the clubs or even at private parties to which my husband and I were invited. I reached the point where I was half afraid to go out where I would meet attractive men. I was starved for romantic love, and completely contrary to my moral standards, I found that I quickly became the 'sucker for a line' if a man offered me one.

"For a while my relationship with men was on a superficial, flirtatious level. Then a man came along with whom I fell in love and who fell in love with me. Our relationship reached the stage of intimacy and, during the five months he was stationed there, we saw each other regularly. He was everything I needed; we had so much in common and in every way got along smoothly. In many respects, it was a happy experience; however, I was left obsessed with morbid fear that Jack or the folks at home would find out about me. I also wondered if Jack weren't going out with other women. We weren't spending very much time together and even when we were together we didn't seem to have anything to share."

After fourteen months in Chicago, Mr. and Mrs. B. moved back to their home and took up their former pattern of living. Mrs. B. found that she became increasingly ill at ease when with friends. She feared that a slip of the tongue might reveal too much or arouse suspicion concerning her life in Chicago. There was always the possibility that someone from home may have seen her in Chicago in the company of her friend. As a result, she began to withdraw from groups; she stayed at home, using all kinds of excuses to explain her absence from social functions. While at home alone, she yearned for the freedom which she had enjoyed in Chicago. She spent hours daydreaming about what had been and what could be possible under different circumstances. But even phantasy she could not fully enjoy because, as she said:

"I hated myself for it all—I felt so guilt-stricken, and I often wondered how I had ever let myself get so involved. And yet that short span of real companionship I had experienced gave me a taste of what it could be all the time. And right now, when Jack and I go out with our crowd, I feel downright envious of couples who are happy together. Maybe some of them aren't really happy but only act as if they are, as we do, but I know some of them are madly in love with each other, share everything, and have real fun living together. I guess I easily catch the spirit of the crowd, because when I'm at a gay party, I can be the peppiest person there. Then when we reach home, the old slump hits me again. It makes Jack so angry to see me change— he knows I don't have as much fun with him alone as I can with other people. As a matter of fact, he has always been very jealous of me— even at the university. Once we'd agreed to going steady, I never dared look at another fellow. I think he has always been extreme in that respect. He has often shown jealousy when there was no basis for the feeling."

In subsequent interviews, Mrs. B. said that for at least three years she had tried to gain enough courage to ask Jack for a divorce. She believed that he, too, was desirous of making a permanent break. Her courage, however, always weakened when she realized what it would mean to their reputation. The small town where they lived was conservative concerning divorce; their families would be shocked; the church with which they were affiliated did not condone divorce; and Jack's future position might be endangered if it were known that his family relations were unstable. Still more important to her than all other reasons for not getting a divorce was her obligation to the three children. Of them Mrs. B. said:

"My anxiety is so much more intense now. I'm afraid the children are getting old enough to discover the true state of affairs between Jack and me. Martha—that's our older daughter—is now thirteen. She makes a remark or asks a question ever so often which shows that she observes rather closely. I don't know how much I should share with her; it's making a barrier between us, in a sense. Maybe when the children are old enough to understand, they'll appreciate the sacrifice I've made by sticking it out all these years. On the other hand, I often wonder if they would turn against me in favor of their father if we did separate. It seems so unfair to place on the children the burden of making a choice between us; I would never want them to feel that they have to line up on one side or the other in terms of loyalty. That really isn't the problem. We both love the youngsters and I know they love us.

"I say I love them and I really do, although sometimes I feel so guilty in my feelings toward them. At times I almost wish they didn't exist, because I know if it weren't for them I wouldn't be so conscientious about staying on with Jack. It's unbelievable but I almost resent my parents too. They are strict, and I know they would never give in to my getting a divorce. It sounds so terrible when I say it, but I know it's true; if it weren't for the children and my parents, I am sure I could leave Jack. As it is, I feel forced to go on and on like this.

"I'm so mixed up, I don't know what to do. In fact, I'm ill. About three years ago I started having headaches. During the past year, they have been getting worse and worse. Nothing helps to ease them. I always have to go to bed. My doctor tells me he doesn't find anything to cause them and suggests that I rest when I get these attacks. Another thing that worries me is the way my heart pounds and, in addition, I find breathing difficult. Just last week I had a physical checkup and the report shows my heart and lungs are all right."

When Mrs. B. was questioned concerning her eating and sleeping habits, she answered:

"I probably don't eat any more than average, but I eat irregularly— I eat between meals all the time and not so much at the table. I always have something handy to nibble on, and sometimes I just stuff myself on something I happen to like real well. Then, of course, I end up with my old spells of indigestion. I frequently have indigestion. As for sleeping, well, I seem to need a lot of sleep and yet I don't sleep very well. I have horrible nightmares, and when I come out of them my heart is thumping hard. I dream such stupid things—of my children or my parents. And one dream that haunts me so frequently is that I'm being attacked by men. Over and over I wake up from a dream in which I am running frantically up and down the streets in Chicago or New York. This isn't about sleep, but recently I've begun to wonder if I'm losing my mind. Not only are my nightmares silly but I do such foolish things when I'm working around the house. I forget things so easily—not occasionally but every day I do something that is almost unbelievable. I honestly wonder if something is happening to my mind. I've reached a stage where I am so confused I don't know what to think. I don't know which way to turn. I've been reading quite a bit lately about the effects of emotional disturbance on the body—so many of the difficulties I read about sound like me—in fact that's what made me come to talk to you about my condition . . ."

THE EFFECTS OF DIVORCE ON MATES

This topic has already been touched upon briefly in Chapter 1, pages 6–7. Here we shall present it in greater detail. First, the number of persons involved in divorce should be noted. There has been a steady increase in the divorce rate of our country from 1870 to 1946. In the latter year there were slightly over four divorces per 1,000 population. The accompanying graph indicates the trend.

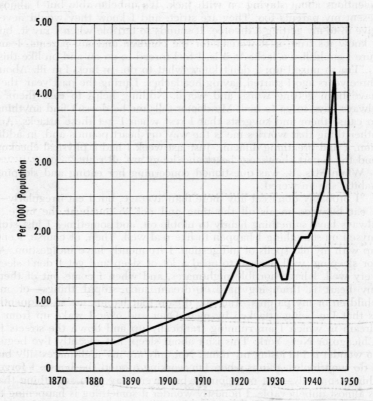

FIGURE 21. Divorces in the United States per 1,000 population, 1870–1950.[8]

In any discussion of the effects of divorce, one must take into account a number of factors: (1) The persons involved, their age, education, economic status, religious affiliation, familial background, and ability or strength to face serious problems. The

[8] Taken from *Statistical Abstract of the United States*, 1952, p. 59, as reproduced in Ernest W. Burgess and Harvey J. Locke, *The Family*, 2nd ed., New York, American Book Company, 1953, p. 475. Reprinted by permission.

same cause may not have the same effect on each individual.
(2) The length of the marriage. (3) Whether or not there are
children and, if so, their ages. (4) The degree of unhappiness up
to the time of divorce. (5) The willingness or unwillingness of
both mates to obtain a divorce. (6) The reaction of relatives and
friends. (7) The nature of the divorce trial—how much ego-hurt
was involved. (8) Prospects for remarriage.

There are individuals who can hardly wait to receive the
decree in order to be able to marry someone else. In contrast, others find divorce such a great relief that no matter
how unpleasant single life may be, they harbor no desire to try
marriage again. Thus, what is said here about the effects of
divorce is not true for every divorced person. Furthermore, such
effects for some may be temporary, while for others, they may be
permanent. We have in mind a typical or average divorced
couple. Such a couple has been married from three to seven years,
may have one or two children and has exerted a sincere effort to
make their marriage work; and yet, in their estimation, they have
failed. Let us now look at the possible effects which divorce
might have on such couples.

Feeling of Relief. After the divorce is granted, there is usually
a feeling of relief which comes from the strains and tensions
prior to and during the divorce proceedings. It is a reaction
which can be embodied in the words "now, at last, it is all over."

Feeling of Emptiness. There may follow an intense feeling of
emptiness, for it is impossible to get out of an intimate relationship without sensing a loss. When the lives of two persons become interwoven, it is difficult to separate them without leaving
in each mate a sense of incompleteness.

Feeling of Remorse. Doubts may arise about the wisdom in
having taken such a serious step. There may be a feeling of
remorse—a feeling that perhaps one should have gone on and
tried harder to bring about adjustment.

Self-accusation. There is often self-accusation of having been
too egocentric, a feeling that perhaps one should have paid more

attention to what people think and believe or to what religion teaches about the willingness to sacrifice. After all, there was a promise for better or for worse.

Feeling of Defeat. The feeling of defeat in marriage which was already present before divorce now becomes aggravated, because one has admitted publicly that, no matter for what reasons, he was incapable of making a success of marriage. Getting married was a public announcement of the belief in one's ability to achieve happiness with a certain mate, and divorce is an open admission of failure. There is a loss of status, of prestige, for just as there was pride in the ability to gain a mate for marriage, so there is now a feeling of humiliation at having lost one. This experience may necessitate a reorganization of the self-concept —and the experience may be traumatic.

Reliving the Past. A reliving in memory of the whole relationship may be experienced. The fact that the two mates are physically apart does not mean that there is a complete psychological break. At first, the unpleasant memories tend to predominate; they may be so much out of proportion that they overshadow all pleasant memories. But as the unpleasant memories are discharged through thinking, talking, or doing something about them, they may lose their effectiveness. The pleasant memories may then predominate, with a feeling of longing and desire to go back to the conditions under which they originated. It is not unlikely that there will be daydreams and night dreams about the marriage. Especially for the mate who was not eager to have the divorce, there may be a reliving of the enjoyable months or years spent together. Such reminiscence may lead to depressed moods if the person has not begun to find a new pattern of living.

Bitterness. There may be a reaction of intense bitterness against the mate who was willing to go through with the divorce. There is no coming back and trying to make up, as in many quarrels prior to the divorce. There may also be bitterness against friends and relatives who did not put forth more effort to stop the divorce procedure; and out of this bitterness may develop a desire to get revenge, to hurt the former mate and even his or her friends.

Self-pity. A divorced person may consider himself a victim of circumstances which were too forceful for any human being to master. The result may be a feeling of persecution and intense self-pity. Reaction formations (behavior just the opposite of one's true feelings) are not uncommon, for no matter how depressed and inwardly hurt a divorced person may be, he may try to put forth a bold front and an "I-don't-care" attitude.

Affectation. A divorced person, once freed from what were considered to be unjust and unfair restraints, may seek "to have his fling, to really taste life." He may be in a state of elation, always gay and hilariously happy. (Such reactions account in part, no doubt, for the well-known expression "a gay divorcée.")

New Life Role. A divorced person must learn to play a new role in life. It was pointed out above that marriage difficulties often arise because marital roles lack clarity of delineation. This deficiency is aggravated for a divorced person, because the roles he is to play are extremely vague and contradictory. Society is slow in formulating such roles, not only because of the relative newness of widespread divorce, but also because of mixed feelings about it. There seems to be a strong resistance toward formulating rules by which a divorced person should live. The whole situation is disturbing to a divorced person, because he must change so many habits and action patterns. Everything he does or does not do becomes a major decision involving careful examination of all consequences and ramifications. He must seek the approval of society without knowing what society approves or disapproves. No wonder divorced persons go through periods of severe tensions.

Feeling of Isolation. More or less intense feelings of isolation and loneliness are not uncommon. The individual is out of step with society, so to speak, and there is likely to be some degree of change in relation to friends. Mutual friends before divorce may present a serious problem. To associate with them as a single person seems somewhat unnatural and awkward. He does not fit well into the group because the former social life was organized around couples. Certain friends may have been half-hearted in their approval of a divorce, and to associate with them means to put oneself on the defensive. The divorced may be forced to find new friends, and sometimes circumstances make this step difficult.

The divorced husband, as a rule, does not have as great difficulty as does the divorced wife. In our society, he is much freer to look around, and it is quite common for his friends to find him at least a temporary companion for social functions. The excess of available women as compared with men makes his lot a comparatively easy one. The ex-wife has a much more serious problem, because she is not so free to make friends, and, of course, there are fewer men available. Nor do her friends show the same degree of eagerness to secure a temporary companion for her. What makes her plight still more unpleasant is the fact that many married women regard a divorcée as a potential rival for the affection of their husbands.

Marriage on "the Rebound." There may be a strong tendency to "save face," especially on the part of the mates who were not willing to obtain a divorce. They may rush into a new marriage primarily to prove that they have adequate and desirable personalities. They can get a new mate on short notice. In common parlance, they marry "on the rebound."

Financial Problems. Divorce may put a financial strain on husband and wife because of the expense of legal proceedings and the increased living expense after divorce. The husband may have to pay alimony, though this is not so common as it was formerly. Courts seldom grant alimony to a young wife who has no children, except when the husband is wealthy. For the less wealthy husband, an alimony becomes a great burden, especially if he should remarry and have to support a new wife and possibly children. For the average wife, complete loss of support or even decreased support from her husband means that she will have to find employment in order to meet her expenses. For the wife who has been working before marriage or who may possess special skills, the problem is not so crucial, but it becomes a serious one for the wife who lacks previous work experience and training in skills.

Unnatural Attitude toward Children. In divorces where small children are involved, additional problems present themselves. Who shall be given custody of the children? Shall the children remain continuously with one parent or shall they be shifted from one parent to the other at stated periods of time? In either case there is too often an attempt to win the children to one's side. Also, when children develop behavioral problems (and it is not unusual under such circumstances), each mate blames the other for them. When the wife has exclusive custody of the children, she may either shower them with too much affection or may regard them as a hindrance to her chances at remarriage and therefore reject them.[9]

EFFECTS ON CHILDREN OF PARENTS' INABILITY TO ADJUST

It has been stated repeatedly in previous sections that the foundations of personality are laid in the home, especially during the first five years of a child's life. An unstable or broken home can have endless undesirable effects upon a growing child.

Effects of a Discordant Home on Children. In former years, it was the practice to advise parents not to get a divorce for the sake of their children. In recent years, there has been a change to some degree in this point of view. Magoun says, "Where there are children, many people believe the parents should stay together for the sake of the children. I used to think so. Parents may be able to fool the neighbors as to the tottering condition

---

[9] For a more detailed study of the effects of divorce, see Willard Waller, *The Old Love and the New*, New York, Horace Liveright, 1930.

of the home, but they cannot possibly keep the children from feeling and being affected by their incompatibility. . . . It is far better to live with one parent in peace than to live with two parents on the battlefield of a quarreling home." [10] Harper states: "The old argument of staying together for the sake of the children is of doubtful validity in many marriages which would otherwise end in divorce. It is not at all certain that the divorce of their parents will harm children more than continued living with incompatible parents." [11]

The authors are fully in accord with these two statements and call attention to the following detrimental effects of a discordant or disharmonious home:

(1) A child finds very little security in a discordant home, no matter how much the parents try to hide the true state of affairs from him. Children are highly sensitive to an emotional atmosphere long before they understand words. They can sense it from tone of voice, facial expression, and gestures. A discordant emotional atmosphere makes it impossible for a child to take "permanent roots" in his environment.

(2) One must remember that for children parents are demigods; having no existence outside of the home, very young children are completely dependent upon parents and are at their mercy. Conflict between parents, therefore, will give a child the feeling of not being wanted and of not being loved. He feels rejected because he recognizes that parents are more concerned about themselves than about him.

(3) The child may feel that he is in the way of his parents' happiness. He may become aware of the fact that his parents do not care for each other and that they remain together only because of him.

(4) In his childish way, he may attempt to reconcile his parents with each other, only to be defeated again and again. Made to face the unpleasant side of life long before he is ready to cope with it, he may develop a strong inferiority feeling in interpersonal relationships.

[10] F. Alexander Magoun, *Love and Marriage*, New York, Harper & Brothers, 1948, p. 329. Reprinted by permission.

[11] Robert A. Harper, *Marriage*, New York, Appleton-Century-Crofts, Inc., 1949, p. 236. Reprinted by permission.

(5) He is also prevented from expressing his affection for either parent for fear of being rejected by the other. Deprivation early in life of the opportunity to express a natural, outwardly turned love may mean that the child will never learn to express love for others.

(6) As compensation, the child may withdraw from his environment by living in a world of phantasy and daydreams in which he pictures his parents as not being his "real parents," or he may idealize imaginary parents, perfected as he wants them.

(7) He is prevented from being himself; the normal urge for self-realization is frustrated and blocked.

(8) He may learn the trick of getting his way by pitting one parent against the other. He finds that he can play upon their already disturbed emotions.

(9) He is in danger of becoming too dependent upon the mother and too much attached to her because of her tendency to transfer to him all the affection she may possess for the father.

(10) If the father senses this overattachment, he may become jealous of the child and use him to revenge himself on the mother. For instance, he may be overly strict in disciplining the child.

(11) As a consequence, the child may feel very hostile toward the father and, being prevented from expressing such hostility, he may direct it toward any form of authority outside his home, such as camp counselors, teachers, and officers of the law.

(12) Young children learn about life and about adjustment to people by identifying themselves with the parents, who become their models. When children are deprived of such models, they experience great difficulty in learning normally expected techniques of adjustment.

(13) It has been stated above that happily married couples ordinarily come from happy homes. Conversely, children who come from unhappy homes are handicapped in making good marital adjustments later. Either they may become afraid of getting married because of their childhood memories of marriage or, if they should marry, they may put forth too much effort to make it a success, so much so that life becomes a strain. They may excessively magnify minor misunderstandings, or they may be too sensitive to withstand the ordinary, normal conflicts.

EFFECTS OF DIVORCE ON CHILDREN

Accurate statistics as to the total number of children affected by divorce in the United States are not available, but a fair estimate can be made on the basis of a number of sources of information. According to the 1950 census, there were 44,600,000 children under 18 years of age living with one or both parents; 866,000, or 1.9 per cent, of these were living with a divorced parent.[12] This does not include all children of divorced parents, since a considerable number live with other relatives, friends, adopted parents, or in institutions. Another source of information states that the number of children under 21 years of age affected by divorces secured in 1948 was about 313,000.[13] On the basis of information supplied by these two sources, one may estimate that there are at present in our country at least several million children who have been affected by divorce.

The effects of divorce on children depend on a number of factors. It is obvious that not all children are influenced in the same way. There are great individual differences between children themselves. One and the same event will affect different children in various ways. Much depends upon the age of a child. Other things being equal, the older child is better prepared to face the divorce of parents than the younger one.

The conditions prevailing in the home prior to divorce are also important. In some cases, a divorce may be as much a relief for a child as it is for a parent. In other cases, where a child was only slightly aware of the severe conflict between parents, divorce may come as a shock. To these factors must be added the conditions under which a child will live after the divorce.

Living with the Mother. The majority of children of divorced parents live with the mother, at least for some time. According to the 1950 census, about 92.6 per cent of such children lived with

[12] Bureau of the Census, "Children and Youth," *Current Population Reports, Population Characteristics,* Series P–20, No. 32, December 4, 1950, p. 17.
[13] Metropolitan Life Insurance Company, "Divorce and the Size of Family," *Statistical Bulletin,* New York, 1950, 31, No. 2, p. 1.

the mother. On the whole, therefore, the mother is more responsible for the rearing of children than is the father. Much will depend upon the mother's personality, her skill, her attitude toward children, and the time she can devote to them. Under favorable circumstances, she can do a highly commendable job in raising the children. Yet the children will still be deprived of the father's example, his love, and his guidance. Boys may suffer more from this loss than girls. A boy will have to look to other men to find an ideal to copy, or he may identify himself with his mother and become effeminate. In other instances, a boy may try to play the father's role at a time when he is still quite immature. Both boys and girls may undergo much suffering from a belief that their father, since he has not remained with them, does not love them. Sometimes this feeling is aggravated by the tauntings of other children.

The conditions are much worse when the mother is unstable; when she is ill-prepared to raise children; when she uses children to express her hatred toward her ex-husband; when she showers them with too much affection because of the lack of love in her own life or because of guilt feelings; when she looks upon them as a great personal or financial burden; or when she regards them as a hindrance in finding a new husband. In such cases, children may feel completely rejected and may react either by fighting back or by withdrawing into seclusion.

As a rule, divorce means a lowering of standard of living for the children, since the amount of money paid by the ex-husband for support of children is seldom equivalent to what was available before divorce. Children may be deprived of comforts which they had before: they may not have as good clothing and food; they may be forced to move to a poorer neighborhood; they may have to find part-time work; they may leave home to seek full employment early in their life and possibly be deprived of higher education. All of this may result in hate for the father, especially in those cases where there is difficulty in collecting support money.

Living with the Father. According to the 1950 census, only 7.4 per cent of the children of divorced couples lived with the father; still, the total of such children was 64,084. All of these children were deprived of the mother's care and affection. In many cases, they were undoubtedly cared for by other women as long as they were small. However, the disadvantages for a child living with a divorced father are so many that society approves in most cases that the mother be awarded custody of children. Probably the greatest handicap the father has in trying to care for children is that he has to spend most of the normal waking hours of a child away from home.

Living Alternately with the Father and Mother. This arrangement is invariably entered into more to pacify the quarreling parents than to benefit the child. It usually signifies that the parents are antagonistic toward each other. The child is deprived of security as well as a free expression of love and affection. He cannot feel permanently secure in his physical environment. He is constantly torn from one social environment and transplanted into another. He cannot let himself be fully attached to either parent for fear of antagonism. In the long run, he is likely to feel uprooted, rejected, and isolated.

Living with Relatives. If a child lives with grandparents, it usually results in his being spoiled or being subjected to discipline too strict for him. If the child lives with other relatives, his welfare will depend upon their attitude toward him. He may be fully accepted, especially when such relatives have no children of their own. Or he may be merely tolerated as an additional burden. He may become the cause for family quarrels as to what should be done for him and what should be expected of him.

Living in Foster Homes, Boarding Schools, etc. Foster homes, boarding schools, and orphanages offer many advantages for children deprived of their parents. They are generally better equipped, however, for satisfying a child's physical needs than his personal and emotional needs. Limited finances make it difficult for some institutions to obtain enough adequately trained personnel to meet the psychological needs of the children. In such cases, children may feel unwanted, unloved, and emotionally starved. It should be noted, however, that an increasing number of our present-day institutions are fully cognizant of this need and are striving diligently to create real homes of unity and stability for children who otherwise would be homeless.

Living with Stepparents. Many children who lose a parent through divorce are happy to get a new parent when their divorced father or mother remarries. The children themselves may be wholeheartedly accepted. However, a child often is unable to accept a new parent either because of a feeling that he is not really wanted by the new parent or because of loyalty to a real parent. A child with such an attitude may break up a new marriage. A case in point is that of a divorcée with a seven-year-old son. When she married the second time, the boy made life so miserable for the couple that during the next six years his stepfather left his mother seven times and finally got a divorce. When his mother married another man, the boy's opposition started again. When the son finally moved to a distant part of the country, his mother and stepfather made a good adjustment to each other. Of course, sometimes a husband or wife cannot accept children from a previous marriage. Such conditions invariably cause a great deal of suffering to everyone concerned. Should either parent or both parents have children by a previous marriage and in addition later have children together, the stage is often set for intensely unpleasant interpersonal conflicts. Envies, jealousies, and even hatred frequently aggravate the whole relationship.

The over-all effect of divorce on children is not necessarily detrimental, at least not any more so than the loss of a parent through death. To conclude that children will necessarily manifest behavior problems or personality inadequacies is an oversimplification of cause and effect relationship. When a boy or girl from a broken home gets into some moral or legal difficulty, one must not jump to the conclusion that divorce is the cause of it. After all, delinquents come from all kinds of homes. When society blames broken homes for delinquency, it is not surprising that sometimes young people from such homes will not exercise as much restraint in their antisocial drives as they might otherwise do, or that when they get into difficulty, they will shake off responsibility by blaming their unfortunate background.

INTERPRETATIVE SUMMARY

1. Inability to adjust in marriage will affect not only the marital union as such, but also each mate and any children of the union.

2. When a marriage turns out to be unsuccessful, a couple may go on living with each other in various degrees of disharmony, or they may dissolve their marriage.

3. For whatever reason a couple may prefer to live in disharmony rather than dissolve their marriage, the effects of such a decision are detrimental and painful for all persons concerned.

4. Marriages are dissolved through separation, desertion, annulment, and divorce. While all of these methods break the marriage tie, the most common and drastic is divorce.

5. Whether or not a couple will get a divorce when the real meaning of their marriage has vanished depends not only on them as individuals but also on many other factors, such as religion, relatives and friends, children, occupation, education, economic conditions, and place of residence.

6. One significant sociological phenomenon in recent years has been the remarriage of a husband or wife while the divorced mate is still living. Such a state of affairs often results in highly complex interpersonal relationships, clashing loyalties, and many inner conflicts. In spite of these conditions, many couples achieve quite satisfactory adjustments.

7. The effects of divorce on mates and on children are varied and complex. They range all the way from being harmful to physical and mental health to being more or less beneficial in every way to everyone concerned.

THOUGHT QUESTIONS AND PROJECTS

1. Using members of the class as sources, compare urban and rural attitudes toward divorce.

2. What are some possible effects of divorce on the couple involved?

3. If you have read John Galsworthy's *The Forsyte Saga,* what are the difficulties and effects of divorce as presented in this novel?

4. If members of the class whose parents are divorced or separated wish to volunteer to discuss the effects of these conditions on children as they see them, it may be helpful to hear opinions from primary sources.

5. Why does a home where there is continuous disharmony tend to create in the children feelings of insecurity and problems of loyalty toward parents?

6. What may be the social problems of persons who are definitely separated, but not divorced, from their mates?

7. Discuss the advantages and disadvantages if an unhappy couple remains married for the sake of the children.

8. Do you think divorce has more disadvantages for the man or for the woman? Explain your answer.

SUGGESTED READINGS FOR FURTHER STUDY

Bowman, Henry A., *Marriage for Moderns,* 3rd ed., McGraw-Hill Book Company, 1954.
    Chapter 16. Divorce.
Baber, Ray E., *Marriage and the Family,* 2nd ed., New York, McGraw-Hill Book Company, 1953.
    Chapters 1, 3, and 14. Divorce.
Despert, L., *Children of Divorce,* Garden City, New York, Doubleday & Company, 1953.
Ernst, Morris L., and David Loth, *For Better or Worse,* New York, Harper & Brothers, 1951.
Goode, William J., "Problems in Post Divorce Adjustment," *American Sociological Review,* 1949, 14:394–401.
Slade, Frances, *Divorce If You Must,* New York, Coward-McCann, 1938.
Waller, Willard, *The Old Love and the New,* New York, Liveright Publishing Corporation, 1930.
Young, Kimball, *Personality and Problems of Adjustment,* 2nd ed., New York, Appleton-Century-Crofts, 1952.
    Chapter 17. Some Problems of Marriage and Divorce.

20

FUNCTIONING AS A UNIT

CO-OPERATION

A social unit is characterized not only by adjustment among the elements which make it up but also by co-ordinated action toward common goals or objectives. Marriage should be viewed not only as *mutual* adjustment between husband and wife but also as a goal-directed undertaking.

This united action does not just happen; it must be achieved, since everyone begins life as a dependent and self-centered individual. Egocentricity is greatly minimized as one attains emotional maturity and becomes more concerned about the welfare of others. It is questionable, however, whether one can reach a stage of development in which he relinquishes self-interest completely. Therefore, this vestige of self-concern, no matter how small in degree it may be, remains an important factor in adjustment throughout life.

Marriage is an intensive training in supplanting "I" by "we." The attainment of this objective is made still more difficult in our society because of our general emphasis on competition. The spirit of competition pervades almost every aspect of our social life, education, occupation, and even recreation. Everywhere the emphasis is on getting ahead of the other person. It is true that there is considerable emphasis on teamwork, but the team must win and the highest recognition is given the one who does most for the team. In the final analysis, even with teams the individual effort is singled out for recognition.

In marriage, there must be co-operation, without thought even of who contributes what: each should give to the maximum of his capacity. The important fact is the achievement of mutually satisfying goals. Ideally, neither husband nor wife seeks individual credit, nor do they place individual blame. A simple but rather significant example illustrates the point: The husband noticed, in getting the cups from the pantry, that one hook was vacant. He asked his wife what happened to the cup. She responded: "Oh, we broke it." Although she had broken it, she was not aware of saying "we." In their relationship, the "we" feeling was so natural that there was no hesitation in automatically saying "we" instead of "I."

An analysis reveals three aspects of co-operation: common goals, common means or methods, and common action. Goals are based upon needs. A husband and wife will have many of these in common, physiological as well as psychosocial, just because they are human beings. These needs are not always felt at the same time and in the same degree, however, so that adjustments are necessary. Adjustments are necessary also when the needs differ because of differences in sexual training. In order to attain common objectives, there must be accommodation and assimilation. The methods depend upon innate capacity, knowledge, skill, and emotional control; each mate will function according to his ability.

Actions are the central feature of co-operation. Actions may speak louder than words, but words are also involved in co-operation. They are necessary for the interchange of ideas. Actions are usually in the form of work—which is activity, not for its own sake as in play, but activity in which the goal to be achieved is of primary importance. The activity, as such, may be strenuous and therefore not pleasant in itself. It is for this reason that one or the other mate may fail to complete his part of the responsibility. One, by leaning too much on the other, may become a burden rather than a help. He or she may exploit the other, or live a parasitic life.

The satisfactions derived from co-operation are many. A significant form of satisfaction is the feeling that one's needs are important, not only to himself but to his mate as well. Other satisfactions arise out of the opportunity given for self-expression and self-realization, the sense of security because of another's interest, the conviction of not being alone, and the feeling of being strengthened by another.

We shall consider now six areas in which, especially, husband and wife must function as a unit.

EARNING A LIVING

In our society, there is a well-established division of responsibility between husband and wife for supporting the household. The husband works outside the home, the wife within the home. While this arrangement is generally accepted by the majority of couples in our society, it can be a threat to unity in that such division of labor may lead to division in other respects. To prevent this result, each mate must share in the other's function and participate to whatever degree is possible. A wife establishes her social status almost exclusively on the basis of her husband's occupation. Whether she is the wife of a day laborer, clerk, lawyer, doctor, educator, or executive, she must be able to accept her husband's job status and, having accepted it, must be willing and able to live up to it. Insofar as she is able to do so, she becomes a source of strength, support, and comfort to her husband; otherwise, she can do him a great deal of harm in the eyes of his associates and friends. To minimize or prevent such harm, husband and wife should be alike in as many ways as possible. It is also important that the husband keep the wife informed as much as possible about his work, so that she may act in a manner that is a credit to him. Since her own work is, as a rule, more confining, her life will be enriched by such communication.

Working Wives. It is becoming more and more common for wives to participate actively in earning a living outside the home. The following are some of the reasons for this trend: (1) The income of the husband is so low that the wife must help provide the family's bare necessities of life. (2) The wife may work only until children arrive in order to accumulate larger savings.

(3) She may work in order to have extra money for her family or herself. (4) She may work to retain her skill in order to be able to care for herself in case of need. (5) She may have time on her hands, either because there are no children or because the children have grown up. (6) Since her work at home is not paid for in money, she may feel like a parasite and insist on working. (7) Keeping house may be distasteful, and the wife may want to build up her ego by some gainful employment outside the home. (8) She may possess some talent or special education which she must use and express in order to be happy. (Whatever a person can be, he must be in order to be happy.) (9) She may work to realize some ambition. There may be a combination of these reasons, of course, or some unusual, personal reason.

Problems Connected with the Wife's Gainful Employment. There is still a strong feeling that a woman's place is in the home; therefore, a working wife may incur the criticism of many friends and of her husband's associates. Her husband also may feel he is losing respect because he cannot support a wife. It is difficult to find suitable work for a working wife. On the whole, employers strongly prefer to hire the single woman, who has fewer responsibilities. (Conditions during World War II, of course, somewhat altered this practice.) Also, pay ordinarily is less for a woman than it is for a man doing the same type of work. Her work, plus responsibilities at home, may be so fatiguing to a wife that she cannot perform well as either wife or worker. All of these conditions indicate that others beside herself are involved in what she is doing. The decision to work should, therefore, be arrived at by both husband and wife. If the wife feels she must work in order to express herself more fully, or if her self-respect demands that she work, the husband should realize that she has this right, conventions or no conventions. To help her, he may share the housework. This co-operative plan often works out well.

The problem of caring for the children is more serious. Their rearing should not be handed over to a grandmother or a maid. A good solution is to send children to a nursery school if they are of proper age. While there, the child will get physical and psychological care. Among other things, he will have opportunity to be with children of his own age under supervision. Early in life, he will learn to be at ease in social situations. He will be freed from too great attachment to his mother, and he will adjust better to adults. A good nursery school will not only instill sound habits and attitudes, but also in many cases solve such

"I'm afraid you'd better give up trying to combine marriage and a career."

Gustav Lundberg and The Saturday Evening Post.

problems as bed wetting, faulty eating habits, and temper tantrums.

Mrs. S., a young divorcée, came to discuss the problem of what to do with her three-year-old son. It was apparent that she would have to work, at least part time, in order to supplement her income. She had found a position, but it meant that she would be away from home from nine until four. Who would take care of her child? Mrs. S. commented:

"My mother lives with me but she isn't good for him—she's so nervous and becomes irritated at him. She's so inconsistent. One minute she treats him as if he were a helpless infant and the next she expects him to act like a grownup. She isn't very well; I'd hate for him to become a burden to her."

When asked if she had considered sending him to a good nursery school, she replied:

"But he's so shy, he doesn't take to strangers very well."

As she continued describing the child's behavior, it became apparent that he had several symptoms of an emotionally disturbed child. To get him to eat had become an ordeal, he refused to take naps, bed-wetting was an every-night occurrence, and recently he had begun to stammer. Mrs. S. was advised to place the child in a nursery school. She later reported that the first day he cried violently when she left him, but that each successive day their separation became easier for both of them. After one week at the nursery he was eager to go and shed no tears when he told his mother good-by.

Three months later she returned to report progress.

"It was really hard for me to send him away from me like that, but the experience has made a new child of him. Now he eats exceptionally well, sleeps regularly, enjoys playing with other children, and his bed-wetting has stopped completely. And he is anything but timid now! I'm amazed at how much he has learned during these three months."

Reluctantly, she confessed—

"It does hurt my pride a little, however, to think that others could help my child in ways which I myself could not do."

There are mothers, like Mrs. S., who suffer from ego-hurt in such situations but at the same time realize that the ultimate welfare of the child is uppermost in importance. It is possible that the type of mother who feels hurt most easily in such parent-child relationships is the very one least prepared to handle the emotional problems of her child at this age.

MAINTAINING A HOME

To keep up a home requires management and physical labor. It is the latter to which so many wives object, not because it requires time and energy but because of the types of chores involved. The husband, in order to understand his wife's feeling, should be aware of the following characteristics of housework:

(1) *It is boring*. The work is repetitive and seems unending. Three meals a day means 1,068 a year, 10,680 in ten years. Every

meal requires washing and drying dishes. Then there are washing and ironing and repairing clothes over and over again. No sooner is the house cleaned than the cleaning process must start again.

(2) *It is solitary.* The satisfaction of working with someone beside you is absent in the home. There is no stimulation. No wonder women find it necessary "to take out" and talk with the neighbors over the back fence or become ardent supporters of soap operas, gruesome mysteries, and gossipy chit-chat on radio and television programs.

(3) *There is no promotion.* Many jobs in other fields are well done because of the prospect of recognition through promotion. What can a wife be promoted to? More of the same! Quite often she does not even get verbal appreciation for a job well done. Her work is taken for granted—it is her duty!

(4) *Work without pay.* Her work is, of course, worth money, but only in terms of saving money that would have to be paid to someone else. Concrete remuneration is lacking.

(5) *Low-level activity.* The routine work in housekeeping is of such a nature that it requires little intelligence as compared with many other types of work. Consequently, anyone with some practice and accumulated information can do a good job. It is, therefore, not ego-building for an intelligent woman.

(6) *Hard to evaluate.* The work is of such a nature that no satisfactory criteria exist whereby to judge the quality of work accomplished. The quality of housekeeping may be below the standard held by some friends but above that held by others.

It is important for a husband to understand these points about housework, so that he will appreciate the wife's lot and be willing to relieve her of as much drudgery as possible. He may come to think that outside help might well be engaged in order to give the wife some sense of relief even when she herself has time for the work. He will also come to realize that household equipment which will eliminate some routine function or simplify housekeeping should be obtained as soon as finances permit.

Management of the Home. The management of the home is of an altogether different nature and is much more stimulating because it taxes a person's intelligence and knowledge. In a

successful marriage, the wife is ultimately responsible for proper
management of the home. Important matters are discussed, but
final decisions are left to her. There is practically no limit to the
ingenuity and skill she can use in the aesthetic appointment of
the house, in the economical buying of everything pertaining to
housekeeping and in the orderly and systematic running of the
house. The expense involved in her work, as a rule, accounts for
the spending of the major part of the income. She assumes,
therefore, great responsibility. If she is not well prepared for
her work, she is subject to much criticism. Since it is not easy
for the majority of people to earn money, they are very much
concerned about proper spending. They become sensitive about
money matters. According to many authorities, most family quarrels concern economic questions in one way or another—when
either the wife or the husband spends too much.

In order to avoid many quarrels or misunderstandings along
this line, husband and wife should agree on some basic principles
on the handling of their money. The following methods are used.
(1) The husband handles all the money. He decides what should
be bought and what price to pay. The wife has to ask for every
dollar she needs. (2) The husband puts the wife on an allowance.
She receives a fixed amount of the monthly income and must do
the best she can. (3) The husband is on an allowance. (4) The
husband and wife have a joint bank account, on which each can
draw as money is needed. From the viewpoint of mutual respect
and confidence, the last method is undoubtedly the best. However, this plan implies equal knowledge and skill in the management of money. Actually, the best method for a couple is the one
mutually decided upon and acceptable to both. This method
should be arrived at by fundamental agreement and, once agreed
upon, should be retained. Such procedure alone can eliminate
misunderstanding about money matters.

In discussing a joint bank account, Mrs. G related the following story:

"Prior to our marriage, I was working and, of course, had my own
bank account. Naturally, my husband had his. For a few months after
marriage we continued the same plan, since I didn't give up my job
until some time later. Soon we realized that separate accounts had no
advantage. We were sharing everything else, so why not the bank

account? Since we had no business entanglements which in any respect required separate records, we opened a joint account. Each month we went over all canceled checks together; we often discussed the nature and amount of our expenses for that particular month; we were aware of exactly how we stood financially. We had the utmost confidence in each other's judgment when it came to handling money. For several years now I haven't worked, but we have continued our joint bank account. I think sharing our funds during those early years of marriage taught us many things, such as a system in handling our finances, a sense of values in spending our money and, above all, what it means for a husband and wife to place complete trust in each other. By using this method, each of us has known our financial status at all times; we have known whether or not we could afford to buy certain items. It gives me a sense of dignity to know that the checking account is equally mine, even though I no longer bring home a monthly check. For myself, I prefer this system to the allowance plan. Naturally, I realize that some women must have their zeal for spending curbed by the method which sets a definite limit. I am inclined to believe that husbands and wives should start early in their marriage to share the economic problems and responsibilities of home management and that the joint bank account will help them to be informed concerning their financial status."

Any couple with a family budget not only eliminates misunderstanding but also uses the income more wisely. The value of such a budget can be seen by keeping a detailed record of income and expenses for a period of three to six months and then examining the expenditures. A glance suffices to show where the money has gone. From such a record, the couple can determine how much must be allowed for various items; they also may see whether they are spending too much money for unessentials. In addition to their own efforts at budget planning, they may wish to compare their plans with acceptable planning aids obtainable through the government printing office, through the home planning services of various reliable publications, from financial counselors or banks, and so on. Obviously, any intelligent, mature couple will so plan their budget that some savings can be set aside. A bank or investment advisor is helpful in determining the percentage of income any couple should be able to save. Budgetary advisers usually suggest that 10 to 15 per cent of one's income be set aside as savings. Perhaps the important point for young couples is that they learn early the habit of making systematic savings, whether large or small.

REARING CHILDREN

The proper attitude toward a child is to regard him as a new member in the union who, for a certain period of his life, must receive from the other members more than he can give but who, nevertheless, has just as many "rights" as the others. He should never be regarded as a plaything or as a means to an end. The child should never be regarded as a plaything to be loved when he gives satisfaction but disliked when his needs become a burden. He is being treated as a means to an end when parents use him to realize their unsatisfied ambitions.

A case in point is that of the father who wanted to become a physician but did not attain this goal and now wants to achieve it through his son. A mother may try to live her life vicariously through her daughter's life. Now and then, children are used as a means to carry on a family tradition, a vocation, a business, or a profession. In such cases the child's capacity and wishes are disregarded. Whenever a child is used for self-aggrandizement of any kind, he is regarded primarily as a means to an end rather than as an end in himself. Too often "I am proud of my son," means "He is doing what *I* want him to do."

Joys and Responsibilities. A child is a source of great joy to parents under normal conditions, but also a responsibility. The joys are many and varied. A child may be a concrete manifestation of the love between parents. He is the embodiment of the blending of the parents' physical and mental traits. It is as though a part of each has been separated from them and become a new being. They can see in the offspring a fulfillment of their desire for immortality and the immortality of their love. The capacity of a child to enrich their lives for many years is almost unbounded.

On the other hand, the responsibility that parents assume when giving birth to a new life is great. Their responsibility consists not simply in taking care of him as a living organism, but especially in making him a useful member of society. Other members of society play an important role later in his life, but the contribution of parents is the most basic and most important, for it is they who lay the foundation of his personality in the first five years or so of his life. Authorities agree unanimously on this point.

Guidance in the Growth of Personality. The reader might with profit read again the chapter on personality, realizing that the shaping of personality is intricate and complex. While our scientific knowledge about the foundation of personality is still limited, it is inestimably better than the haphazard information possessed by the average parent. It certainly is ridiculous and yet true that many parents believe they possess the knowledge of how to rear a child simply because they were able to procreate one. "Mother knows best" is taken almost as an axiom; yet in most cases mother does only what her mother did, and she did what her grandmother did, and so on indefinitely. It is in this manner that ignorance and superstition are perpetuated. Fortunately, more and more parents recognize their limitations and the limitations of their parents before them and are anxious to learn. For detailed information about parenthood one must consult special sources; here we can mention a few basic points.

It is essential to be familiar first with a few *principles which underlie child guidance*. At the center of child guidance is the child—his welfare and happiness. This may sound trite, and yet in practice what the child is often expected to do or not to do is motivated by the idea of keeping up a certain standard. The rules, the principles are more important; they are sacrosanct, and the child is used merely as a means to effect cultural perpetuation. (More will be said later on this point when we discuss discipline.) If the child is to be the center, parents must know the child as well as the culture they wish to perpetuate.

To *know* the child means to be aware of his needs, his abilities, and his limitations. (The physical needs of a child are fairly well known, but the psychological needs are relatively unknown.) These needs, which were discussed in Chapter 3, are merely mentioned here. They include security, love, recognition, self-expression or self-realization, and exploration. The satisfaction of these for healthy growth is just as important as soil, air, sunshine, and rain are for the growth of a plant. The abilities in a child—physical, emotional, and intellectual—are more potential than actual. They must await maturation and learning for their full development. To regard a child, therefore, as a mature being is a grave mistake. The limitations, which are many, may be summarized in two concepts—dependency and autonomy. Gardner Murphy has given graphic description of dependency in early childhood:

> "After the flush of excitement, pride, and responsibility, the parents settle down into their new stride. From the baby's own 'point of view' —as fast as he acquires one—he is little, helpless, ignorant; these big hulks go and come as they please, make the rules, administer the 'sanctions.' But retaliation is possible. The baby can kick and scream, he can be cute and winsome; he holds plenty of aces. He controls much of what father does, and nearly all of what mother does. His rule is capricious but despotic. It is a constitutional monarchy, to be sure; he can be controlled by parliamentary methods. But he cannot abdicate; and though he can be ignored at times, his powers cannot be clipped below a very clear—and large—grant. As he grows, he learns how to rule more effectively, more powerfully; he learns the weaknesses of this parliamentary control, especially on all points on which parliament is divided. He learns how his weakness, as well as his strength, can command the field. But not only does he learn the sense of power; the self is undergoing development, and he learns to note his own worth. His parents evidently find him important, a supreme value. Since they know all about things, they are probably right, so he concludes very reasonably that he must be very, very valuable." [1]

For the child, growing up largely means outgrowing his dependency on others for the satisfaction of his needs and overcoming his egocentricity—the feeling that the world revolves around him. Parents must aid the child to become independent of them as soon as possible. In this respect they can learn from animals, who rush their offspring into self-reliance. Dependency is often prolonged by parents because of "love." They want to do things for the child, to make his decisions, to protect him from mistakes. The motive may be good, but the end result is undesirable. The child is "spoiled"—that is, he thinks of others only in terms of how they can serve him. Instead of love for the child, the parents have only self-love. They want to be needed, to be important to the child. By treating him in this manner, they do not

[1] Gardner Murphy, *Personality*, New York, Harper & Brothers, 1947, p. 586. Reprinted by permission.

set their child free. Rather, he is forced to remain "tied to mother's apron strings."

In this connection, we are reminded of a certain mother who has three married daughters and an eight-year-old son. Perhaps the great disparity in age between her earlier children and the boy causes her to overprotect him. She constantly refers to him as "our baby" and "the little one," instead of calling him by name. She sends him to a small private school so that he can have more individual attention. She works outside the home in order to supplement the family income, but she must work where the hours allow her to take the boy to school in the morning and to get him in the afternoon. They live only four blocks from the school, but she is afraid to let him cross the streets alone. Little does she realize that she is literally depriving the child of the opportunity to learn how to be self-sufficient and that later he may grow to resent her because of her overprotectiveness.

Self-centeredness is prolonged by parents who pamper their children. In many cases, a child is rudely forced to surrender his throne when the second child arrives. If not prepared, the first child will feel rejected and may react with jealousy and aggression toward the newborn. If autonomy—that is, the self-centered desire to satisfy his will at all times—is not overcome in childhood, it may cause problems of adjusting during adolescence, problems which may be prolonged even into adulthood and the married state.

The almost universal method used in making a child into a social being is *reward and punishment*. We cannot discuss the philosophy and psychology implied in this technique except to say that in using this approach parents must be absolutely fair and just and at no time arbitrary. They must realize that for their child they are demigods. He depends completely upon them for everything he needs for a long period of his life. Any unfairness on their part may affect him throughout life. The following point is important: punishment should never be inflicted just because the parent is angry. In fact, it should never be inflicted *when* the parent is angry, because the child then associates anger with punishment. He should be made aware that an unpleasant consequence is connected with a violation of a rule—

as pain follows being burned. The punishment should call attention to the fact that something was wrong, that certain forms of behavior do not meet approval and that specific reasons can be given for this disapproval. But at the same time, the child must know that he is still loved and can regain his former relation with the parents. Punishment must always be in proportion to the offense. Since the memory span of young children is very brief, punishment should follow the act as soon as possible after the parent has regained composure. If punishment is used, it should not make any difference who administers it—father or mother. We believe it is completely wrong to leave all punishment to only *one* of the parents, whether it be father or mother. The writers know several fathers who refuse to punish at any time because they are afraid their children will dislike them; but these same fathers will demand that the wife mete out punishment. Rearing children is in any case a responsibility of *both* parents, and in front of the children they should always be in agreement. If there is disagreement between parents over disciplinary matters, it should be discussed in private.

It goes without saying that the principles of fairness and justice imply that there should be no favoritism in treatment of children. It is difficult to avoid rivalry and even jealousy between siblings in any case. Partiality on the part of parents or either parent toward any child, no matter for what reason, is extremely unwise.

The principle of *consistency* in child rearing has been implied in some statements above, but it is of such importance that it must be stressed separately. In simple terms, it means that when the parent says yes, it must be *yes;* when he says no, it must be *no.* Consistency requires careful consideration of the point at issue before a decision is made. As any parent knows, such decisions are often difficult to make, but they nevertheless must be faced very frankly. At times, such behavior on the part of a parent may appear autocratic, yet in acts which are definitely wrong the child can never learn that they are wrong if they are sometimes tolerated or even looked upon as "cute." It is cruel, yet true, that fire always hurts, whether a child likes it or not. If nature were as inconsistent as so many parents are, this world would be utter confusion. We could never learn to predict or control anything. Consistency is not a great problem if parents remember always to punish a misdemeanor so that a child learns to connect punishment with a forbidden act, just as he learns to connect pain with fire.

Authority, Self-control, Self-direction. The whole problem of child guidance will be facilitated if parents help the child to attain self-direction as soon as possible. We have mentioned above that any person will roughly go through three stages in the regulation of his behavior. The first is the period when a child, because of immaturity, must be told from moment to moment how to behave. Second, as he grows older, he learns the rules of behavior. Insofar as he tries to live by them, he controls his behavior. And third, when he understands the reasons for the rules, or the principles which underlie them, he directs his pattern of behavior insofar as he makes them a part of himself. He then has achieved self-direction. The period of authority should be as brief as possible.

SOCIAL LIFE

Many young couples feel, when they fall in love, that from then on they do not need anyone else in the world; they want to live by themselves and just for each other. They wish they could go to some distant island, away from everyone. Occasionally there is a couple who, after marriage, will live apart from other people. Such behavior invariably causes some resentment. People regard the couple as being "stuck up," too good for others.

Value of Friends. Most normal couples sooner or later feel a need for the companionship of others. Contact with friends will serve two useful functions. First, the couples' lives are very much enriched. Every husband and wife must recognize that neither can satisfy all needs of the other. They must have others to satisfy their need for recognition, and especially their need for new experience. Only an unenlightened marriage partner cannot appreciate the fact that a mate also needs friends and becomes jealous when the mate obviously derives pleasure from them. Second, if a couple is in love, contact with others will enhance their appreciation of each other. Every new experience with friends will help them realize how much more they find in each other than anyone else could give them.

Sources of Friends. Roughly speaking, there are three sources of friends for a couple: (1) the individual friends they had before they knew each other; (2) the common friends they had when they were married; and (3) the new common friends they make after marriage. All of these friends are valuable to them when they are stimulating to both. Perhaps most individual friends can be made common friends to the great satisfaction of both, and whenever possible this should be done. However, there is no good psychological reason why husband and wife may not have some separate friends. It manifests lack of appreciation of the mate's judgment when he or she states (as sometimes happens) after marriage: "I want you to give up all your friends. I do not like any of them." Individual friends should be given up when there is good reason to believe that their retention would interfere with the couple's satisfactory adjustment to each other. Such friends are usually the young man's girl friends or the young woman's boy friends to whom they were close before they knew each other. A former boy friend or girl friend must be discarded if he or she, for selfish reasons, tries to come between the couple. The reason for giving up a friend should never be mere jealousy, for such a reason causes resentment and lack of respect for the jealous mate. An honest and straightforward discussion invariably will do a great deal of good.

Sometimes, too, a husband or wife may have legitimate interests not shared by the other. Under such conditions, there is no reason why either of them may not have friends with whom such interests are shared. Such friendships will be of value not only because they enrich the mate's life but also because such enrichment can serve to stimulate and enlighten the other.

Friends of Opposite Sex after Marriage. Can husbands have individual women friends and can wives have men friends without their marital happiness being affected? We believe that no general answer can be given to this question. A number of factors are involved. (1) How happy is the couple in its marital adjustment? If mates are well adjusted, such friendships will not make the other mate feel insecure. (2) If the basis of friendship is common business or professional interest, such a relationship can be accepted by the mate. (3) If the friendship is based upon common recreational interests, it is usually fraught with some danger to marital happiness. The mate, as a rule, finds it difficult to accept such friendship without some resentment or jealousy. (4) Much will depend upon how close and how prolonged such friendship may be and upon how well the friends of one mate are known to the other. (5) How other people will regard such a friendship is important. A husband or wife may accept the other's friends, but mutual friends, relatives, or society in general may disapprove. In such a case, the reputation of both mates is at stake. The question is again one which requires serious mutual consideration and agreement. It is also one which becomes more and more acute because of our changing society. We have more single women than ever before and more married women who are engaged in activities outside the home; men and women associate more and there is greater freedom of communication between the sexes.

In-laws. Most young people not only create their own family when they marry but also marry into one. Contrary to the impression created by jokes or stories about the mother-in-law, the new relationship created by marriage is usually a happy one for everyone concerned. Most parents accept a son-in-law or daughter-in-law as though he or she were their own child. They love him or her and extend as much help as they can. Ordinarily, too, the young man or young woman accepts the mate's parents fully and wholeheartedly. In such cases, there is an extension of personal satisfaction and great mutual happiness. The effect sometimes is greater when in-laws have only one child, son or daughter, or only sons or daughters. For parents who have wanted an additional child for years, a marriage often means getting a son or daughter. They feel that their life has been made more complete.

The social life of a young person often is expanded when he marries a mate who has brothers and sisters. Under favorable circumstances, the newcomer is welcomed and, in turn, the mate's siblings are accepted as friends. In such cases, the union between husband and wife becomes closer, is strengthened, and made more secure. The feelings of oneness, belonging, sharing, and participating take on deeper and wider meanings. To the extent that the parents, the young married couple, their brothers and sisters, and the latters' wives and husbands are forged and shaped into one large family, there emerges a greater sense of power for each of them. All in all, marrying into a family can be and is for many an experience which enhances their personal values and elicits and develops their capacities as no other experience can.

When the in-law relationship is not satisfactory, however, the harm to everyone concerned can be as great as, if not greater than, the happiness which can be derived from a good relationship. The difficulties are in no sense due to the in-law relationship but to the personality of persons who enter into it. The causes may be either with the parents or with the son- or daughter-in-law. The following are typical attitudes on the part of parents which may interfere with the marital happiness of their children:

Faulty parental attitudes toward married children. (1) Parents who are unhappily married may not believe that anyone else can be happy in marriage. Having been disillusioned about love, they constantly expect their children to have the same experience. They look for evidence, and are inclined to magnify the slightest misunderstanding their son or daughter may have with his or her mate.

(2) They may think so much of their son or daughter that they believe no one is good enough for them as a mate. To prove their point, they are constantly on the lookout for faults. A somewhat extreme case of this type was brought to the attention of the authors by a young woman of 28. She had one gentleman friend after another, because her mother constantly disapproved just as soon as she expressed intentions of marrying. When the daughter finally decided to get married in spite of her mother's disap-

proval, the mother had a heart attack. When the illness appeared not to affect the daughter, the mother actually struck her in the face, beat her, and said: "When you are married, I never want to see you, or any children you may have. I never want to see you even when I am dying. I don't want you to come to my funeral." Undoubtedly this mother had other motives besides the one stated.

(3) In some cases, parents show jealousy or envy toward the marriage of their children. Jealousy was very likely one reason for the mother's behavior in the case just mentioned. It is known that the father of Elizabeth Barrett Browning was jealous of the marriage of any of his children, particularly so of his invalid daughter's marriage.

(4) When parents reject their children, there is likely to be in-law trouble. If the daughter is rejected, the son-in-law may be rejected for the same reason. In extreme cases, the mother actually tries to take the husband away from her daughter, and sometimes succeeds. The young man falls in love with the daughter and ends by marrying the mother, or divorces the daughter and marries her mother. In other cases, such mothers succeed only in making the son-in-law antagonistic to his wife. A father can cause similar difficulties for his son.

(5) Overattachment of parents to their children may also cause trouble. Unhappily married women, divorced women, or widows quite often cause such difficulties. Cartoonists and jokesters have frequently used the following situation for their humor, but it was stark reality to Mrs. J., who needed help with her marital problem. She said:

"The problem with my mother-in-law began on our honeymoon. My husband and I had decided to make a trip by car to California. As soon as my mother-in-law learned where we planned to go, she told us she had never been to California, that she had some friends living there and suggested that she might drive along with us. Naturally, I was greatly surprised by such an idea and resented it. On the other hand, I did not want to cause trouble, and so I complained to my husband, though very mildly. I hoped he would sense how I felt about it but at the same time not be hurt by my reaction. On the contrary, he interpreted my very slight degree of protest as meaning the next thing to approval and was happy that he could take his mother along. We started out with her sitting in the back seat, but before long she became car-sick and asked to move to the front seat. Her size made it uncomfortable for the three of us in front, and so I sat in the back seat. By the time we reached California, I was thoroughly disappointed in and disillusioned about my marriage. Since then, my mother-in-law has been sitting in the driver's seat for everything. When we returned home, she was too lonesome to live away from her children. She also knew exactly how to prepare the proper meals for her son, and so on and on."

(6) Parents are sometimes reluctant to give up their authority over their children. They insist upon making all important decisions for them after they are married because "they do not want them to make any mistakes." So they decide for them where to live, how to spend their money, whether or not to have children, how many children they should have, and how to rear them. One mother insisted that her daughter have an abortion when she became pregnant against the mother's wishes.

(7) There are parents who just do not like the son-in-law or daughter-in-law and therefore cause difficulties. Some of the reasons given for this dislike are low social status, financial status, race, nationality, religion, political views, family background, occupation, and "low character."

(8) Occasionally, in-law problems may be due to the fact that parents prefer one child to another. When this preference is extended to either son-in-law or daughter-in-law, the less favored will resent not only the parents but also the favored one. Sometimes the husband of the less favored daughter may even turn against her.

(9) Any of the above attitudes may be manifested by an older brother or sister, who may act as a parent surrogate. Uncles and aunts or grandparents may play similar roles and, in many cases, tend to play the role even more severely than would the real parent.

If one or more of the above conditions prevail, it is a severe strain on marital ties. But whether the attitudes manifested are intense or mild, the young couple should always act as a unit. Sometimes this is difficult, because of unjustified guilt feelings or a false sense of loyalty. Parents are never justified in trying to regulate the lives of their children who have attained maturity. The young couple must be permitted to seek their happiness as best they can. If, in the opinion of parents, their children are not equipped to regulate their own lives, the parents must have done a poor job of rearing them—and if they have not succeeded so far, there is no guarantee that they will succeed now. In addition, if parents try to regulate their children's marriage, they also try to dominate their children's mates, over whom they have no conceivable authority. To parents it must be said: You may express your opinion, you may suggest, but beyond that, let your children decide and act for themselves. Young people, in turn, while they should treat their parents with respect, should regard them as good friends, whose advice they may accept or reject.

Faulty attitudes of married children toward parents. There are in-law problems resulting from undesirable attitudes on the part of married children.

(1) Sometimes a son-in-law or daughter-in-law may be too sensitive about any kind of interest shown by parents. With few exceptions, parents have the welfare and happiness of their children at heart. Being human, they make mistakes; but their motives usually are good, and this fact should be recognized.

(2) There are some sons-in-law and daughters-in-law who wish to exploit their parents. They become careless about their finances and expect to be pulled out of debt, or they may feel it is their parents' responsibility to take care of grandchildren.

(3) Now and then, a husband or wife is so dependent upon parents that he or she feels it necessary to discuss every problem with a parent before coming to a decision. Such practice is usually resented by the mate, not only because it shows immaturity, but also because it indicates lack of respect for the mate's opinion. In some marriages, no phrase is more annoying than either "my father says" or "my mother says." A young couple should be happy to be able to consult parents who have more experience about certain problems, but they should consult jointly and then only to gather more information before making their own decision.

Acting as a Social Unit. In conclusion, it must be emphasized that in the interest of social adjustment a married couple should act as a unit in all social situations. They must decide mutual problems together. It is poor taste to single out a mate's inadequacy in any form for public criticism. And nothing seems as painful as to be held up to ridicule in front of friends or relatives. Such ego-hurts are hard to forget, as is clearly indicated by the case of Mr. K., who complained:

> "I don't object to being criticized when it's justifiable. I know I make plenty of blunders and I realize I am far from perfect, but I'd rather be told so in privacy. My wife has always taken advantage of the social situation to bring up negative criticism of me. She seldom starts a quarrel when we are alone, but just let us have guests at the house and she strikes out at me. Or if we are invited out, it's the same—she seems to save up all grievances until she can air them in front of our friends. As a matter of fact, we are losing friends because of her behavior. Much as I dislike quarreling in front of people, I can't control my temper when she starts one of her critical tirades, and so we invariably end up with a verbal battle. My brother told me recently that two couples with whom we used to play cards frequently told him they no longer come to our house because they couldn't stand the tongue-lashing that goes on between us. It's embarrassing for outsiders. I recognize the fact that we have some problems to solve between us, but not in the presence of our friends and relatives."

RECREATION

Recreation is any pleasurable activity which involves relaxation from work. It is activity for activity's sake, whereas work is activity for the sake of attaining a goal. The essential difference is the attitude one takes toward the activity. If it is enjoyable, it is play; if it is done with mental effort only as a means toward an end, it is work. For this reason, the same activity may be work for one person and play for another.

There are many recreational activities which husband and wife can enjoy together. Some of these are more intellectual; others more emotional; and others physical. Not all will appeal to every couple and their selection is a matter of background and training.

Reasons for Recreation. (1) Because of the division of responsibilities between husband and wife, they need to pursue some activities in common. Recreations are well suited for this purpose. There is greater need for shared recreational activity at present than there was for our grandparents, many of whom spent practically all their waking hours together. Being together most of the time, grandfather and grandmother each could go his way when it came to recreation. But if their grandchildren, who are apart at work all day, also are apart at play, they are in danger of becoming strangers to each other—as indeed too many couples have become strangers after several years of marriage.

(2) Playing together is an excellent method of learning to know each other. In play, everyone is more himself, tries to enjoy himself, and therefore throws off most of his inhibitions. There is less acting, less conforming in play than in work. He can discover what a person is really like, can see into the deeper layers of his personality.

(3) Since each one is playing for self-enjoyment, one can see how much opportunity he gives the other person to enjoy himself at the same time. Will he think only of his own enjoyment? In a competitive game, is he so set on winning that he is a "poor sport" when he loses?

(4) When husband and wife play together, there is a conscious or unconscious reminiscence of the "good times" they used to have together before marriage. The present recreation, therefore, has an additional glow and prevents them from forgetting their previous experiences.

(5) Each period of recreational enjoyment will be added to their storehouse of pleasant memories and thus will give them a feeling of oneness and belonging.

(6) Engaging in various types of recreation will provide opportunities for a couple to make mutual friends.

In addition to the joint recreational program enjoyed by mates, it is often wise for the husband to participate in some forms of recreation which are strictly stag and for the wife to belong to women's organizations. Such participation does not mean that their lives become paralleled. On the contrary, they have an opportunity to share with each other experiences which they have enjoyed separately.

For all these reasons, recreation has become a necessity for a modern couple, especially if they live in a city, where life becomes ever more impersonal. Money, time, and energy spent in recreation are a good investment in greater mutual happiness. That this is true is indicated by the research of Burgess and Cottrell, who found that husbands and wives who shared all outside activities had fifteen times the chance for happiness as those who shared only a few.[2]

POLITICS AND RELIGION

It is generally easy to start a quarrel about either politics or religion. This fact holds true for a husband and wife who have strong convictions about these two fields and different backgrounds in both. One important source of possible conflict is removed if they belong to the same political party or are members of the same church (denomination). When their orientations happen to be divergent, if they are to function as a unit in these areas, it is desirable to agree to disagree. This means that each follows his or her own convictions and beliefs, and that these are not merely tolerated by the other mate but fully respected and appreciated. It is not difficult to follow this arrangement when it is realized that not all truth is found in one political party or in one particular religious organization. All beliefs are based partly on reason and partly on emotion. When we *believe* something, it is an indication that we are convinced we have some evidence for our belief. Moreover, it also gives us satisfaction to accept it. The satisfaction is usually based upon our conviction that those who gave us our belief were fine and intelligent people. And most people, at present, get their political and religious views in this manner; they acquire them by social heredity, so to speak. When people come to a conclusion themselves about these matters, it is not that they have absolute evidence for them, for there is no such evidence, but because they do not like to doubt. A state of doubt is unpleasant; it produces tensions. It is more satisfying to believe, and so they accept what evidence they can and have the satisfaction of being at peace.

[2] Ernest W. Burgess and Leonard S. Cottrell, Jr., *Predicting Success or Failure in Marriage*, New York, Prentice-Hall, Inc., 1939, p. 62.

Beliefs differ from each other in the amount of reason or emotions they contain. Thus, beliefs may be based upon 25 per cent reason and 75 per cent emotion, on 50 per cent of each, or 75 per cent reason and 25 per cent emotion. Unless a person has made a thorough study of politics and religion, beliefs about them are largely emotional. We are reminded of a young man who got into a debate about his religion. He was certain he was right and the other person wrong. After the debate, he went to his minister and asked him "Why am I a Baptist?" The minister gave him ten reasons. Afterwards the man advanced these ten reasons for being a Baptist. He failed to realize that he was not reasoning but rationalizing.

When a husband attempts to change his wife's opinion about religion by reasoning, he cannot and will not succeed. One can never reason an emotion away. If the husband had a very strong dislike of his wife's form of religion, probably he should not have married her. The same applies to political alignment, although political views, as a rule, are not so firmly held. Again, any couple, though of widely different political or religious background, can act as a unit in these areas only if they really and truthfully respect each other's beliefs.

INTERPRETATIVE SUMMARY

1. Marriage involves not only adjustment between husband and wife but also co-operative action toward common goals or objectives. Six such goals are discussed. The key word in all of them is co-operation.

2. Usually a husband works outside the home and the wife within the home, although at present many wives are gainfully employed, often part-time, outside the home.

3. Management of home and money often causes misunderstanding between husband and wife. The best solution seems to be joint overall responsibility, but with each mate ultimately responsible for those areas which he knows best.

4. Perhaps the most important co-operative function performed by a husband and wife is the rearing of children, since

the foundation for personality is laid in the home and continues to be shaped there throughout the formative years. Parents not only must create the proper atmosphere but also must know how to guide their children in development and growth.

5. No matter how well adjusted a couple may be to each other, they still cannot satisfy all of their needs merely between themselves. They must have friends. The most important point for them to remember is to function as a unit in all social relations. This is especially true with reference to in-laws, who may be valued as the best of friends, but not more than friends.

6. Joint recreational activities are as essential for a couple after marriage as they were before marriage—perhaps even more essential.

7. Since politics and religion are usually charged with a great deal of emotion, a wise couple will try to learn how to handle these areas of conflict in their lives with a minimum of friction.

THOUGHT QUESTIONS AND PROJECTS

1. What does co-operation imply with reference to mates functioning as a unit?

2. On what bases are goals selected and evaluated by husband and wife? In what respect does disparity in goals and values affect unification?

3. Obtain class opinion on (a) the issue of "working wives," and (b) the participation of husbands in housekeeping chores.

4. What financial arrangement would you favor for husband and wife who have separate incomes? If the wife has no separate income, how should finances be handled?

5. Suggest a constructive program of activities for a wife who finds housework boring but who cannot be gainfully employed.

6. The following ten reasons are often given by women for their continuing to work in addition to maintaining a home and family. Each student should interview five employed women and ask them to select from the list the three reasons most applicable to them. They should mark *1* as the most influential, *2* as next in importance, and *3* as having some significance. Lists should have

no personal identity, and should indicate only educational level attained—grade school, high school, college, professional.

Give the checked lists to a committee for tabulating to determine which reasons rank first, second, and third in importance. Note the number of times each reason was checked. Which reason has the lowest count? Is there a relationship between educational level and the reasons checked?

(List of Reasons)

__(a) To supplement husband's income in order to meet necessary family expenses.

__(b) To increase savings until a family is started.

__(c) To have extra money in order to buy special items for the home and family.

__(d) To retain skills in earning a livelihood in the event that conditions might some day make it necessary.

__(e) To utilize extra time because there are no children.

__(f) To occupy free time, since children have grown up and gone away.

__(g) To satisfy personality needs, since the routine of housekeeping is insufficient challenge.

__(h) To use special education or talents.

__(i) To work toward the fulfillment of a life-long ambition.

__(j) To satisfy some unusual personal reason (need not be expressed).

Formal education: __grade school; __high school; __college; __professional.

7. Point out specifically how husband and wife can work together in the rearing of children. In what ways can differences of opinion about how to rear children affect the marital harmony of husband and wife?

8. Find out what local provisions are made for the education in child care of "prospective mothers and fathers."

9. Review the major areas in which a husband and wife can function effectively as a unit. How can a couple who function well as a unit contribute to the welfare of their community and how can this experience in turn enrich their own lives?

10. Interview a couple known for their ability to function as a unit and ask them to explain to you what they consider to be "the secret of their success."

SUGGESTED READINGS FOR FURTHER STUDY

Baber, Ray E., *Marriage and the Family,* 2nd ed., New York, McGraw-Hill Book Company, 1953.
   Chapter 8. Parent-Child Interaction.
   Chapter 9. Parent-Child Interaction (Cont'd).
   Chapter 10. The Status of Women: Occupational.
Bigelow, H. F., *Family Finance,* New York, J. B. Lippincott Company, 1953.
Burgess, Ernest W., and Harvey J. Locke, *The Family,* 2nd ed., New York, American Book Company, 1953.
   Chapter 11. Family Unity.
   Chapter 14. Criteria of Marital Success.
Burgess, Ernest W., and Paul Wallin, *Engagement and Marriage,* New York, J. B. Lippincott Company, 1953.
   Chapter 14. The Dynamics of Marriage.
   Chapter 18. Marital Adjustment.
   Chapter 19. Adaptability.
   Chapter 21. Children and Marital Success.
Harper, Robert A., *Marriage,* New York, Appleton-Century-Crofts, 1949.
   Chapter 15. Family Unity In An Individualistic Society.
Landis, Judson T., and Mary G. Landis, *Building a Successful Marriage,* 2nd ed., New York, Prentice-Hall, 1953.
   Chapter 14. In-Laws and Marriage Adjustment.
   Chapter 15. Religious Attitude and Family Life.
   Chapter 16. Finances and Adjustment in Marriage.
   Chapter 17. Getting Your Money's Worth.
   Chapter 19. Family Planning.
   Chapter 22. Bringing up Children.
   Chapter 23. Sex Education.
Magoun, F. Alexander, *Love and Marriage,* New York, Harper & Brothers, 1948.
   Chapter 13. Religion in the Home.
Merrill, Francis E., *Courtship and Marriage,* New York, The Dryden Press, 1949.
   Chapter 8. Economic Roles: The Homemaker.

APPENDIX A

SELECTED BIBLIOGRAPHY

Adams, Clifford R., and Vance O. Packard, *How to Pick a Mate*, New York, The Macmillan Company, 1937.

Adams, Clifford R., *Preparing for Marriage*, New York, E. P. Dutton & Company, 1951.

Adams, Clifford R., *An Inventory for Measuring Marital Happiness and Sexual Adjustment*, Chicago, Science Research Associates, 1951.

Adler, Felix, *Incompatibility in Marriage*, New York, Appleton-Century-Crofts, 1930.

Allport, Gordon W., *Personality: A Psychological Interpretation*, New York, Henry Holt & Company, 1937.

Anderson, John E., *The Psychology of Development and Personal Adjustment*, New York, Henry Holt & Company, 1949.

Anshen, Ruth Wanda, *The Family, Its Function and Destiny*, New York, Harper & Brothers, 1949.

Baber, Ray E., *Marriage and the Family*, 2nd ed., New York, McGraw-Hill Book Company, 1953.

Bachmeister, Rhoda, *Growing Together*, New York, Appleton-Century-Crofts, 1947.

Baruch, Dorothy, *Parents Can Be People*, New York, Appleton-Century-Crofts, 1944.

Becker, Howard, and Reuben Hill, eds., *Family, Marriage and Parenthood*, Boston, D. C. Heath & Company, 1948.

Bergler, Edmund, *Divorce Won't Help*, New York, Harper & Brothers, 1948.

Bergler, Edmund, *Unhappy Marriage and Divorce*, New York, International Universities Press, 1946.

Bernard, Harold W., *Toward Better Personal Adjustment*, New York, McGraw-Hill Book Company, 1951.

Bigelow, H. F., *Family Finance*, Philadephia, J. B. Lippincott Company, 1953.

Binkley, Robert C., and Frances W. Binkley, *What is Right with Marriage*, New York, Appleton-Century-Crofts, 1938.

Birk, Neuman B., and Genevieve B. Birk, *Understanding and Using English*, rev. ed., New York, The Odyssey Press, 1951.

Bowman, Henry A., *Marriage for Moderns*, 3rd ed., New York, McGraw-Hill Book Company, 1954.

Brown, Fred, and Rudolph T. Kempton, *Sex Questions and Answers,* New York, Whittlesey House, 1950.

Burgess, Ernest W., and Leonard S. Cottrell, Jr., *Predicting Success or Failure in Marriage,* New York, Prentice-Hall, 1939.

Burgess, Ernest W., and Harvey J. Locke, *The Family,* 2nd ed., New York, American Book Company, 1953.

Burgess, Ernest W., and Paul Wallin, *Engagement and Marriage,* New York, J. B. Lippincott Company, 1953.

Burkhart, Roy, *From Friendship to Marriage,* New York, Harper & Brothers, 1938.

Cameron, Norman, and Ann Magaret, *Behavior Pathology,* Boston, Houghton Mifflin Company, 1951.

Carroll, Herbert, *Mental Hygiene, The Dynamics of Adjustment,* 2nd ed., New York, Prentice-Hall, 1952.

Christensen, Harold T., *Marriage Analysis,* New York, The Ronald Press Company, 1950.

Clark, Le Mon, *Emotional Adjustment in Marriage,* St. Louis, The C. V. Mosby Company, 1937.

Cole, Lawrence E., *Human Behavior,* Yonkers-on-Hudson, World Book Company, 1953.

Cuber, John F., *The Marriage Counseling Practice,* New York, Appleton-Century-Crofts, 1948.

Davis, Katherine B., *Factors in the Sex Life of 2,200 Women,* New York, Harper & Brothers, 1929.

Dickinson, Robert L., and L. Beam, *One Thousand Marriages,* Baltimore, The Williams and Wilkins Company, 1931.

Dickinson, Robert L., *Techniques of Conception Control,* Baltimore, The Williams and Wilkins Company, 1950.

Dreikurs, Rudolf, *Challenge of Marriage,* New York, Duell, Sloane and Pearce, 1946.

Duvall, Evelyn M., *Family Living,* New York, The Macmillan Company, 1950.

Duvall, Evelyn M., and Reuben Hill, *When You Marry,* rev. ed., Boston, D. C. Heath & Company, 1953.

Ellis, Havelock, *Studies in the Psychology of Sex,* New York, Emerson Books, 1933.

English, O. Spurgeon, and G. H. J. Pearson, *Emotional Problems of Living,* New York, W. W. Norton & Company, 1945.

Ernst, Morris L., and David Loth, *For Better or Worse,* New York, Harper & Brothers, 1951.

Everett, Millard S., *Hygiene of Marriage,* rev. ed., Cleveland, World Publishing Company, 1948.

Fishbein, Morris, and Ernest W. Burgess, eds., *Successful Marriage,* New York, Doubleday & Company, 1947, 1955.

Ford, Clellan S., and Frank A. Beach, *Patterns of Sexual Behavior,* New York, Harper & Brothers, 1951.

Foster, Robert G., *Marriage and Family Relationships,* rev. ed., New York, The Macmillan Company, 1950.

Fromme, Allan, *The Psychologist Looks at Sex and Marriage*, New York, Prentice-Hall, 1950.

Goldstein, Sidney E., *Marriage and Family Counseling*, New York, McGraw-Hill Book Company, 1945.

Goldstein, Sidney E., *Meaning of Marriage and Foundations of the Family*, New York, Bloch Publishing Company, 1942.

Grant, Dorothy F., *So You Want to Get Married*, Milwaukee, The Bruce Publishing Company, 1947.

Groves, Ernest, *Marriage*, rev. ed., New York, Henry Holt & Company, 1941.

Groves, Ernest, *Conserving Marriage and the Family*, New York, The Macmillan Company, 1946.

Groves, Gladys, *Marriage and Family Life*, Boston, Houghton Mifflin Company, 1942.

Hamilton, Gilbert V., *A Research in Marriage*, New York, Albert & Charles Boni, 1929.

Harper, Robert Allan, *Marriage*, New York, Appleton-Century-Crofts, 1949.

Hart, Archibald, *Twelve Ways to Build a Vocabulary*, rev. ed., New York, E. P. Dutton & Company, 1939.

Hart, Hornell, and Ella B. Hart, *Personality and the Family*, Boston, D. C. Heath & Company, 1935.

Hayakawa, Samuel I., *Language in Thought and Action*, New York, Harcourt, Brace & Company, 1949.

Healy, Edwin F., *Marriage Guidance*, Chicago, Loyola University Press, 1949.

Hill, Reuben, *Marriage and the Family*, Boston, D. C. Heath & Company, 1942.

Himes, Norman E., *Your Marriage, A Guide to Happiness*, New York, Rinehart & Company, 1940.

Horney, Karen, *The Neurotic Personality of Our Times*, New York, W. W. Norton & Company, 1937.

Horney, Karen, *Neurosis and Human Growth*, New York, W. W. Norton & Company, 1950.

Hutton, Isabel, *Sex Techniques in Marriage*, New York, Emerson Books, 1942.

Johnson, Wendell, *People in Quandaries*, New York, Harper & Brothers, 1946.

Jordan, Helen M., ed., *You and Marriage*, New York, John Wiley & Sons, 1942.

Jung, Moses, *et al.*, *Modern Marriage*, New York, Appleton-Century-Crofts, 1947.

Keyserling, H. A., *Book of Marriage*, New York, Harcourt, Brace & Company, 1926.

Kinsey, Alfred C., W. B. Pomeroy, and C. E. Martin, *Sexual Behavior in the Human Male*, Philadelphia, W. B. Saunders Company, 1948.

Kinsey, Alfred C., W. B. Pomeroy, C. E. Martin, and P. H. Gebhard, *Sexual Behavior in the Human Female*, Philadelphia, W. B. Saunders Company, 1953.

Kirkendall, Lester A., *Understanding Sex*, Chicago, Science Research Associates, 1948.

Kirkendall, Lester A., *Sex Adjustment of Young Men*, New York, Harper & Brothers, 1940.

Kling, Samuel G., and Esther B. Kling, *The Marriage Reader*, New York, The Vanguard Press, 1947.

Koos, Earl L., *Marriage*, New York, Henry Holt & Company, 1953.

Landis, Judson T., and Mary G. Landis, *Building a Successful Marriage*, rev. ed., New York, Prentice-Hall, 1953.

Landis, Paul, *Your Marriage and Family Living*, New York, McGraw-Hill Book Company, 1946.

Lane, Bess B., *Your Part in Your Child's Education*, New York, E. P. Dutton & Company, 1949.

Larrabee, Harold A., *Reliable Knowledge*, New York, Houghton Mifflin Company, 1945.

Lee, Irving J., *Language Habits in Human Affairs*, New York, Harper & Brothers, 1941.

Levy, John, and Ruth Monroe, *The Happy Family*, New York, Alfred Knopf, 1938.

Lindgren, Henry Clay, *Psychology of Personal and Social Adjustment*, New York, American Book Company, 1953.

Locke, Harvey J., *Predicting Adjustment in Marriage*, New York, Henry Holt & Company, 1951.

Lockwood, Lemo D., and Mary E. N. Ford, *Youth, Marriage and Parenthood*, New York, John Wiley & Sons, 1945.

Mace, David R., *Marriage: The Art of Lasting Love*, New York, Doubleday & Company, 1952.

Mace, David R., *Hebrew Marriage, A Sociological Study*, New York, Philosophical Library, 1953.

Magoun, F. Alexander, *Love and Marriage*, New York, Harper & Brothers, 1948.

McClelland, David C., *Personality*, New York, William Sloane Associates, 1951.

McKinney, Fred, *The Psychology of Personal Adjustment*, 2nd ed., New York, John Wiley & Sons, 1949.

Mead, Margaret, *Sex and Temperament in Three Primitive Societies*, New York, William Morrow & Company, 1935.

Mead, Margaret, *Male and Female*, New York, William Morrow & Company, 1949.

Meerloo, Joost A. M., *Conversation and Communication*, New York, International Universities Press, 1952.

Menninger, William C., *Understanding Yourself*, Chicago, Science Research Associates, 1949.

Merrill, Francis E., *Courtship and Marriage*, New York, The Dryden Press, 1949.

Mowrer, Harriet E., *Personality Adjustment and Domestic Discord*, New York, American Book Company, 1935.

Mudd, Emily H., *The Practice of Marriage Counseling*, New York, Association Press, 1951.

Munn, Norman L., *Psychology,* 2nd ed., Boston, Houghton Mifflin Company, 1951.

Murphy, Gardner, *Personality,* New York, Harper & Brothers, 1947.

Mursell, J. L., and R. B. Cattell, *Personality: A Systematic and Theoretical Study,* New York, McGraw-Hill Book Company, 1950.

Novak, Emil, *The Woman Asks the Doctor,* 2nd ed., Baltimore, The Williams and Wilkins Company, 1944.

Overstreet, Harry A., *The Mature Mind,* New York, W. W. Norton & Company, 1949.

Overton, Grace S., *Love, Marriage and Parenthood,* New York, Harper & Brothers, 1939.

Phelps, William Lyon, *Marriage,* New York, E. P. Dutton & Company, 1940.

Pilpel, Harriet F., and Theodore Zavin, *Your Marriage and the Law,* New York, Rinehart and Company, 1952.

Popenoe, Paul, *Marriage, Before and After,* New York, Funk and Wagnalls Company, 1943.

Popenoe, Paul, *Modern Marriage,* rev. ed., New York, The Macmillan Company, 1945.

Rice, Thurman, *Sex, Marriage and Family,* Philadelphia, J. B. Lippincott Company, 1946.

Ruch, Floyd L., *Psychology and Life,* 4th ed., Chicago, Scott, Foresman & Company, 1953.

Ruesch, J., and G. Bateson, *Communication: The Matrix of Psychiatry,* New York, W. W. Norton & Company, 1951.

Sadler, William S., *Courtship and Love,* New York, The Macmillan Company, 1952.

Sargent, S. Stansfeld, *Social Psychology,* New York, The Ronald Press Company, 1950.

Scheinfeld, Amram, *The New You and Heredity,* Philadelphia, J. B. Lippincott Company, 1950.

Scheinfeld, Amram, *Women and Men,* New York, Harcourt, Brace & Company, 1944.

Schmiedeler, Edgar, *Marriage and the Family,* New York, McGraw-Hill Book Company, 1946.

Seward, Georgene, *Sex and the Social Order,* New York, McGraw-Hill Book Company, 1946.

Skidmore, Rex A., and Anthon S. Cannon, *Building Your Marriage,* New York, Harper & Brothers, 1951.

Stagner, Ross, and T. F. Karwoski, *Psychology,* New York, McGraw-Hill Book Company, 1952.

Stagner, Ross, *Psychology of Personality,* 2nd ed., New York, McGraw-Hill Book Company, 1948.

Stokes, Walter F., *Modern Pattern for Marriage,* New York, Rinehart & Company, 1948.

Stone, Hannah M., and Abraham Stone, *A Marriage Manual,* New York, Simon & Schuster, 1952.

Sweeney, Esther E., *Dates and Dating,* New York, The Woman's Press, 1948.

Terman, Lewis M., and associates, *Psychological Factors in Marital Happiness,* New York, McGraw-Hill Book Company, 1939.

Thorpe, Louis P., *The Psychology of Mental Health*, New York, The Ronald Press Company, 1950.

Van de Velde, T. H., *Ideal Marriage*, New York, Random House, 1943.

Vaughan, Wayland F., *Personal and Social Adjustment*, New York, The Odyssey Press, 1952.

Waller, Willard, *The Family, A Dynamic Interpretation*, (revised by Reuben Hill), New York, The Dryden Press, 1951.

Waller, Willard, *The Old Love and the New*, New York, Liveright Publishing Corporation, 1930.

Wieman, Regina W., *The Family Lives Its Religion*, New York, Harper & Brothers, 1941.

Winch, Robert F., *The Modern Family*, New York, Henry Holt & Company, 1952.

Young, Kimball, *Personality and Problems of Adjustment*, New York, Appleton-Century-Crofts, 1952.

APPENDIX B

LIST OF RECOMMENDED FILMS

The following films can be used in connection with topics discussed in this book. The list is not an exhaustive one but represents at least some of the possibilities which the authors have found applicable to the content of the text. It is strongly recommended that the user preview each film to determine suitability to subject matter as he wishes to present it. The numbers at the end of each film description suggest the chapters with which the film might be shown.

For additional films, consult the annual edition of *Educational Film Guide* and its quarterly supplements published by H. W. Wilson Company. For several of the films, film strips are also available; inquiry should be directed to producers or to rental libraries.

Sources of motion pictures are given at the end of the film list. A directory of local and state film libraries which lend or rent films can be obtained at slight cost from the Superintendent of Documents, Washington 25, D. C. The booklet is called a *Directory of 2002 16 mm. Film Libraries.*

All films listed below are 16 mm. sound.

Are You Popular (Coronet; 10 minutes)

Although this film deals with the dating of teenagers, it enables students of college age to review earlier behavior and conduct. (9)

Are You Ready for Marriage (Coronet; 15 minutes)

A young couple receives a "practical checklist" from a marriage counselor to determine whether or not they are ready to marry. (8)

Choosing for Happiness (McGraw-Hill; 20 minutes; made to correlate with *Marriage for Moderns,* by Henry A. Bowman)

Shows a girl's critical attitude toward several boys, her final rejection of all with the result that she, too, suffers rejection; the old problem of the perfectionist. (7)

Choosing Your Marriage Partner (Coronet; 13 minutes)

Factors worthy of consideration when selecting a mate. (7, 8)

Communication and Interaction in Three Families (Kinesis; 80 minutes)

Data gathered through camera on nonverbal communication within the family circle. Three families are shown to illustrate behavior and interaction. Résumé of interpretations is included. (18)

Dating: Do's and Don'ts (Coronet; 14 minutes)

Presents a teen-age date with the typical problems of an early stage of courtship. College students may be able to analyze present problems by way of retrospection. (9)

Don't Get Angry (Encyclopaedia Britannica; 12 minutes)

Points out anger as an emotion which cannot be entirely subdued but which should be controlled in a mature way. Physiological changes during attacks of anger are indicated. (15)

Emotional Health (McGraw-Hill; 20 minutes)

Examples of emotional disturbances common among young people which if allowed to continue can damage future mental health. (7, 8, 15)

Endocrine Glands (Encyclopaedia Britannica; 12 minutes)

Stresses the nature, functions, and interrelationship of the endocrine glands. (3, 15)

A Family Affair (New York University; 19 minutes)

Presents problems faced by an average middle-class family. Stresses roles taken by members of the family in their community relationships. (20)

Family Circles (National Film Board of Canada; may be purchased from McGraw-Hill; 31 minutes)

Presents three situations stressing the interrelationship between school and home, how attitudes are learned, and to what extent family attitudes affect school progress. (3, 20)

Family Next Door (Methodist Publishing House; 30 minutes)

Three episodes of Christian family life are presented to show how religion can make a difference. (20)

Going Steady (Coronet; 12 minutes)

Points for and against "going steady" are presented. Although high-school students are shown in the film, their problem is similar to the one faced by college students. (10)

Heredity and Prenatal Development (McGraw-Hill; 20 minutes)

One of a series correlated with *Child Development*, by Elizabeth E. Hurlock. It traces step-by-step developments prior to and following fertilization, the role of genes and chromosomes, structural changes, and reflex responses. (3, 17)

The High Wall (McGraw-Hill; 32 minutes)

A case study of intense prejudice resulting from economic frustration; it shows how attitudes and strong feelings are learned and handed down from one generation to the next. (3, 14, 15)

How Do You Know It's Love (Coronet; 12 minutes)

A simplified version of the meaning of love and whether or not the kind presented is mature enough for marriage. (6)

Human Reproduction (McGraw-Hill; 21 minutes)

Detailed factual presentation about human reproduction; included in the film are the menstrual cycle, the male and female reproductive organs, and the growth of the embryo from fertilization to birth. (4, 16)

In Time of Trouble (McGraw-Hill; 14 minutes; made to correlate with *Marriage for Moderns*, by Henry A. Bowman.)

A wife, worried over her husband's excessive drinking, sees no relationship between it and her domineering perfectionism. The family minister gives helpful guidance. (14, 15)

It Takes All Kinds (McGraw-Hill; 20 minutes; made to correlate with *Marriage for Moderns*, by Henry A. Bowman.)

Young couples are shown reacting to diversified emotional situations; the quality of their reactions is related to marital success or failure; stresses careful mate selection. (7)

Jealousy (McGraw-Hill; 16 minutes; made to correlate with *Marriage for Moderns,* by Henry A. Bowman.)

An overly emotional wife projects her dissatisfactions on her husband, whom she accuses of infidelity. (15, 17)

Make Way for Tomorrow (New York University; 17 minutes)

A situation which deals with the problem of in-laws. (14, 20)

Marriage and Divorce (McGraw-Hill; 15 minutes)

Effects of broken homes and divorce. (1, 20)

Marriage Is a Partnership (Coronet; 15 minutes)

Emphasis is given to the problems which may arise during early years of married life and to the significance of joint efforts by husband and wife to solve them. (13, 14)

Marriage Today (McGraw-Hill; 22 minutes; made to correlate with *Marriage for Moderns,* by Henry A. Bowman.)

This film should follow the presentation of *This Charming Couple* since it answers problems raised in the latter. Shows how two couples have made a success of marriage. (14, 20)

The Meaning of Engagement (Coronet; 13 minutes)

Depicts the meaning of the engagement period as it contributes to further preparation for marriage. (11)

Mental Mechanisms Series (National Film Board of Canada; may be purchased from McGraw-Hill or rented through various film bureaus.)

Presents cases of individual maladjustment and the mechanisms used to meet life situations. The films stimulate discussion as to how personality problems affect marital happiness:
(1) **Breakdown** (40 minutes)
Case study of a young woman who has a schizophrenic breakdown; film follows her course of treatment through the clinic and mental hospital and ends with her discharge to complete habilitation at home as a member of her family. (1, 20)
(2) **Feelings of Depression** (30 minutes)
Case of a young man, jealous of his brother's success. Guilt feelings follow which affect his relationship with his wife and friends. (15)
(3) **Feelings of Hostility** (27 minutes)
A case history of a girl whose childhood experiences build up resentment in her toward others. Getting and giving love is unsuccessful, and she overcompensates through intellectual achievement. (3, 8)

(4) **Feelings of Rejection** (23 minutes)
A case study of a neurasthenic; a girl dominated and rejected who develops physical ailments as a means of adjustment until she gains insight into her problem. Shows effect on boy-girl relationships. (3, 9)

(5) **Overdependency** (32 minutes)
The case of a young man whose pampered childhood and overattachment to his mother result in feelings of inadequacy and undue concern over health. His marriage and position are in jeopardy until he receives treatment. (13, 14, 15)

A Planned Parenthood Story (Mayo; 18 minutes)

Presents reasons for spacing the birth of children and explains the services of the Planned Parenthood Federation of America. (16, 20)

Preface to a Life (Castle; 28 minutes)

Stresses the effects on children of emotionally insecure parents; shows importance of adequate personal adjustment if parents function as a unit in the rearing of children. (20)

The Story of Human Fertility (Ortho; 34 minutes)

A highly technical film made for medical schools, showing the anatomy and physiology of sex. Methods of birth control are included. (4, 16)

This Charming Couple (McGraw-Hill; 19 minutes; made to correlate with *Marriage for Moderns,* by Henry A. Bowman.)

A young couple through courtship so romanticize their relationship that they are utterly blind to signs of incompatibility. Adjustment to marriage is inadequate. (10, 19)

Wednesday's Child (New York University; 11 minutes)

The effects on children of parental inability to adjust and of the eventual divorce. (20)

What's On Your Mind? (McGraw-Hill; 11 minutes)

Shows how some people in an effort to solve personality problems and to know themselves better seek help from unscientific sources such as phrenologists, palm-reading experts, fortune tellers, and pulp magazines. (8)

Who's Boss? (McGraw-Hill; 16 minutes; made to correlate with *Marriage for Moderns,* by Henry A. Bowman.)

The attempt of a young married couple, both with forceful personalities, to combine careers with marriage. Misinterpretation of husband-wife roles leads to competition and conflict. Finally, co-operation solves their problem. (18, 20)

Who's Right? (McGraw-Hill; 18 minutes; made to correlate with *Marriage for Moderns,* by Henry A. Bowman.)

A quarrel between husband and wife who misinterpret each other; to her, he is dictatorial; to him, she is extravagant. (15, 18, 19)

Woman Against Woman (New York University; 20 minutes)

The problems of divorce and remarriage. (20)

The Wrong Way Out (Association Films; 20 minutes)

Problems of "those early years" of marriage are presented. Special emphasis is given to the economic factor in adjustment. (14)

SOURCES OF MOTION PICTURES

Association Films, Inc.
    347 Madison Avenue, New York 17, N. Y.
    79 East Adams, Chicago, Illinois.
    351 Turk Street, San Francisco, California.
Castle Films Division, Inc.
    445 Park Avenue, New York, N. Y.
    605 West Washington, Chicago, Illinois (c/o United World Films, Inc.).
Coronet Instructional Films
    65 East South Water Street, Chicago, Illinois.
Encyclopaedia Britannica Films, Inc.
    450 West 56 Street, New York, N. Y.
    1150 Wilmette Avenue, Wilmette, Illinois (Sales)
    1125 Central Avenue, Wilmette, Illinois (Rental)
Kinesis, Inc.
    566 Commercial Street, San Francisco 11, California
Mayo Films
    400 Madison Avenue, New York 17, N. Y.
McGraw-Hill Book Company, Inc., Text-Film Department
    330 West 42 Street, New York, N. Y.
Methodist Publishing House, Audio-Visual Department
    810 Broadway, Nashville 2, Tennessee
New York University Film Library
    26 Washington Square, New York, N. Y.
Ortho Pharmaceutical Company
    Linden, New Jersey.

APPENDIX C

LIST OF COUNSELING AGENCIES

Individuals or couples who have premarital or marital problems may want to consult professional help, as has been suggested several times in this book. While there are many counseling centers available throughout the country, it is not feasible to list all of them here because addresses may change from year to year; also, new centers are continuously being organized. For the latest and most reliable information about local services in a particular community, it is suggested that the reader write to one of the following national organizations. (It should be clearly understood that these national organizations do not deal directly with marriage problems but serve as referral agencies.)

Family Service Association of America
    192 Lexington Avenue, New York 16, N. Y.
Dr. Robert W. Laidlaw, Secretary, American Association of Marriage Counselors
    270 Park Avenue, New York 17, N. Y.
National Council on Family Relations
    5757 South Drexel Avenue, Chicago, Illinois.

The following agency supplies the names of medical specialists who can offer guidance concerning child spacing or supply information pertaining to the problems of human fertility:

The Medical Director, The Planned Parenthood Federation of America
    501 Madison Avenue, New York, N. Y.

GLOSSARY

Abient. Tending to withdraw the organism from a source of stimulation in order to avoid unpleasant effects.

Accommodation. Adjustment of differences between groups or individuals by stressing points of agreement rather than points of disagreement.

Adient. Tending to approach a source of stimulation for continued contact.

Adjustment (Marital). An effort on the part of mates to satisfy each other's needs by the process of give-and-take.

Adolescence. The period of a person's life between puberty and adulthood.

Adrenal Glands. Paired endocrine glands located above the kidneys secreting primarily cortin and adrenalin.

Adultery. Voluntary intercourse by husband or wife with a person of opposite sex other than mate.

Affect. A general term for feeling and emotion.

Afferent Nerve. A nerve leading toward the central nervous system.

Afterplay. Acts of endearment following sexual intercourse.

Ambivalence. Simultaneous existence of either conscious or unconscious contradictory impulses or attitudes (such as love and hate) toward the same person.

Ampulla. A membraneous sac or vesicle.

Annulment. A religious or legal pronouncement that a marriage was void from the beginning.

Anus. Posterior outlet of the alimentary tract.

Anthropology. Science of man; comparing man throughout history with reference to physical and racial characteristics, language, habits, and culture in general.

Artificial Insemination. Inducing pregnancy by depositing semen through the use of instruments.

Asocial. Deficient in intimate human relationships.

Associative Neuron. Neurons linking afferent and efferent fibers located primarily in the central nervous system.

Astrology. A pseudo science which assumes that human beings and affairs are influenced by the stars.

Attitude. A learned mental and emotional predisposition for action or a readiness to engage in some type of activity.

Autonomy. A law unto itself or self-rule.

Autonomic Nervous System. That part of the nervous system which supplies the vital organs, smooth muscles, glands, and blood vessels with their efferent innervation. It is composed of the sympathetic and parasympathetic divisions.

Autoeroticism. A method of obtaining sexual satisfaction from the self.

Autosomes. A name for chromosomes which enter into the structure of the body as differentiated from sex chromosomes.

Bartholin Glands. Lubricating glands located near the entrance to the vagina.

Biophysical. Pertaining to the biological and the physical.

Birth Control. Voluntarily limiting the number of offspring.

Caesarean Section. Removal of the child from the mother's womb by cutting through the walls of the abdomen and the uterus.

Canalization. Establishment of a basic permanent connection between a need and a satisfier.

Case History. An intensive study of an individual's entire life from the prenatal period to the present by means of interviews, records, tests, and personal documents for the purpose of understanding his behavior.

Cervicitis. Inflammation of the cervix.

Cervix. The neck of the womb.

Central Nervous System. That part of the nervous system which includes the brain and the spinal cord.

Character. That aspect of personality which can be evaluated as good or bad, right or wrong.

Choleric. Characterizes a temperament given to rapid and intense emotional changes especially in reference to anger or rage.

Chromosome. Microscopic body containing chromotin and observable in the nucleus during mitotic cell division.

Circumcision. The act of cutting off the prepuce or foreskin of males or the labia minora of females.

Climacteric. That period of life centering on the menopause during which pronounced physiological changes take place in the human organism. It also refers to glandular and bodily changes at a later period in the male.

Clinical Psychologist. A psychologist trained in the techniques used in the treatment of personality disorders.

Clitoris. A small organ embedded at the top end of the labia minora which corresponds to the penis (or more specifically, the glans penis) in the male.

Code. Any systematic body of law such as a moral or religious code.

Coitus. Sexual intercourse.

Conception. The fertilization of an egg by the spermatozoon.

Conditioning. The establishment of a response to a substitute stimulus.

Contraceptive Devices. Artificial means for controlling pregnancy.

Copulation. Sexual union.

Cortex. The outer layer of gray matter covering the cerebral hemispheres and the cerebellum.

Cowpers' Glands. Glands located near the base of the urethra secreting a lubricating and alkalizing substance.

Cryptorchism. A condition in which testicles have not descended into the scrotum.

Culture. Anything man-made or an inclusive term which stands for capabilities and habits, such as morals, laws, customs, beliefs, and knowledge in general, acquired by man as a member of society.

Customs. An organization of conventions, usages, and practices which regulate social life.

Dominance. Controlling the attitudes and behavior of another person.

Ectomorph. One of Sheldon's somatotypes characterized by linearity, flatness of chest, and delicacy of body and in whom somatic and visceral structures are slightly developed.

Effectors. A unit of the body which is either activated or innervated by efferent fibers.

Efferent. Carrying impulses from the central nervous system to the muscles and glands.

Efferent Neurons. Neurons which carry impulses from the central nervous system to the effectors.

Ego. Sometimes used synonymously with the self but more specifically refers to the central part of the self, namely, that part which maintains its identity throughout life.

Egocentric. A person who is overly concerned with his own self and is inclined to interpret every experience in the light of his personal interest.

Ego Concept. A person's evaluation of himself.

Ejaculation. The expulsion of semen by forceful innervation of the propellent muscles of the penis.

Electra Complex. An excessive emotional attachment of the daughter to the father, often involving conscious or unconscious incestuous desires and frequently accompanied by hate for the mother.

Embryo. Term applied to the first eight weeks of prenatal life of an organism.

Emotion. A disturbed state of the organism which characteristically involves the activation of the autonomic nervous system.

Empathy. A process of recreating within oneself the feelings and emotions of another person.

Endocrine. Secreting internally.

Endogamy. A custom or tribal law which prescribes marriage to a member of one's own group or clan.

Endomorph. One of Sheldon's somatotypes in which the body structures are rather weak and undeveloped while the digestive viscera are massive and highly developed.

Envy. Unpleasant feeling or attitude aroused in an individual when viewing or contemplating anything possessed by another person which he himself lacks but which he would like to own.

Epididymis. An elongated mass consisting chiefly of efferent tubes of the testicles located between the testicles and the vas deferens.

Erection. Distended or rigid condition of the penis.

Erogenous Zones. Those parts of the body which cause sexual excitement when touched or stroked.

Ethics. A social science which is concerned with the evaluation of behavior from the point of view of moral values.

Exhibitionism. Usually a compulsive tendency to display one's genitals to other persons for the purpose of experiencing sexual pleasure.

Exogamy. A custom or tribal law which stipulates that one must marry a person not belonging to his own group or clan.

Extrovert. A person who is preoccupied with interests in and attitudes toward external environment and social relationships.

Fallopian Tubes. A pair of tubes which extend from the womb to the ovaries.

Fertility. The ability of an organism to reproduce its kind.

Fertilization. The act of impregnation of an ovum.

Fetishism. A deviation in which an individual achieves sexual satisfaction by looking at or touching any object belonging to a person of opposite sex such as hair, underclothing, shoes, handkerchiefs.

Fetus. Term applied to the prenatal state of an organism covering the period from eight weeks to birth.

Folkways. Traditional or conventional forms of behavior which have the sanction of a certain group.

Frigidity. Either the absence of sexual desire on the part of a woman or the inability to achieve sexual satisfaction.

Frustration. Internal and external barriers which prevent an individual from achieving satisfaction of his needs and desires.

Gene. A factor in the germ plasm which determines the hereditary endowment of an organism.

Genetic. Pertaining to heredity.

Genitalia. The reproductive organs.

Genius. A person who possesses a very superior mental capacity or whose I.Q. is 140 or above.

Germ Plasm. A substance which contains the hereditary characteristics of a new organism.

Glans Penis. Anterior part of the penis ordinarily covered by the prepuce or foreskin.

Gonad. A general term for both ovary and testis.

Graphologist. A person who specializes in the investigation of handwriting.

Gynecologist. A physician who specializes in diseases peculiar to women.

Habit. A learned behavior pattern which has become automatic.

Hemophilia. A hereditary tendency to excessive bleeding.

Heredity. Traits transmitted through the germ plasm.

Heterosexuality. Social and sexual interest in the opposite sex.

Homocidal Mania. A compulsive urge to kill.

Homogamy. Marriage between two persons of marked similarity in physical, social, and personality characteristics.

Homonomy. Primitive satisfaction of needs or drives in the presence of others.

Homosexuality. Sexual interest in a person of the same sex and often accompanied by actual sexual relationship.

Honeymoon. An attitude of pleasing the mate; a trip taken immediately after the wedding.

Hymen. A membrane partly closing the opening to the vagina.

Id. A term used by Freud to cover all pleasure-seeking instinctive impulses which drive the individual to seek satisfaction without regard to future effect on himself or on others.

Identification. Conscious or unconscious effort to put oneself in the place of another individual or to play his or her role for the purpose of participating in the experiences of that person.

Impotence. Inability on the part of the male to achieve erection or to complete successfully the sex act.

Industriousness. A strong self-motivation to work.

Infatuation. A state in which one imagines oneself in love with another person when in actuality he or she is enamored with the process of the love experience.

Inferiority Feeling. Strong sense of insecurity and inadequacy which affect a person's total evaluation of himself, especially in comparison with others.

In-group. A group characterized by strong coherence, solidarity, and common interests. Individuals belonging to such a group closely identify themselves with each other. In-group is used as the opposite of out-group.

Inhibition. Blocking or restraining a process from starting or continuing.

Infertility. Inability to produce one's kind; barrenness.

Insight. Ability to view oneself objectively, without bias; also, ability to perceive relationships.

Insomnia. Persistent inability to sleep.

Inspectionist. A person who has a tendency or compulsion to view secretly nude persons in order to obtain sexual satisfaction (popularly known as a "Peeping Tom").

Intelligence Quotient (I.Q.). The ratio between the mental age and the chronological age. Mental age is determined on the basis of the Binet or some other standardized intelligence test. The mental age is then divided by the chronological age of the person tested.

Interaction. Reciprocal interrelationship between individuals or groups. A relationship in which the behavior of one individual or group affects and is affected by the behavior of other individuals or groups.

Interest. Interests are positive attitudes toward objects or conditions which possess the capacity of satisfying one's needs or desires.

Innervation. The nervous excitation necessary for maintenance of the life and functions of an organ.

Integration. Process of organizing or unifying parts into a greater whole.

Introception. Adoption by an individual of attitudes, interests, standards, and beliefs from his environment and making them part of his own motives and desires.

Introjection. Reacting to external events and persons as though they were a part of oneself.

Introvert. A person who is preoccupied primarily with his own feelings, thoughts, and imagination; he, therefore, tends to withdraw from external environment.

Intuition. Direct or immediate knowledge—knowledge arrived at without the awareness of any mental processes having intervened between stimulus and response.

Jealousy. Unpleasant feeling resulting from fear of losing a desired object or person to another.

Kleptomania. Compulsion to steal objects for which one has no apparent use.

Labia Majora. The two outer lips or folds of the vulva.

Labia Minora. The two small inner folds or lips of the vulva.

Leucorrhea. A liquid substance secreted from the vaginal tract which has the color, consistency, and general appearance of the white of an egg; usually caused by some form of inflammation.

Masochism. A sexual deviation in which a person derives sexual pleasure by being maltreated or having pain inflicted on him.

Masturbation. Self-induced orgasm by means of artificial stimulation of the genitalia.

Maturation. The gradual unfolding of innate capacities during the period of development and growth.

Melancholia. A type of temperament characterized by frequent and prolonged states of depression.

Menopause. Permanent cessation of menstruation occurring at the climacteric.

Menstruation. Periodic discharge, usually monthly, of mucous membrane; connected with the reproductive functions of the female.

Mesomorph. One of Sheldon's somatotypes. A person characterized by pronounced skeletal and muscular development who is usually active, energetic, and aggressive.

Metabolism. The integrated life processes concerned with the building up of tissues (anabolism) and the tearing down of tissues (katabolism).

Microcosm. A miniature world. This term is sometimes applied to man to indicate his extreme complexity and ordered structure.

Mixed Marriages. A marital union between two persons of radically different religious or racial backgrounds.

Monogamy. A form of marriage in which one husband is married to one wife at a time.

Mood. An affective state which persists after the original emotion has subsided; thus, when a person has been angered by some experience, he may remain in this state for a considerable length of time afterwards. During this period, a slight stimulus is sufficient to re-arouse the original anger.

Mores. A set of inflexible rules regarding right and wrong, good and bad conduct having group sanction. Their violation is followed inevitably by group condemnation.

Motility. An organism's performance of complex and co-ordinated movements; also, movement from place to place.

Motivation. The application of some incentive to induce an organism to activity; the determination, in part, of an organism's behavior by its own internal needs or structure.

Motive. A goal-directed drive.

Narcissist. A person who is so much in love with himself that he is incapable of loving anyone else.

Neuron. A unit of the nervous system consisting of a cell body and its processes.

Neurotic. A person who suffers from a mild functional personality disorder and who has a tendency to react with excessive emotion, especially fear, to almost any situation.

Nymphomania. Exaggerated degree of sexual desire on the part of the female.

Obstetrician. A physician specializing in the science dealing with all aspects of pregnancy.

Oedipus Complex. An excessive emotional attachment of the son to the mother, often involving conscious or unconscious incestuous desires and frequently accompanied by hate for the father.

Organismic Level. Behavior of an individual motivated by desires originating primarily from his biological needs.

Orgasm. The intense pleasurable excitement experienced as a climax in sexual intercourse.

Orifice. An opening, as applied to the aperture leading into the vagina.

Out-group. A group to which a person does not belong, as contrasted with the in-group.

Ovaries. Reproductive glands in the female which produce ova and other internal secretions.

Overt. Outward; open to view.

Oviduct. Another name for Fallopian tube.

Ovum. A female germ cell; an egg.

Palmistry. The practice of judging personality traits and of foretelling the future by studying the palm of the hand.

Parasympathetic Nervous System. The cranial and the sacral sections of the autonomic nervous system which regulate the vital functions when an organism is in a state of well-being.

Parathyroid Glands. Small endocrine glands located in the neck near the thyroids.

Pedophilia. A sexual deviation in which an adult either desires or actually engages in sexual relationship with an immature child.

Penis. The male reproductive organ.

Perception. Immediate interpretation of a sensation.

Peripheral Nervous System. An over-all term for all the efferent and afferent nerves.

Perversion. Deviation from the normal.

Phlegmatic. Temperamentally indifferent and passive.

Phrenology. A theory that mental capacities, character, and personality traits are shown by the conformation of the skull.

Physiognomy. A theory that psychological attributes of a person can be deduced from facial features.

Pituitary Gland. An endocrine gland located at the base of the brain secreting several types of hormones. Since it possesses a regulating power over the other endocrine glands, it is often called the "master gland."

Polyandry. A form of marriage in which a woman is married to two or more men at the same time.

Polygamy. A form of marriage in which one man is married to two or more women at the same time, or one woman is married to two or more men at the same time.

Polygyny. A type of marriage in which a man is married to more than one wife at a time.

Potency. Man's power of procreation.

Prepuce. The fold of skin which covers the glans penis; foreskin.

Projection. An ego defense mechanism in which a person blames others for his own failures or his difficulties or attributes his own unethical desires and impulses to others.

Promiscuity. Sexual intercourse with many partners.

Prostate Gland. A muscular and glandular body surrounding the posterior portion of the urethra in the male.

Psychiatrist. A medical doctor who specializes in the treatment of mental and emotional disorders.

Psychoanalysis. A method of psychotherapy developed by Freud and a system of psychology based upon his clinical experience.

Psychopath. A person who suffers from character disorder. He appears to be constitutionally incapable of conforming to the rules of society. He has practically no sense of responsibility and is almost completely governed by his "id" drives. In many ways he behaves like an immature child.

Psychotherapy. Treatment of the personality and emotional disorders by the use of various psychological techniques and methods.

Puberty. That period in a person's life at which the sex organs attain reproductive powers.

Pubic Area. That part of the body which includes and surrounds the genital organs.

Pyromania. A compulsive urge to set fires.

Rating Scale. A method used for plotting the degree to which a person possesses a specific trait. A point is indicated at an appropriate place on a scale between the two extremes that show the possible range of degrees of a particular trait.

Rationalization. A process of finding socially acceptable reasons in order to hide or justify one's egocentric or antisocial motives.

Reflex. A simple innate response pattern consisting of sensory, associative, and motor fibers, such as the contraction of the pupil of the eye to light.

Regression. A defense mechanism in which an individual, when confronted by a problem situation, retreats to forms of behavior characteristic of early childhood or adolescence.

Rhythm Method. A method of birth control which consists of avoiding sex intercourse during a woman's periods of fertility.

Role. The process of interpreting and carrying out tasks and functions expected of an individual by the group to which he belongs.

Sadism. A type of sex deviation in which an individual reaches sexual gratification while causing bodily pain to another.

Safe Period. The days during the month when a woman is incapable of conception.

Sanguine. Endowed with a temperament characterized by action, a sense of well-being, and enthusiasm.

Satyriasis. An exaggerated sex desire in the human male.

Scrotum. External bag or pouch containing the testicles.

Self. A person's ultimate concept of himself especially with reference to his identity and his relation to his environment.

Seminal Vesicle. A small sac located close to the end of the vas deferens.

Sex Deviate. An individual who does not conform to the sex mores of his group.

Sibling. One of two or more children of either sex produced by the same parents.

Skene's Gland. A mucous gland located in the female urethra.

Skill. A goal-directed system of learned behavior pattern.

Spermatozoon. A male sperm cell.

Stereotyping. Treating or regarding all members of a class as if they were alike in all aspects of their personalities.

Sterility. Inability to reproduce one's kind.

Sublimation. Unconscious process of channelizing the sex impulse to nonsexual and socially approved goals.

Submission. Act of yielding to power or authority.

Superego. A Freudian term used to designate that part of personality which is due to moral and ethical learning; roughly equivalent to conscience.

Superiority Feeling. A conviction that one excels his fellows in one or more physical or mental traits.

Sympathy. Shared attitudes, feelings, or emotions.

Sympathetic Nervous System. The central segment of the autonomic nervous system which usually is in ascendance when a person is under stress.

Testicle. A male genital gland.

Thyroid Glands. Two ductless glands located near the upper end of the windpipe which secrete thyroxin and in part control metabolism.

Trait. Any biological or psychological characteristic by means of which one person can be distinguished from another; also, a generalized habit or attitude.

Typology. A system of classifying individuals into groups on the basis of significant traits or characteristics.

Unconscious. A general name for all psychic processes which lie beyond the awareness of the individual and can be reached only by special methods of psychotherapy.

Urethra. A tube or duct through which urine is discharged from the bladder.

Uterus. The womb; a sac-like organ in women in which the embryo is nourished and developed until birth.

Vagina. Genital canal leading from the orifice to, and surrounding the anterior portion of, the uterus.

Value. Any object or condition which is sought after because of its capacity of satisfying some need.

Vas Deferens. A canal which leads from the testes to the ejaculatory duct.

Venereal Disease. An infectious disease which may be transmitted through or contracted by sexual intercourse.

Virgin. A man or woman who has had no sexual intercourse.

Virility. Power of procreation on the part of the male.

Voyerism. Synonymous with inspectionism.

Vulva. External parts of the female genital organ.

INDEX